ISSUES IN
BUSINESS DATA PROCESSING

ISSUES IN
BUSINESS
DATA PROCESSING

Edited by

Elias M. Awad

and

Data Processing Management Association

PRENTICE-HALL, INC., Englewood Cliffs, New Jersey

Library of Congress Cataloging in Publication Data

Main entry under title:
Issues in business data processing.

     Includes bibliographies.
       1. Electronic data processing—Business—Addresses, essays, lectures.
I. Awad, Elias M.   II. Data Processing Management Association.
HF5548.2.I79   658'.05'4   75-8991
ISBN 0-13-093906-4

Printed in the United States of America

10 9 8 7 6 5 4 3 2 1

PRENTICE-HALL INTERNATIONAL, INC., London
PRENTICE-HALL OF AUSTRALIA, PTY. LTD., Sydney
PRENTICE-HALL OF CANADA, LTD., Toronto
PRENTICE-HALL OF INDIA PRIVATE LIMITED, New Delhi
PRENTICE-HALL OF JAPAN, INC., Tokyo
PRENTICE-HALL OF SOUTHEAST ASIA (PTE.) LTD., Singapore

Contents

PART 3

Trends in Data Entry and Output Devices   *83*

PART 4

The Make-up and Impact of Minicomputers *147*

PART 5

Operating Systems *165*

PART 6

Real-Time Data Processing *173*

PART 10

Data-Processing Management *287*

PART 11

Computing in the 1970's *343*

Preface

The primary objective of materials in this book is to present selected issues relevant to key areas in business data processing. Unlike technology- or time-bound publications, this book emphasizes several continuing areas of interest and is expected to save the instructor much of the time he otherwise would spend reviewing the literature and selecting articles to provide timely materials as supplemental reading for his basic data processing course.

This book is designed to supplement introductory texts in data processing, including Awad's *Business Data Processing, 4th edition* and *Automatic Data Processing,* both by Prentice-Hall, Inc. Most of the articles are from 1970 to date, although a few classic articles are prior to that time. The book is divided into eleven parts. Part one is about computer uses and misuses and the broad areas of the social impact of computers. Part two presents the major steps in program preparation, beginning with systems analysis and following through systems design, systems implementation, and systems operation. The readings also include discussion of the systems-management relationship, the various forms of systems organization, and the impact of virtual memory on systems design and operation. Program and systems flowcharting are also discussed.

Part three discusses the areas of direct data entry and OCR devices, illustrates how POS systems facilitate a more effective relationship between retailer and consumer, and explains the concept of ultrafiche and the makeup of a microfilm jacket. Part four is an overview of minicomputer structure, the impact of minicomputers on industry, and the ways of choosing the "right" computer. Part five is a summary of operating systems.

Part six elaborates on the concepts of and the critical factors in the implementation of a real-time system. Part seven covers time sharing techniques and the success factors in time sharing services, with a close look at trends in the field. Part eight discusses management information system and the data base concept. Part nine is about computer security and the issue of privacy, with emphasis on the issue of the computer as a threat to individual privacy.

Part ten covers the topic of data processing management. In particular, it discusses the issues of computer productivity, computer and personnel selection, and personnel management. Finally, part eleven is a discussion of computing in the seventies, with attention to the social implications of the vast nationwide information networks and the threats they pose to the individual's privacy. The concluding article by Campise speculates on the future role of data processing and its impact on society in the next decade.

The authors express their deep appreciation to the various publishers and journal editors for granting us permission to use their material. Mr. Paul McKenney, production editor, and his staff deserve special credit for their interest and dedication to the production of the manuscript.

Elias M. Awad
and
Data Processing Management Association

ISSUES IN
BUSINESS DATA PROCESSING

PART 1

Computer Uses

Selected High School Students Describe How Computers May Fashion the World . . . and the Society . . . in Which They Live

ON THE MACHINE

The computer is one of the newest and most versatile of man's tools. However, its ubiquitous presence in our society has not occurred for the same reason as the steam engine in the 19th century or the internal combustion engine in the first half of the 20th, these inventions being the major technical advances of those eras. The computer, unlike those advances of human control over nature, does not handle the material world in large amounts or carry large loads, but controls tiny amounts of electricity which represent bits of information.

Computers are the extension of man's ingenuity, as opposed to extensions of his body such as airplanes. They are still tools, however. This is their potential for the future, then: Computers will be used or misused as humanity's tools have always been.

Quest for knowledge has led man to fantastic ideas beyond the rules of simple logic. But a computer has no such drives. Unlike man, the computer is always satisfied with what it already knows. It has no desire to learn more and it never wonders about the great tomorrow.

The computer adds more than lightning calculation and fact storing to man's brainpower. It also makes a man think.

A man cannot instruct a computer to perform properly until he first has thought through what he wants to do and how he wants to do it. This applies to businessmen, government officials, military leaders, doctors, educators—in fact, to everyone who works with computers. As a result, wherever the machine is used, it is enormously improving the quantity and quality of human thinking, thus enabling man to understand and apply more readily the benefits of the world around him.

In the past, population, gross national product, military and natural resources were used to measure national power. Now, however, economists have another way to measure national power. They use computer power.

Source: Reprinted, with permission, from *Data Management,* October 1971, pp. 44-46, published by the Data Processing Management Association, Park Ridge, Illinois.

Into a washing machine goes the dirty clothes. Approximately 30 minutes later, out come the clean clothes. Again, the computer's sequence of operation: input, processing, output. A washing machine is really "programmed" for certain duties. One button may be pushed for a cold wash, another for cold rinse, another for presoaking. Each button, or cycle, is actually a program. Choose the program that is needed for the clothes, add soap, and you are all set.

The computer's potential is not founded in its future as an electronic marvel. To the contrary, the computer's real future is founded in development as a useful and necessary tool to be used by many. We find more and more people using computers in new and different ways. Its future is limited only by the imagination of the people who use it.

Computers in this day and age are high-priced. Because they are always changing and it isn't profitable to own one unless it can be constantly used, most firms rent them for certain periods of time. But in the time to come, a computer will be made that will be considered standard and made in such a way that only minor changes will be needed to modernize it. Then every place of business will own one. Owners will be taught how to repair and maintain the computer themselves, thus eliminating more employees.

If people will get acquainted with technical terms, they will be able, eventually, to build an inexpensive computer at home. It will help them with their shopping and other minor things around the house.

ON WHAT COMPUTERS MAY DO

In the future there might be computers that could diagnose any disease a person might have if a sample of his blood was put into them.

Another computer of the future might, after several tests, be able to estimate the mental capacity of a new born baby. It might also be able to tell what is needed to improve his mental capacity. Another computer might be able to check the baby's hearing and sight and then recommend any necessary treatment.

Maybe someday the computer will be able to help in finding a cure for cancer.

A computer would make a wonderful translator, and by this, it would break the language barrier. We then could converse with anyone and could make friends with people in other countries. This would also help diplomatic relations.

If nations would accept it, a computer could be used as an impartial judge to settle disputes among nations.

With these different types of computers to do the work of many men, we can put our minds to more pressing problems like pollution and war. No computer can solve these problems directly, at present.

We have computers for the defense of our nation, which we hope will never be needed. Maybe some day someone will design a computer that will do away with war—a "peace computer." This idea of a peace computer may seem completely impossible, but think back before World War II, how impossible it seemed for man to walk on the moon. Computers have accomplished many tasks which at one time or another were thought to be impossible.

Government operations will be much more efficient with computers. They will be able to keep accurate census records, and elections will be faster and more efficient. People need not even leave their homes to vote. It will be so convenient and easy that everyone could vote, and thus the results would represent all the people.

COMPUTERS IN EDUCATION

Students, simply because of human nature, will probably always prefer learning from another human being instead of a computer. Computers aren't really appealing to most students because they aren't apt to make mistakes, and if they do, it is very rarely. This can easily make students feel lowly as compared to the computer, and this can take much enjoyment out of learning and even help a student to develop an inferiority complex.

A computer cannot realize a student's efforts, his struggles with various types of school work. The computer is a box full of an assortment of tubes, wires, screws, bolts, etc.; it is not a person the student can relate to, go to for guidance, or really enjoy learning from. To learn from one of the same kind is always rewarding in the end because, among other things, an understanding or a realization of one's endeavors is communicated from teacher to student at many intervals in the years of educating done at school. The student learns to accept responsibilities more fully, and usually learns to lead a proper and meaningful life, by relating to another person. The teacher is the person who introduces and bestows much of the everyday, routine responsibilities upon many students. A machine such as the computer could not sufficiently do this and so, not only from this aspect of computers in the classroom, but from other similar ones it is easy to realize that some of the very valuable things taught in school, aside from material in textbooks, would be lost.

ON WORKING WITH COMPUTERS

Our future growth as a society will depend greatly upon how we make use of the computer. Every individual, regardless of his educational, economic, or racial background, will be affected by the way America's leadership makes use of the computer. In other words, our future rests in the hands of the people who make the computer work.

To place a telephone call is perhaps one of the simplest procedures for anyone who has been exposed to telephones. In essence, though, we could all be considered computer programmers. By dialing the numbers or pressing the buttons, we are giving the machine the information it needs to execute our call.

"The age of the computer" is definitely on its way. When we, the youth of today, hear our children using such words as bit, cybernetics, debug, flow chart, macro, magnetic drum, etc., we won't get alarmed, but we'll only get out our dictionaries and try to understand what they are talking about.

What is the computer's potential in solving the problems of today's society? The computer offers the career of the future. Its ultimate contribution to society, however, is solely dependent on the hopes, the aspirations, and the wisdom of man. It is within the power of mankind to use the computer to enrich his world or to destroy it.

ON THE BENEFITS OF COMPUTERS

Some people are wrong when they say computers are built to overtake people. Instead of being here to overtake people, they are here to help people make a stronger, better, and easier-to-live-in world. I think when this day comes, people will be grateful for the men and women who worked on computers. Then the people will realize the computer's fantastic potential in society.

In order to initiate the further development of the "marve" machines, each of us will have a load to carry. I think the youth of today will play a very instrumental part in this development. We are an inquisitive group, always seeking answers to things that puzzle us, and wanting these answers quickly. Since these are two things the computer can do—give us solutions to problems and give them out rapidly— youth should find the computer especially helpful.

ON THE "DANGERS" OF COMPUTERS

The most efficient totalitarian government would be run by a computer. It would be programmed to evaluate the quotient of an individual's disloyalty and, when an individual's quotient reached a certain level, he would be liquidated.

And there is always the possibility that the computer, like so many other of man's inventions, will become an ominous threat to safety or privacy rather than an asset. It is a risk one has to take, and you can rest assured that man, who is a gambler at heart, will take that risk.

But is it not true that any tool that is sharp enough to be useful is sharp enough to hurt? In simpler form, if the computer is used properly, it will be a tremendous boon for mankind; however, if used improperly, it will do serious harm. This statement can be made, of course, about every important element of our society, past and present . . . but will it apply to the future?

It is false thinking to believe that a computer system will prevent losses from fraud and errors. On the contrary, the computer probably lends itself to embezzlement on a scale greater than has ever been known. With the speed that automation can attain, even honest errors can become compounded to enormous amounts in a short period of time. Unless properly controlled, the records can be manipulated and the manipulation would be difficult to detect because the transactions pass through relatively few human hands and irregularities may be disclosed only by accident.

American society teaches that everyone should be employed. It holds that moral fiber is developed by honest work. Some feel that having machines do the brainwork will demoralize and make slaves out of man.

Thousands of workers and their families that are out of work because of computers are surrounded with the sight and sound of prosperity, increasing their despair. Sometimes human destruction is apparent and measurable. After the Hudson Motor Car Company folded, 15 auto workers committed suicide and the marriages of more than 300 broke up. Most of the suffering is private and unrecorded.

Ever since it emerged from the mists of time, the human race has been haunted by the notion that man-made devices might overwhelm and even destroy man himself. Frankenstein's frustrated monster (who tortured and destroyed his creator) and many other examples all play upon the age-old fear that man's arrogant mind will overleap itself. And now comes the electronic computer, the first invention to exhibit something of what in human beings is called intelligence.

Not only is the computer expanding man's brainpower, but its own faculties are being expanded by the so-called artificial intelligence.

The fears are several and related to each other, but three major ones encompass the lot.

The one that worries the columnists and commentators is that the computer will hoist unemployment so intolerably that the free enterprise system will be unable to cope with the problem and that the government will have to intervene on a massive scale. It is enough to repeat here that the computer will doubtless go down in history, not as the explosion that blew unemployment through the roof, but as the technological triumph that enabled the U.S. economy to maintain the secular growth rate on which its greatness depends.

The second fear is that the computer will eventually become so intelligent and even creative that it will relegate man, or most men, to a humiliating and intolerably inferior role in the world. This notion is based on the fact that the computer already can learn, can show purposeful behavior, can sometimes act "creatively" or in a way its programmer does not expect it to, and on the probability that artificial intelligence research will improve it enormously on all counts.

The third fear is that the computer's ability to make certain neat, clean decisions will beguile men into abdicating their obligation to make the important decisions, including moral and social ones.

In my opinion, computers will improve only as man improves his understanding of the thinking process, and his ability to control the mechanical brain will increase to the extent he increases his own understanding; so I don't think that two of the three fears are justified. Meanwhile, the prospect for instructing the computer to behave like a real human is remote, and this is precisely why some fear that the machine's role as a decision maker will be abused.

But computer intelligence is not human, it does not grow, has no emotional basis, and is shallowly motivated. These defects do not matter in technical applications, where the criteria for successful problem solving are relatively simple. They become extremely important if the computer is used to make social, business, economic, military, moral, and government decisions.

In my opinion, these defects are very small, perhaps too small. That's why I think that the computer is here to stay; it cannot be shelved, any more than the telescope or the steam engine could have been shelved. Taking everything together, man has a stupendous thing working for him, and one is not being egregiously optimistic to suggest he will make the most of it. Precisely because man is so arduously trying to imitate human behavior in the computer, he is bound to improve enormously his understanding of both himself and the machine.

DISCUSSION QUESTIONS

1. Search the data processing journals and write a 500-word essay on any of the six areas included in the article. Confine your search to articles written within the last three years.

2. In your opinion, what are the two most significant contributions computers have made in each of the following areas:
    a. education
    b. medicine
    c. industry
    d. government

3. List and explain in some detail one of the dangers resulting from the use of computers.

4. Given the knowledge you have about computers, what do you think are the chances that man will find himself a slave rather than master in future decision-making? Why?

WHAT USE IS A COMPUTER?

Edmund C. Berkeley

Joe: What use is a computer? Tell me in simple words.

Ed: Well, a computer is a machine that handles information and solves problems—and that's useful.

Joe: What do you mean by information, and handling it? You can't handle information the way you can handle potatoes. Tell me in simple words.

Ed: Well, I'll try to use simple words: information is facts and guesses, words and numbers, letters and digits, marks and pictures, questions and answers. Handling means copying, storing, looking up, calculating, reporting, etc.

Joe: OK, I think I have an idea. You mean to tell me that machines can take in facts and guesses and give out answers to questions?

Ed: Yes.

Joe: Then I can talk to a computer the way I can talk to a person? and the computer will answer questions for me?—tell me facts that I can believe in and tell me guesses that I might or might not believe? Is that so?

Ed: No, you can't talk to a computer the way you would talk to a person.

Joe: Then what the devil use is a computer to me—all sorts of things that I might want to know—and I can't talk to it!

Ed: But you can talk to a computer with another machine, for example, an electric typewriter connected to the computer, or some other gismos like that.

Joe: That's interesting. How come I have to talk to a computer with a typewriter and not with spoken words?

Ed: To tell you the truth, Joe, the boys who have been all excited about computers for the last 25 years still have not made a computer that people can talk to—but they can make computers that do lots of neat tricks if people give them written words with a typewriter.

Joe: But I use the hunt and peck system, and so it will take me a long time to say anything I want to say to a computer that way.

Ed: But they have computers that will ask you questions, and you read the questions that the computer types out on paper, and then you can for example type Y for "Yes" or N for "No" or DK for "I don't know," etc.—and so you can have a kind of one-sided conversation with a computer that way.

Joe: But how am I to explain to a computer what I am really worried about, the real questions I want answers to—like, what made the Americans give a landslide vote to Nixon when he has dropped more bombs on people that any other man in history?

Ed: A computer can't answer that kind of question.

Joe: Well, if a computer won't answer that question, how about this one—how can I "get rich quick" in the stock market?

Source: *Computers and Automation,* February 1973, p. 6.

Ed: A computer can't answer that question either.

Joe: Oh? How about this problem: what should I do this year, next year, and the year after that, so that I can earn much more money than I am now earning, what with prices going up and up and up and up? Ed, it is going to be damn hard for my present income to continue to pay even my present expenses.

Ed: I am sorry, Joe, a computer can't answer that kind of question either—but a computer could throw a lot of light on it.

Joe: Huh! How about this one—what will the weather be on Friday, March 16 this year, when I want to start driving from South Dakota to Oregon?

Ed: I'm sorry, Joe, a computer can't answer that question either.

Joe: Wow! A know-nothing on that question, too! Well, what are the kinds of questions a computer can answer?

Ed: They can tell American Airlines whether that airplane seat you want for arriving in Sioux Falls on the morning of March 16 can be surely reserved for you, and they can tell the Collector of Internal Revenue how your 1972 reported income compares with what other people said they paid you, and they can tell the National Aeronautics and Space Administration when and for how long to fire a rocket on a spaceship, so that an astronaut can land on a particular spot on the moon, and then can tell . . .

Joe: One crumb of useful information for me, and a stack of useful information for the government!

Ed: Not exactly, Joe. I have a list right here, of 2300 fields where computers can be applied, where lots of detailed answers to lots of detailed questions can be obtained by a computer.

Joe: (shaking his head): The computer reminds me of the story of the idiot genius who could add all the numbers on the freight cars as they went past a railroad crossing in Indiana, at 70 miles an hour—but he did not know how to tie his own shoelaces.

Ed: I am sorry to say that although the computers are marvelous, and very useful, and have done much useful work, and have a wonderful public relations image—on net balance they may be doing as much harm as good—because of their side-effects.

They are being used by people and organizations who have money and resources, and who want and need good images and more profits—in order to keep on doing the often thoughtless, and occasionally wicked, things that they are doing.

And so far as I know there is nobody, no organized group, in the computer field or out of it, in government or outside of it, really making sure that the power of computers is being used to help solve the really important problems of society.

Joe: Gee! If you ask me, I think computers are for the birds!

Ed: If the birds had computers, they might well be worse off.

Thoughtless technology is a curse, because the side-effects are on such a large scale.

MANAGEMENT, THE COMPUTER, AND SOCIETY

Martin Ernst

Seventeen years ago the first attempt was made to put a computer to routine industrial use. In 1953, General Electric tried to place their local payroll on a computer at Appliance Park. It took many months; major difficulties were encountered; and, all in all, it was a very painful process.

If you want to buy a computer today, Neiman-Marcus will be glad to supply you with a Honeywell machine for home use—if you can figure out what you want to do with it. So, computers have moved from a rarity to something we encounter almost every day in one form or another.

COST REDUCTIONS

Growth in the computer business has been fed by technological advances that have made computing equipment cheaper and better each year; and technological progress is definitely going to continue at a high rate for at least another decade. For example, we can expect approximately a doubling in speed of large central processors, during the next five years or so and a halving in cost per unit of computer power. Even more dramatic improvements in minicomputer cost-effectiveness seem assured. Gains by a factor of as high as ten may be possible prior to 1980.

For a long time, high speed core memory has been an expensive item in computer configurations. These memories will probably improve in access time by a factor of four in the next decade, and their costs will probably decrease by a factor of between four and eight. Low speed memory in the past has tended to be monopolized by magnetic tapes or by fairly clumsy random access equipment. Now it is technically possible to build devices that, for all practical purposes, have infinite memory capacity and modest costs, although they will be relatively slow of access.

CHEAPER PERIPHERALS

With these equipment cost reductions under way, peripherals such as input/output terminals have become a major factor in the cost of modern installations; but even these are going to become cheaper as we move from mechanical devices, with their high production and maintenance costs, to all-electronic systems. Finally, there is a strong likelihood that the entire data insertion process will be revolutionized before the end of the next decade through the introduction of voice control mechanisms and inexpensive, broadly useful character recognition equipment.

Source: *Computers and Automation,* September 1971, pp. 8-11ff.

STAGE THREE

As equipment is becoming more diverse, more efficient, and cheaper, we are entering what sometimes is called Stage Three of computer usage. We have passed through the earlier periods, when the computer's capability was limited to performing simple clerical operations, or to producing routine decisions in areas such as inventory control. Now the primary excitement is in how computers can aid in major management decisions.

SOCIAL PROBLEMS OF COMPUTERS

Rather than discussing the problems of using computers for management decision-making, the social problems associated with the use of computers deserve even more attention.

We have had early warnings of the social dangers in the growth of computer usage; for example, Norbert Wiener raised important questions many years ago in his first book on cybernetics. However, until recently these warnings meant very little—computers played too small a role in society to make their unpleasant aspects very painful. Our period of grace is now coming to an end. It would be good to give you a well structured and orderly statement of the origins of our problems and their potential cures. But, I don't believe we have reached a stage in understanding that permits this. The best I can do is to share with you some examples, ideas, and suggestions that are still in a formative stage, in an effort to begin more productive thinking.

To help present these tentative ideas, I have divided computer impact into three broad areas: depersonalization, talent bias and vulnerability. These terms can best be explained by citing some examples.

DEPERSONALIZATION

The origins of depersonalization lie in the high degree of standardization needed to use computers efficiently. As computer activities spread their influence, individuals tend to feel that they are being molded to fit the computer's needs rather than that the computer is being employed to meet their needs. It probably is no accident that, during the first of the major campus riots at Berkeley, resentment was directed to the punch cards and computers that students claimed made them feel more like numbers than like people.

AIRLINE SYSTEMS

A more concrete example lies in airlines reservations systems. A few of the largest airlines have been able to plan and develop computer reservations systems tailored to meet their own particular needs, but this process is difficult and expensive. Smaller airlines have no choice but to select an existing package of programs and attempt to modify them to fit their own character and style. I know of one case where a review indicated a need for some 60 significant program changes in an available package if the resulting system was to match the operating procedures and philosophy of the airline. When the effort for performing such a surgical operation was investigated, the airline decided it could afford almost none of these desirable changes. It now operates like every other airline employing the same basic system and has lost a bit of its special personality and flavor.

BILLING OPERATIONS

Another unpleasant encounter with computers, which I am sure we all face, involves dealing with a company that has automated its billing operations. At first I had faith that this would be a transient situation but during the preparations for this talk I found that this is not the case. One associate of mine is currently going through the excruciating process of unsnarling his financial obligations to a success-ful, widely known and highly efficient organization, while another associate went through exactly the same process—and for the same reasons—with the same com-pany as much as six years ago. The problem arises from the fact that it is always difficult to insert an exception into a computer run. This difficulty is compounded if an organization seeks to get by with minimum training of the clerical staff that examines the customer input of payments and complaints about misbilling. The final result is that the customer writes letter after letter into a non-answering void, with resentment growing at each cycle.

There are ways for the individual to deal with these mis-billings and to achieve fairly prompt satisfaction. However, it's probably only the more sophisticated of our population who will learn these methods. The poor and the less educated are ill-prepared to deal with these situations; they are far more apt to accept errors and try to pay, but they do this with a sense of resentment and growing dissatisfaction.

DEALING WITH EXCEPTIONS

Planning to deal with exceptions has been completely inadequate in the design of most computer billing systems and their associated manual procedures. There seems to be little excuse for this. Very few companies have difficulty picking up changes of address in the blank spaces provided for this purpose on most bills.

LOAD BALANCING

There are many other examples associated with standard customer-business rela-tionships. We are all subject to some of the penalties of load balancing, which has become an important requirement of all major computer installations. Instead of consistently getting bills to be paid by the tenth of the month, as was the case in my father's day, bills keep streaming in throughout the month as various service installations attempt to keep their computers loaded evenly. With delays in com-puter output and mail delivery, and interest penalties for slow payment, one has to keep the checkbook constantly on hand.

These are all minor matters if viewed singly, but, when accumulated, they boost our frustration level alarmingly and seem to chip away at our individuality and personality.

PRIVACY

A second area of depersonalization concerns privacy. Privacy considerations occur most frequently in regard to credit information, though even more serious invasions may occur in the collection and transmission of health, employment and other information. We have collected and employed credit information for a very long time, but never with the degree of completeness and nationwide access made possible by high speed communications and electronic data processing equipment. I wonder how many of you are completely satisfied that the information concerning your own credit is based on appropriate inputs? How many of you would like to see this information, to make sure that failure to pay a bill during some past period because the circumstances justified your delay does not appear on your records as a negative mark?

RIGHTS OF INDIVIDUALS TO DISCOVER WHAT CREDIT ORGANIZATIONS HAVE ON FILE ABOUT THEM

Fortunately, some solid steps have been taken in this area of credit information. A national law now gives significant rights to individuals to discover what information concerning themselves is being held on file. Some of the better credit associations took equivalent or even stronger steps prior to the passage of this law. Unfortunately, as with most legal steps, there are a number of loopholes; and we again face the problem that the least sophisticated among us are not apt to discover and apply their rights even though they are the ones who probably suffer most from the system.

Further, credit information is by no means the only area of concern. There are many reasons for developing good medical data banks but the issues of privacy and access must be solved before these banks can be made effective. The subject of psychiatric information is a particularly difficult one since, without proper safeguards, it could be used for blackmail purposes.

DISPLACEMENT BY COMPUTERS

A third area of depersonalization has to do with the opportunities for white collar workers to get started in business. The current situation is one wherein more and more clerks are being displaced by computers. So far, this displacement has been largely made up for by the increasing numbers of people needed to handle the input and output information, to design computer programs, and to undertake the variety of services necessary to use computers effectively. However, one very large component of this work force—the personnel responsible for preparing input—is threatened by the development of efficient and economical character recognition devices. I feel that in the next decade a significant component of the current work force in this area will be eliminated. This means that a certain type of starting job for the white collar worker will disappear in much the sense that the automatic elevator removed a kind of starting opportunity for the least trained blue collar workers. We do not seem to have particularly good alternatives available for the starting clerical worker, so a certain range of opportunities is going to be cut off and there undoubtedly will be resentment about this process.

DISENFRANCHISEMENT OF PEOPLE THROUGH CREDIT CARDS

Finally, and an extreme case, the use of computers can lead to a form of disenfranchisement of people. This possibility shows up most clearly in the area of credit cards, a phenomenon whose growth is closely tied to computers. The use of these cards is increasing at a rapid rate, and over a period of time, we can visualize approaching an almost cashless society. One can ask the question: what happens then to a man who cannot get credit and cannot obtain a credit card? Will he, in a valid sense, be banned from a form of equal opportunity in our society?

The beginnings of this type of disenfranchisement in the credit card area are already beginning to be evident. When one registers at a hotel in a number of U.S. cities, there is a sign behind the registration desk to the effect that the local innkeepers' association "requires" that guests either provide an acceptable credit card or pay for their room in advance. This may make good business sense for the hotels, but it is also a minor indignity. The passing of blame for the act to an innkeepers' association has a ring of phoniness and deprives the consumer—and, at least in theory, the hotels—of their freedom of choice in the market.

TALENT BIAS

A second broad area of social impact by computers concerns the extension of an existing talent bias—a bias in favor of technical training and experience as opposed to the humanities. As we move into Stage Three of the computer revolution, there will be changes in the requirements for talent to serve business effectively. Previously, computers have been devoted to clerical areas which, by their nature, already had to be routinized within a given company. Management decisions are not standard and we rarely have a library of procedures available that can be programmed into a computer. If we wish to use the computer effectively, we are going to have to develop new techniques. We will have to acquire large numbers of personnel for developing these techniques and analyzing the output of computer runs. For example, a lot has been written and some excellent work has been done on the role of simulations in the decision-making process. But just a few minutes of time on a computer, running a complex simulation, can call for many man-months of analysis to understand the implications of the output. One result will be enormous requirements for analytical skills in business staffs.

ANALYTICAL SKILLS NOT BACKED WITH PRACTICAL EXPERIENCE

Analytical skills unbacked with realistic experience can lead to a variety of difficulties. Our military organization has often been a leader in trying new techniques; so it is worthwhile taking a quick look at what has been happening recently in the Pentagon. During the McNamara era, enormous emphasis was placed on employing analytical techniques to establish and justify expenditure levels. There were many cases in which these techniques were not well employed because we did not have the skills available yet. Failures due to misapplication have caused a very strong reaction to the analytical approach for developing expenditure budgets. These skills are now being employed far less by the military.

We face a situation where competition will demand effective employment of skills in short supply. Either the performance will be poor, leading to backtracking and loss of efficiency, or new procedures will be necessary for providing both a larger supply of technical skills and a basis for combining these skills with practical experience.

ADDICTION OF PLAYING GAMES WITH COMPUTERS

Another area of talent bias arises in training and education. Some months ago *Datamation Magazine* published a rather interesting science fiction-type article which, among other things, discussed a future period where playing games with computers had become a sociological disease equivalent to narcotics addiction. It was an amusing article but it lost some of its humor when we made a recent survey for a major university concerned with planning for their development and use of computers. We encountered a number of students who had become so fascinated with the computers made available to them that they lost all interest in their courses and were devoting essentially all of their time to playing with the computers!

NEW DEMANDS FOR SKILLS

We face a number of problems in educational institutions in that the future demands of business call for certain talents to a greater extent than they probably are naturally present in the human race. These demands tend to cut down the stature and role of the student studying humanities as he visualizes his position in future society. The new demands place great emphasis on mathematical and analytical skills and tend to split the student body into two components—technically-oriented and humanities-oriented. I believe this split is resented, and some evidence of a rather emotional getting-together of the segments of the student body was quite visible in the recent riots and protests. It should also be pointed out that a significant number of faculty members in most of our schools have an extreme distaste or even fear of the computer. Some of this will begin to come through to the students that they train, as the computer develops a bigger and bigger role in university and daily life.

LOSS OF A TRAINING GROUND FOR MANAGEMENT

The talent bias also has an impact on management training. The use of computers has often led to elimination of some echelons in the organization of companies. This may achieve greater efficiency, but you also can lose a very important training ground for future management. The result may be an increasing trend for progress to senior managerial positions to come through staff rather than line positions. There are some reasons to suspect that over time, this trend could have disastrous results. As the computer plays more and more of a role, there will be less and less opportunity to develop junior and intermediate management skills. This must be faced as a real threat for the future.

VULNERABILITY

The third general topic is that of vulnerability. There are a number of forms which this can take. First, I do not think we have even begun to see the extent to which fraud can take place through the use of computers. There have been a limited number of examples, but skills in manipulating computers can unquestionably be employed in ways we have not yet visualized to milk companies and to perpetrate fraud or thefts. This subject has not received adequate and serious study.

RELIABILITY PROBLEMS

Second, we are going to face a variety of reliability problems. I was once told of an occasion when the head of the American Airlines automated reservations systems paid a visit to the U.S. Air Defense Command. During a discussion, one of the officers turned to him and said in effect: "You know, you people really have the reliability problem. Our equipment can go down for an hour or so, and if the Russians don't choose that period to attack, we bring it up again and nobody knows anything has happened! But if you go down for an hour or so, you have got a lot of angry customers who are aware that you have been having difficulties." We can extrapolate this further. There has been a lot of attention paid to the problems of floor automation on Wall Street. To my mind, one of the most legitimate barriers to progress has been the reliability of equipment. An airline may get into difficulty if its reservations equipment goes down for an hour. On the trading floor, a five minute failure of a computer can lead to nearly disastrous results.

INCREASED VULNERABILITY

In the future we are going to be faced with problems as our banking system, our mutual funds, our stock exchange and other institutions make increasing use of electronic records. We already have cases where records were destroyed by mistake or were lost; a small mutual fund, for example, has had the embarrassment of having to write its customers to find out how many shares they owned! No system is perfect in reliability; and no matter what steps we take, sooner or later there are going to be errors and failures. As we build bigger systems and become more dependent on them, we face increased vulnerability. The size of the largest organization in a given field of endeavor tends to approach the maximum that is manageable. The use of the computer increases the manageable size of a company; but it also increases the vulnerability of that company if something happens to the computer.

SABOTAGE

There is also the question of sabotage. It is probably no accident that quite a number of efforts of the radical left and students in their bombing attempts, building seizures and such, have involved computer systems. We are not too vulnerable now, but in the future these actions can cause far greater difficulties.

INDUSTRIAL ESPIONAGE

In addition to straightforward sabotage, I think we have to look forward to problems of increased industrial espionage. If it is known that a company bases its marketing plans very heavily on a simulation it has developed, the simulation itself can become a target for a competitor. And it is not too difficult in normal situations to arrange for the disappearance of a program or the disappearance of input data from most of our current computer systems.

MORE FILTERING OF DATA FOR DECISION MAKING

Finally, we face the fact that management itself will become more vulnerable in its decision making. As we use more complex decision making tools, and as we rely more heavily on large data banks, there will be more filtering of information by management staffs before materials for decisions are presented to the senior management. Even today, I feel that a large fraction of the decisions of senior managers are not made by them. They are forced on them by the selectivity of their staffs in providing data and in presenting arguments. As the staffs grow bigger and the data base more complex, the filtering mechanism will expand and senior managers will find it more difficult to exercise effective personal control.

BUSINESS WILL SUFFER FROM FAILURES TO DEAL WITH PROBLEMS

In this brief review, I have described some of the problems of computers I have encountered in a variety of work for business, universities and governmental organizations. The list is obviously not complete. Though the examples range from fairly trivial to moderately serious, all are characterized by the fact that they will become far more extensive and very likely far more dangerous as our use of computers broadens. At the moment, these problems don't hurt us very much. I don't believe they will be painless for much longer, however, and I do believe businessmen have an important responsibility for helping solve these problems. If they do not, business will certainly be among the first groups to suffer from our failure to deal with them.

DISCUSSION QUESTIONS

1. What can the consumer do about the department store computer that makes mistakes? Which is the problem, the store or the computer? Why?

2. The author discusses three broad areas of social impacts by computers. Do you agree with his views? Explain.

3. What areas of depersonalization have been generated as a result of the use of the computer? Which area(s) do you believe to be the most crucial to the average citizen? Explain.

4. Assume that wide use of credit cards has led us to a virtually cashless society. What can be done about those who cannot get credit cards? Discuss.

5. Elaborate on this statement: "As we build bigger systems and become more dependent on them, we face increased vulnerability."

MAYBE THE COMPUTERS CAN SAVE US AFTER ALL

Edward Yourdon

We have known for several years that mortal men are incapable of managing large cities to the general satisfaction of their constituents. The 1970 elections have shown us that this pervasive feeling of disgruntlement has spread to the state level, and the 1974 elections may very well show evidence of a "throw the rascals out" mood at the national level. Perhaps then we will all agree that our society has grown too complex to be effectively managed by mere human beings.

LOSING FAITH

Before this national disenchantment became so strong, most Americans had what so many generations of men before us have had: *faith*. Men must have faith in themselves, in their social order, their leaders, and their government, or we would never have progressed past the point of feudal kingdoms.

Somehow, we seem to be losing that kind of faith today, for reasons that are not entirely clear. Perhaps it is because political faith, like religious faith, depends on the faithful being kept relatively uninformed and unenlightened.

Perhaps our disenchantment is caused by the fact that faith seems to work only when surrounded by ritual, by familiar day-after-day repetitions of the same facts, the same speeches, the same political ceremonies. Maybe we have lost faith because Alvin Toffler's "future shock" has destroyed such comfortable rituals for us.

WHAT CHOICES DO WE HAVE?

Given this state of affairs, there seem to be several choices open to us. The most obvious choice, of course, is to avoid doing anything at all. We lack a prophet who

Source: *Computers and Automation*, May 1971, pp. 21-26.

could tell us with certainty what will happen if we fail to make some basic changes in the form and structure of our government; at the very least, it would appear that we can look forward to great periods of restlessness and instability.

There are more drastic choices: we can attempt to bomb our outmoded society into oblivion, or we can simply run away from it. However, despite the wild antics of a few revolutionaries, I think the vast majority of Americans are profoundly committed and dedicated to this country. We were born here; we grew up here, for better or for worse. Despite the way we move restlessly from city to city, America is, in the very deepest sense of the word, our home.

Still another choice is represented by the hippie communes and the "back to the earth" movement currently in vogue with the young. While this is a viable alternative for those who simply cannot cope with the Establishment, or for those who can afford to buy a farm in Vermont, it does not seem likely that the great mass of Americans would be either willing or able to settle down to the quiet rural life our forefathers knew. It is difficult to imagine that a rural economy would be capable of supporting 200 million Americans in the lavish style to which they have become accustomed.

There is yet another choice, though it seems to arouse violent feelings of paranoia whenever it is mentioned: we can attempt to make our government more automatic, more organized, and more responsive with the use of computers. At the moment, the vast majority of government computers are nothing more than glorified adding machines, used to spit out bills and process tax reports. We have made little or no use of the computer's ability to organize and retrieve *information*, information which could be used to help legislators govern more effectively, and which might help the average citizen better understand what is going on in government. There are a multitude of *major* changes which could be effected with computers, including the six which follow.

1. Voter Registration and Vote Processing

Computers have occasionally been used on the local and state level to help automate both voter registration and the actual counting of votes. While these efforts have been only partially successful, there is reason to believe that a *national*, unified computerized voting system would remove many of the inequities in our voting process. Since the computer would be capable of keeping tabs on every citizen, it would be easier to relax residency requirements so that *everyone* could vote in the national elections, if not in the state and local elections. The voting booths could be connected directly to a central computer complex, so that an individual's vote would be registered immediately. This would make it more difficult for political bosses to rig an election, though the possibility of fraud would not be completely eliminated.

2. Improved Information for Legislators

A good deal of the actual legislative work at the state and national levels is done by staff organizations. Even with this staff help, though, the legislator must often make snap decisions in areas where he is relatively uninformed. A computerized information retrieval system would make it possible for a Congressman or a

Senator to obtain information on any subject with a minimum of effort. The same kind of system might be used to provide *citizens* information on various subjects, as we shall discuss in detail presently.

3. Optimum Scheduling of Services

At the city and state level, it often seems that things like garbage collection, snow removal, road repair, bus schedules and street cleaning are performed on an inflexible, if not completely random, basis. Computers could be used to *optimize* such services on a relatively dynamic basis, so that as conditions changed, the services could be re-scheduled.

4. More Up-to-date Information on the State of the Economy

At the moment, there are a number of economic indicators which give government officials a rough feeling for the direction in which the economy is moving. In addition to the fact that these indicators are often contradictory and subject to different interpretations, there is a problem caused by the *delay* from the time the economic phenomenon occurs until it is noticed; and then the delay from the time it is noticed until something is done about it; and finally, the delay from the time some action is taken until the time the effect of that action is felt. The total delay can easily be as little as six months or as much as two years, and it can cause a great deal of economic damage.

What we need is a computerized *model* of our economy, an idea which has been of fundamental interest to economists for several years. To have any validity, the model would have to have several thousand inputs, including such things as the production and capital expenditure figures from major corporations, money supply and interest rates of the major banks, and employment, wages and spending figures of the American citizen. The output from the model could help economists and lawmakers review the state of the economy on a weekly, or even a daily, basis. Instead of taking six months or a year to react to an economic crisis, we would be able to take action within a matter of days.

Even more important, a comprehensive model would allow economists to *simulate* the effects of various proposed economic activities. The effect of a General Motors strike could be predicted by the machine, as well as the effect of a decrease in defense spending.

5. More Streamlined Administration of Government

It is conceivable that a large number of clerical tasks carried on by local, state and Federal administrations could be eliminated with a computer. Programs like Social Security, unemployment benefits, the processing of marriage licenses, and so forth, could almost be completely automated; exceptional cases, of course, would continue to be handled by people.

Computers do not ask for raises, do not go on strike, and do not take long vacations. Since the cost of computing equipment has been decreasing as a result of improved technology, and since labor costs continue to spiral upwards, it might be wise for many administrators to re-examine the economics of automation.

6. Better Determination and Control of National and State Priorities

A common complaint in these times of tight money is that our *priorities* are wrong—we should be spending more on urban problems and less on foreign aid, or more for foreign aid and less for defense. The final decisions must, of course, be made by people, and the decisions often take highly political considerations into account. Nevertheless, a computer might be able to help in the decision-making process. The computer could, for example, easily tell a legislator how many extra schools or hospitals could have been built with the money being spent in Cambodia; it could tell how many jobs would be affected if $1 billion was shifted from defense work to mass transit or pollution control.

Equally important, a computer might be able to help *control* these priorities, once they were determined. It could point out cases of fraud and embezzlement, as well as pork-barrel projects and cases of extreme nepotism.

WHY HASN'T GOVERNMENT BECOME MORE COMPUTERIZED?

Some of these projects have been attempted on an experimental basis—the city of Wichita Falls, Texas, for example, is almost completely computerized. However, there has been very little concerted effort on the part of the Federal and state governments to move in this direction, and things are even more primitive at the city level.

Part of the reason for this backwardness is that many of the projects are difficult to define and specify. Most computer people know little or nothing of the *application* they are attempting to computerize, and they fail to program the computer for the exceptions that are inevitably present. On the other hand, applications-oriented people—the economists, legislators, and administrators—often have a difficult time describing their application in sufficiently precise detail for the computer people. Fortunately, there has been a growing familiarity with computers in these professional disciplines, and there is some hope that they will be willing and able to participate in more ambitious computer projects in the near future. Computer people, by the same token, are beginning to specialize in specific applications, and they should eventually be able to converse more intelligently with legislators and economists.

PEOPLE FEAR COMPUTERS

There is one obstacle, however, that will be more difficult to overcome: the ordinary man in the street is deathly afraid of computers. To many Americans, the word "computer" is a reminder of incorrect bills, all-digit telephone numbers, and the indignity of having to use one's Social Security number as a prime means of identification; to other more sensitive souls, "computer" evokes memories of George Orwell's *1984* or Karel Capek's *R.U.R.*

There is no doubt that a computer can bungle simple things like bills and invoices. In fact, when it comes to resolving an incorrect bill, we seem to be finding that a computer can be more petty, more arbitrary and more obstinate than any human bureaucrat. On the other hand, computer technicians are quick to point out that these problems are rarely, if ever, the fault of the computer *per se;* what has happened is that somebody has *programmed* the computer in a petty, arbitrary and obstinate way. If someone took the trouble to program a computer to be sweet, apologetic and understanding, much of the ill will toward computers would disappear.

For example, consider the fact that many current computer systems use *numbers* as a prime means of identification. When dealing with Blue Cross, American Express, or the local gas and electric company, one must know one's *account number* or there is no hope of getting anywhere with either the computer or its human attendants. Account numbers are used primarily because it is *easier* for the programmers to deal with a well-known 9-digit decimal number than it is to deal with a variable-length string of numbers and letters that he would find in a name and address; in addition, the programmer can be sure that the account number is a *unique* identification of the customer, while the name "John Smith" may not be unique. Nevertheless, the programmer *could,* if he wanted to make the computer system a little more palatable to its customers, dispense with the ubiquitous numbers forever.

MISUSE OF COMPUTERS

Unfortunately, this does not dispel the deeper fear of computers felt by laymen and scientists alike: the fear that the computers will eventually "take over" and start running our lives. If this happens, it will *not* be the result of the computer having acquired some innate intelligence of its own—while we can get computers to play a reasonably good game of tic-tac-toe and checkers, we computer people have all but given up hope, for the present time at least, of building a truly "intelligent" computer like *HAL* in the movie *2001.* The really important danger, as Norbert Wiener has pointed out in books like *God and Golem* and *The Human Use of Human Beings,* is that an unscrupulous leader can use a powerful computer to help subjugate his people, or that a thoughtless leader might abdicate some of his decision-making powers to a computer. The appearance of computerized war games, computerized military strategy-making systems like WIMMIX, computerized defense systems like SAGE, and the growth of computerized surveillance files certainly lend credence to these fears.

It would be absurd to minimize the dangers to this kind of misuse of computers—dangers that seem potentially far greater than those posed by the computers that generate incorrect bills. Since it is ultimately *people* that misuse the power of a computer, just as it is people that misuse atomic energy, a great deal more attention should be given to systems of human checks and balances to ensure that the rights and privileges of American citizens (and citizens of the rest of the world, for that matter) are not being endangered by computers.

CAN WE HAVE FAITH IN COMPUTERS?

It seems, then, that computers could bring about a tremendous improvement in various phases of government . . . if one has *faith:* faith that the computers will work properly, faith that they will not be as petty and obstinate as many of the current computer systems, faith that they will not be misused by scheming politicians or over-zealous bureaucrats. We seem to have come full circle, first indicating that men had lost faith in their human leaders, and now suggesting that things will be better if they have faith in a cold-blooded mechanical computing machine.

In the long run, the advantages of computers will hopefully become self-evident. If, twenty years from now, people become generally aware that it is a *computer* that gets the garbage picked up on schedule; a computer that makes the telephone work properly; and a computer that keeps unemployment at a minimum, then they may gradually begin to feel a little more benevolent towards the machines.

OPINIONS: A MIXTURE OF FACTS AND FAITH

In the meantime, the garbage *isn't* being picked up, the telephone *doesn't* work, and unemployment is by no means at a minimum level. To make matters worse, even the pitifully primitive computer systems that currently exist don't work half the time. As a result, many of us are perpetually disgruntled, and do not feel kindly towards politicians, computers or the government. Our *opinions* on these subjects are a curious mixture of facts and faith, and the proportion of the two seems to differ from one generation to the next, from one neighborhood to the next, and from one ethnic group to the next. It is important to realize, I think, that our opinions and our views of the world are a function of our environment. Most of us have certain social and political attitudes formed and influenced by our parents, our friends, by the type of education we received, by the type of work we do, and by the newspapers, movies, and television shows that we happen to watch.

One of the problems in forming an opinion is that there is simply too *much* information available on any particular subject. On the other hand, there are times when desperately needed information is not available to the average American. Listening to a debate between any two political candidates, for example, can be a highly frustrating experience—each accuses the other of having wrongly opposed or supported critical legislation, and it is extremely difficult, given the resources and the patience of the average citizen, to detect who is telling the truth. The "truth," such as it is, may be scattered through various official documents and reports, or it may be withheld from the public for reasons of national security and/or political expedience. It is highly ironic, given the nature of our national malaise, to hear leaders implore us to "have faith" that their programs will work out well.

A COMPUTER IN THE HANDS OF THE PEOPLE

One way of improving the situation would be to put a computer in the hands of the people. If, as we have suggested above, part of the average citizen's feeling of impotence is caused by a lack of organized and readily available information, would it not be possible to put such information at his fingertips with a computer?

I believe that it would be feasible, both economically and technically, to create a National Information Bureau, whose sole purpose would be to provide information to any citizen on any issue.

CREATING A NATIONAL INFORMATION BUREAU

An example will illustrate the possibilities of such a system. Suppose a local citizen's group wanted more information on welfare, so that it could form an intelligent opinion of local political candidates. Not knowing where to begin, it might ask the National Information Bureau what information existed on welfare. The Bureau might respond that its files on welfare are broken into six categories:

1. Welfare legislation
2. Welfare statistics
3. History of welfare in the United States
4. Sociological and psychological effects of welfare
5. Attitudes towards welfare—speeches, interviews, etc.
6. Bibliography

Each of these categories could, of course, be broken down further. The local citizen's group could then request summaries of books, copies of articles, speeches and so forth. Similar information could be maintained on such subjects as Vietnam, defense spending, the economy, and crime. Information would be available in as much or as little detail as desired.

The major purpose of the National Information Bureau would, of course, be to serve as a central source of information on any subject of reasonable interest. However, it would also serve to illustrate the inconsistencies and the contradictions that exist in areas like the Vietnam war. If a political figure made one speech in the North and another contradictory one in the South, it would become evident in the files of the National Information Bureau; if his voting record in Congress was at odds with his public speeches to his constituents, it would also be recorded by the Bureau. If a politician quoted statistics or made charges that were contradicted by other reputable sources, that, too, would show up in the files.

HELPING TO DISTINGUISH BETWEEN FACT AND FAITH

The National Information Bureau could also help people distinguish between matters of fact and matters of political faith. In addition to showing what the public figures really believe in, the files of the Bureau could also show what "faiths" are involved in the major issues of the day. It might show, for example, that the question of welfare really boils down to an emotional argument between the liberal and conservative attitudes: the liberal feeling that *everyone* in a civilized country has a right to a decent amount of food, clothing and shelter, and the conservative feeling that *everyone* should work hard enough to be self-supporting. In other situations, the Bureau might show that there are five or six sides to an issue, each of which has its own combination of facts and faith.

The National Information Bureau would essentially be a large computer system. It would receive newspaper articles from every major newspaper in the country; speeches by all major public figures; books; polls, news analyses by television and radio commentators, and so forth. All of this would be filed, categorized and summarized automatically. The source material might be kept on microfilm; summaries, analyses and indexes could be kept on faster forms of storage. For those who merely wanted to "browse," information could be displayed on devices called *CRTs*, which look like television screens. Copies of source documents could be made on high-speed printers or microfilm reproduction equipment.

In computer parlance, such a system is known as an "information retrieval system." A number of business organizations use information retrieval systems to extract information about their employees or about sales, production or inventory. Scientists often use information retrieval systems to find literature on a particular subject of interest. Even the government data files which pose such a potential threat to our privacy are, for the most part, information retrieval systems. The National Information Bureau would simply be an information retrieval system designed to handle a different kind of information for a different clientele.

FINANCING THE NATIONAL INFORMATION BUREAU

Since computers are so expensive, financing such a system might well be a problem. It would be desirable to avoid government financing, since that would pose a number of thorny problems. On the other hand, it is not at all clear that the National Information Bureau could be self-supporting. To do so, it would have to charge its customers for the information it provided, and this would certainly discourage both the poor and many of the middle-class Americans who desperately need it. The only approach that seems viable, at the moment, is to provide financing from an independent, non-profit foundation.

FALSE DATA

There are other potential problems that should be explored before any money is invested in such an ambitious undertaking. For one thing, it is quite possible, if not almost *certain,* that false data would be supplied to the system at various times. Economic or military figures which would prove embarrassing would probably be "adjusted" before being released to the public and to the files of the National Information Bureau. This, of course, is already being done, but the exposure that would be provided by the Bureau would make it even more necessary. It might also make politicians attempt to withhold more information from the public.

This would not cause any great harm to the information retrieval system unless it took the form of a complete national conspiracy. There are still some politicians in this country with opposing viewpoints, and there is still some free flow of information; since *all* available information would be digested by the Bureau, the deceptions or inconsistencies of any one politician would soon become apparent. However, if the entire United States Government undertook a concerted effort to hoodwink the American people, it is conceivable that they could engage in such a massive propaganda campaign that even the National Information Bureau would be fooled.

THE BUREAU MIGHT BE BIASED

There is also the possibility that the Bureau itself might be biased. If the computer were programmed by a rabid segregationist, for example, the resulting system might reflect that bias. Since the National Information Bureau would be dealing with the categorization, the summarization and, to some extent, the analysis of information, it would be easy for even the most subtle personal prejudice to work its way into the computer. Hopefully, this problem could be resolved by subjecting the system to a constant scrutiny by people of varying political and philosophical attitudes.

CRITICISM AND PRESSURE

It is almost certain that the system would be subjected to extreme criticism by any individual or group that felt it was being unfairly portrayed by the Bureau. Financial and/or political pressure could certainly be brought to bear on the system by lobbies, companies, individual politicians or even the entire government. If this happens, and if the pressure is strong enough to shut down the National Information Bureau, then we will indeed be in as much trouble as the young revolutionaries say we are.

THE GREATEST DANGER: LACK OF INTEREST

The greatest danger of all is that nobody will be interested in such a system. No matter how available the information is, there will certainly be some people that will be too lazy or too uninterested to obtain it. There may also be a number of people who will not want to have anything to do with the Bureau because it only seems to tell them bad things. The "it's-about-time-we-heard-what's-right-with-America" philosophy might find it very difficult to cope with a National Information Bureau that refused to sugar-coat the material it collected.

It is not really clear, then, whether such a system would work or would have any value. It *is* clear, though, that computers are here to stay; technology is here to stay; the information explosion is here to stay. American society will continue to become more complex and more technological in nature. No one seriously expects Americans to move back to the farms *en masse* in order to solve the ecology problem. Similarly, no one really expects the telephone company to give up its all-digit dialing system, or the government to give up on its attempts to reduce everyone to a social security number.

We have already spawned the monster; now all we can do is attempt to control its growth and its appetite. We can try to control the way technology is used, so that it becomes easier, not more difficult, for people to cope with the complexities of our age. The National Information Bureau might well be a first step in that direction.

DISCUSSION QUESTIONS

1. If you were to summarize this article in one or two sentences, what would you say?
2. According to the author, in what ways does a computer effect major changes in our society and government? Do you agree with all of them? Why?
3. Suppose you were selected to serve on a national committee to develop a National Information Bureau. What problems are you likely to encounter? How would you handle each problem? Be specific.
4. From reading the article, how optimistic would you say the author is in terms of the government's acceptance of a National Information Bureau? Give reasons for your answer.
5. List and discuss briefly two major areas (other than those listed in the article) where a centralized information retrieval system might be useful.

SELECTED REFERENCES

Books

Awad, Elias M. *Business Data Processing.* 4th ed. Englewood Cliffs, N.J.: Prentice-Hall, 1975, Chapter 1.

Davis, Gordon B. *Introduction to Electronic Computers.* 2nd ed. New York: McGraw-Hill Book Co., 1971, pp. 33-51.

Desmonde, William H. *Computers and Their Uses.* Englewood Cliffs, N.J.: Prentice-Hall, 1971, pp. 1-10.

Wirthington, F. G. *The Use of Computers in Business Organizations.* Reading, Mass.: Addison-Wesley Publishing Co., 1966, pp. 1-48.

Articles

Autry, V. M. "Computer: Boon or Downfall?" *Data Management,* January 1974, pp. 26-29.

Drucker, Peter F. "What the Computer Will Be Telling You." *Nation's Business,* August 1966, pp. 84-90.

PART 2

Steps in Program Preparation

INTRODUCTION

The topic of systems analysis and design is a key area of interest in making business problems operational through the computer. It is a specialized area requiring (1) a thorough understanding of basic system concepts and (2) competence in the use of special tools for implementing system projects.

Comprehensive coverage of systems analysis and design is to be found in the many books written on this subject over the past decade. Given the space constraints, the attempt here is merely to explore the primary concepts and the role and requirements of systems analysis in business organizations.

Every organization needs accurate and timely processing of the information affecting its operations. When certain problems restrict proper information flow, they can threaten the organization's survival or at least limit its potential for growth. The difficulties that plague an information system range from specific, easy-to-handle problems to those reflecting a general breakdown in the system's ability to function. Regardless of scope, however, solving an organization's information processing problems requires complete involvement with the organization's total requirements for information. In other words, it is necessary to understand the purpose, the structure, and the overall operation of the organization.

Frequently, systems analysis entails a preoccupation with automated procedures without relating data requirements to functions and objectives. Too many systems have been designed to solve problems that do not exist. To eliminate this waste, a systems study formally sets out to define the problem and seeks to develop an optimum solution, aimed at establishing an effective framework of an operating information system. From the analysis phase through the implementation phase, objectives must be formulated, reviewed regularly, and revised as necessary.

In prescribing a methodology of systems analysis and design, certain phases and their sequence can be listed. However, a mechanistic approach of this kind tends to be somewhat artificial. There is no clear-cut moment when an analyst has completed the analysis phase, for example, and has begun the design phase. Even at the stage of receiving a given assignment which he may have helped to write, the analyst may have begun to formulate ideas about the manner in which the new system should function. Thus it is difficult to deliberate on a problem situation without thinking of possible solutions even before all the supportive facts have been gathered and reviewed. The assumption here is that the analyst is expected to consider the total system resources. Failure to do so can lead to the design of an ineffective system or a fragmented system that is redundant and productive of conflicting information.

THE SYSTEMS LIFE CYCLE

Analysis of a system is a part of what has come to be called the *life cycle* of a management system. Although there may be variations in detail, the key elements of the life cycle are essentially the same. The cycle is viewed as consisting of three stages:

1. Study of the present system and design of a new system.
2. Implementation of the new system.
3. Operation of the system.

The analysis and design stage concerns itself with a study of the present system in the light of how it is geared to the accomplishment of management's goals and objectives. It is performed for clearer recognition of the problems of the present system and for determining the requirements of the new system. Once the requirements have been established, a solution is proposed. Thus the end product of the first stage is a proposed solution in the form of a report.

The primary purpose of the second stage is to prepare the necessary details for conversion to the new system. This involves explaining the details of the system design, designing the input/output files, writing the necessary programs, and so on. The new system is then tested and debugged and its outputs compared to the old system. Finally, a full conversion to the new system is carried out.

The third stage in the life cycle is system operation, evaluation, and modification. In this stage the outputs of the new operating system are evaluated on a day-to-day basis and modified where necessary to make sure the system meets its initial specifications. Modifications may be required owing to changes in management's initial goals as well as external environmental changes. Personnel also must be continually trained and equipment maintained.

The Primary Phases of Systems Study and Design

The study and design stage in the life cycle involves five major phases: (1) understanding the present system, (2) determining systems requirements, (3) design, (4) implementation of the new system, and (5) system documentation and maintenance. Phase one calls for a general review of the present system: its adequacy, its level of performance, how well it meets the organization's present and future requirements, its strong and weak points, and its overall contributions to the profitability of the organization. Once completed, the findings are presented to management in the form of a detailed report.

The report serves as a description of the organization and a valuable means for gaining management's respect for the systems team's competence. Furthermore, it can identify other problems usually not considered within the scope of this study, providing material for future study. The report resulting from phase one becomes an input for phase two—determining the system requirements.

Phase two is, in essence, a feasibility study with the objective of defining the goals of an alternative system and establishing its practical and economic feasibility.[1] In determining the requirements of the proposed system, a look into the future is made by forecasting the impact of new products and services, volume trends, competitive products, and design and process innovations. Much analysis, synthesis, and simulation is carried out in establishing the system's present and future requirements.

Once the systems analysts and management have reached an understanding of the goals and the present and future requirements of the new system, activity definitions are then reshaped and the inputs and outputs of each activity are designed to fit the new goals. These details are developed and formulated through interviews and discussions with the prospective users and others who are in a position to provide relevant information about the system.

The result of phase two is a formal report documenting the system's requirements. It may include an input/output sheet, required operations sheet, and resource list of present and projected hardware, facilities, and files. The report provides a takeoff point for phase three, dealing with the actual, detailed design of the new system.

Systems Design

The design phase should produce the system's general flow: specifications of the format of outputs, inputs, files, and computer procedures; a tentative work schedule; and an estimate of operational costs. Other details include: (1) a design of specimen documents for inputs and specimen layouts for printed outputs; (2) an implementation procedure for conversion and file setup requirements and time schedules; (3) an operating plan including priorities, file security, and equipment utilization; and (4) a project proposal report to the user and the systems department.

Basic in phase three is the selection of system equipment. Equipment selection is aimed at satisfying design requirements and constraints. Evaluation of equipment may result in changes in the configuration of the system, which in turn affects program design. These and other factors must be carefully weighed before a final decision is reached on the adoption of the new system. Some of the key factors to be reviewed include: (1) business growth, (2) personnel selection and training, (3) availability of specialists by computer manufacturers, and (4) other business applications and their ease of implementation. These factors may result in further modification of the system design.

Once the new system has been designed and the proposed equipment selected, a report describing the new system is presented to management for approval. The

---

[1] A substantive part of the work given to the feasibility study covers an examination of current and proposed costs to justify the proposed expenditure on a full systems study and to provide a basis against which performance can be monitored. Additional considerations are made regarding the cost of present and proposed equipment, the cost of operating present and proposed systems, personnel costs affecting the proposed system, file conversion costs, and system maintenance costs.

objectives of the report are to provide management with a clear understanding of the new system's economic value to the organization and with supportive information for proper evaluation by the company's specialists.

System implementation. The implementation phase serves to ensure that the system is fully implemented as intended and is producing the desired output in an accurate and timely fashion. The user is a key individual here. He must be involved with the supply of test data and must agree with the expected results as well as the results based on the use of the test data. He must also be involved in planning for pilot and parallel running and in the education and training of his staff. User participation should be maintained throughout the changeover to a new system so that there is a minimum disruption of existing procedures and a smooth transition to new ones.

System testing is a critical stage in putting a new or revised system design to work. The test's purpose is to validate the accuracy of the system's output. Given the use of the data prepared by the user, it tests (1) the information flow within the system, (2) the manual paper handling by the user's staff, and (3) the links between programs as well as man–machine links. Finally, the test reflects to the analyst and the user that control totals are maintained throughout all processing operations to ensure that transactions have been processed and have been related to their appropriate records.

In constructing test data, a data item dictionary or similar document should be prepared. The contents should include: (1) the name of the data item as it appears on the input form; (2) a brief description of the data (whether it is alphabetic or numeric, the size range of the number, etc.); (3) the destination of the data; and (4) what happens to the data item along the way (is it added to other data items or is it merged onto a new master tape?). The data item dictionary and the input and output formats are all that is needed to begin preparing test data.

System documentation and maintenance. Once the analyst is satisfied that the system is working to his and the user's expectations, it is time to prepare the final documentation. Good documentation safeguards the integrity of the system and provides a vital communications link with others who may need to work with the new system design. Generally, documentation of the final system design will include the assignment authorization form, investigation and working files, the feasibility reports, a system definition, the computer operations guide, and operating instructions. The documentation must be consistent in form, understandable, and free from the technical jargon that might be a source of confusion involved in its interpretation and use.

Problems in Systems Work

Of the several problem areas that affect systems work, the ones most frequently mentioned are related to problem definition, communication, personnel, education, and management participation. The first three areas account for approximately 50 percent of the problems and the last two areas for roughly 25 percent. The remaining 25 percent fall into the areas of scheduling, documentation, vendors, and so on.

At the problem definition stage, some users are uncertain about what EDP can do or what information reports should include. Poor problem definition results from the prospective user's failure to realize the importance of conveying all aspects of the problem, from his reluctance to take adequate time to provide accurate and pertinent information in defining his requirements, or from his uncooperative attitude. Such attitude has much to do with the user's fear of losing his job, worry about his status, or gripe about the present operation, often leading the analyst to conclude falsely that the user "has no immediate need for a new system."

Thus, for effective, accurate definition of the problem at hand, both the user and the analyst should work together in an atmosphere of mutual trust, exchanging views and sharing the kind of information that would contribute in a positive way to efficient design of a new system.

Good user-accepted systems can be developed if users and top management are encouraged to play their proper role in the development of their own systems. A research report by McKinsey & Company, Inc. shows that organizations which are more successful with systems work are requiring their line managers to "identify computer opportunities, specify their payoffs, staff and/or manage their systems development efforts and also be accountable for the results."[2] The report further suggests that the key to success is a strong thrust of constructive interest from corporate operating executives who have put their own staffs to work on computer development projects.

To have the active involvement of managers requires that their interest be stimulated along these lines and that they receive some additional education in systems. Usually, this can be accomplished through seminars and lectures in a relatively short time. Top managers must recognize the need for them to work together with users and systems analysts when developing systems. They must be taught how to do their own thing within a framework of togetherness. Here, communication plays a critical role. It becomes important to know who communicates, when they communicate, what they communicate about, and how they communicate.

Well-established communication links enable everyone involved to maintain open lines so that a pulse of both the progress and problems involved are known and so that user-managers become meaningfully involved when they are called upon to make suggestions and decisions.

Systems analysts also have the responsibility of facilitating proper communication by maintaining an attitude which reflects their willingness to meet the user at his level of understanding and accommodate him in ways which encourage the user to "return the favor" in terms of feeding the analyst the information he is after. Thus what is needed is a system team composed of user personnel from the department which the proposed system will serve. In this respect, (1) users (and, indirectly, their supervisors) and systems analysts become involved in the project on a joint and equal basis; (2) analysts can more readily understand the problem and thereby design a more effective system; and (3) to some extent, systems people will be kept from making management decisions (telling management what kind of system it should have).

In summary, most systems problems result from poor problem definition and poor communication between the user and the analyst. Too frequently, analysts

[2] Arnold Barnett, "The Process of Effective Data Systems Development," *Barnett Data Systems,* 1971, p. 3.

may inadvertently make management decisions as a result of poor communication. The key to effective systems analysis and design is user-management involvement. With a team effort, participating members can help one another to perform their respective functions more effectively.

CONCLUSION

The future success of systems analysis and design as a management tool depends largely on its wider use and acceptance, as well as upon innovations in methodology. As there is increased emphasis on systems education, and as more managers gain experience with the application of systems analysis and design, there will be a growing appreciation of its potential. Furthermore, as specific areas related to systems analysis and design are improved, its use will become more sophisticated.

The systems staff and the users must work together to upgrade their understanding of user needs. The problem is one of relating each user's needs to systems objectives. The user often sees his requirements as unique and of primary importance. The systems analyst may view a particular user's requirements as only one of many demands made on the organization's information processing system. It is the responsibility of the analyst to recognize the users' legitimate information needs and to fit them within the framework of the entire system. A closer and more frequent working association between the systems staff and the users will do much to foster a better understanding of the users' needs.

Translating information needs into a responsive information processing system within a reasonable time period can be a major problem. Because most large-scale organizations have a growing appetite for new and timely forms of information, pressure will increase upon systems people to design and implement new systems more rapidly than ever. It is hoped that automated system building techniques such as *TAG*[3] and *ISDOS*[4] will provide part of the answer. Other means of speeding up the systems analysis and design process will depend on the creativity of individual systems analysts and equipment manufacturers. The analysts will have to work with the new devices and equipment to convert raw data into automated information processing networks as close to the source as possible.

In an effort to implement realistic and timely systems, the systems staff will need to be even more cognizant of the organization's entire systems network. New and revised systems will have to blend into a more complex network than now exists in most organizations. As new systems are added, their interrelationships will expand. The chances for duplication of information processing modules could go on increasing unless precautions are taken to provide for an orderly and logical growth of information systems.

There is no panacea for this problem of accommodating growing information system requirements. Systems managers and their staffs will have to devote more

[3] *TAG* (Time Automated Grid) is based on a series of *IBM* programs to help the analyst develop large-scale systems.

[4] *ISDOS* (Information System Design and Optimization System) is a contemporary system design being developed by the University of Michigan. Its major concept is the separation of user requirements from decisions on how these requirements should be implemented. With automated system design, a much more responsive information processing system should develop.

attention to short-range and long-range planning of the organization's systems needs. Once the systems staff and the organization's management recognize the need for planned systems growth, there is reason to believe that the information network will develop into a vital and responsive management tool.

The readings section consists of four parts: In the first part (systems analysis and design), Senensieb's article discusses the principles of systems analysis and design. Yorks' article clarifies the systems-management relationship and explains in some detail the various forms of systems organization. Wallace's article presents the problems that often exist between the analyst and the user, and offers suggestions for bridging the communication gap between them. Lee's article is a summation of the qualifications found in high-caliber systems analysts. Finally, Cotter's article explains the impact of virtual memory on systems design and operation.

Part two deals with program flowcharting. Part three is about decision tables. Part four consists of Bellotto's article on documentation. It summarizes the characteristics of a good documentation, the key information it should include, and its importance in computer installations.

PRINCIPLES OF SYSTEMS ANALYSIS AND DESIGN

~ *N. Louis Senensieb*

Systems analysis and systems design are the heart of all information systems work. Neither function can be performed in a vacuum. Basic steps must be completed before analysis can be performed on the data related to a problem or system under review. Likewise, creative design of a new system or a modification of an existing system does not automatically put it into operation. Therefore, it is necessary to consider systems analysis and design as key phases within a broader cycle of systems development. This cycle can best be described as the systems study.

The basic purpose of the systems study is (1) to review the adequacy of existing systems to meet operating requirements, or (2) to investigate specific operating problems, developing and implementing improvements that will provide an optimum solution to those problems, thereby contributing to the establishment of an optimum framework of operating information systems.

Scope of the Systems Study

The key to conducting any systems study is to recognize that it represents a broad cycle of systems work. This cycle consists of the following phases:

1. Survey initiation—defining the problem and planning the study project.
2. Fact gathering—collecting all pertinent data on the problem or situation under study.
3. Analysis and synthesis—evaluation of the facts and the creative design of a proposed systems improvement.
4. Selling—overcoming resistance to change and gaining acceptance for recommendations.
5. Formalizing—the necessary documentation for the acceptance, implementation, and operation of the new systems.
6. Installation—implementation of the actual operation of the new systems.
7. Follow-up—review to see if performance of the new system is according to plan, and identifying any modifications required.

The tools of systems work may be a decisive factor in systems improvement. However, their effective use depends on having all pertinent facts available. Only then can an effective job of analysis and systems design be undertaken.

Source: Reprinted, with permission, from *Data Management,* September 1970, pp. 19-23, published by the Data Processing Management Association, Park Ridge, Illinois.

Survey Initiation

Awareness of the problem. The initiation of a systems study may be the result of (1) a request from some operating group that has a problem, (2) management desire to review and revamp certain operations, (3) problem identification in previous studies by systems personnel, (4) periodic systems audits. Whatever the means of recognition and method of starting the study, two key factors must be understood and resolved:

1.   The true nature of the problem.
2.   The scope of the study.

Frequently, there is some obvious overt symptom which appears as the cause of an immediate operating problem. Yet the real problem may be hidden—consciously or unconsciously—and may be of a far more serious and widespread nature than the overt symptom. Often, perceived symptoms can be adjusted in such a fashion that the basic problem remains unrecognized and continues to fester.

Furthermore, managers may ignore or deemphasize problems which do not immediately affect their status and position in the company. Thus the key consideration of the survey initiation phase is comprehensive problem definition. This often will require some sort of preliminary survey to determine whether the known symptoms constitute the actual problem in its full scope.

The scope of the systems study. Once we have identified the true nature of the problem, the required scope of the systems study can be determined. Here we must consider such factors as whether a broad companywide study is required for a problem of companywide nature or implication, or whether a study limited to a specific operation or department is sufficient. We also must consider how formal or informal such a study should be to accomplish its specific objectives.

The scope of a systems study also is affected by whether the objective is one of merely patching an existing system or one of developing the best possible new system. The availability of company resources to support a systems study may well affect how much manpower can be spared by both the systems staff and operating personnel assigned, and what kind of systems revision can be afforded. These factors certainly will have to be taken into consideration in determining the scope and scheduling of any systems study.

The depth and breadth of the systems study also will indicate the types of fact-gathering techniques to be used.

The systems study plan. A systems study should be governed by a definite plan that indicates who is responsible for its conduct, the objectives to be obtained, who else is affected, and a schedule for the start and completion of all steps. The initiation of such a plan should be tied to attainment of necessary management approval to conduct the study question.

The systems study plan should be formalized into some type of project and study assignment for the specific guidance of the systems analysts and other parties concerned. Any such project plans should indicate at least the project title; the analyst(s) assigned; summary of objectives; scope of the project; any other parties involved; necessary background information; a starting and completion schedule indicating major phases of the study; cost and savings estimates; the anticipated reports and proposed plans, procedures, proposals, etc.; to whom they should be presented; and the approval authority for the study. Where periodic reviews and/or progress reports are required, that fact also should be indicated on the plan.

Fact Gathering

While the detailed fact-gathering phase can be considered to follow the survey initiation phase, some of it is concurrent. After all, facts are needed to define the problem. Furthermore, facts obtained later may shed additional light and may require the modification of the earlier problem definition.

Choice of technique. The choice of technique and the extensiveness of the fact-gathering phase depend on the type and scope of problem being studied. We may have (1) a general survey that covers broad problems crossing organizational lines; (2) organization studies limited to reviews of organization structure, relationships between different organizational functions, and divisions of responsibilities; (3) work measurement studies concerned with specialized job analysis and the establishment of work standards; (4) specialized surveys for forms control and records management programs; or (5) extensive feasibility studies for the installation of major new systems and automated tools such as electronic data processing.

Elements of data. Using a general survey as the more common example, this phase of the systems study concerns itself with gathering different elements of data to see the complete problem picture. While each problem may require a different set of facts for subsequent analysis, in-depth data probably will be needed on the following:

1. The organization structure, with stress on definitions, functional breakdowns, and divisions of responsibilities between them, including the names of people manning key positions in regard to the problem under study, their authority, and possibly even knowledge of the different job classifications involved.
2. Details on the policies and procedures in existence for comprehension of what is being performed by whom, when, how and why, and within what guiding and limiting policy parameters.
3. Details on actual work flow between components of the organization.
4. Quantitative data on volumes of work, man-hours required, personnel strengths, degree of stability of volume and work flow, and costs of performing key functions.
5. Qualitative factors on requirements of accuracy and limits of acceptance.
6. Identification of problem areas, e.g., uneven work flows, uncontrolled or excessive costs, unacceptable quality, or overlap of functions and duplication of work.
7. Inventory of equipment used and identification of areas where mechanization would be beneficial.

All the above elements of data are required so that we can get a picture of what actually is being done and what the real problems are. Do not accept all you find at face value. Organization charts and manuals may not be up to date, or may not reflect the actual but possibly informal authority structure and divisions of responsibility behind the scenes. Similarly, systems and procedures actually may bear little resemblance to those in the procedures manuals. Therefore, all vital information must be checked first-hand. Furthermore, even information obtained personally must be double-checked and cross-checked with other personnel and against other relevant data to assure its validity. After all, on these facts will rest subsequent conclusions and their synthesis with other pertinent considerations into new systems designs. If the facts are incomplete or inaccurate, solutions based on them cannot be much better.

Fact-gathering techniques. The basic fact-gathering techniques are the interview and the questionnaire, although rarely would one or the other be used exclusively.

The interview provides the opportunity for face-to-face contact and for possible exploration in depth of any key segment of data that the interviewee can provide. However, an interview must be planned. The interviewer should have a prepared list of key questions to which he wants answers. Without such a predetermination of subject matter to be covered, there is a danger that important aspects may be overlooked.

Besides this aspect of planning, the interviewer should follow a few other basic rules to assure optimum results:

1. Explain to the interviewee why the information is needed and how it will be used, overcoming at the outset any suspicion by taking the mystery out of the subject.
2. Conduct the interview in a friendly and informal manner and indicate a genuine interest in the other person's work and problems.
3. Don't dominate the conversation—you want the other fellow to talk and provide information.
4. Use care in phrasing questions in order not to elicit what the interviewee may interpret as desired answers, and don't express opinions or amazement that in turn may cause defensive reactions or resentment.
5. Be considerate of the other fellow's time.
6. Do not spend time on capturing voluminous notes during the interview. Take brief notes and then schedule time right after an interview to write up more details from memory.

Cross-check all information. Take no one's word, including that of the supervisor. Cross-check with his subordinates, as things may differ from what a supervisor believes is the current practice.

The interview, if properly conducted, also can be an opportunity to plant the seeds for proposed change as part of the selling phase.

The questionnaire is the other basic tool of fact gathering. It has the advantage of unlimited range of what can be covered and is more economical than a personal interview. It is most useful in posing questions that can be answered briefly and factually, e.g. To whom do you report? Who reports to you? However, this technique has serious disadvantages. It is difficult to secure replies from everyone, and the replies may be inadequate. People may also be willing to talk about controversial matters, but unwilling to put them in writing. Then there is the matter of different interpretation of the questions and of the answers.

In developing a questionnaire, observe certain ground rules:

1. Determine carefully what questions are required to get the desired information.
2. Visualize the person(s) from whom answers are desired.
3. Ask no objectionable questions.
4. Avoid long or involved questions.
5. Phrase questions to avoid misunderstanding or to avoid giving clues to an expected answer.
6. Arrange questions in a logical sequence.
7. Make questionnaire as brief as possible and as easy as possible for the recipient to answer.

Frequently, these techniques are combined in some manner, depending on the information to be obtained, the type of situation and personnel involved, and the abilities and time limits of the systems analysts. .

The two basic techniques can be supplemented, as appropriate, by detailed checklists outlining data required, collection of printed procedures, reports, organization charts, production statistics, cost control, and, where applicable, work sampling techniques.

The flow chart. A flow chart can provide an effective overall pictorial representation of a system. It assists the systems analyst in effectively gathering all the necessary data to describe an existing system. In step-by-step graphic representation, it can help to determine whether all steps of a system are accounted for, and its use of symbols and flow-lines reduces the volume of written descriptive material and cross-reference notations required. (Subsequently, in the analysis phase, flow charts can provide graphic analysis of work flow; facilitate the spotting of bottlenecks, duplications, and unnecessary operations; and provide for pictorially comparing the systems.)

Decision tables. To supplement flow charts, decision tables are often used. They display the logic of complex interrelationships and alternatives in simple table matrix form. Like flow charts, decision tables also are a tool for the subsequent analysis phase. They are a valuable technique for expressing computer program logic. Software techniques exist that permit acceptance of program coding in decision table format.

As shown in Figure 1, the basic format of a decision table consists of four parts:

1. The condition stub—containing a series of conditional statements pertaining to a problem.
2. The condition entries or rules—various rules which satisfy the conditional statements and which can be answered by yes (Y) or no (N) entries in the table.

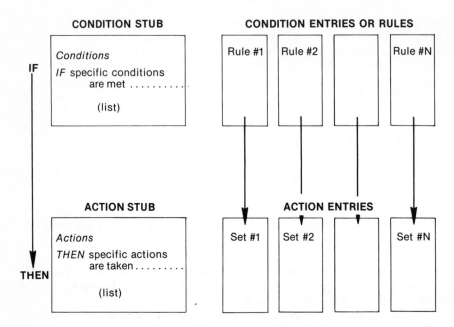

Figure 1. Basic Format of a Decision Table

3. The action stub—all possible actions which can be taken as a result of the conditional statements.
4. The action entries—all the action or actions that can be taken for each specific condition entry or rule.

Analysis and Synthesis

In this phase of the systems study all the facts are reviewed and set in perspective. Requirements of the business are synthesized with knowledge gained about its present operations, permitting the dynamic creation of a new systems design or modification of an existing system to meet the predetermined objectives of the study.

Basically, the raw materials for this phase are the objectives of the study, the problems defined, and all the facts gathered to date. Keep in mind that there is no cutoff in fact gathering. As different aspects of a problem come to light, more data may be required. Finally, from the scrutiny of all data on hand, a new systems design can be created to overcome the noted problems and meet predetermined objectives for the system.

Modern systems concepts have introduced a complicating factor. No longer is it sufficient to come up with just a solution to an isolated problem. We now recognize that modern organizations are an intricate network of numerous integrated systems and subsystems. As a result, one of the challenges of effective systems design is the integration of these organizational components and the effective channeling of information between them. In terms of the systems study, this emphasizes the need to review the interrelationships and effects that the existing system has on other systems, and to assure that the new systems design takes such interrelationships into full consideration. This may require more delicate compromises to assure an overall optimization of systems than if we were only concerned with the limited scope of one system or subsystem, or only one component of the organization.

No systems tool provides a greater assistance than the flow chart in this key analytical and creative phase of systems work. The other sources of analysis consist of five questions: What? Where? When? Who? How? which invariably lead to the sixth question, Why?

The use of these questions can be summarized as follows:

What is done? *Why* is it done at all?

Where is it done? *Why* is it done there, and where should it be done?

When is it done? *Why* is it done then, and when should it be done?

Who does it? *Why?* And who should do it?

How is it done? *Why* is it done this way, and how should it be done?

Having examined each part of the existing system and answered the above questions on each, we can apply the following work simplification steps:

Eliminate all unnecessary operations.

Combine operations, forms, and records that lend themselves to it.

Change the sequence, location, or grouping of operations.

Simplify the method of operation for optimum work and information flow.

The problem of synthesis is compounded by the fact that the new systems design should implement only real operating requirements. Determining such requirements calls for considerable analysis. It will call for knowledge of the objectives of the organization and how the system in question helps to implement them within the parameters of applicable legal and contractual obligations, company policies, and other related systems and procedures. In turn, the new systems design must have built in the review of operating results against pre-established controls for accuracy and validity and the feedback of pertinent information on operating results for managerial evaluation and decision making.

These areas make up the core of the systems cycle (Figure 2).

DECISION MAKING

Figure 2. Total Business Systems Cycle

The view of such an overall systems cycle, coupled with the recognition of an organization being composed of interrelated systems and subsystems, is commonly referred to as the total systems approach. It can provide a valuable intellectual discipline of systems design under the influence of which:

1. Objectives are the foundation for formulating a basic policy framework for the organization.

2. Logical operating procedures govern performance toward the attainment of objectives within parameters of applicable policies, and related procedures are integrated into logical systems.

3. All mechanization is systems-oriented and utilized where feasible.

The last point is of major importance. Logical steps, such as are contained in procedures, can be performed by computers. Combined with logical policy parameters, such computerized procedures can form the basis of powerful new management information systems.

Mechanization of this type can be economical, however, only where such systems and procedures are indeed designed ligically to form an integrated network. Then the computer can become the heart of an integrated management information system which accepts masses of input; edits, validates, and stores the data; and combines them into meaningful relationships as information extracts for rapid dissemination to management. The implication here is that today's systems analyst must be fully knowledgeable of the computer as a systems tool, and must be capable of knowing where it can be used economically in designing integrated systems networks.

Selling

The best, most efficient system is useless if it cannot be sold to those who must use it. Therefore, basic to all systems work is the awareness of the need to master salesmanship and the motivational techniques.

Systems must be sold to various levels of an organization: employees, supervisors, middle and top management, staff personnel—anyone who may be affected. Systems also may have to be sold in a variety of atmospheres; friendly, neutral, hostile.

Basic to implementation of all systems changes is the normal problem of overcoming human resistance to change. This is best done by involving those directly concerned in the new systems design so that the end product can be considered as having been designed by "us," not just by "you" or "them."

The selling phase does not have a definite beginning or end. It can start concurrently with the fact-gathering phase, where that phase involves planting the seeds of the ideas for necessary and desired changes. Certainly, it should be in full swing as the new system design is created. It must then continue beyond the stage where formal approval is required, and through to the vital installation phase.

Formalizing

This phase is concerned with the preparation of the required formal procedures, proposals, and reports for obtaining formal management approvals, orientation of all concerned, and providing guidance for all affected individuals during and subsequent to the installation phase.

Installation

More systems failures stem from muddled or slipshod installations than from any fundamental defects in the design. The systems analyst's job is not complete upon gaining acceptance of his proposals. He must now be the major helping hand to line management in actually installing the new system. Even though the authority and responsibility for operating the new system belong to line management, the systems analyst must play the leading role as the coordinator between all affected parties.

Like any other operation, the installation must be planned with scheduled dates for implementing key steps. These schedules must take into consideration procurement lead times for equipment and forms, accounting and holiday schedules, peak load considerations, time required for orientation and training, and learning curve considerations. In all these considerations, the systems analyst should be a prime adviser, coordinator, or participant, backed by his knowledge of the requirements of the system he designed.

The systems analyst also should advise and help implement the optimum method of installation: the all-at-once, piecemeal, or parallel operation type.

Certainly, as problems develop in the installation phase, the systems analyst should be on hand to help overcome them. This also is a phase during which selling has to continue. It is here that people finally come face-to-face with the actual change and may need continual convincing of its necessity and the benefits the system is designed to offer.

Follow-up

The fourfold purpose of the follow-up phase is to (1) assure consolidation of gains made by the new system, (2) provide the minor modifications that actual operating experience indicates are necessary, (3) assure the smooth working of the new system, and (4) eliminate any backsliding to the old system.

Without follow-up, the systems analyst cannot really be assured that the new system is being used. By detecting and implementing those modifications that operating experience shows to be advisable, he assures optimum implementation and performance of the new system and eliminates an excuse for returning to the old system. It is only when follow-up indicates the completion of an optimum implementation of the new system that the study's objectives are considered attained.

DISCUSSION QUESTIONS

1. What is the primary purpose of a systems study? What phases does it include? Explain each phase briefly.
2. What is the relationship between the formalizing and the installation phases of a systems study?
3. Suppose you were asked to conduct a systems study; what tool(s) would you use? Why?

4. Based on the details contained in the article, explain why it is important for the systems analyst to be a convincing salesman.

5. What factors do you consider important for successful interviewing? What approach would you use? Why?

THE SYSTEMS-MANAGEMENT RELATIONSHIP

Robert A. Yorks

The "systems–management relationship" is an exciting phrase until one investigates its meaning. The term management conveys many different functions. This term has been scrutinized by experts who have agreed to disagree. The summation of many such investigations was made in Harold Koontz's famous article, "The Management Theory Jungle," in which Koontz identifies five different schools of management thought. One of the many conclusions to be drawn from the article is that the term management has many valid meanings.

In the environment of the computer, one deals with managers who epitomize the different schools of management theory. However, to draw boundaries around this discussion, the theory by which management operates will be ignored. Instead, management will be identified by the type of task it supervises. Specifically, management will mean the supervision of the data processing area, the functional policy makers, or the functional user. The systems function will interface with these three types of management and, most often, the interface is different. With this understanding of the term management, let us examine the term systems.

One of the most nebulous of the decade, the term systems is said to have been defined "by so many different people in so many different ways that as a term, it is meaningless." This is a caustic but true comment.

The definition of systems that applies to this discussion is the one contained in the standard vocabulary for information processing. It states that a system is an assembly of procedures, processes, methods, routines, or techniques united by some form of regulated interaction to form an organized whole.

This definition, like most, permits individual interpretation. Thus, many practitioners view the systems function as merely "extended data processing" or the totality of functions which interface with a computer. Here totality of functions include people, procedures, communication networks, development tasks, and much more. So the relationship of systems to management can exist at almost any level and with any function. Limiting the systems function, for purposes of discussion, to the actions of analysis and design, let us consider what the relationship is between management (the types previously mentioned) and the systems

Source: Reprinted, with permission, from *Data Management,* September 1970, pp. 25-27, published by the Data Processing Management Association, Park Ridge, Illinois.

tasks necessary for the development of a computer based system. Three major areas will be explored: (1) systems analysis and systems design, (2) management involvement in each task, and (3) management and systems.

SYSTEMS ANALYSIS AND DESIGN

Who needs systems analysis and systems design and why? The immediate answer is everyone. But a closer examination shows that this is mostly lip service on the part of the computacrats and functional specialists. Clarification of this is needed since "design" is always accomplished. But what good is this design? It is not possible to perform systems analysis and systems design at the same time. However, it is possible to perform "some analysis" during systems design. Management should not equate "some analysis" to systems analysis. The point is that classical systems analysis of the present system is necessary to increase the probability of success for systems design. Too many systems have been designed to solve problems which do not exist. The design may end up being exotic, but not relevant.

Many organizations are faced with obtaining a computer for their systems work. There are two general approaches to computer selection, hardware-oriented and non-hardware-oriented. The hardware-oriented approach selects the computer and subsequently does the development work. This usually means no systems analysis. The non-hardware-oriented approach requires a systems analysis and systems design as the basis for computer selection.

The former approach focuses on the hardware and the latter on the system. It has been the policy of the U.S. Air Force to follow the latter approach. This was done in the belief that more cost-effective systems would result. We believe that has been true largely due to the requirement for systems analysis and systems design for all management supporting systems. Those in the systems business must insist on a thorough systems analysis and a meaningful systems design as a minimum.

The focus has been on the need for systems analysis and systems design. If they are so important and necessary it should not be required to "sell" them. Since the favorable sides of the tasks have been examined, the unfavorable sides must also be exposed. There are two factors militating against doing these tasks. First, the proper execution of systems analysis and systems design requires many resources. The resources are not only people, facilities, and money but also include time. *Probably more than any other factor, excessive time requirements have been the greatest obstacle to sound systems work.*

The second factor that feeds the argument that systems analysis and systems design are not needed is less tangible. It arises from the instant solution syndrome prevalent in systems work today. The reasoning goes something like this: "The problem is apparent to all and the solution even more so." It follows that the "resource eating task" of systems analysis is not needed since the answers are known. The only conclusion that can be drawn from this type of reasoning is that the complexities of the systems business have been seriously underestimated.

There are many forms of systems organizations (SYSORG). One which will serve as an example contains both computacrats and functional specialists. Computacrats include programmers, systems analysts, systems designers, operators, and management. The functional specialists are the representatives of the users assigned to the SYSORG. These personnel are representatives of the user but are organizationally independent. They are part of and under the direct control of the SYSORG. They include technicians, analysts, and management pertaining to their specific functional area. A SYSORG of this structure is generally located as a separate, independent agency within a firm or command.

The roles of the two types of personnel reflect the nature of the SYSORG. In addition, it is from these roles that the systems-management relationship evolves.

The role of the functional specialist is singular. He must represent the user in such a manner that outputs of the system properly reflect the user's needs. The functional specialist is responsible for, and indeed, must perform the systems analysis. That is, he must examine the user's environment and identify the areas of concern. If systems analysis leads to systems design, it is the functional specialist who furnishes the computacrat with the data needed.

Even though the functional specialist becomes subordinate to the computacrat during systems design, he must maintain an active entity. He serves as the connecting link between the computacrat and the functional policy makers. The SYSORG is constituted so that little direct interface is necessary between the user and the computacrat. The functional specialist fills this need.

The functional specialist needs to possess certain qualifications. First, he should have a thorough, complete knowledge of his functional area. Second, he need not be "knowledgeable" in data processing. This statement needs further clarification. If you could assign the number 100 to indicate the sum total of a man's job knowledge, a functional specialist would have 90-95 in the functional area and the remainder in data processing. This means that he would have a "communicating knowledge" relative to data processing. He would know that a compiler is not a piece of hardware but would not need to know that a COBOL program needs a procedures division. It is the computacrat who will need the detail data processing and systems knowledge.

The roles and qualifications of the computacrats are relatively straightforward. The computacrats will be primarily programmers, systems analysts, or systems designers. In addition to the known qualifications of these types of personnel, management should be sure they are oriented to the equipment generation being used or considered. A computacrat working with third generation equipment and systems should have a complete understanding of multiprogramming, for example. A problem with many SYSORGs is that they have lost their zeal for maintaining their professionalism. Some systems personnel still view computers as faster 407s.

MANAGEMENT INVOLVEMENT

Who is management? In this instance, management is the functional policy maker of a company or command. It is this management who instigates systems works. They levy a requirement for systems analysis on the SYSORG. They will request that a feasibility study be performed. To aid the study, they will establish objectives and guidelines with the SYSORG. In coordination with the SYSORG, a target date will be scheduled for completion of the study. It is important that the SYSORG be informed about present conditions and future management plans.

The SYSORG has the responsibility to provide a realistic plan to management for the systems analysis phase. But, it is ironic that a profession which develops MIS

(Management Information Systems) for functional units cannot develop one for itself. Some SYSORGs cannot even identify the tasks required let alone time schedule the task. This is not to suggest naively a detailed set of standard tasks and times, but we can do better. . . .

The final interface in the systems analysis phase is the presentation of the study results to management. It is management who will determine future action and will decide whether to further expend resources of the SYSORG to do the design.

Whereas management is active in the initial stages of systems analysis, it should be relatively passive in the initial stages of systems design. The SYSORG must take the initiative and define the system requirements for management. This means that the SYSORG, since it performed the systems analysis, need not go to management and ask the age old question, "what do you need in your new system?" The SYSORG should assume its responsibility and provide management with the initial system requirement, which should stimulate a systems-management dialogue on the new system. The SYSORG will not have final authority on the system requirement but should influence the content of it.

Once the system requirement is in focus, management becomes the activist, and must be especially careful not to abdicate its responsibility to the SYSORG. Management will decide on the final content of the system requirement and subsequently, on the content of both the system output and input. That is, the ball is in the SYSORG court but it must be played by management.

The SYSORG suffers from a credibility gap in systems design similar to systems analysis. It has little data on which to base project schedules. However, management can aid the SYSORG by exercising a control over the development. Systems design has identifiable tasks, i.e., output, data base design, input, etc., which lend themselves to positive control. That is, they do not actually control the SYSORG design effort but they do set its tempo.

The SYSORG has a responsibility to management during systems design. It must not only design an effective system but, more important, it must keep management abreast of its actions. Computacrats suffer from a malady which prohibits them from communicating with noncomputacrats. They assume that everyone has the same fervor for the computer environs as they. For example, why brief a general systems flowchart when you have a micro programming flowchart. This is what causes barriers to effective communication. The SYSORG and management must function as a team during systems design.

MANAGEMENT AND SYSTEMS

Management must become actively involved with the systems function. The SYSORG is a service organization for the functional area. It must not be permitted to set its own pace. Management needs to exert its influence in the twin functions of planning and control. No area in systems work needs greater emphasis. Companies have come to realize the economics involved in systems and they no longer ignore this function. Vast amounts of money and other resources were being expended with little or no management control. Firms now realize that they must apply the same management techniques to systems as they do to other functions.

The absence of sound management practices in the systems area can be traced to two factors. First, the top management of many SYSORGs are really technicians, not managers. Second, the lack of a systems or cybernetic view by functional management has resulted in tunnel vision. But improvements are being made in both these problem areas. One of the more forward looking solutions is to involve the managers in a cybernetic training experience. The objective is to have management outside and inside the SYSORG assume individual and collective responsibility.

DISCUSSION QUESTIONS

1. What is the main theme of the article?
2. Who are the computacrats? the functional specialists?
3. The author cites two approaches to computer selection. Explain each approach. From a managerial point of view, which one makes more sense? Why?
4. In what ways do line management and the author's systems organization work together toward a given project? Explain.

IMPROVING COMMUNICATION BETWEEN SYSTEMS ANALYST AND USER

John B. Wallace, Jr.

Communication flow between the systems analyst and the data processing user has been one of the most critical and long standing problems plaguing the field of data processing. Both groups share the objective of creating efficient and effective data processing systems, and whenever the purpose of a data processing application is to reduce the clerical cost of doing what must be done, the systems analyst and the user generally can make valid estimates of the cost savings which will result. But whenever the benefits of the new application are in the form of better information than was previously available, the communication problem becomes acute.

The systems analyst must spend a great deal of effort to understand how he can help the user make better decisions, and the user has difficulty understanding how the technical options available to the systems analyst can improve his decisions. Communication breaks down. The systems analyst is tempted to let the user specify his information needs in isolation rather than attempt to discuss the problems and assist in generating options for the user on the assumption that the

Source: Reprinted, with permission, from *Data Management,* June 1972, pp. 21-24, published by the Data Processing Management Association, Park Ridge, Illinois.

user should know what information he needs. In the same way that fish were probably the last to discover water, decision makers generally are hard pressed to specify how decisions are made and upon what they are based.

A language based upon a set of concepts which relates the systems analyst's options to the user's requirements is needed. With this language the costs and benefits of an information system can be explicitly identified. Once identified, the costs and benefits can be manipulated to compute standard financial measures of desirability such as payback period, rate of return, net present value, or expected annual savings.

In the framework to be developed in this paper, the systems analyst's options determine the cost of designing, implementing and operating a data processing application. The user's needs determine the benefits of the system to the organization.

The benefits of quality information are often considered intangible. Systems are justified on the basis of tangible cost reduction and the intangibles usually are considered to be by-products. But new clerical cost reduction applications are rare today. The cream of the new applications has been skimmed over the decades.

As information technology enters maturity, new data processing applications increasingly must compete for funding on the same basis as other projects such as a new punch press or truck fleet addition. To compete on this basis, intangibles must be made tangible. Quality must be quantified.

By relating cost to value, the users and systems analysts can jointly negotiate and design an information system with a maximum return to the organization. During this negotiation the users can better understand the costs of desirable features and determine how much they are worth. The user should be encouraged to regard this negotiation process in the same way he buys a car or company plane. Low maintenance or faster trips have quantifiable value just as accurate and timely data have. To refuse to estimate these values is to engage in sloppy thinking.

BUILDING LANGUAGE

The first step in bridging the communications gap is to construct a list of options open to the systems analyst and relate that list to the benefits which the user desires. The concepts which form the basis of the language through which the user and systems analyst can negotiate are the intersections between the systems options and user benefits.

These concepts can then be used as one classification scheme for the information sciences.

Of course, different sets of concepts are possible. Some lists of concepts are longer than others in the same way that one manager may break his job into five functions while another manager may classify the same set of tasks under only three headings. A good set of concepts would contain all of the relations (exhaustive), but would not overlap (the property of being mutually exclusive).

Not only must the set of concepts meet the requirements for a good classification scheme, they also must be relevant to the jobs that information systems perform for managers. Thus the concepts should encompass the three elements of information systems for managers: (1) faster awareness of problems and opportunities, (2) reduction in the amount of manual clerical effort, thereby freeing more time for managerial planning, and (3) information to evaluate more alternatives.

Consider the following set of five concepts to meet the objectives stated. The set of concepts which are the foundation of our language are *accuracy, responsiveness, timeliness, orientation,* and *flexibility.*

Accuracy

A clear concept of the value of accurate information must be based upon the two distinct ways in which information processing machines produce accurate information. First, the use of machines reduces the opportunity for clerical mistakes and second, provides cheap number crunching capacity for computing accurate answers for decision makers to replace "gut-feel" estimates. To compute the value of error reduction, the user and the systems designer must consider both the number of man-hours that can be diverted from searching for and correcting clerical errors and the improved organization performance which can come from a reduction in uncaught errors.

The systems designer can influence the amount of error reduction by his decisions on such alternatives as the place and method of capturing the data in machine readable form, the use of document reading devices, and the design of input editing programs.

Decision making information of improved accuracy generally results from the combination of fast, cheap computing capacity and management science techniques such as linear programming, inventory control, scheduling algorithms, and conversational corporate simulations. The cost of this type of accuracy includes the amortized purchase price or programming cost and training cost and the periodic cost of updating the data base and running the management science program.

The value of decision making accuracy is estimated by predicting the improvement in organizational resource utilization. For example, the value of a sophisticated forecasting package for customers' calls by hour of day is the reduction in wages resulting from the ability to handle the same level of demand with fewer clerks.

Responsiveness

Responsiveness refers to the time interval that occurs between the recognition of a need for information and the satisfaction of that need. In general, responsiveness can be improved by assigning high priorities to significant decisions (or decision makers), and reducing the distance between the user and the source of information through in-house experts, libraries, and desk-top consoles. For computer systems, the use of random access storage devices, conversational time-sharing, utility programs and general purpose languages to reduce the time required for programming a response to a specific inquiry, and training users to get answers quickly can improve responsiveness.

Information delay in any type of system can be modified by changing the distance information must travel, the speed at which it travels, or the number of delay points. Without using a computer, a manager may reduce delays on certain types of information by assigning priorities or reducing the number of links in the chain of command. Distance also can be reduced by physically relocating the information sources and users. Speed can be modified through the use of different media such as closed-circuit TV monitoring of charts of operating information. The responsiveness of a computer-based information system can be modified in similar ways. Turnaround time can be reduced for some applications through priority assignments and multiprogramming; distance can be reduced through the placement of remote consoles; and delays in searching can be reduced through the attachment of inquiry devices to on-line files.

Increasing the responsiveness of an information system has value if the productivity of resource is increased, expected waste or damage is reduced, or more profitable sales are made through the improved accessibility of information about the services of the organization. A responsive information system improves the productivity of resources by reducing nonproductive waiting time. Lower idle time will appear on the income statement in the form of lower costs for the same amount of productive work or more productive work for the same amount of resources. The productivity of an organizational planner can be improved by providing him with a set of responsive, conversational simulation programs that will allow him to test the profitability of more alternative plans than would be possible with pencil and paper or with a batch system. Additional productivity may result from the increased involvement which can accompany the capability to work conversationally with a computer without long waiting periods in which the planner often forgets about the plans.

What is often of interest is the value of each unit of improvement of responsiveness. For example, consider the Toll Charge Inquiry System of a large telephone company which helped the operators handle inquiries faster and also resulted in an annual saving of $250,000 in operator wages. Since operators were able to handle inquiries on the average of 30 seconds faster, each second of improved responsiveness was worth about $8,333 per year. This type of information can be used by systems designers to assess the possible profitability of improvements in information system responsiveness.

Reducing waste and damage through improved responsiveness is often accomplished by installing systems which quickly signal the occurrence of an out-of-control condition and either request or take corrective action. Examples of such applications include process control, critical patient care, and quality control. For example, the IBM typewriter plant in Lexington, Kentucky installed an early example of an on-line quality control system which resulted in lower scrappage rate and rework costs. Each inspector prepared a card whenever he found a defect. The computer system made control chart computations and indicated immediately the occurrence of a suspected out-of-control condition.

Airline and theater reservation systems and railroad boxcar inquiry systems are examples in which the responsiveness of an information system was exhibited in more profitable sales because customers spend less time acquiring the product or service. People prefer certainty to uncertainty, they prefer making productive use of their time, and they are often willing to pay for these preferences as evidenced by the price differentials inherent in reserved seats.

But the systems analyst should avoid the temptation to apply measures of the value of responsiveness in one situation to another situation without careful thought. For example, the fact that a thirty second reduction in inquiry time is worth $250,000 to a company a year does not necessarily imply that a sixty second reduction is worth $500,000. With respect to customers, reducing the time to answer an inquiry may have very nonlinear impacts due to "balking" behavior. That is, the typical customer may be relatively indifferent to waiting for twenty to thirty seconds but may choose another service if the response time grows to 45 seconds. The delay he will tolerate is closely related to what he expects. If he is told he will have to wait 35 seconds, but only has to wait 30 seconds, he may be highly pleased while if he is told he will have to wait 15 seconds and has to wait 30 seconds he may be highly displeased and choose another service the next time.

Timeliness

Timeliness refers to the correspondence between the age of stored data and the relevant status of the entity to which the data refer. Accuracy and timeliness are similar but they should be considered separately because they are achieved in different ways. The systems designer influences the accuracy of a system through techniques which keep the data in step with reality by keeping it error-free. He influences timeliness by updating the data to make certain that reality doesn't get out of step with the files. The cost of various levels of timeliness is primarily the per period costs of updating data files.

The value of timeliness comes from the same source as the value of accuracy; the improvement in capacity to make accurate inferences about the relevant status of some entity. The relevant status of a resource usually takes the form of where, or how many in order to determine its present or future availability. For example, since prospective airline passengers want to know the future availability of a seat, the airline updates its seat inventory upon each transaction.

In computing the value of timeliness, the systems designer must consider the influence of various updating schemes upon the accuracy of inferences about the relevant status of an entity. The value of timeliness usually increases with more frequent updating, but the amount of increase depends upon the predictability of the resources. Predictability depends upon such attributes as visibility, scarcity, and regularity of change of an entity. Piles of iron ore or gondolas of coal are usually more visible to the user than vacant airline seats on future flights or the level of working capital, therefore, it is more valuable to record the relevant status of the latter two resources than the former. Rarely is it valuable to be able to infer the relevant status of a plentiful resource. For example the value of a timely airline reservation system diminishes when reservation clerks can safely assure a passenger of a seat without referring to the file. Thus, if a resource is scarce and its value fluctuates in a complex, hard to predict manner, a timely information system is likely to be valuable.

If the location of an entity is its relevant attribute, then the value of timeliness is related to the cost of searching and the cost of not knowing. For example, in a job shop the location of each batch may be entered through a remote terminal whenever the batch is moved. If an engineering change or quality check must be made on the batch, the value of knowing the location of a batch can be estimated by considering the man-hours required to search for the batch and any lost production or damage which may occur before the batch is located.

If the display strategy and updating strategy are interdependent, the systems designer may not wish to estimate the value of responsiveness separately from the value of timeliness. For example, if the system is designed to update the file whenever a transaction occurs (real-time) and make the information immediately available to the user through a remote terminal then the value and cost of responsiveness and timeliness are too interdependent to be worth separating. However if the display strategy is separate, and the problem is to determine how often to update the files, then the value of timeliness should be estimated. For example, railroad boxcar location applications collect data whenever a train passes a terminal, but the on-line files may be updated remotely or by batch every two, four, or six hours. Since it is easy to predict the future location of a train by considering its movements over a twenty-four hour period, batch updating is reasonable.

Orientation

Orientation refers to the amount of effort the user must expend in searching for and transforming data to suit his needs. The systems designer influences the orientation of the system through the amount of relevant detail and the dimensions in which the information is presented to the user. Using exception reporting techniques and computing the statistics which the user needs are techniques for improving the orientation of the data.

The value of orientation can be estimated by considering the expected total man-hours which must be expended by the users searching for relevant data, calculating statistics, adjusting for incompatibilities, and making comparisons. The orientation value of the system is directly proportional to the degree to which the users are relieved of these burdens.

Flexibility

Flexibility is a measure of the ease of modifying the information system to meet varying requirements. It represents a tradeoff between current programming and operating efficiency and the cost of future changes. The systems designer influences the flexibility of the information system by specifying the type and amount of documentation, the modularity of the programs, the level of the programming language, the file size and record sizes. Initial systems costs usually are directly related to the amount of documentation and the degree of modularity of the programs and indirectly related to the program-language level. (Compiler-level languages such as COBOL, FORTRAN, and PL-1 are examples of higher level languages than are the machine-oriented assembler languages.) Periodic operating costs usually are directly related to the degree of modularity, the level of the language, and the file and record sizes.

The most important factors influencing the value of flexibility are advances in information technology, changes in the information needs of users, and programmer turnover. Large records and files leave room for additional data to meet new informational needs and to allow for growth in volume of transactions processed. This reduces the expected cost of modifying the information system in the future. Program modularity, complete documentation, and the use of high level languages also generally lowers the expected future costs of reprogramming the system to meet new information needs.

USING THE LANGUAGE

A comparison of the options available to the systems analyst in conjunction with the benefits desired by the user of an information system results in a set of concepts which can be used to improve the way in which information systems are designed. The user has a better idea of what he is getting and how much it will cost and the system analyst has a better idea of what the user really needs.

Classification is one of the early steps in the development of any science. If the realm of Management Information Systems is to become scientific so that knowledge of the techniques can be taught in an orderly way and new knowledge can be added rationally, then relevant classification schemes must be proposed, evaluated, modified or discarded.

DISCUSSION QUESTIONS

1. What suggestion(s) does the author offer in bridging the communication gap between the systems analyst and the user? Do you agree? Explain.
2. Explain the set of concepts suggested in the article for improving information systems design.
3. How does one improve or modify responsiveness of a computer-based information system?
4. What factors determine the amount of savings realized from improved responsiveness of a given area?
5. In terms of the contents of the article, what is the difference between responsiveness and timeliness?
6. Suppose that a large retail store redesigned its credit card information so that the two employees in charge can now handle incoming inquiries in one-half the average time it took under the old system. What are the factors of responsiveness in the customer complaint department of the same store? Discuss.

PROFILE OF AN EFFECTIVE DATA PROCESSING SYSTEMS ANALYST

J. R. Lee

If one were asked to identify the distinguishing attributes of an outstanding systems analyst, the initial response would probably be "he has good technical knowledge" or "understands how to use computers effectively." Then a long pause would follow in search of other traits.

Just what traits do good analysts have in common? For example, two equally effective systems analysts can have substantially different approaches to problem definitions and solutions. What is it then that makes both of them good analysts?

Many managers rely heavily on technical competence as the primary indicator of probable success when faced with the prospect of selecting a systems analyst or project leader from a group of candidates for the positions. Too little attention is given to the personal qualities that can significantly influence the productivity of the analyst.

While technical competence forms a solid base necessary to support effective project leadership, it does not appear to be the critical factor that distinguishes the outstanding analyst from the mediocre one. Many analysts possess good technical qualifications but do not produce superior results. Other analysts produce quality work with only average technical competence.

My objective here is to isolate and examine certain non-technical qualities which are frequently found in the best systems analysts. Of course, all of these traits will not be found in every analyst.

• *The more effective analysts spend much effort on the problem identification phase of the project.* They are acutely aware of the possibility of solving the "wrong" problem. For example, they do not want to design a sales analysis system that merely produces clerical savings when the critical need is for a sales forecasting system. Consequently, the analyst goes to considerable length to insure that the apparent problem to be solved satisfies the basic management need.

• *The systems analyst/project leader sees the EDP system as only one element or component of the total system.* He recognizes that "overemphasis" on the automated phase of a system is an occupational hazard that frequently can be avoided only through conscious effort. Recognizing that he is often the only individual who clearly sees how all pieces of the completed system will relate, he assumes full responsibility for both the manual and automated phases of the system.

• *The better analyst believes in the synergistic capacities of a team approach to problem solutions.* He does not follow the philosophy, "I can do it better myself." This is, in part, because of the importance he places on the training and development of other persons assigned to the project. But, primarily, this attitude stems from his confidence that ideas generated and tested in a group environment will achieve superior results.

• *The effective analyst has the ability to design the system to operate in not only the current environment but also the environment of the future.* This is a difficult aspect of his job, an important and distinguishing hallmark of outstanding work. Systems designed for the future can be identified by such features as the absence of restrictions imposed by table sizes, few programs approaching maximum core size, file designs that do not have a maximum capacity (except in extremely unusual circumstances), etc. The analyst designs the system with as much flexibility for future growth as possible.

• *He believes that the elements of work involved in project conception and*

Source: Reprinted, with permission, from *Data Management,* September 1970, pp. 24-25, published by the Data Processing Management Association, Park Ridge, Illinois.

implementation can be scheduled to a reasonable and realistic degree. Consequently, he plans and controls the project with a well organized and detailed work plan. In essence, he replaces artistic management with planned professional management techniques.

• *He assumes that it is his responsibility to present alternative solutions to the user as well as provide a meaningful basis for decision-making.* He does not automatically assume that the user always knows exactly what he wants. Rather, the analyst provides meaningful ideas of what can be obtained. He then works patiently with the user to select most desirable alternatives.

• *The analyst designs the system to help operations, and to use the personnel function effectively.* For example, automatic file purges, thorough edits, elimination of operator controlled decisions, etc., are typical features of his systems. The system is, in essence, designed to help prevent problems as well as detect them.

• *The analyst will dig deeply to acquire and use valid suggestions from users for design characteristics, special features, input producers, etc.* This is perhaps the prime method employed by him to acquire rapid user acceptance and support of the newly implemented system. The analyst insists upon user participation in design, and upon management support of the entire effort. These, he recognizes, are basic to successful systems.

• *He assumes that most problems in the initial operation of the system are his responsibility.* As problems occur, he closely reviews the training plan and documentation for weaknesses, inaccuracies and omissions. He is quick to make revisions and improvements or increase the scope of training. A willingness to provide comprehensive assistance in the inital operation of the system can be a critical factor in overcoming any resistance to a new system.

• *He considers training a major element of his job and, consequently, allocates a major block of his time to training operations personnel as well as user personnel.* He is continually engaged in training activities on both a formal and informal basis, because he assumes most user problems can be corrected by training.

• *He exhibits leadership qualities and is able to motivate the project team to accomplish goals and to function at a superior level of individual performance.* A considerable source of his personal satisfaction comes from helping others to move forward as individuals and as professionals.

• *He keeps both the user and data processing management informed of progress, and of anticipated problems.* Routine problems are, of course, handled by the analyst, but management is given as much advance notice as possible of problems that may affect the implementation schedule.

Some will weigh these points differently, deleting some and adding others. Hopefully, this examination of the salient traits exhibited by effective systems analysts will be useful as a tool for personnel training and selection.

IMPACT OF VIRTUAL MEMORY ON SYSTEMS DESIGN AND INSTALLATION

Herbert E. Cotter

Virtual storage can be viewed as another step in the continuing evolution of data processing systems. Virtual storage, stated very simply, is the apparent extension of memory size beyond the available real memory.

For example, a real computing system may have one million positions of real storage, but has an apparent memory size that is much larger, perhaps ten million positions. It becomes the responsibility of a software and hardware combination to allow large programs to operate on a smaller real machine size.

The issue becomes one of why virtual storage is needed. What is virtual storage going to do within the data processing profession and what will it do to the relationship between data processing and the rest of a corporation?

MAN AND MACHINES

Viewed from within, data processing departments have been striving for a balance between the costs of computing equipment, and the costs of people to implement the computer systems. They have, in effect, been solving a linear program. The two variables have been man and machines, and they have been solving the linear program for minimum cost.

Early computers, like the IBM 650, were very expensive by today's standards. Many firms chose to have a balance that was labor intense in order to maximize machine utilization. As machines became less expensive, the balance began to shift. Input/Output Control Systems (IOCS) became more popular, but often made less efficient use of the machine. High level languages, and job stream monitors have been significant factors in changing the balance between machine overhead and manpower productivity. Multiprogramming was the next step in this evolutionary process, enabling the hardware to be utilized more effectively.

Virtual storage becomes yet another step in this continuing evolution. It has a twofold advantage for the data processing community. First, the machine's storage resource will be better utilized with the virtual concept, allowing a higher degree of multiprogramming. Second, virtual storage allows systems designers and programmers to become more productive by concentrating more on the needs of the end user and less on the needs of the computer.

Source: Reprinted, with permission, from *Data Management*, September 1973, pp. 47-51, published by the Data Processing Management Association, Park Ridge, Illinois.

TRADITIONAL SYSTEMS

Many older, traditional systems have been balanced with a cost displacement technique. How many people can be replaced with a new payroll, accounts receivable, or general ledger system? The justification of newer systems has become more difficult when dealing with intangibles such as information value or customer service. These new requirements bring about broad new terms, data base systems, data communications systems, and information systems. This change in emphasis has been reflected by many data processing departments changing their names to information services or information processing departments. Many have become divisions or separate corporations rather than just departments of a corporation. This reflects the growing emphasis on the information needs of today's modern business. These large complex information systems become difficult to justify because they use massive quantities of real storage.

Virtual storage provides a vehicle for extending the power of the computer into the user departments through the implementation of advanced data base and data communications systems. There is a massive quantity of new applications waiting to be implemented on computing equipment and the lessened concern for storage requirements will make the justification easier.

CONSTRAINTS OF GROWTH

Returning to a view from within the data processing department, virtual storage can help the data processing profession in the design and implementation of systems.

Machine costs have undergone radical changes in the last ten years. As an example, the IBM 1401 cost about $125 per 1000 positions of additional memory per month, while today the IBM 370 line of computers have some models where that same 1000 positions of memory cost only about $5.00. In terms of central processing unit (CPU) power the number of instructions that can be executed per dollar has gone up dramatically.

While machine costs have been going down, the cost of people has been increasing at a significant rate. Data base and data communications systems are being implemented with an eye towards increasing the productivity of people by providing standardized interfaces to files and terminals. In addition, many small users have not been able to take advantage of the full high level language compilers because of their large real storage size. Many more data processing departments will be able to take advantage of these advanced function packages to reduce personnel costs. Systems can be designed that solve user needs rather than the idiosyncrasies of the computer.

As the cost of computing equipment has decreased, users have been willing to devote an increased portion of the hardware to system related functions. Trade-offs have been made in the past to achieve a balance between the man and machine relationship. These system functions were installed to make the machine easier to use.

IMPACT ON SYSTEMS DESIGN

The systems designer has several goals in mind when he creates a system. They can be identified as developing:

- Useful applications
- Open-ended applications
- Economical applications
- Meet timely development schedules
- Design systems that are easy to implement

Obstacles in the way of these goals are the real machine constraints of the available computer system.

Systems have always been designed with real machine constraints. Unit record equipment was constrained by the function of the machine, and its capacity. One machine could sort, another collate, a third tabulate and summarize, etc.

The introduction of computers removed many of the functional constraints but left a capacity constraint which was expressed primarily in terms of machine size.

Systems were designed that took many steps to perform a rather straight-forward application. A job was broken down into many steps so that it would fit into the available machine size. Systems are still being designed today as if they are to execute in a "unit record" mode.

Virtual storage allows systems to be implemented which satisfy a business requirement, not an artificial program size requirement from the data processing department. The high availability of storage should be viewed as the removal of an artificial constraint on the systems designer.

Data files are another area that should be considered when viewing virtual storage. Generally, data files have been kept on an external storage medium because of the expense involved in keeping them all resident in real program storage. Virtual storage allows a greater capability to consider data to be tables in the memory of the machine rather than a special external file. When data is viewed as a table in the program rather than as a file, the presence or absence of that data in real storage is determined by the software system supporting the virtual storage hardware. The data can be brought into real storage on demand by the paging supervisor and removed from real storage when the use of the data becomes low.

A considerable amount of time is spent designing systems that fit in a particular hardware environment. This is primarily a memory size constraint. As larger computers are installed, the old application continues to execute in the "unit record" form of operation. The time and manpower to re-program a job to fit more logically into a larger partition or region size is not easy to justify and the inefficiencies continue for 'a prolonged period of time. When working with a virtual storage environment, the application is designed to meet a user function. The application can execute on small and large machines.

Multidivisional corporations that run common systems on different hardware sizes are limited by the smallest of the installations in nonvirtual systems. Compromises will often be made in system design so that the small systems can be accommodated. Virtual storage enables applications to be designed to solve the user department need, instead of the machine need. An application will usually run faster on a larger system while not compromising the capabilities of that larger system. The same application will run slower on the smaller division's equipment, but, with virtual storage, it can still be designed as a full function system.

In summary then, it can be seen that virtual storage systems help the systems designer in five areas:

- Wider availability of generalized packages such as high level compilers, data base, and data communications systems to ease application design and implementation.
- Ability to design full function systems that run on a variety of machine sizes.
- Ability to design systems that take advantage of changing real machine environments.
- Ability to consider data as tables in memory rather than external files.
- Increased ability to design systems that meet used department requirements rather than machine constraints.

IMPACT ON IMPLEMENTATION OF SYSTEMS

Virtual storage impacts the system implementation process in a number of significant areas. A programmer, as well as a designer, has a number of goals that he strives to achieve. These can be identified as:

- Write straightforward programs
- Create programs that are easy to modify
- Use available development tools to make full use of his time.

In dealing with the systems design process the increased availability of generalized packages was considered. These data base and data communication systems, as well as full high level language compilers, can also significantly impact the implementation effort.

An additional area that cannot be overlooked is interactive computing. A wall has been built around data processing departments because it has become too expensive to allow hands-on test time. Interactive computing systems can break down the wall and allow programmers to become more productive. It is important to move the programmer closer to the computer to make him more productive, just as it is important to bring user departments online to speed their flow of information.

BETTER TEST TURNAROUND

Virtual storage can improve the productivity and morale of programmers by providing better testing turnaround. Programmers often are assigned multiple programs with a potential loss of productivity when moving from one program to another. This is done to balance the workload while a programmer is waiting for the results of a test shot. Crisis situations often occur in which a programmer becomes even more constrained by test turnaround time and operates at less than maximum productivity during the crisis period.

In addition, programmers often have to work off-hours to test nonstandard size programs. Virtual storage may allow this oversized program testing to take place during the day shift.

The application impact must be viewed to complete an analysis of virtual storage on the implementation process. Today, a designer lays out a system, specifies record layouts and program modules and then hands off to the programmer who will spend a considerable amount of time coding the system. The programmer may have had a general idea regarding the ultimate size prior to compilation. It is not until compilation that the programmer finds out, for the first time, whether the program will fit in the assigned real storage constraint. When the programmer finds that he has violated the installation standard he has several alternatives.

- He may request an exception to the standard size because of the complexity of his particular program.
- He may simply overlay the program, with its resulting inefficiencies in execution of the program.
- He may decrease the size of his file blocking factors to reduce the size of the program.
- He may reduce the number of buffers used by his program, making the performance less efficient.
- He may spend considerable amounts of time reworking the program, breaking it up into several steps to perform the required system objective.

Once the program is complete, additions will start the cycle over again. All of these problems are more likely to occur on a complex program and, because of the complexity, problems are difficult to correct. The impact of virtual storage on these areas is significant in that none of these remedial actions will have to be taken. The system can handle the overlay problem more efficiently through paging. There will be no violation of standards and, therefore, no reason to change blocking factors to meet memory constraints. Virtual storage removes the constraint of memory from the list of worries of each programmer. He now spends more time concentrating on his goal of creating a code that is easy to modify, meets his implementation deadlines, and, most importantly, satisfies the user department requirements.

In summary then, it can be seen that virtual storage is an aid to the programmer in the areas of:

- Greater accessibility of packages to ease the programming burden.
- More users will now be capable of taking advantage of interactive computing.
- Better turnaround can be provided for programmer testing.
- Storage becomes a much smaller consideration in the implementation of systems.

OPERATIONS

It is imperative that a reasonable operating environment be provided for the testing and productive running of applications.

An operations department has the goals of: meeting schedules, making efficient use of the machine, handling peak demands.

The operations manager is perhaps best termed a "juggler." He has limited machine resources and unlimited demands from many people. Virtual storage removes one of the main scheduling constraints, that of machine size. Now jobs may be introduced to the system based on their requirements for completion, and their use of peripheral devices, not the artificial requirement of partition or regions size.

In terms of making efficient use of the machine, wasted storage is found in the nonvirtual machine environments in existence today.

If a job step requires, for example, 120K of storage for execution, various phases of that step require only a portion of the partition or region for productive use. There may be buffers used infrequently during the execution of the job, exception routines used only at certain times of the year, routines only used for data exception, etc. A virtual storage system will automatically remove these infrequently used portions of code from the system and replace them in real storage if and when they are required.

The operations department is often called upon to provide "hot job" service for those jobs that must be turned around quickly. Whenever these have hit the existing nonvirtual systems, drastic action sometimes had to be taken. Initiators had to be stopped and perhaps long running jobs would have to be canceled to make way for the "hot job." With a virtual storage, the system automatically removes less critical jobs from real storage and allows the hot jobs to acquire the appropriate quantity of real storage to meet the immediate requirement.

If a batch computer goes down for a period of time, the knowledge can be contained within the department. Only the most prolonged outages will be known back in the user departments. As more systems become terminal oriented, the presence of the computer becomes a concern to people outside of the data processing department. Virtual storage provides a more agreeable method of backing up large on line systems. Nonvirtual systems have needed matching CPU's to back up online computers. Now virtual storage makes it easier to back up a large computer with a smaller model, providing backup where there was none in the past.

In summary, virtual storage aids the operations department in the areas of: "hot job" scheduling; better utilization of CPU memory resource; small machine backup for larger real-time computers.

CONCLUSION

Virtual storage has been viewed from several angles. It is another step in the evolution of data processing opening up new areas for computer use. It has specific advantages in the individual departments of design, programming and operations.

Virtual storage systems provide a basis for additional enhancements to operating systems. IBM is utilizing virtual storage techniques to provide new teleprocessing access methods, new file access methods, and many of the performance improvements that our users have requested.

DISCUSSION QUESTIONS

1. Based on the reading of the article, explain the concept of virtual storage. What are its real advantages?
2. What impact does virtual memory have on systems design? Explain.
3. In what areas does virtual memory affect system implementation?
4. "Virtual storage can improve the productivity and morale of programmers by providing better testing turnaround." Do you agree? Explain.

WHAT IS A PROGRAM FLOWCHART?

Elias M. Awad

Program analysts or systems analysts apply special-purpose tools in planning a computer program. Atlhough card, tape, disk, and storage layout charts have been used to depict the logical flow of data and the operations related to them, the two most commonly used tools for program planning are program flowcharts and decision tables. The use of either tool carries with it the assumption that the programmer is aware of (1) the procedures to be followed in solving a given problem, (2) the system resources needed for the operation, (3) the required input data and file procedures, and (4) the processing operations of the proposed project. Once these things are made clear, the analyst can proceed to develop the necessary set of computer instructions for processing data.

A program flowchart is a graphic representation of the operations and decision logic and the order in which they are to be handled. It enhances communication and aids the programmer/analyst in visualizing the sequence of operations. Once debugged, it becomes a part of program documentation, serving as a primary source for future reference.

Symbols and Uses

Terminal. A terminal (flat oval) symbol normally designates the beginning and the end of a program. It can be used elsewhere in the flowchart for specifying error conditions such as parity checks or detection of invalid characters. In this case, manual intervention is required (Figure 1).

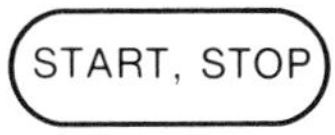

Figure 1. A Terminal Symbol

Direction-of-Flow. The direction-of-flow (flowline) is indicated by a line and an arrow (Figure 2). These may cross, form junctions, or connect any two symbols to establish a logical, meaningful relationship.

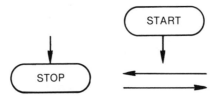

Figure 2. Direction of Flow

I/O symbol. Describes a program operation. It stands for an instruction to either an input or an output device (Figure 3).

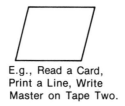

E.g., Read a Card,
Print a Line, Write
Master on Tape Two.

Figure 3. Input/Output Symbol

Process symbol. Denotes an operation involved in the actual processing of data (Figure 4).

Figure 4. Process Symbol

Conditional and unconditional looping. A computer system is often instructed to alter the sequence of its program execution (loop) for handling special conditions. Most functional programs include one or more loops to test various conditions or to decide on a particular course of action based on the test. This decision-making ability is symbolized by the logic operation symbol shown in Figure 5.

Conditional looping relates to situations where the computer takes an alternative path in program execution based on a predefined condition. For example, in "test for last card," the computer stops the program upon detection of the last

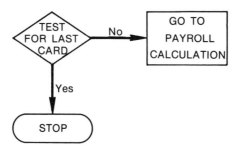

Figure 5. Logic Operation Symbol

card. Otherwise, it branches to the next sequential operation. If the program does not provide for conditions to be tested by the computer, unconditional or endless looping takes place. In the case of a last card processing, the card input device effects a halt of the total system.

Annotation symbols. Is an open rectangle with a broken line connecting the symbol to another flowchart symbol. It does not signify any action in the program but is used to give descriptive comments for clarification (Figure 6).

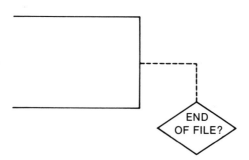

Figure 6. Annotation Symbol

Predefined process. This symbol represents a named operation not explicitly detailed in the program flowchart (Figure 7).

Figure 7. Predefined Symbol

Instruction modification. Is a specialized process symbol used in specifying an instruction or a set of instructions that alters the program's course of execution (Figure 8).

Figure 8. Instruction Modification Symbol

Fixed and interpage connectors. A fixed connector symbol is a nonprocessing symbol used to connect one part of a flowchart to another without drawing flowlines. It denotes an entry from or an exit to another part of the flowchart (Figure 9).

Figure 9. Fixed Connector Symbols

An interpage (or off-page) connector is used to indicate an exit from one page to another (Figure 10).

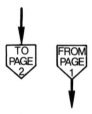

Figure 10. Interpage Connector Symbols

Figure 11 serves to illustrate the use of the symbols introduced in this section.

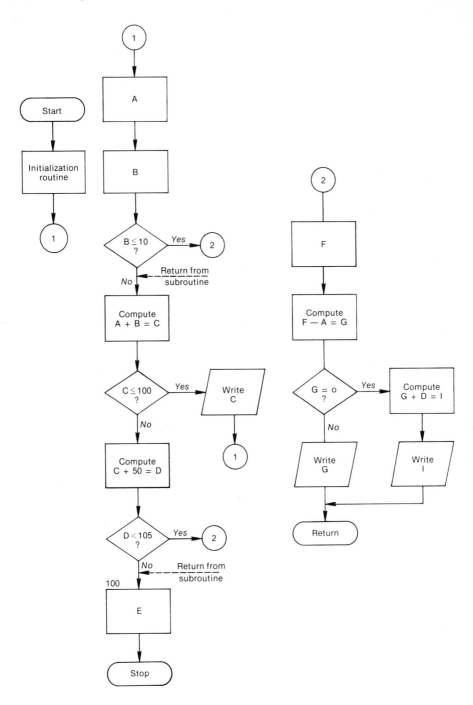

Figure 11. A Hypothetical Program Flowchart

DECISION TABLES AS A SYSTEMS TECHNIQUE

Wilfred C. Chesebrough

Suppose you heard about a new systems technique that provided better communication with programmers and was also understood by users and management—a universally applicable presentation piece written in English and in tabular form.

This technique is called decision tables. It serves as an aid to creative analysis and expresses a business situation in cause and effect relationships. It is easy to learn and its fundamentals could be taught in less than one workday. Its format is easy to draw, easy to read, and is its own free standing documentation. It possesses the latent ability to go directly to the computer without flowcharting and coding.

Decision tables are being accepted and used by analysts who are seeking to improve their effectiveness and obtain more personal satisfaction from their work.

TWO KINDS OF TABLES

Tables in themselves are not new. People have used them for centuries, and "table lookup" is a phrase that gets instant recognition in the world of data processing. Familiar examples exist in the income tax tables, insurance rate tables, mileage tables, mathematical tables, railroad time tables, and the others that we see every day. Two dimensional, they give a constant result based on two variables, hence are often called *"passive"* or "inert" tables.

Results tables use an IF-THEN relationship as the basis of their construction. For example, IF you earned $5000 and IF you had 5 dependents, THEN your tax is $76. IF the angle is $30°$ and IF the function is the sine, THEN the value is .500. IF the train number is 502 and IF the railroad station is Boston, THEN the departure time is 6:54 a.m. In all of these examples, two variables produce a single result.

Decision tables are a more powerful adaptation that prescribes actions in response to one or more conditions. They are of matrix construction and are not restricted to two variables or to a single directive but can specify any number of them.

Decision tables use the IF-THEN relationship but in an *active* sense whereby a course of action is indicated. For example, IF the gauge says EMPTY, THEN put in some gas. IF the alarm clock goes off, THEN get up, close the window, and get back in bed. Unlike results tables, we are not restricted to two IF statements and a single THEN statement in decision tables. The parameters are limited only by the creativity of the analyst working within a set of basic standards.

Source: *Computers and Automation,* April 1970, pp. 30-33.

DECISION TABLE SYMBOLOGY AND CONSTRUCTION

A decision table has four quadrants, separated by two sets of double lines at right angles to each other. The quadrants are called (1) condition entry, (2) condition stub, (3) action entry, and (4) action stub. (See Figure 1.)

The condition stub, in the upper left quadrant contains the IF statements that define the variables that affect the decision-making process. Sometimes called "tests," the statements are arranged horizontally in rows in logical descending order. Rows are identified by letters.

The action stub, in the lower left quadrant, contains the THEN statements, also in horizontal rows, that describe the possible and/or desirable responses to the situation. If there is a sequential dependency, the arrangement should be in that order.

The condition entry, in the upper right quadrant, has the possible responses to the list of if statements in the condition stub. The responses can be yes or no in a limited entry table, or can be descriptive such as (1) red, yellow, green, black, and white, or (2) Indian, Negro, Chinese and Caucasian, or (3) steam, gasoline, diesel and electric in an extended entry table. Limited entry can have only the two responses, but extended entry can have as many as the analyst chooses in defining his situation, subject only to the size of the paper.

Although limited entry tables tend to be longer than extended entry tables, limited entry tables are binary and naturally suited to computer applications. This is especially important if you are considering machine processing of decision tables, and this discussion will only deal with limited entry.

The condition entry responses are arranged in vertical columns called rules, each one identified by a number and having a unique series of yes or no responses.

The action entry, in the lower right quadrant, contains an X at the intersection of each row and rule if the action should be taken as a consequence of the responses in the rule. If the action is not prescribed, a • is put there. There are no blanks in the action stub since a blank indicates that the action or inaction decision has been overlooked instead of specified.

The table header is a box located immediately above the condition stub. It contains a descriptive name or title of the decision table (Figure 1).

SITUATION DEFINITION

We have determined what a decision table is, that it exists to communicate information, and that it is action oriented. Now we can demonstrate the ability of decision tables to aid in situation definition by analyzing a typical business problem in narrative form.

The ticket seller at an airlines counter uses these guidelines in serving customers. There are two classes of tickets—first class and coach. If the request is for first class and if space is available, reserve a first class seat. If the request is for coach and space is available, reserve a coach seat.

```
┌─────────────────────┐
│   TABLE HEADER      │
└─────────────────────┘
```

CONDITION STUB	CONDITION ENTRY
ACTION STUB	**ACTION ENTRY**

Figure 1. The Four Quadrants of a Decision Table

Analysis tells us there are four if statements or conditions to be put in the condition stub.

1. request first class
2. request coach
3. first class available
4. coach available

We can reduce these to two conditions by judicious examination of the responses in the condition entry. Since there are only two classes of service, a yes for request first class is a positive response. A no response tells us that the request is not for first class and by logical deduction that it is for coach. Similarly, we rephrase conditions 3 and 4 to "requested space available" and satisfy both classes, depending on the previous rule. Having defined the possible conditions, we now add the two actions listed in the narrative. We put the appropriate X or • codes in the action entry and our table is as shown in Figure 2.

However, in looking at what we believe to be a completed table, we can see that no action is specified for the conditions where the response to space available is no. This presents a problem to the ticket seller because he has no instructions for this plausible condition. Our assumed status of completeness is untrue even though we have converted the given narrative to conditions and actions. We have discovered one of the benefits of decision tables, i.e., we know whether we have satisfied all the possible combinations and if not, which ones must be analyzed further.

AIRLINE TICKET CLERK		1	2	3	4
A	REQUEST IS FIRST CLASS	Y	Y	N	N
B	REQUESTED SPACE AVAILABLE	Y	N	Y	N
C	RESERVE FIRST CLASS	X	•	•	•
D	RESERVE COACH	•	•	X	•

Figure 2. Initial Airline Decision Table

In our airlines problem, we could add another action statement, "place on standby," as a means of getting a "hit," but since one of our business goals is to fill as many seats in the plane as possible, we ask the customer another question, such as, "Would you accept the alternate class of service?" This has a yes or no response and we ask one more question, "alternate available?"

Now, we can subdivide place on standby into first class, coach, or either and add the actions to the action stub.

We have expanded our table to cover four conditions and their possible action. Now we direct our attention to enlarging the condition area to supplement the enlarged stub area.

EXPANDING THE CONDITION ENTRY QUADRANT

In our initial table building work, we intuitively recognized that as conditions increase, the number of rules must also increase.

Some practical conventions exist to help us in determining the number of rules and the arrangement of the yes-no responses in the condition entry. Given the number of conditions in the table, the number of rules will be 2^n where n is the number of conditions. Thus a two condition table has 2^2 or 4 rules, a three condition table has 8 rules and so on. This convention is called the 2^n factor.

Once we know the number of rules, we can begin to fill in the yes-no responses. Here, another simple guide permits us to proceed with confidence, irrespective of the logic contained in the conditions. Start at the row directly above the action entry (the bottom row of the condition entry) and write a series of single Y and N responses across the row. Then move up one row and enter responses in pairs. (Y Y N N etc.) The next row is in fours, the next in eight, sixteen and so on. By following this pattern in conjunction with the 2^n factor, the analyst is assured that

1. Every possible combination is included
2. There is no duplication of rules

This arrangement, called "bifurcated," or two-branched, is especially helpful in larger tables.

COMPLETING THE ACTION ENTRY QUADRANT

The remaining quadrant, the action entry, is filled by logically moving down through each rule and placing an X in the row if the action statement is to be done and a • if it is not. There can be more than one X in any rule.

Remember, there must be *at least* one X in every rule or the problem has not been solved, since no action has been specified for that particular combination of yes-no responses. To complete the solution, the analyst must specify an action and add it to the action stub with the appropriate X or • added to every rule. Thus, the analyst is assured that he has prescribed a complete solution to the situation before coding begins, a feature not included in conventional flowcharting.

In our airlines problem, the 2^n factor tells us that there will be 16 rules, and we can complete the condition entry in bifurcated form. Then, we can complete the action entry, creating the decision table in Figure 3.

Examination assures us that the decision table is complete, since there is a "hit" for every rule. We have utilized the 2^n factor and bifurcated form in the condition entry, giving us assurance that we have considered every possible combination.

COMPRESSING THE DECISION TABLE

Thus far we have been concerned with building completeness of problem definition and ensuring that we consider all possible happenings in our business situation.

Now that we are assured that every combination of responses is visible, there is the possibility that analysis will reveal opportunities to compress the table. Once more, we can draw on methodical guidelines for assistance.

Looking back at Figure 3, the airlines problem, we observe that rules 7 and 8 prescribe the same action even though the responses to the alternate available condition are opposite. It is obvious that the response to this condition doesn't make any difference in the outcome.

This has been formally expressed as the redundancy concept, stating "When two rules result in the same action(s) and the condition entry responses are the same except for the last condition, this difference has no effect on the outcome, and the test can be ignored and the two rules combined into one." A dash (−) is put in the condition entry to represent the redundant test.

Thus, we can condense airlines problem rules 7 and 8 into one rule. Further analysis indicates we can condense rules 1 and 2, 3 and 4, 9 and 10, 11 and 12, and 15 and 16 into single rules. Then, we can apply the redundancy concept again and shrink rules 1-2 and 3-4 and rules 9-10 and 11-12 into single rules. Figures 4 and 5 illustrate the tests that are found to be redundant and Figure 6 illustrates the resultant compressed decision table. It is common practice to renumber the rules after compression is completed.

Another method of removing rules is to examine each rule to ensure that the situation described can logically exist. If a railroad ticket table has four conditions, e.g., one way, round trip, 10 rides weekly and 12 rides monthly, a yes response to more than one condition cannot logically exist and the rule can be eliminated. Similarly, a fuel tank cannot be full, half full, and empty.

Since illogical conditions can be detected without referencing the actions, illogical rules can be eliminated before the action entry is constructed.

INTUITIVE CONSTRUCTION

There is another method of constructing the condition entry that does not demand the discipline of the 2^n factor or the bifurcated form of yes and no responses. It relies, instead, on the skill and knowledge of the analyst to develop rules at random. These rules follow no pattern but are intuitively constructed according to plausible combinations of yes and no responses in the business situation. After these are written in, one final rule called the "else" rule is noted (but not filled in with yes

AIRLINE TICKET CLERK	1	2	3	4	5	6	7	8	9	10	11	12	13	14	15	16
A REQUEST IS FIRST CLASS	Y	Y	Y	Y	Y	Y	Y	Y	N	N	N	N	N	N	N	N
B REQUESTED SPACE AVAILABLE	Y	Y	Y	Y	N	N	N	N	Y	Y	Y	Y	N	N	N	N
C ACCEPT ALTERNATE CLASS	Y	Y	N	N	Y	Y	N	N	Y	Y	N	N	Y	Y	N	N
D ALTERNATE AVAILABLE	Y	N	Y	N	Y	N	Y	N	Y	N	Y	N	Y	N	Y	N
E RESERVE FIRST CLASS	X	X	X	X	•	•	•	•	X	X	•	•	X	•	•	•
F RESERVE COACH	•	•	•	•	X	•	•	•	•	•	X	X	•	•	•	•
G PLACE ON STANDBY, FIRST CLASS	•	•	•	•	•	•	X	X	•	•	•	•	•	•	•	•
H PLACE ON STANDBY, COACH	•	•	•	•	•	•	•	•	•	•	•	•	•	•	X	X
I PLACE ON STANDBY, EITHER	•	•	•	•	•	X	•	•	•	•	•	•	•	X	•	•

Figure 3. Interim Airline Decision Table Illustrating Use of the 2^n Factor and Bifurcated Form

AIRLINE TICKET CLERK	1	2	3	4	5	6	7	8	9	10	11	12	13	14	15	16
A REQUEST IS FIRST CLASS	Y	Y	Y	Y	Y	Y	Y	Y	N	N	N	N	N	N	N	N
B REQUESTED SPACE AVAILABLE	Y	Y	Y	Y	N	N	N	N	Y	Y	Y	Y	N	N	N	N
C ACCEPT ALTERNATE CLASS	Y	Y	N	N	Y	Y	N	N	Y	Y	N	N	Y	Y	N	N
D ALTERNATE AVAILABLE	Y	N	Y	N	Y	N	Y	N	Y	N	Y	N	Y	N	Y	N
E RESERVE FIRST CLASS	X	X	X	X	•	•	•	•	•	•	•	•	X	•	•	•
F RESERVE COACH	•	•	•	•	X	•	•	•	X	X	X	X	•	•	•	•
G PLACE ON STANDBY, FIRST CLASS	•	•	•	•	•	•	X	X	•	•	•	•	•	•	•	•
H PLACE ON STANDBY, COACH	•	•	•	•	•	•	•	•	•	•	•	•	•	•	X	X
I PLACE ON STANDBY, EITHER	•	•	•	•	•	X	•	•	•	•	•	•	•	X	•	•

Figure 4. Interim Airline Decision Table Illustrating Applications of the Redundancy Concept

and no), and an action is specified to cover all combinations that have not previously been specified.

It can be claimed that intuitive construction with the else rule works as well as the 2^n factor and bifurcated form, especially in small tables. It is even possible that the resultant decision tables will be the same in many situations regardless of which method is used.

On the other hand, intuitive construction is risky when analysts move into real business situations. The else rule becomes an expedient way to convert haphazard system study into table form, and missing actions only come to light after the system is installed when it is too late. The intuitive method lacks the mathematical certainty that all possible conditions have been considered. Furthermore, most analysts will find that after a short learning period the 2^n factor and bifurcated form are faster and easier as well as more reliable.

SOLVING LARGE PROBLEMS WITH DECISION TABLES

Our discussion and work thus far have been concerned with single tables and our problems have been simple enough to be solved within this constraint. While this has provided a climate of stability in which to learn the basics, it is obvious from the 2^n factor that real business problems quickly outgrow a single decision table.

Earlier, we determined that a decision table is not complete unless there is at least one action prescribed for each rule in the table. In the airlines problem, we added conditions and actions to meet this requirement within the boundaries of a single table. In other situations, it is better to construct a network of separate but interrelated tables to describe the logic of the situation.

This is especially true where one set of conditions remains relevant and another set becomes redundant based on early responses. For example, the career of a young man takes totally divergent paths depending on the response to "draft notice received?" and "physical examination passed?" Similarly the course of action for an automobile driver on the turnpike is drastically altered depending on his response to "destination Hartford?" and "take Hartford exit?" In cases like this,

AIRLINE TICKET CLERK		1	3	5	6	7	9	11	13	14	15
A	REQUEST IS FIRST CLASS	Y	Y	Y	Y	Y	N	N	N	N	N
B	REQUESTED SPACE AVAILABLE	Y	Y	Y	Y	Y	Y	Y	N	N	N
C	ACCEPT ALTERNATE CLASS	Y	N	Y	Y	N	Y	N	Y	Y	N
D	ALTERNATE AVAILABLE	—	—	Y	N	—	—	—	Y	N	—
E	RESERVE FIRST CLASS	X	X	•	•	•	•	•	X	•	•
F	RESERVE COACH	•	•	X	•	•	X	X	•	•	•
G	PLACE ON STANDBY, FIRST CLASS	•	•	•	•	X	•	•	•	•	•
H	PLACE ON STANDBY, COACH	•	•	•	•	•	•	•	•	•	X
I	PLACE ON STANDBY, EITHER	•	•	•	X	•	•	•	•	X	•

Figure 5. Interim Airline Decision Table Illustrating Effect of Redundancy Concept Application

AIRLINE TICKET CLERK		1	5	6	7	9	13	14	15
A	REQUEST IS FIRST CLASS	Y	Y	Y	Y	N	N	N	N
B	REQUESTED SPACE AVAILABLE	Y	N	N	N	Y	N	N	N
C	ACCEPT ALTERNATE CLASS	—	Y	Y	N	—	Y	Y	N
D	ALTERNATE AVAILABLE	—	Y	N	—	—	Y	N	—
E	RESERVE FIRST CLASS	X	•	•	•	•	X	•	•
F	RESERVE COACH	•	X	•	•	X	•	•	•
G	PLACE ON STANDBY, FIRST CLASS	•	•	•	X	•	•	•	•
H	PLACE ON STANDBY, COACH	•	•	•	•	•	•	•	X
I	PLACE ON STANDBY, EITHER	•	•	X	•	•	•	X	•

Figure 6. Final Airline Decision Table After Elimination of All Redundant Rules

separate tables are more effective since they permit us to access the conditions that still have impact on the situation and eliminate repetition of redundant tests.

An exit routine is used to get from one decision table to another when no action has been specified and/or because we want to bring the logic of another decision table into play. The exit routine always uses the table header of the accessed table as a destination.

Given a table with a table header called Inventory that we wish to access, one form of exit routine is to add a row to the action stub specifying go to inventory with appropriate X or • signals in the action entry. This is especially efficient when a majority of the rules exit into the same table, but requires an additional row for every additional table that is accessed.

Many analysts prefer to use a different instruction, exit to—which is an extension of the rule and unique to that rule. It requires that a destination be specified for every rule, but permits assignment of different destinations in the same space as if a single destination applied. Figure 7 shows this method.

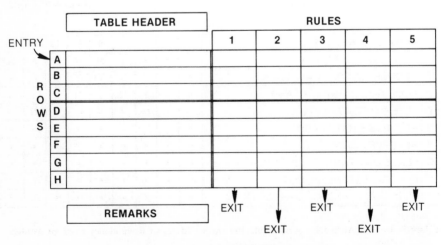

Figure 7. Decision Table Elements

The choice of exit routine is an analyst's option although you should not combine the two types in one table or in one network of tables.

SUMMARY

The preceding paragraphs have discussed decision tables as a method of business problem analysis. The symbology and format have been supplemented by examples of business problem narratives and conversion to decision tables. Lack of space and time have forced me to allude to certain communication and documentation features rather than describe them in detail. Hopefully, the reader has been equipped and stimulated to begin work and develop the skill and familiarity that come with experience.

Not everyone will respond to decision tables. They suffer the same handicap as any new tool, invention, or technique in that they must overcome people's inherent resistance to change.

On the other hand, the simplicity and straightforward nature of decision tables permit an analyst to become proficient in their use very quickly.

After research into networks of tables, he will begin to accrue the benefits of decision tables in system analysis, design, and presentation. Then his wisdom and judgment can be concentrated on problems that have successfully resisted solving in the past. In combination with computers, decision tables will enable us to reach new levels of professional attainment and personal satisfaction.

DISCUSSION QUESTIONS

1. Explain (a) the redundancy concept; (b) bifurated arrangement in decision tables.
2. What methods are used in removing redundant rules from a decision table?
3. What methods are used in constructing the condition entry? Which method poses the greatest risk? Which method(s) is the fastest and most reliable?

DOCUMENTATION: EDP'S NEGLECTED NECESSITY

Sam Bellotto, Jr.

Documentation for the computer is essential. So say a mushrooming number of small, medium and large EDP users in a wide variety of organizations across the country. Getting all the pertinent data processing information down in complete,

Source: *Administrative Management,* January 1971, pp. 24-26.

yet concise black and white form can save an organization large chunks of money and man-hours. But what are the techniques needed?

Before any kind of documentation can be established, the term itself should be defined. While there are many opinions on the subject, most EDP authorities agree that documentation is, very basically, the transcription of everything prior, during and following a computer program into print. But why bother with this procedure at all?

Because something might go wrong. A data processing manager of a New York based firm explains that before they considered documentation, "every time we had a problem with the computer or job, we also had a problem trying to understand the basic programming. We called in the manufacturer's representative, but he knew less than us!" The outcome was a waste of time and tedious effort scrutinizing reams of computer print-out for programming errors.

A Boston based manufacturing firm recently replaced its manager of data processing along with the assistant programmer. The company felt the wallop of almost no documentation six months later when snowballing program changes created chaos in a once smoothly operating data processing department. "At first we made program patches to cope with minor changes as they cropped up," says a company spokesman, "but soon the staff was working 12 and 14 hours a day, trying to make changes and reassemble programs. Within months, his confidence gone, our new manager quit."

These case examples are not unique and illustrate the strongest argument for documentation: if your data manager leaves the company for any reason, you don't want him taking along thousands of dollars in computer systems information as well. If you want to revise an aging program, documentation provides immediate reference to how the program was originally set up. Training new programmers with documentation saves vital man-hours. And in the case of a fire or other disaster, some means of reconstructing destroyed programs is available if they were properly documented.

What good is documentation to the organization with a crack data processing team and a happy, high-paid, healthy EDP manager?

For one, effective documentation will aid in clarifying the job, identifying the methodology at the roots and spotlighting any important changes in procedure. This clarification also forms an invaluable reference to personnel who are working on more than one job over a length of time.

Granted the importance of documentation, the question remains—how to do it? The best system depends on the individual firm, but an overview parallels the typical "scientist's notebook." A good, general documentation skeleton is fleshed with: (1) *clarity*, employing standardized format and ample diagrams giving the big picture at a glance; (2) *relevance to the job being done;* and (3) *simplicity*, enabling changes to be made in the documentation quickly and without becoming a book of hieroglyphics.

A data processing specialist for a major firm sees documentation as "primarily an operating procedure." He offers the following guidelines in preparing your material.

Include information relating to the following areas:

- Run description and systems description.
- Input/output processing charts.

- Input records.
- Output records.
- Printed output.
- Cards output.
- Informal and external controls, also describing audit trails.
- Halt lists, explaining what to do when the computer halts.
- An operator's guide, which is a "how to" manual for operation and programming.

Some users are going one step further and including a sample printout run with the documentation. A manufacturer of documentation binders says, "a proof run of the program itself is kept as a check, a comparison for other runs. The whole binder package contains program work sheets, the documentation and the finished printout sample."

Advice from other experts varies. Spokesmen for IBM present an extremely thorough policy of setting down documentation. "Records generated during the pre-installation period should be compiled in an individual binder, with index tabs for each section." The tabbed sections keep at fingertip convenience: (1) discussions and ultimate agreements between management and data processing staff; (2) finalized objectives, scope and purposes of each job in essay form; (3) systems flowcharts, clearly labeled; and (4) record layouts, sample forms and "any other material needed for clear understanding of the system."

A separate binder should then be prepared for each program or group of programs run, advocates IBM, "most of this material developing as a by-product of programming and testing." This material consists of run descriptions, general flowcharts, detailed flowcharts, record layouts, sample forms, and program listings and history.

Incomplete documentation, most experts agree, is as bad as no documentation at all. But too much documentation may become burdensome and inefficient. One of the most elemental ingredients needed to brew a capable documentation system, then, as echoed by IBM, "is determining just how much documentation is needed."

It is a narrow path to tread. For example, many smaller firms delude themselves by believing that since they have a small EDP system, one man is capable of supporting the total burden. And in large firms the job is enormous; one man can't know it all. "The first goal is to establish your needs," states one administrative executive, "then you develop standardization, and finally, you can carry the ball into documentation."

DISCUSSION QUESTIONS

1. What is documentation? How is it related to standardization?
2. According to the article, what are the characteristics of a good documentation?
3. What key information should documentation include?
4. In your opinion, how important is documentation in small (compared to large-size) computer installations? Why?

SELECTED REFERENCES

Systems Analysis and Design

Books

Awad, Elias M. *Business Data Processing.* 4th ed. Englewood Cliffs, N.J.: Prentice-Hall, 1975, Chapter 15.

Barnett, Arnold. *The Systems Man's Role in Systems Development.* Rockville, Maryland: Barnett Data Systems, 1971.

Byrne, Brendan; Mullally, Alan; and Rothery, Brian. *The Art of Systems Analysis.* Englewood Cliffs, N.J.: Prentice-Hall, 1972.

Cohen, Bernard J. *Cost Effective Information Systems.* New York: American Management Association, 1971.

Matthies, Leslie H. *The Quest for Systems Principles.* Colorado Springs, Colo.: Systemation, 1970.

Articles

Ackoff, Russell L. "Towards a System of Systems Concepts." *Management Science,* XVII (July 1971), pp. 3-11.

Awad, Elias M. "The Dilemma of the Systems Analyst." *Computer and Automation,* August 1970, pp. 34-38.

Chu, Albert L. C. "Shortcut to Computer Power." *Business Automation,* September 1971, pp. 16-22.

Greenwood, F., and Ilas, T. "DPMA System Analysis Problem Study." *Data Management,* April 1968, pp. 30-33.

Head, Robert V. "Automated Systems Analyses." *Datamation,* August 15, 1971, pp. 22-24.

Hoschild, Alan. "Disciplines Systems Development." *Data Management,* September 1971, pp. 32-36.

Hudson, Miles H. "A Technique for Systems Analysis and Design." *Journal of Systems Management.* May 1971, pp. 13-15.

Shays, E. Michael. "The MSP: A Master Plan for Systems Design and Development." *Data Management,* November 1971, pp. 17-23.

Suter, Albert E. "Optimization of Business Operations." *Data Management,* September 1970, pp. 23-24.

Teichoew, Daniel, and Seyani, Hason. "Automation of System Building." *Datamation,* August 15, 1971, pp. 25-30.

Vander Noot, T. J. "Systems Testing . . . A Taboo Subject." *Datamation,* November 15, 1971, pp. 22-25.

Flowcharting

Books

Bohl, Marilyn. *Flowcharting Techniques.* Chicago: Science Research Associates, 1971.

Chapin, Ned. *Flowcharts.* Princeton, N.J.: Auerbach Publishers, 1971.

Farina, Mario. *Flowcharting.* Englewood Cliffs, N.J.: Prentice-Hall, 1970.

Flowcharting Symbols and Their Usage in Information Processing. ANSI X35-1970. New York: American National Standards Institute.

Glenn, George A. *Program Flowcharting.* New York: Holt, Rinehart and Winston, 1970.

Passen, Barry J. *Approaches to Business Data Processing Logic.* New York: John Wiley & Sons, 1972, pp. 23-52.

Price, Wilson T. *Introduction to Data Processing.* Corte Madera, Calif.: Rinehart Press, 1972, pp. 302-318.

Saxon, James A., and Steyer, Wesley W. *Basic Principles of Data Processing.* 2nd ed. Englewood Cliffs, N.J.: Prentice-Hall, 1970, pp. 142-164.

Schriber, Thomas J. *Fundamentals of Flowcharting.* New York: John Wiley & Sons, 1969.

Decision Tables

Books

Decision Tables Tutorial Using Detab-X. Instruction Task Force CODA-SYL Systems Development Group. ACM Headquarters, 1130 Avenue of the Americas, New York 10036.

Decision Tables—A System Analysis and Documentation Technique. Form F20-8102. International Business Machines Corp., 112 E. Post Road, White Plains, N.Y. 10601.

Gildersleeve, Thomas R. *Decision Tables and Their Application in Data Processing.* Englewood Cliffs, N.J.: Prentice-Hall, 1970.

Hughes, Marion L.; Shank, Richard M.; and Stein, Elinor. *Decision Tables.* Wayne, Penn.: MDI Publications, 1968.

Documentation

Books

Gray, Max, and London, Keith R. *Documentation Standards, 2nd edition.* Princeton, N.J.: Brandon/Systems Press, Inc., 1974.

Articles

Ehle, Robert C. "Documentation of a Computer System." *Software Age,* July 1970, pp. 14-18.

Gunderman, Richard E. "Hard Look at Software Documentation." *Journal of Systems Management,* June 1971, pp. 35-37.

Navolta, Glorino M. "Adapting the Use of Documentation." *Journal of Systems Management,* May 1971, pp. 39-41.

Power, Joel. "A Crash Documentation System.' *Software Age,* July 1970, pp. 10-13.

Tatman, James C. "Achieving Proper Program Documentation." *Journal of Systems Management,* November 1971, pp. 40-41.

PART 3

Trends in Data Entry and Output Devices

The introduction of each new generation of computers has brought with it faster and more powerful processors, coupled with high-speed printers and other output devices. However, emphasis on the speed of internal processing and output presented a problem at the data input stage, especially with increasing volumes of data to be processed. This data input bottleneck was further accentuated by such factors as high personnel turnover, tight deadlines, shortage of keypunch operators, absenteeism, and queuing delays. Thus the picture in its totality makes it clear why more than one-third of the EDP dollar is spent on data entry.

With the foregoing orientation, alternative data entry devices had to be developed. The keypunch is still the primary data entry machine today, with some 500,000 units in use in the United States. For the small user with standard data, the keypunch continues to be the way to prepare data input. Aside from the traditional keypunching advantages (inexpensive, easy to operate), the punched card is an expensive data entry medium. Not only is it difficult to store, cumbersome, and slow, but its input cost is greater than other methods of data entry. The alternative methods of data entry are the verified (buffered) keypunch, key-to-tape, key-to-cassette, key-to-disk devices, optical scanning, and point-of-scale (POS) devices.[1] On the output end, computer-output microfilm (COM) is also discussed.

The verified keypunch is designed to store two card records in its core memory, allowing the punching of one card while the operator is keying the next. This feature means that verifying and punching can be done on one unit. Furthermore, the operator can now backspace over errors and correct them prior to

---

[1] Data entry is used here to refer to the method of data input to a computer system. This usually involves converting human-readable data into machine-readable language. From a systems viewpoint, data entry includes the staff, equipment, procedures, and communication required for converting source data into computer-readable form. The three types of data entry systems are: (1) The keypunch system where the operator retranscribes the source data by punching them into standard-size cards. (2) The keypunch replacement system, which essentially involves the use of a key-to-tape or key-to-disk system to replace the keypunch. Either replacement system allows faster data entry and lower input costs. (3) Source data automation (SDA) captures data at the point of origin directly into computer-readable language, eliminating any retranscription, especially keypunching. Most data entry services could, in some respect, be used in an SDA mode, although the optical character reader exemplifies a typical SDA device. Point-of-sale terminals are also found under this category.

punching. Skipping and duplicating data are also done at electronic speed, as compared with mechanical speed in the traditional keypunch.

The key-to-tape device allows direct recording of input data on magnetic tape in the same format in which it was entered. This means that the computer can act immediately on processing the recorded data, eliminating the card-to-tape conversion needed under the keypunching system. Data processing departments using key-to-tape units can expect:

1. Reduction of data processing time by up to 25 percent, since the key-to-tape device is electronic and is as fast as the operator could handle. Its backspacing feature for error correction further improves data preparation speed.

2. Higher operator morale due to noise reduction and better appearance of the system layout.

3. Greater accuracy of data preparation and faster verify search procedure of traditional files such as accounts receivable, inventory, and payroll.

The key-to-cassette is a direct outgrowth of the key-to-tape. Input data are entered directly on a magnetic tape cassette which is later converted to full-size magnetic tape for computer processing. This form of data entry operates at electronic speeds and eliminates the need for separate verifiers, and the equipment can be moved to the area where data originates.

Key-to-disk devices (also called shared processors) offer the advantages of (1) virtually unlimited record formats and lengths, (2) reformating stored input data prior to computer processing, and (3) editing and validating records off-line. A key-to-disk system can handle up to 64 keystations. It provides the best cost/performance ratios when used in handling large volumes of data. Thus, it is generally restricted to the largest users.

OPTICAL CHARACTER RECOGNITION (OCR)

A more promising approach to solving the data entry bottleneck has been optical character recognition (OCR) devices, first introduced in the mid-1950s. For some time it was widely predicted that OCR would "stamp out" the keypunch as the primary method of data entry. OCR's growth pattern, however, shows that not more than 1,000 units are in commercial use, handling roughly 2 percent of the total data entry volume. Its slow acceptance has been blamed on several factors: (1) EDP systems were originally designed around the traditional punched card; (2) those who replaced the keypunch with OCR devices failed to make appropriate reorganizational changes for effective implementation; and (3) there was a lack of acceptance of the OCR idea by administrations. Despite these setbacks, the OCR industry predicts that by 1975, OCR will constitute 25 percent of all data input equipment.

Oil companies and banks were among the early users of OCR equipment. Today, a staggering volume of gasoline credit card purchases are processed by document readers at speeds reaching 80,000 documents per hour. Most large commercial banks also use optical scanners for branch-to-central transactions. One first national bank, for example, uses two OCR installments for its 165 branches; one installation handles regular banking transactions and the other processes stock transfer details. The latter installation is capable of issuing over 40,000 stock certificates in less than ten hours, which amounts to reading 63,000 lines of copy on 2,600 pages.

For OCR to gain acceptance, several key problems have to be settled. First is the problem of font standardization. The American standard OCR-A is uniformly used in the United States. In contrast, the international standard font, OCR-B, contains characters not easily detected by the scanner. The future of OCR is in mass production, which will become feasible once the standardization problem is settled. The second problem is the limited tolerance of scanners, especially with regard to imperfectly formed (including handwritten) numbers. The third problem is cost; practically all OCR readers carry a high price tag. Page readers sell for $160,000 to $400,000, while document readers are priced from $100,000 to $220,000. Even journal tape readers sell for an average of $100,000. One manufacturer estimates a breakeven point of 17,000 bills per day to justify the cost of a $200,000 OCR reader. All this means that when it is used to capacity, a typical OCR installation can match the productivity of 100 keypunch operators.

Even when and if these and other problems are worked out, the ultimate decision to adopt an OCR system rests with the executive. While optical scanning has not caught the fancy of upper management, it has to date generated growing interest.

POINT-OF-SALE (POS) AUTOMATION

Point-of-sale (POS) automation refers specifically to integrated terminals designed to record sales transaction data at the time of purchase. In addition to recording sales, new POS terminals validate a customer's credit and handle merchandise control as well as accounts receivable and payable chores. Their use is most dominant in the retail and grocery industries.

A typical POS terminal is similar to a key-to-tape or a key-to-disk terminal. It performs five key functions:

1. *Data entry.* Through a keyboard, POS data are entered manually, although data related to credit purchases can be automatically recorded from the customer's credit card. Manual data entry handles information related to the type of item sold, the price of the item, and merchandise adjustments, if any.

2. *Arithmetic.* Each POS terminal is a self-contained calculator, in that it calculates details related to the price of the item, amount of sales tax to be collected from the customer, and discount calculations.

3. *Credit checking.* A check on the credit status of a given customer is performed almost instantly. When the credit card is presented to the sales clerk, the terminal reads the bar code on the back side of the card, facilitating on-line verification of his account. Average time for receiving a reply after feeding in the necessary information is approximately one second.

4. *Inventory control.* The terminal's ability to record each transaction sold allows management to keep tabs on the status of such items in stock. In doing so, the amount of inventory to be ordered or available for sale can be more effectively controlled. Thus management can expect real-time data on overall store operation and performance.

5. *Output function.* Most POS terminals are designed to produce printed sales receipts, journal tape, and/or visual developing of the data entered by the sales clerk.

Most POS systems share similar characteristics. They involve on-line registers (stand-alone terminals) linked to a minicomputer or a data controller located on the premises. The terminal has a built-in sequence control and instructions which tell the sales clerk what to key in through a given sales transaction. The average price of POS terminals varies between $2,700 and $3,500.

COMPUTER-OUTPUT MICROFILM (COM)

While each successive generation of computers introduced faster and more powerful processors, little has been done in the way of developing compatible input/output devices. The discussion so far has concentrated on developments at the input stage involving direct data entry devices. On the output end, an alternative to the line printer which has been gaining in popularity is computer-output microfilm (COM).

COM's biggest potential lies in its use with the computer. Since the computer's main function is to store and manipulate data and COM's function is to store and miniaturize data, these two technologies share a common relationship in data handling. In operation, output information becomes available on-line from the computer or off-line from a tape driven by means of a microfilm process, using a COM recorder. This process operates at many times the speed of the fastest line printer. The layout and details of output data on microfilm appear the same as those on a regular printed page.

Among the advantages of COM as an output device are lower data processing costs, fast information retrieval and storage, high-speed throughput, compact storage, reduced computer time in producing output, and unlimited copies of a single computer run at a fraction of the cost of the original. The main disadvantages of COM are high cost of the COM recorder, inadequacy in applications where contents of the data base change frequently, restricted use with the presence of a microfilm reader, relatively difficult retrieval techniques, questionable hardware reliability, and limited input format.

Many differences exist among the various COM systems available today. In choosing a COM system, management should conduct a thorough preliminary study of both its own needs and the COM applications that can be made. Furthermore, evaluation of factors related to character quality, serviceability, throughput, and price of the COM system(s) under consideration are also important. Whatever decision is made, it must be one which commits the organization to a COM system that would best serve its needs—short term and long term—at minimum cost.

The readings section on direct data entry consists of five short articles. Each article explains briefly what the data entry devices can and cannot do, with an overview of the status and potential developments affecting each device.

The section on OCR systems revolves around three interesting articles. Reagan's article, "Should OCR Be Your Data Input medium?" discusses the areas where OCR can be used to advantage, explains how an OCR system operates, and attempts to evaluate the performance of OCR readers. Gray's article, "Optical Readers and OCR," describes the operation of optical readers, evaluates OCR input versus conventional key input devices, and outlines the various OCR applications in business, industry, and government. Sheinberg's article assesses the OCR market and applications potential for the seventies.

The section on POS systems is based on Shaffer's article which essentially illustrates how POS systems facilitate a closer, more effective relationship between the retailer and the consumer. Merowit's article shows how supermarkets benefit from POS. The last section concentrates on COM systems. Boulanger's article explains the concept of ultrafiche, and the makeup of a microfilm jacket. Chu's article presents data to show the cost disparity between COM and the line printer in both in-house and service center.

AN INTRODUCTION
TO THE INTELLIGENT TERMINAL

Staff Report

"I don't even know what the damned things are," scowled one executive, "but they seem to be part and parcel of every new idea that comes up from dp." The gentleman was referring to intelligent terminals, and his position is far from unique. This man, at least, was unafraid to admit his ignorance, but many executives offer quite another story. Even those who know some of the current buzzwords of the "smart tube" business seem to be confronted by sets of specifications that are contradictory or, worse, bear no relationship to each other.

An intelligent terminal isn't really that complicated a machine. There are, however, enough differences between models to make for large price and performance variations. Fundamentally, an intelligent terminal is a keyboard/crt terminal to which a user-programmable processor has been added. In addition, there may be facilities for the connection of various peripheral devices, including unintelligent "slave" terminals, which are coordinated by the processor in the central, or "master," terminal. The consolidation of the processor and the terminal into a unit leads to economies that cannot be matched by the addition of a minicomputer to a single unintelligent crt or sometimes even a cluster of such devices. In addition to cost savings, users are often better off with systems that can be carried around if necessary—although none of the terminals now on the market is small enough to be truly a take-home item.

YOU CAN SIZE 'EM UP

The best measure of the power of an intelligent terminal is its processing capability. Unlike most computer hardware, intelligent terminals are not generally used with high-speed peripheral devices, nor are they likely to find their way into number-crunching applications. Most of the jobs that go on under the skin of an intelligent terminal are limited by the speed of its human operator.

The processing power of the intelligent terminal, though, makes a big difference when the user develops application software. A more powerful terminal will require less programming effort and less memory for a given program. An exception to this low-load situation may occur when there are clusters of slave terminals to be driven from one intelligent master. The raw hardware power of the tiny computer inside the smart tube may then be used to its limit.

But even in clusters, memory storage efficiency and instruction (or language)

Source: Reprinted by permission of the publisher from *Computer Decisions*, January 1974, pp. 32-34.

sophistication are better measures than cycle time. If you have a good idea what you are going to be doing with an intelligent terminal, you may find that one or more of the vendors will offer you software packages or languages that really can cut down your installation costs. Some vendors may supply you with free custom software if your order is large enough, but you should be aware that your needs may grow larger than the friendliness of the vendor. You should not expect support to continue indefinitely unless you have arranged to pay for that support.

LOOK FOR EVERYTHING YOUR HEART DESIRES

The development of a product for a broad market that can sell at a realistic price demands some tradeoffs. As vendors mature, they are beginning to offer different models or plug-in options to enable customers to purchase only as much terminal as they really need. While it is not necessary that every terminal you consider be capable of solving any problem you might imagine, a plan that characterizes your projected needs for two to four years is a good measure of the upward mobility you will need. Physical features that provide more value in an intelligent terminal include peripheral device capability, display size and clarity, keyboard quality and layout, memory expansion capability, and service.

Peripheral device capability: Most intelligent terminals use crt displays. If you need hard copy, you will have to get a printer. There are both line- and character-printers available for most intelligent terminals, and they have a wide range of prices. In most applications, one printer can service more than one terminal. Often, the printing you need can be done offline, and the simplist approach is to move data from the terminal to another system via phone lines or by hand-carried magnetic tapes.

Tape cassettes, generally the Phillips-type, are a popular offering of intelligent terminal makers. Single-drive units are not as good as dual-drive units for single-terminal installations. In multi-terminal installations, two terminals may be connected for offline tape duplication or editing. In any event, the cassettes are strong enough for regular use, but fragile enough so that you should have some way to back them up. Some systems load programs, even compile them, from tape. Others may be loaded via any input device, including the host system.

Other peripherals available include floppy disks, for storage, autodialing modems for remote batch jobs, and even plotters and card readers similar to those used with unintelligent terminals. Independent peripheral makers haven't yet made a strong showing in this market, but as the number of intelligent terminals goes up, so will the number of competitors.

Display size and clarity: Your jobs may only require a few lines of text at a time, or they may take up a huge screen. Look for those features that you really need, such as special characters, intensity control for forms work and editing, useful cursor commands, and both upper- and lower-case letters. At least one terminal-maker offers the Katakana alphabet and others will give you other symbol sets on request. These goodies will cost, but enable you to use the same terminals wherever you do business.

All intelligent terminals allow you to keep some text in memory, and you should try to plan your applications for only as large a "window" as you need—larger letters drastically reduce operator fatigue.

Keyboard quality and layout: If you have a special job, get a special keyboard. Most makers have keyboards that are "read" by the processors so that a key can be interpreted any way you want under software control. Count both training and usage savings against the cost of special keyboards.

Memory expansion capability: The amount of text or software that a terminal can store is largely a function of memory size. Processors can compress data, and good ones require few instructions to do most user programs, but you will be comfortable with a terminal only if it has enough capacity for the toughest job you have to do. Many of these products let you add memory, but check with vendors to make sure that the job is straightforward. You may find that some models offer more expansion capability than others. If you really need a lot of storage, you are better off with a disk or tape unit, or maybe both: semiconductors used in terminal memories cost a lot more per bit than magnetic tape.

Service: When a terminal breaks down you should be able to get it fixed on the spot in a matter of hours. If you use several terminals, it's wise to plan for a spare. If you have only one intelligent terminal, you should clearly specify your service needs when you install the system, in writing. Even though these units are quite reliable in a statistical sense, they may serve in a critical capacity. Try to put a price on your service demands and factor it into any purchase decision you make. In particular, watch out for the mechanical components of a system, which are in the peripheral devices. Tape cassette drives, the cassettes themselves and printers all go down much more frequently than the circuitry inside a terminal. Keyboards, generally very reliable, fall between peripherals and electronics in their stability. Most vendors or their service agents carry enough spare parts to keep you on the air, but a check with them is much better than a guess or a generous interpretation of a salesman's promises.

INSIDE THEY'RE SIMILAR BUT DIFFERENT

The components of an intelligent terminal are the keyboard, the display unit (or printer), the processor, the memory, and the input/output interface. Each performs the same function in every terminal on the market, but each model of terminal is designed differently. If you understand the way these pieces function, individually and with each other, you may be able to cut through some of the jargon that accompanies most manufacturer's product descriptions: what is shorthand for engineers is often longthought for users.

Keyboards have one moving part per key. Those that don't depend on mechanical action, because they use a magnetic effect or because they break a light beam, are likely to last longer without trouble than those with mechanical contacts.

The keyboards are generally read by a scanning technique—the processor polls each key, electronically debouncing and testing for multiple depressions. Try to fool the terminal with simultaneous pressures and rapid typing; a good design will be foolproof.

The display unit of an intelligent terminal is identical to that found in any other crt and very similar to that in a home television receiver. Some crt terminals even offer video output that may be put over a closed-circuit television system.

Contrast and clarity are a property of the display system, and your expectations should be high. If the terminal is to be used with high ambient light, you may want a dark faceplate which most makers can supply if it is not already a standard part of their system. You may have some choice of phosphors, the chemicals that determine the color of a display. If you think you'd like a green phosphor, ask about it—you may be surprised to find that the tube you want is a standard item for the terminal maker, even if it's not shown. Extra-large or extra-small tube faces may be available for systems that will sit in a special cabinet if you want them. All such items cost money once, and will save money in the long run if you have special problems at your installation.

PRODUCTS IN TRANSITION

The processors used in most intelligent terminals fall into two categories these days: those made up of many integrated circuits, and those dependent on a microcomputer, a large-scale integrated circuit. While the technical difference should not concern you if you plan to purchase only a few items, a bulk purchase should involve some consideration of the technology involved.

To date, the processors made of standard integrated circuits are faster than the LSI versions. In the long run, most intelligent terminals are expected to use large-scale integration for the heart of their processors, because production economies make such an approach cheaper.

Today, there are firms that supply raw processors to the makers of intelligent terminals, and they specify product performance. If they are using separate integrated circuits today, there is no reason they will not switch to LSI tomorrow as long as they can get processors that do the same job. The reliability of LSI is a bit greater than that of equivalent functions performed by standard integrated circuits, but the difference will not be perceptible to the average user. In any event, the processor may have an instruction set that looks like that of a mini, or it may have instructions specifically tailored to the needs of a terminal, with more editing commands and fewer arithmetic operations.

Of the several terminals on the market using LSI, most employ the exact same microcomputer as a processor, and will thus offer identical performance, from a hardware standpoint. The distinguishing characteristics between these terminals lie in software, and sometimes in additional special circuitry.

The memory within an intelligent terminal is made of LSI circuits, similar to that used in IBM 370's, although arranged differently for the particular use to which it is put. Images and programs are stored in the same memory, which is usually expandable up to the capacity that minicomputers offer. This all means that most of the capabilities of a mini can be found in an intelligent terminal, but the terminals will be slower because the processors are somewhat slower.

One byte of memory is used for each character position on the screen in some terminals, and you should then compute the memory capacity you need on the

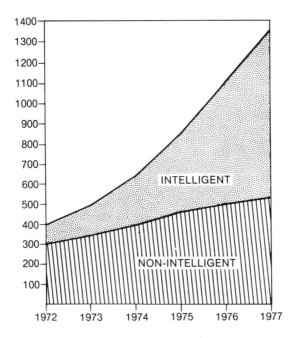

Figure 1. Spreading intelligence. Intelligent terminal sales (millions of dollars) are expected to grow rapidly during the next few years, exceeding sales of nonintelligent terminals in both dollar volume and units installed, according to a study made by Quantum Sciences. As acceptance widens, the industry is expected to trim the marketing territory now held by remote batch terminals.

basis of screen-loads, not actual characters. You should, however, check with vendors to determine if they only use memory for actual characters displayed; you might save a bit of memory with terminals that don't fill up memory with blanks.

Because peripheral devices are currently available for most intelligent terminals, you will want an input-output interface that permits add-ons of whatever type you choose to purchase. There is yet no industry standard for peripheral interfaces. But increasingly, makers of these terminals are designing peripherals that use the same conventions that the terminals use for tie-in to a modem or computer. The standard commonly used is called RS-232, and it specifies the kinds of signals that pass data between modem and terminal.

Intelligent terminals offer several data rates, and will generally let users choose either the ASCII (a sort of standard) code or EBCDIC (IBM's code) for communications, although nearly all terminals use ASCII codes for their own data storage and programming languages. Check with vendors to determine the specific capabilities of the terminal you have in mind before you plan for interfaces that may indeed cost extra or simply be unavailable.

Finally, in selecting an intelligent terminal for your operations, think ahead. This sector of the industry is young but growing rapidly, and the products offered will improve greatly during the next few years. Plan financing that will let you trade in or return items that will limit your potential, even if they more than meet your present needs.

DISCUSSION QUESTIONS

1. What is an intelligent terminal?
2. List and briefly describe some physical features that improve the effectiveness of intelligent terminals.
3. Explain the main components of an intelligent terminal.

THE VERIFIED KEYPUNCH

Robert E. Steele

Keypunching an 80-column card continues to be the most common form of data transcription. Even with the entry of key-to-tape, key-to-disc, OCR devices, and CRT display screen devices, the death knell of the punched card has yet to be sounded.

The punched card is a discrete record which can be read by machines and, when interpreted, by humans. It has the psychological advantage, both in transcription and in processing, of being a visual and understandable record. Data processing personnel still somehow prefer holes in cards to magnetic recordings on a disc or tape for source data input. The punched card is unique in special applications where data is written on the card and the same information is punched into it.

Thus, the punched card has often been referred to as the most flexible accounting document. With the introduction of the Univac 1700 Series keypunches in late 1968[1] punched card techniques were upgraded with the first significant improvement in several decades, the concept of the verified keypunch.

The verifying keypunch provides the user with unprecedented speed and economy in data transcription. In brief, the user retains all of the advantages of the familiar punched card and gains the advantages of electronically buffered key-to-tape and key-to-disc devices, without being encumbered with the disadvantages of these other key devices. For example, training an experienced keypunch operator on Univac's 1710 VIP averages about two hours. The VIP incorporates automatic printing as part of keypunching or verifying. It also provides for separate interpretation of 80-column punched cards. The VIP combines the functions of a keypunch

Source: *Data Systems*, May-June 1971, p. C4.
[1] More recently, IBM introduced its 129 buffered keypunch that has a monolithic memory.

and verifier. It assures the fastest and most accurate means of keypunching, verifying and correcting 80-column punched cards in the industry.

It is easy to become sidetracked by a feature for feature comparison when the vital concern should be directed to these three points:

Total production capabilities
Total costs
Total installation balance

In addition to increasing throughput 25 percent or more—on the average—combining punching and verifying into the same unit gives the user additional benefits. In conventional installations of keypunches and verifiers, the machines usually outnumber the operators. Further, there are idle operators—waiting to use a keypunch or waiting for keypunching to get ahead of verifying.

The verifying keypunch accommodates work load balancing, with a one for one ratio of operators and machines. Depending on the need at the moment, at the flip of a switch all operators can keypunch, or all can verify, or jobs can be divided. This assures clearing priority work to computer input on schedule. All personnel are utilized. All machines are in use.

Although there continues to be a significant increase in distributive entry—capturing the data as close to the source as possible (graphic displays, terminals, etc.)—an even greater increase is occurring in transcription entry. The Univac 1700's capabilities provide the defenders of the keypunch method of transcription with additional support when confronting the key-to-tape, key-to-cassette, or clustered off-line systems.

All keypunching is initiated in the normal manner. However, instead of each keystroke causing the card to be punched, data is entered into core storage.

During verification, the entire card image is read into storage. Constants are verified automatically: the operator just keys the variables on each card. If all information is correct, the card is fed to a stacker containing verified cards.

Operators no longer have to write the correct data on each error card—and keypunch a complete new card and refile corrected cards. This is due to the "in-line correction feature."

The inclusion of core storage can provide additional operating advantages. The keying of one card can start without operator hesitation, since the operator is keying into input storage while the previous card is being punched from output storage. Since the keying is to storage, the operator can backspace and correct an error when she senses it. And . . . if an error is discovered after punching, just re-key the correction and feed another card. Information remains in storage until replaced by new data.

The basic punching rate of 47 columns/second allows 35 cards/minute to be punched with a full 80 columns of information on each. The use of core storage increases throughput by making it impossible for the operator to overrun the keyboard in a burst mode. Cards are visible and stationary during data entry. Skipping, duplicating, keyboard shifting and right justification proceed in microsecond speed.

A variety of control keys and mode switches offer complete operator control. Without moving hands from the keyboard (except to load cards), the operator can keypunch or verify in the manual or automatic mode, correct punching errors or gang punch 35-60 cards per minute. When interpreting, 40-60 cards are processed per minute. Programming the verified keypunch is generally easy. Operators can change from one program to another in a matter of seconds. Program storage is maintained until a new program card is inserted.

Constant data for repetitive punching can be loaded in much the same way as a program. The operator enters only the significant characters for any given field. Depending on which justify key is used, the operator can automatically shift characters to the right of the field and automatically identify negative fields. The vacant column(s) to the left of the number are filled with zeros or spaces depending on a switch setting.

Many users report 25% to as great as 40% improvement in keypunching and verifying production over electro-mechanical devices. Increased production equates to cost reduction in data transcription. So the verified keypunch provides the means of realizing cost reduction.

Because of this, the punched card will be with the computer installation for a long, long time.

GLOSSARY

Buffer: A storage device designed to compensate for the variations in data flow during transmission from one device to another.

CRT: An electronic vacuum tube containing a TV-like screen on which information can be displayed.

Key-to-Cassette: A special input device which records input data in a 16-millimeter tape cartridge for direct computer processing.

DISCUSSION QUESTIONS

1. What advantages does the verified keypunch offer compared to the traditional keypunch? Explain.

2. Do the advantages of the verified keypunch offer enough argument in favor of their replacing the present keypunch? If not, what other factors should be considered? Be specific.

3. Suppose you head a data processing department where you have 50 keypunch machines in operation. You are considering a more efficient way of preparing the card input data for processing, knowing that the verified keypunch offers unique features. Answer the following questions:

    a. What is the first step that you would want to take?

    b. How much emphasis would you place on the keypunch operators' probable reaction to their keypunch replacement?

    c. What financial and economic factors are involved in adopting the verified keypunch over the regular keypunch?

    d. At what phase of the decision process do you begin to inform your operators of a possible change in the equipment? Why?

CUT INPUT COSTS WITH KEY-TO-TAPE DEVICES

James H. Bauch

Since 1950, the number of computer installations in the United States has increased from 600 to more than 70,000. Along with this increase has come vast improvements in machine speed and efficiency. To take advantage of these improvements, more people have been required to keypunch data for input. The result: almost one out of every 100 employees is involved in keypunching data—a total of more than 600,000 people in the total U.S. work force of 70 million. For the large-scale user, these labor charges have shot the cost of data preparation upwards at a rate of about 20 percent per year, with anywhere from 30 to 50 percent of the total budget of most EDP installations spent for input charges.

The problems of skyrocketing input charges and the need to keep pace with the rapidly increasing amounts of data required by newer computer systems resulted in the creation of key-to-tape devices, a concept introduced in 1965 by Mohawk Data Sciences Corp. with their Data-Recorder.

KEY-TAPE MACHINES COME IN VARIOUS VERSIONS

There are various types of key-tape devices available today. All, however, are characterized by certain common features: all are used to key-record data onto a tape which can then be read by a computer; all include a tape-transport mechanism; all employ a keyboard for recording data—either one similar to that of a keypunch machine, or similar to that of a typewriter; all include a display—usually coded—which permits the operator to view what is on the tape (with some units, the operator has a CRT display, and can view the entire record); all key-tape devices have some kind of control console so that special functions, such as setting record formats, can be performed. Two different types of key-tape configurations are available to users: stand-alone and key-to-central-tape. Stand-alone devices such as the Singer-Friden 4300, the Honeywell K-900 and the Mohawk 6400's comprise the majority of key-tape units on the market. They are self-contained, and each has its own tape unit built into the data-entry station. These units are generally of two types, depending on function:

First are keypunch replacement devices which normally have identical keyboards, and are found typically in a central keying office where they replace keypunches on a one-for-one basis. These key-tape devices use standard one-half-inch computer tape, cartridges or cassettes, depending on the manufacturer. While half-inch magnetic tape can be used directly by the computer, generally the

Source: Reprinted by permission of the publisher from *Computer Decisions,* May 1971, pp. 36-39.

individual reels are "pooled" onto one reel to cut down on set-up time. In operation, data that is keyed on these machines is generally stored temporarily in a buffer. When the entire record has been keyed, it is written on the tape from the buffer. This technique is used in order to make possible appropriate packing densities on the tape (for example, one user may require 800 bits per inch, another 1,600 BPI). Some units, however, key directly to the tape.

The second type of stand-alone device is used for recording of source data, a function commonly served by a combination of a standard typewriter and a magnetic-tape cassette or cartridge unit. The typewriter not only produces hard copy, but records data on tape simultaneously. It has applications, wherever data is created, and can generally be used by a typist, without special training. The chief advantages of using a cassette or cartridge are: easier operator training and handling (no loading procedures for the operator to worry about), and the larger flexibility provided by keying in relatively small batches. A typical example is the Data Action Typescribe which interfaces to a standard IBM Selectric Typewriter. This device employs a cartridge tape which is converted to standard one-half-inch tape for processing.

The key-to-cartridge (or cassette) manufacturers offer a number of different approaches. Some use a standard Philips cassette which is of the same type used on small tape recorders. This cassette usually contains 300 feet of tape which has a capacity of 200,000 characters of data. Other companies utilize a special cassette designed especially for use in their particular product. Normally the data keyed is temporarily stored in a buffer as with computer tape.

If this equipment is chosen by the user, however, he must carry out a pooling process to transfer data to one-half-inch machine-compatible tape. A special pooling device is usually supplied for a minimal monthly rental.

SHOULD YOU USE KEY-TAPE?

The decision to put in a key-tape system involves comparing the benefits and costs of these systems with other input means, particularly the keypunch. Let's look first at the important advantages of key-tape: A key-tape system becomes profitable once a user gains a production increase of about 15 percent over keypunch machines. The principal reason for increased production is that the key-tape device is electronic, rather than mechanical. Another point should be considered, however: regardless of the device used, an operator's fingers will only move so fast. But key-tape devices allow increases in operator speed by expanding record sizes to more than 80 characters, as required by the keypunch.

Nearly all key-tape machines offer record sizes greater than 80 characters, with some machines offering capacities of up to 720 characters. Some also can "step" through a record format, giving a literal definition of the data field instead of a "field position," as on a keypunch. This eliminates time-consuming operator decisions.

Most time loss in a keying situation comes from "error recovery" or error correction. Both of these are relatively simple and quick with key-tape. When in the "Write" mode, the operator merely backspaces and re-keys the correct character. With the exception of newly announced "buffered" machines, a keypunch error necessitates the re-keying of the entire card.

COMPARING KEY-TAPE AND KEYPUNCH

The punched card, however, remains the major entry medium in data processing, principally because of compatibility with most existing data processing systems. It also has obvious advantages in situations where the card itself serves as a working document, for example, in turn-around-document applications such as billing, and in inventory control. Other advantages include the ability to utilize tab equipment as well as the security provided by the user's ability to isolate, hold, read and replace records.

The main disadvantage of punch-card equipment is cost, including costs for ordering, storing and handling cards. The 80-column limitation of the cards forces format compromises which reduce the efficiency of the operator, and a dropped deck can be disastrous. Error correction is cumbersome. Finally, the noise and mechanical nature of the keypunch make working conditions for the operator less than ideal.

KEY-TAPE VERSUS KEY-DISK

The shared-processor or key-disk concept was introduced in 1967. In these systems each key station is tied to a minicomputer which stores the data temporarily on a disk and then dumps the information onto one-half-inch computer tape which is suitable for use as a mainframe input. This approach promotes increased speed and efficiency of handling of all input data through a central controller, without the additional step of handling intermediate magnetic tape as is required on the newer key-tape devices.

The shared-processor concept is most successful in large installations with very high-volume applications—if the user can isolate specific large jobs for his shared-processor installation, significant benefits can be realized. The most obvious limitation lies in the requirement for the minicomputer to do editing and validating while servicing the remote key stations. As a result, each manufacturer makes use of elaborate software to handle necessary data manipulation.

EVALUATING YOUR INPUT NEEDS

The computer user should evaluate his data preparation methods not only to provide a more efficient and less costly system today, but to provide for orderly growth. Here's one way to approach these evaluations, using a chart with the following columns:

- **Job:** List all of the jobs currently being processed in order of volume, using characters per month as the common measure. The availability and accuracy of this information will be a good indication of the quality of data-preparation control.
- **Volume (char/mo):** For each job, how many characters per month are processed?

- **Information source**: Where does the information to be processed originate? time card, pre-punched, handwritten inquiry, typed form, journal tape, etc.?
- **Computer preparation I**: How is the information prepared for machine reading? keypunch, Flexowriter, key-tape, shared processor, etc.?
- **Computer preparation II**: Where is the information prepared for machine reading? at the source, remote keying pool, local keying pool, etc.?
- **Key verification (percent)**: If applicable, what percent of the record is key verified?
- **Maximum record size**: What is the maximum record size (in characters) that can be entered?
- **Batch control**: Is the data currently batched and controlled so that all records must be error free before any information is processed?
- **Current input time**: This is the total elapsed time beginning when the information is under control of the company until processing begins.
- **Desired input time**: Be realistic, obviously it is desirable to have everything done instantaneously.
- **Audit trails**: Are audit trails, such as proof listings, generated to satisfy legal or operational requirements?
- **Processing schedule**: For example: daily, weekly, monthly, annually, etc.

Once the above chart is complete, an objective analysis can be made to determine what input system or systems should be used. In general, the attention should be given to those jobs that cumulatively represent more than 70 percent of the total volume. All time-critical jobs should be given special consideration regardless of volume. With these figures in mind, let's see if key-tape is for you.

Small user. A user who inputs less than eight-million characters per month (equivalent production of about five keypunches) should give careful consideration to stand-alone key-tape machines, assuming he has a one-half-inch magnetic-tape drive on his system. Under these circumstances, a key-tape device can generally save this user money due to increased operator efficiency. However, if any of the following circumstances exist, the justification for using key-tape machines is greatly increased: a large percentage of data entered is contained in records greater than 80 characters; there are large amounts of data in one job or there is a large number of fields being duplicated and skipped; the information source is a typed document, such as a freight bill; computer preparation is currently being done on a type-to-paper-tape device; computer preparation is remote and time is a factor. In this case, key-tape with either a typewriter or keypunch keyboard should be considered.

Medium and large users: Users that input more than eight-million characters per month (equivalent production of five keypunches) should not only consider the use of key-tape devices for recording data either in a central pool or remotely, but they should also consider off-line data-preparation systems being offered with editing and validating features, such as the Mohawk 2400 or the Data Action 1500. With these systems, significant savings may be realized if there is a high percentage of key verification since errors can be detected by an edit program, thereby making key verification unnecessary. A second advantage accrues when audit trails are required as a part of data preparation—they may be generated on the system. Finally, key-tape systems are particularly suited to a growth situation—the user may start small and increase proportionately to volume.

DISCUSSION QUESTIONS

1. What two reasons does the author specify as having contributed to the creation of key-to-tape devices?
2. While various key-to-tape machines are now available, what common characteristics do they share?
3. Distinguish between stand-alone and key-to-central tape. Which type constitutes the major percentage of available key-tape machines today?
4. Explain the two types of stand-alone tape devices.
5. What advantages does the key-to-tape device have over the keypunch? What advantages does the keypunch offer compared to the key-to-tape?
6. What major points should be considered before deciding on the use of a key-to-tape system?
7. According to the author, where and under what circumstances is the use of a key-disk system recommended?
8. What device(s) does the author suggest for use by the small user? the larger user? Do you agree? Explain.

KEY-TO-CASSETTE

James Welborn

With the introduction of key-to-tape systems, users of data processing equipment found they could increase input and improve operating efficiency, and at the same time reduce data entry costs.

The initial key-to-tape devices used standard half-inch computer-compatible tape, and this approach is still being offered by many manufacturers.

But since 1965, when key-to-tape was introduced, a distinctly different approach to input media has been developed. The new type of system employs a cartridge or cassette for storage of input data recorded by the operator of the device.

Source: *Data Systems*, May-June 1971, p. C5.

Although it is but one of several methods of data entry, the key-to-cassette/ cartridge approach offers several distinct advantages, the most important of which is a combination of simplicity and size. This, coupled with an ability to transport information at tape speeds, has created for the key-to-cassette approach a relatively new market—source data capture.

In this approach, the key-to-cassette is used at the district or regional office level and the data is thus transmitted to higher level offices over telephone lines or, an advantage peculiar to cassette and cartridge devices, mailed through the post office. Thus, key-to-cassette devices offer an extension to traditional data entry techniques; the keypunch and key-to-tape devices do not lend themselves so easily to this capability. This is not to say, however, that the key-to-cassette/cartridge approach is not applicable to the larger multi-station data entry installations.

Although manufacturers have taken different approaches in the fine details of recording media, there are two basic types offered. One is the audio cassette type, which is very similar to the cassette used in automobile tape players. The cassette is approximately 2½″ by 4″ and has two reels for feed and take-up. The tape may have from two to eight tracks. The cassette usually has a capacity of approximately 200,000 characters.

The second type of medium is a tape cartridge. IBM and Data Action use a cartridge tape which is offered by several manufacturers, including IBM, Memorex, BASF, and 3M. The tape is sprocket driven, which allows for positive positioning of the tape relative to the read or write head of the recording device. This eliminates the chance of read errors due to skew of the tape as it passes the head. The tape is available in lengths of 100 and 120 feet. It has a capacity of up to approximately 28,000 characters.

Both cartridge and cassette machines are used in conjunction with a pooler to transfer data to half-inch tape. A pooling device is usually offered for a small monthly rental (it is important to note that pooling is also a standard procedure on half-inch devices due to the requirement to consolidate input data contained on many reels for a particular processing run).

In most of the devices using cassettes, data is keyed into a buffer and then dumped to tape. This approach is well suited to applications where bulk storage of data is important.

In devices using cartridges, the data is usually entered directly onto tape as it is keyed, character by character.

Cartridges and cassettes share other important advantages over half-inch computer tape. For one thing, operator handling is much easier because loading is automatic. There are no tape threading procedures for the operator to learn, and there is no requirement for her to spend time spooling tape on the take-up reel. This results in improved operator efficiency and increased production.

Storage is simple and more economical than for other media. Far less space is required for cartridge/cassette tape and important economic benefits can be derived from this fact alone. Just as important is the fact that a girl who is keying (for example) four batches of 300 eighty-character images can easily place the four cartridges directly on her key station.

Virtually no problems can result from accidental mishandling of a cartridge/ cassette. Even if a cartridge is dropped no damage is done. This contrasts sharply with the chaos which results when a stack of cards falls onto the floor, or a reel of tape is dropped and unwinds.

In application, the cartridge/cassette provides a very convenient and helpful method of maintaining batch control. A tape cartridge is perhaps more useful in this regard because of the close correspondence between the capacity of the cartridge and its application in a batch processing environment. In applications where batch control is used, such as processing of rejected checks in a bank, most batches average between 200 and 250 eighty-column records. The cartridge capacity of 350 eighty-character images gives the user batch integrity as well as room for the exception.

Whether or not you use the new cartridge/cassette approach to input depends somewhat on your application requirements, but even this limitation is slipping in importance as some large manufacturers are now offering cartridge/cassette products which are designed to handle almost all data preparation jobs.

DISCUSSION QUESTIONS

1. What unique advantages do the key-to-cassettes offer? How is their use considered an extension to traditional data entry techniques?

2. Explain briefly the two types of key-to-cassette devices. What common advantages do they share?

KEY-DISK SYSTEMS SPEED MAINFRAME PROCESSING OFF-LINE

Barry M. Harder

By putting a minicomputer in charge of several keyboard workstations, users can record large quantities of ready-to-process source data onto a single magnetic tape without the expensive and time-consuming mainframe validation and editing runs normally associated with large-scale input jobs. With these shared-processor, or "key-disk" systems, users can substantially increase the throughput on their mainframe computers, eliminate the maintenance and support of the utility programs formerly needed to perform these editing and validation jobs, and dedicate the main storage and peripheral devices needed for these jobs to other, more productive tasks. However, these systems can be expensive, costing about $200 per terminal per month, or about three times as much as a keypunch machine.

Key-disk systems were developed in 1967 as a result of the low-cost availability of minicomputers and associated disk- or drum-storage devices. Basically, these systems are built around a number of independent keyboard workstations where

Source: Reprinted by permission of the publisher from *Computer Decisions,* May 1971, pp. 42-43.

the source data is physically entered into the system by operators. These workstations also have some form of data display—ranging from a full-tube CRT to a single-character display—for the operator's benefit. Actual editing and validation of the source-data input is handled by the system's central processor, a minicomputer with from 4k to 128k bytes of core storage, depending on the number of workstations, with an attached direct-access device (disk or drum) with from 0.4-million to more than 11-million bytes of capacity for intermediate storage of keyed data. The size of this device is also a function of the number of workstations within the system, and also on the lengths of records being handled and on other factors such as the number of different record formats which are stored. Finally, these systems contain facilities for outputting the edited and validated source data onto a magnetic tape which is then ready for the mainframe-processor run.

In operation, data from source documents is keyed into the system by the operators at the workstations, through the central minicomputer processor and onto the attached disk. The records are held there until verified by the operator— either visually (using the CRT or single-character display), by re-keying (in a manner similar to a keypunch), or through a combination of both. As part of the input process, the minicomputer validates the data and edits it as required and as the data is entered. Some of the validation procedures which can be performed by typical key-disk systems include:

- check digits, which are used principally to insure correct numeric input. For example, in a seven-digit identification number, the last digit could be the "check digit" and could be arrived at by a combination of multiplication and addition of the preceding six digits. The result is checked by the computer. If it corresponds to the check digit, the numeric data is accurate. This tends to eliminate the major numeric-data entry problem—transposed digits;
- high-, low-range checking of a numeric value;
- "must-enter" fields to prevent inadvertent skipping of fields—for example a customer's account number;
- boundary-checking, to prevent overflow into the next field;
- alpha-only or numeric-only checks.

In addition to allowing the user to perform these and many other checks on his data as it is entered, key-disk systems allow searching of files to find and display a record, insertion of records into a file—similar to adding new punched cards, merging of records into new batches (for example, employees formerly listed under two departments are now listed under one department) and the merging of batches into new files.

KEY-DISK IN OPERATION

Let's see how this works: If the records processed by the mainframe were specified as 80-column records (keypunched then put on tape for later validation and editing prior to processing), the user with a key-disk system simply keeps going the way he always has—except for one difference: operator efficiency is noticeably increased since she continuously keys source data from top to bottom, regardless of the format demanded by the punched card. The programs contained in the minicomputer then edit this input into 80-column records, validate the data and prepare a final tape. To the mainframe software, nothing has changed—the input is the same as it always has been. In effect, then, key-disk machines present the user two opportunities: first, he can input data in a form which is convenient to the mainframe; second, he can if needed, permit input in a form which is more productive and convenient to the operator, as mentioned above. In addition, variable length source documents can be formatted to any required length, without any intervention on the part of the operator. In both cases, the "translation" to the format used by the mainframe is accomplished by the software supplied by the manufacturer of the minicomputer within the key-disk systems.

KEYSTATIONS: SOME DISPLAY DATA; SOME DON'T

In keypunching, a card containing an error can be seen by the operator, and can be removed. In key-disk systems, however, the operator can no longer touch the record—she must be given both a method of determining where she is in a record or batch, and a means of correcting mistakes, verifying and editing. To provide her with a means of interacting with the system, a form of display is provided on all systems. One effective way of accomplishing this interaction is via a CRT display at the keystation such as offered on the Entrex 480 and the Inforex systems. This permits viewing of the entire record being entered or verified in context, and with backspace/strikeover capability permits easy correction of mistakes as they occur. Use of a CRT can also speed verifying. For example, verification can be done visually or by entirely re-keying the data, or by any combination of visual and key verification. Other manufacturers, however, offer "blind" entry stations—limited data displays which interpret what the operator needs to know through coded indicators.

Interaction with systems using this method is accomplished via an array of keys or switches. While this approach has the advantage of producing lower hardware costs, it can lead to more complicated training programs for the operators, and may promote a higher probability of keying errors.

The software necessary to perform all these functions, as well as that necessary to edit and validate all input data and to physically transfer this data to the final output tape comes with the system—key-disk manufacturers are normally "bundled." This software, of course, should be configured as closely as possible to the exact needs of the user. For example, whether or not programs to handle one type of validation or edit check are included is a function of whether or not they are required as indicated by the application source document. In short, if the source document has no alpha information on it, then you had best make sure your programs have the capacity to check for alpha characters which may inadvertently be keyed in. Options to the software generally supplied by the manufacturers include those programs which will extend editing and validation procedures beyond those normally supplied—for example, supplying two check digits instead of one.

KEY-DISK AND OTHER INPUT MEDIA

Keypunch machines, of course, are still the major means of converting source data to machine-readable form. However, these machines have obvious limitations. First and foremost, record size is limited by the physical size of the punched card itself; operator efficiency is lower due to the time interval between cards, and errors are costly and hard to correct. Key-disk systems offer users a way to get around these problems. The trade-off, of course, is total cost versus throughput. Key-disk systems rent for considerably more than comparable keypunch machines—for a 10-station system, the average cost may be in the neighborhood of $200-$250 per month per station, compared to $125 per month for IBM's latest buffered keypunch. Standard 029 keypunches rent for even less. These cost figures come down as the number of stations increases—for 25 stations, the average cost can be reduced to about $175. However, key-disk systems can, and have, increased throughput 25 to 75 percent, depending on the application.

KEY-DISK OR KEY-TAPE

Key-disk systems can offer significant advantages over key-tape devices: increased speed and efficiency is promoted in the input process since all input goes directly through the central processor in the system—an approach which eliminates the need to either "pool" the tape from a series of stand-alone key-tape units or to physically transfer it to a system processor for editing and validation before running it through the mainframe. Against these advantages, the user must once again weigh cost per terminal and must contend with scheduling problems if disk capacity is exceeded. Possible downtime of the system should also be considered by those contemplating key-disk systems. Mostly, these will occur in the mechanical parts of the systems such as the tape-handling equipment, and disk rather than the system's central processor. In this case, the user should make sure that his system is capable of inputting directly to the main processor and bypassing either the tape, the disk or the minicomputer if either should be down.

DISCUSSION QUESTIONS

1. Explain the make-up, operation, and advantages of a key-to-disk system.
2. How does a key-to-disk operator correct mistakes on a key-to-disk system?
3. What advantages do key-to-disk systems offer over key-to-tape systems? What factors must be weighed in choosing one system over another?

SHOULD OCR BE YOUR DATA INPUT MEDIUM?

Fonnie H. Reagan, Jr.

One of the traditional bottlenecks associated with computer operations is the problem of getting information into the system in the first place. In the past, this job has generally been done by flocks of keypunch operators reading the data and keypunching it onto cards. Newer methods include key-to-tape and key-to-disk systems, on-line and source data entry, mark readers and optical character recognition (OCR).

Perhaps the greatest advantage of OCR over alternative methods of data entry is its ability to directly encode for processing the same form of data (numbers, characters, symbols) used in written human communications. Ideally, therefore, OCR systems could completely replace the laborious process of manually keying in data.

Although this ideal has yet to be reached, there are economic advantages presently available through OCR technology. Various manufacturers estimate that installations having from 5 to 12 or more keypunches can profitably make use of character readers. Where do the savings come from to pay for this beast?

One place is the lessened cost of labor. Since manual input for the character readers is typically prepared on a typewriter, the hourly wage rate is generally lower than for keypunch operators, while the output is higher and the rate of errors is lower. The ease with which errors can be corrected when preparing typewritten documents contributes to the speed in comparison with keypunching. One user estimates that about 10 percent of the documents processed at his installation contain errors detected and corrected by the operator. Some readers contain special facilities for recognizing a character skip symbol or strikethroughs to further ease correction of errors detected by the typist.

WHERE CAN OCR BE USED TO ADVANTAGE?

Not every installation with a dozen keypunch machines can profit from the installation of an OCR system. In analyzing his application, the user must take into account certain data input parameters. In general, OCR is best suited for those applications which have a very high volume of source documents while, at the same time, having a limited number of different types of documents. Suitable applications include inventory control situations using various types of transaction records (receipts, disbursements, deletions, additions, changes, etc.), and applications involving turnaround documents (utility billing, credit cards, and the like).

Source: Reprinted by permission of the publisher from *Computer Decisions,* June 1971, pp. 19-21.

To estimate the type of configuration which would be necessary for his particular application, the user should take into account several considerations. The first consideration is volume of transactions. This will identify the speed of the OCR reader required. Don't overlook the possibility of two lower-speed readers in place of one high-speed reader. Economics of scale apply here as well as other places, but the sophisticated reader may contain much more in the way of font (type style) selection and document flexibility than is needed for your application, and you would be paying for this as well as for increased performance.

Identification of volume usually implies selecting certain applications. After you get your reader up and running, there's a good chance that additional applications will present themselves, so reserve capacity may be desirable. Long-range planning of this type is difficult, and it is not always wise to go to a large machine in the expectation of finding additional work for it. Perhaps this is the best justification for leasing rather than purchasing the machine, at least until the workload is well defined.

The application for which the reader will be used determines how much machine you need. The essential decisions involve:

- Amount of data per record.
- Type of data to be read.
- Number of different formats required.

The amount of data per record distinguishes between the need for a "form" or "document" reader (one or two lines) and a "page" reader (many lines). If you have been getting along fine with one or two punched cards per record, then a document reader will probably suffice.

Three general types of data can be identified: numeric, alphabetic, and hand-printed (also normally numeric). The more different characters the unit must recognize, the more it will cost. Hand printing has proven itself reliable for numerics and a few letters but, again, it costs more. Hand printing can be used very successfully if the amount of printing per document is kept small and if the manufacturer's rules for forming the characters are carefully followed.

The number of formats necessary is essentially the number of different documents you intend to read. Significant variations require fancier document transports and scanning logic which also adds to costs. A major decision point in document design is whether to hold as closely as possible to previously used forms, or to completely redesign them. Complete redesign usually leads to a cleaner installation, but it does require more effort to implement.

The different type-face fonts you require are also an important cost factor. Some of the less expensive systems can only read one particular font, or part of that font (numerics only, for example). When considering such a system, you must also determine if the font the machine can read is readily available on the typing or imprinting units you are using.

The more expensive systems can read full alphanumerics (sometimes upper and lower case). The potential user should seriously consider standardizing his input forms rather than incurring the expense of these added reading capabilities.

At least two manufacturers produce systems which, although they function as OCR units, are not truly optical character recognition systems. These are Honeywell's DRD-200 which reads "bar code"—a set of vertical lines which can be recognized as letters by human readers, and the Datatype 3800 which reads a line of bars printed below standard-style characters. In certain applications, such units can offer the input powers of OCR without the associated high price tag.

THE VARYING FORMS OF OCR INPUT

The medium used for the input data goes a long way toward determining the type of reader that will be required. While some units, such as the Information International Grafix I, read from microfilmed documents, most OCR readers use some type of paper form as input. Perhaps the simplest of these units are those designed to read data (mainly numeric) from journal tapes. These systems would be used in capturing sales data from cash register tapes or adding machines.

The majority of OCR readers are in the category of forms or document readers. These units are designed to read one or two lines from a form, and are used for credit card billing, utility billing, and other turnaround applications. When comparing these units, an important factor is the amount of data that can be read in one pass of the reader's scanning mechanism. Some devices can read several different lines, but require that the scanning mechanism be manually adjusted. This feature is primarily directed toward accommodating forms with different formats rather than extending the reading capability for one particular document.

A great deal of additional flexibility is obtained if some measure of control (editing and formatting) can be exercised over what can be read from the document. The editing capabilities available range from none to nearly any that a user might desire.

One useful feature is the ability to read a control character and skip over fields or lines where there is no data. This saves time and speeds throughput.

Careful distinctions should be made between the capabilities of on-line systems and those which operate off-line. On-line systems are generally less expensive, but require the user to support their operation with his own computer. To increase capabilities, therefore, he will need to detract from the regular operations of his own computer system. Off-line systems contain their own control computer and are therefore more expensive. However, they do not drain the resources of the user's system. A less flexible method of providing these capabilities is via hardwired plugboards which control the functions of the reader.

HOW THE SOURCE DOCUMENTS ARE HANDLED

The movement of documents from the input hopper (see accompanying idealized illustration of an OCR system) to the output stacker is of critical importance. For low-speed readers, drive rollers are adequate, if only one size of form is to be read. As the need for increased speed or the capability to handle different sized forms arises, more sophisticated techniques are required. Conveyor belts are typically used in higher-speed devices, often with a vacuum assist to hold the documents in position on the belt.

Two problems are outstanding in the area of document handling: double pick-up and jams. If two documents are picked up together they will usually pass

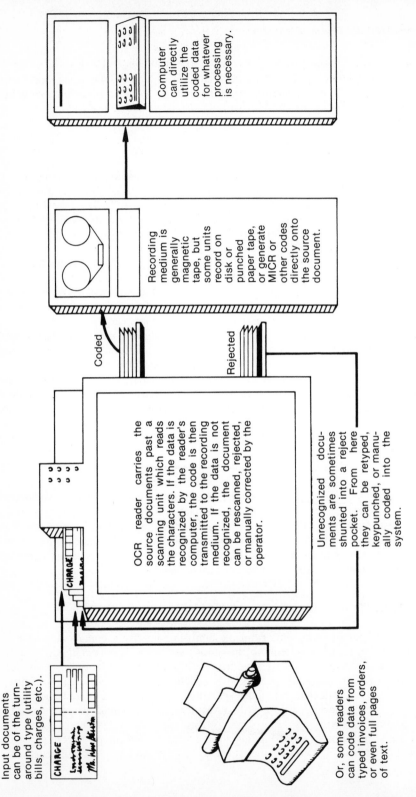

Input documents can be of the turn-around type (utility bills, charges, etc.).

Or, some readers can code data from typed invoices, orders, or even full pages of text.

OCR reader carries the source documents past a scanning unit which reads the characters. If the data is recognized by the reader's computer, the code is then transmitted to the recording medium. If the data is not recognized, the document can be rescanned, rejected, or manually corrected by the operator.

Unrecognized documents are sometimes shunted into a reject pocket. From here they can be retyped, keypunched, or manually coded into the system.

Coded

Rejected

Recording medium is generally magnetic tape, but some units record on disk or punched paper tape, or generate MICR or other codes directly onto the source document.

Computer can directly utilize the coded data for whatever processing is necessary.

Figure 1. How an OCR System Operates

through the readers as one unless special facilities are included to detect this problem. Jams will occur, even with the best and most carefully-designed transports. The problem is intensified if the documents to be read have been handled considerably. The ease with which the document path can be accessed for removal of jams is an often-overlooked factor in selecting equipment.

The range of sizes and weights of documents that can be accommodated by a reader govern your choice of source documents. The limits for maximum and minimum size are fairly obvious criteria—except that not all combinations of sizes in between the maximum and minimum are necessarily acceptable.

ERROR CONTROL CAPABILITIES

Discussion of errors and controls always leads to dissension no matter what area of data processing is being discussed. Advertised (and verified) reject rates of 0.25 to 0.5 percent cause some users to become disillusioned when they see 30 or 40 percent of the documents going into the "reject pocket." Documents in the reject pocket generally must be retyped or entered manually.

There are three principal types of errors of concern to users of optical character readers: ambiguous characters, invalid data, and documents in poor condition.

Ambiguous characters are those for which the reader cannot make a decision about what character each should be. There can be many reasons. Typical ones include broken or poorly formed characters and dirt or other marks that are picked up by the reader. Handling of this situation varies with the reader and with programming. Many readers automatically rescan an ambiguous character. Some substitute a standard character for all unreadable characters and continue. Others display the character on a CRT screen for on-line manual correction by the operator; sometimes adjacent data is also displayed to give the operator more context for making the decision. One unit, the Grafix I, stores a "picture" of the unrecognized character for later identification by an operator.

Users of OCR systems quickly learn that the inclusion of checks in the data is extremely useful for insuring the maintenance of an adequate throughput level by reducing the number of rejected documents. This technique most frequently takes the form of repeated data fields, particularly for numeric entries. The technique is applicable only if the data can be processed and the actions of the reader can be controlled on the basis of the result.

Another commonly employed accuracy check is the check digit. The digits of a numeric field are manipulated, and there are several standard formulas, to generate a check digit. This digit is included in the input. The reader or associated processor generates another check digit while reading and compares it to the one read in. Failure of this check normally causes the document to be rejected.

Another important feature of OCR readers is the type of computer-compatible output they provide. Most units store their coded data on magnetic tape, and a tape drive may be supplied with the system for this purpose. The user should be certain that the mode of output is fully compatiable with his existing system.

PERFORMANCE MEASUREMENT EVALUATION

Attempting to determine performance criteria by which to judge all types of OCR readers is a difficult task. Character or document reading rates would be fine if it were not for the fact that reading speed depends on the quality of the input documents. Also, readers that handle only one size of form or journal tape can be measured much more easily than those which handle different sizes of document.

Of the traditional performance measures (documents per minute, lines per minute, and characters per second), the documents-per-minute rating is usually the most applicable to situations where only one or two lines are being read per document. The lines-per-minute rating is useful for judging journal-tape readers, and the characters-per-second measure is most suited for readers handling whole pages of text.

Careful evaluation of timing information, which often becomes quite complex, is necessary to accurately predict the performance of the more sophisticated character readers. The size of the document, the amount and location of data on the document, and processing of the data read can all affect the rate at which documents proceed through the reader.

In any case, when evaluating the performance of competing OCR systems, it is important to see actual benchmark tests run with documents similar to those that you will be using. There are so many variables involved (reject rate, error rate, document quality, editing capabilities, etc.) that the potential buyer should carefully evaluate the system in action—in addition to studying its specifications on paper.

DISCUSSION QUESTIONS

1. In 200 words or less, explain how an OCR system operates.
2. What economic justification does the author present for the use of OCR?
3. What type of installation do you think would find the use of an OCR system profitable? What considerations must be made? Explain.
4. What factors determine the type and size of OCR device needed in an installation?
5. Explain the pros and cons of on-line and off-line OCR systems.
6. What types of errors are of concern to OCR users?
7. What performance measures are used in evaluating various OCR readers?

OPTICAL READERS AND OCR

Peter J. Gray

Optical scanning is a generic term which includes optical mark, code or bar, and character reading. However, optical scanning is not an accurate term because scanning is only one of the functions of an optical reader. Scanning involves searching a form for marks, bars or characters, and the conversion of the reflected optical impulses to electrical signals. *Recognition* is the process of comparing these signals with matching sets of stored signals in order to determine their identity.

OPTICAL READERS

Optical mark and code readers correlate the position and location of marks, bars, or lines with predefined characters, while *optical characters readers* identify each character by comparing its features or characteristics with those features or characteristics stored in memory. Optical character reading is similar to the reading methods we humans use. When light is placed on a form containing data, we search or scan the form, and the optical image of the characters is reflected on the retina of the eye. These images are transformed into nerve impulses, and transmitted through various logic levels to the visual cortex of the brain. The brain has been programmed through learning to identify and recognize a variety of characters, and put them into context.

SCANNING TECHNIQUES

Among the scanning techniques used in optical readers are mechanical disk, flying spot, photocell or photoarray, Vidicon, and image dissector.

Mechanical disk scanners use a light source which is reflected from the form being scanned, through a series of lenses, and onto a rotating disk containing multiple apertures which slice each character into segments. Light reflected through these rotating apertures and a fixed aperture plate permits a full character to be scanned for each disk revolution. The fixed aperture plate controls the light and directs it to a photomultiplier for conversion into electrical signals. This method is relatively slow (400-500 characters per second), and subject to mechanical problems.

Flying spot scanners use a CRT-generated spot of light which moves across a form to locate characters and trace their shapes. The intensity of the reflected light is measured and converted by photomultipliers and amplifiers. These scanners are of medium speed (1000-2000 characters per second), and have the ability to do

Source: *Modern Data,* January 1971, pp. 67-70.

curve tracing and line finding. However, flying spot scanners do not have the resolution capabilities of some other techniques, and they require strict control to prevent entry of ambient light.

In the *photocell scanner,* a light source is used to reflect a character image onto a series of photocells that are used to sample a number of points adding up to a character slice, or to sample a complete character at a time. The photocells generate signals which are quantized into shades of grey, black, or white. This scanning technique is quite expensive, but scanning speeds of 2400 to 3600 characters per second can be attained.

The *Vidicon* or *TV camera* approach involves scanning characters projected onto the surface of the tube, rather than scanning the form directly. The quantized video signals indicate the degree of blackness or whiteness that exists. This technique is limited by the low number of characters that can be stored on the tube surface.

The *image dissector* method also involves scanning the face of the tube. A high-intensity light source illuminates the read area, reflecting and converging information through a lens and onto the face of the tube. Electrons are activated and directed through an aperture in the tube, where they are measured and multiplied by a photo-electric detector. The image dissector tube is a high-resolution, relatively fast (2000 characters per second) method of scanning.

RECOGNITION METHODS

The most commonly used recognition methods are matrix matching, curve tracing, and stroke or feature analysis.

In *matrix matching,* the electronic signals representing the scanned character are stored in a series of shift registers connected to register matrices. Each matrix represents a single character, and is connected to another register containing a voltage representation of the referenced character. The voltage representations in the two registers are compared, and recognition is accomplished. This technique permits the recognition of full alphanumeric fonts and facilitates font changes.

Curve tracing, in conjunction with flying spot scanning, involves following the outlines of a character and recognizing features to identify the character. However, problems are encountered with broken lines and other character imperfections.

Stroke or *feature analysis* uses selected sizes and positions of strokes to identify a character. The form of the character is matched against a truth table representing each reference character. Some scanners incorporate an image enhancement technique prior to recognition, which permits poor-quality characters to be read and reduces the number of rejects and substitutions.

FONTS

The user of optical readers has a wide choice of fonts in either numeric or alphanumeric character sets. Multi-font readers are available, with most manufacturers offering a basic system and additional fonts as options.

In an attempt to standardize, the United States of America Standards Institute, now known as the American National Standards Institute, adopted OCR-A, a stylized font which consists of alphanumeric characters and a set of special symbols. Similarly, the European Computer Manufacturers Association has adopted another stylized font, OCR-B.

The use of standard fonts by optical readers generally provides higher accuracy than non-stylized fonts because each character has been designed to differentiate it from another character. The use of non-stylized fonts may result in increased reject and error rates. Although there are a number of ways to prevent rejects from occurring, substitutions of one character or symbol for another is a more serious problem, and occurs more frequently with non-standard fonts.

The objection to such stylized fonts as OCR-A is that they are not esthetic, but in reality, the characters are as easily read by the human eye as by scanners. Most users require little or no adjustment to OCR-A, and this font is now used more extensively than any other.

OTHER READERS AND FONTS

For applications where permanent records may be required, optical readers are available that use a microfilm camera to record and index forms while they are being read. Readers are also available that can read microfilm after forms have been imaged during a previous step.

Magnetic ink character readers (MICR) do not read data optically, but pass the magnetized ink characters on a form (such as a bank check) past a read head which magnetically senses each character. The font recognized by MICR systems is known as E-13B, which is limited to ten numeric characters and four special symbols. Some optical readers can scan and recognize these magnetic ink characters, in addition to reading other fonts.

FORMS, TRANSPORTS, AND THRUPUT

A key factor to be considered in evaluating optical readers is the paper-handling capability of the transport. The paper transport moves forms from an input feeder through a read area to output stackers. Most transports use a friction or vacuum feeder with rollers and belts.

The speed and efficiency of the transport, together with the speed and capability of scanning and recognition, determine the thruput rate of the optical reader. The thruput rate of a particular form will depend on the size of the form, the number, type and quality of the characters, and the number of lines to be read. Rescanning characters many times and manual character insertion after display reduce the number of forms rejects, but these methods slow down the thruput rate.

Although most users initially install a scanner to process one or two particular applications, they will want to utilize their systems more effectively by adding other types of forms to be read, such as multi-line documents and pages. Multi-function transports are available, and are capable of handling a wide variety of forms sizes, weights, thicknesses, and textures. Forms design specifications and restrictions are becoming less and less severe; some readers can process forms without reference marks, with formatted or unformatted data, with variable data locations, with no aspect ratio (length to width) constraints.

PRICE AND COST RATIOS

Two popular methods of measuring the relative capability of optical readers are the price to performance ratio, and the cost per character or cost per thousand characters processed during a given period of time. Potential users can best determine thruput rates, price to performance ratios, and cost per character processed by testing their forms on various scanners and comparing results.

TYPES OF READERS

OCR systems can be classified by type of input form processed. There are document readers, page readers, journal tape readers, and multi-purpose readers capable of handling a variety of media.

A *document reader* scans one to five lines of data in fixed locations on a document at a single pass. *Page readers* are capable of scanning many lines of data during a single pass of the form. *Journal tape readers* can process rolls of paper tape generated by adding machines and cash registers.

If the data processing user has a simple, numeric data collection application such as inventory control, or a limited order entry requirement, he might consider using an optical mark reader. Such readers are cheaper than OCR systems, but they restrict the user to a few well-defined applications. Similar restrictions apply to OCR document readers and special-purpose journal tape readers.

For users having a variety of input applications including pages, documents, and sometimes journal tapes, the logical choice should be a *multi-purpose OCR reader* capable of processing a wide range of forms sizes.

A multi-purpose OCR reader should be capable of reading alphanumeric characters from turnaround documents, such as invoices, that are usually computer generated and returned to the issuer for computer re-entry via OCR. In addition, such a device should be able to read and process handprinted information, and handle typed or printed page-sized forms without major modifications to the equipment. Handprinted characters on forms permit direct data entry from the source generating the information. Applications such as sales orders and inventory reports ideally lend themselves to the recognition of handprinted characters; no typing or retranscription is required, with a consequent improvement in the speed and accuracy of data entry.

ECONOMICS

Optical scanning is typically compared to keypunching and verifying or other keyboard data-entry methods. Tangible dollar savings can be established by calculating the costs of manual keying, including equipment, labor, cards or materials, overhead, benefits, and other factors relative to the performance of the equipment, in terms of accurate quantities of data produced. An average keypunch operator can generate 120 to 130 keystrokes a minute, but the effective thruput rate is reduced to between 60 and 70 characters a minute because verification is generally required. In contrast, an average typist can produce data at a rate of 150 to 160 characters a minute. Even if we assumed the total costs of keypunching and typing were equivalent at $5 an hour, the productivity to cost ratio of typists is more than twice that of keypunch operators. For example, the break even point between keypunching and a $4000 a month OCR system reading typed pages is about 15 keypunches and verifiers. When reading computer-generated turnaround documents, the break even point is about 10 keypunches and verifiers.

These comparisons are not fully indicative of the costs involved. Manual key-entry devices of all kinds are labor intensive devices. The costs of hiring, training, turnover, salary increases, benefits, overtime, and other factors must be accounted for. Most optical readers require one operator, or with high-speed readers, only a part-time operator. There are also a number of intangible savings involved by speeding up the data-processing billing cycle, thereby improving the cash flow. Reduced order processing time means faster revenues and reduced inventories, and improved accuracy of data entry means better operating decisions. Pre-editing and formatting of data also helps save CPU time.

A major benefit of using high-speed data entry devices such as optical readers is the improvement in utilization of installed computer systems. Much EDP time is lost in waiting to process key-generated data; this is typical of many installations today, and computer utilization is likely to become even less efficient as users upgrade to larger, more powerful systems. Priority should be given to improving input methods which will, in turn, improve the utilization of main frame systems.

OFF-LINE VS. ON-LINE

In evaluating optical scanners, the subject of off-line versus on-line readers must be considered. The on-line CPU costs of a system should be added to the price of the scanner, because some portion of computer time is dedicated to the operation of the reader, rather than to performing other processing tasks.

Less flexibility in scheduling input jobs, and dependency on the main computer are also restricting features of on-line systems. Remote terminal readers should be priced with the costs of communications lines, modems, and other devices included.

SOFTWARE

An important consideration in evaluating and justifying optical readers is the software, systems, and training support provided with the readers. Some vendors offer complete support within the price of the system, while others are partially or fully unbundled.

APPLICATIONS

A wide range of applications are being processed by the 1500 scanners installed today. Such business applications as billing, order entry, file maintenance, and inventory control are common to all types of organizations.

Scanners are reading specific forms pertaining to individual companies and industries. Publishers are using OCR equipment to read subscription notices and lists, premium forms, and coupons. Manufacturers are reading job tickets and time cards, work orders, production and test reports, and payroll lists. Utilities use scanners to process meter cards, repair reports, and change notices. The retail industry uses readers for price tickets, coupons, route sheets, sales slips, and price changes. Banks process mortgage and loan records, payment forms, stock transfers, trust accounts, dividend checks, and other applications. Insurance companies read premium notices, claims forms, medical records, and accident reports. In the area of education, scanning is used extensively for student tests and records. State and federal governments use scanners for tax statements, payment reports, allotment forms, and many other applications.

DATA ENTRY ASPECTS

Data collection, preparation, and recording for optical scanning may be accomplished in a variety of ways. For example, computer-generated turnaround documents such as bills are prepared by line or drum printers. The return stubs of these documents are read back into the OCR system which, in turn, initiates a file update and new billing cycle. Credit card imprinters are used to generate OCR readable documents for oil companies, retailers, restaurants, and other businesses. Cash registers and adding machines create journal tapes to be optically read by special OCR equipment or multi-function OCR systems with journal tape features.

The office typewriter is commonly used to generate lists or prepare forms for subsequent entry to computers via an optical character reader. Forms may also be generated by hand printing characters or by marking. Sales order slips are filled out at the data source with a date, quantity, description, and prices. These sales orders can be read into the system directly without retranscription. There are a number of other methods of recording data, such as garment tag perforators and notching devices. Another retail application involves point-of-sale scanning devices that automatically read the price or a code from each item purchased, and transmit this information to a computer which calculates taxes and total amounts, and maintains inventory status records.

PARTICULAR APPLICATIONS

The following case studies of users of optical scanners illustrates the power, versatility, and utility of OCR systems.

- *Foremost Foods* is using OCR for routing accounting and sales orders, and saving $350,000 a year.
- *TV Guide* eliminated 13 keypunch and verifier stations, including operators, when it used OCR for subscription fulfillment.
- *McDonnell-Douglas* reduced manufacturing turnaround time, improved systems reliability, and reduced data errors, labor, and equipment costs. Twenty-seven keypunch operators were eliminated, and computer time was reduced, despite an increase in data input workload.

- *The State of Georgia* expects to save $45,000 and months of work by using OCR for direct computer entry of auto registration applications.
- *Imperial Oil* saves $100,000 a year by processing invoices faster and by reducing forms costs.
- *Detroit Ball Bearing Company* reduced its order-inventory cycle time from 62 hours to 45 minutes, using optical scanning rather than punched cards.
- *United Air Lines* saved nearly $25,000 a month in input preparation costs associated with airline tickets and other documents.

CONCLUSION

The selection of an OCR system will depend on the nature and scope of the user's current and potential applications. Many low-cost scanners have severe limitations in their ability to read data reliably, with few rejects and substitutions and at high speeds. On the other hand, some high-priced scanners offer more capabilities than the user requires. With a wide variety of systems to choose from, the user should be able to pick the most versatile equipment available, at a justifiable cost, rather than settle for a machine that can process only one or two immediate applications.

GLOSSARY

Magnetic-Ink Character Recognition (MICR): A process which senses and encodes into a machine language characters printed with an ink containing magnetized particles.

Optical Character Recognition (OCR): A technique which relies on electronic devices and light to detect, and convert into machine language, characters which have been printed or written on documents in human-understandable form.

Optical Scanning: Translating printed or handwritten characters into machine language. Also called *visual scanning.*

DISCUSSION QUESTIONS

1. Where is scanning different from recognition?
2. How is optical character reading similar to the human method of reading?
3. Of the scanning techniques mentioned in the article, which technique
   a. is the fastest?
   b. offers relatively poor resolution capabilities?
   c. can do curve tracing?
4. What factors must be considered in evaluating optical readers?
5. Explain briefly the function of the four types of OCR readers. What factors determine the type of reader that a prospective user needs?
6. How does the author justify the economics of using OCR over key-entry devices?

7. What types of applications are currently processed by OCR systems?
   Can you think of other areas where they might be effectively used?
   Explain.

OCR MARKET FOR THE SEVENTIES

Israel Sheinberg

BACKGROUND

Optical character recognition is often referred to as the most promising means of easing the data entry bottleneck. In fact, this prediction has been made so frequently that it has become somewhat of a paradox. It's a paradox now, at the beginning of the 1970's, because there are still only about 1000 OCR installations in the United States, which account for a small two percent of the total data entry volume for all computer systems.

About 80,000 computers are currently installed, with this figure expected to increase substantially throughout the decade, and the market for data entry devices will be greater than ever. OCR manufacturers will capitalize on this opportunity. There are more companies manufacturing and marketing OCR equipment than ever before; about 18 new ones have been formed within the last two years. During this same period, there have been more new OCR products announced than in all the previous years combined.

COST COMPARISONS

One of the most controversial (and least understood) aspects of OCR is its cost. Although initial expenditures for OCR can be substantial, resulting savings can be even more impressive. Even with large-scale million-dollar OCR systems now installed, users are economically justifying OCR—sometimes saving a quarter of a million dollars annually in direct comparison to costs for other means of data entry. This does not even consider savings in other areas, such as the cost of finding and correcting mistakes.

When compared to costs for preparing data through conventional means, the initial investment in optical character recognition immediately becomes a bargain. Keypunching and verifying costs data processors an estimated $3.5 billion annually, of which $3 billion is for personnel costs alone.

It isn't unusual for the cost of input preparation to exceed the cost of the computers themselves. Twelve experienced keypunch operators on eight-hour shifts could produce about 500 hours of work in a week, or 168,000 cards—assuming 40

Source: *Modern Data,* January 1971, pp. 70-72.

characters per card and no verification. The cost for this productivity, including salaries, equipment, and materials, would approach $4,000 weekly. One new OCR page-reading system can perform equivalent information preparation in about one hour, and its basic cost for one week's work is only $3,000.

Other illustrations of cost relationships between the various methods of input are numerous. The cost per character example is just one. Keypunching costs about 6 cents to 10 cents per 100 characters, depending on the percent of verification, and about eight cents for key-to-tape devices. Large-scale OCR equipment, such as Recognition Equipment's Input 80 page reader, reduces this cost to little more than one cent for 1000 characters. As more technological advances are made, and competition increases, the cost advantages of OCR will be even more evident.

The cost of correcting mistakes that enter the computer—anywhere from 10 cents to $10 each—must also be considered. Generally keyboard-to-tape units provide no greater capability in error checking, and the accuracy of data input is not greatly improved over keypunch input. Therefore, the user's cost of erroneous data entered into the computer system remains high. Another factor is the handling of rejects. Reading reliability depends on the accuracy of the reading machine and on its ability to reject unreadable data, rather than to make random substitutions.

Computer users in the 1970's will give more consideration to OCR as an integral part of the data processing system and not just as an addition to a system or as a direct substitute for a keypunching or a key-to-tape installation. Many computer users will have such voluminous amounts of paper with data to be entered into a computer, that they will not even consider using keypunching or other methods involving an intermediate transcription of data. The cost of this intermediate step will be prohibitive, and direct reading of source documents will be the only practical answer.

MARKET POTENTIAL

According to some predictions, the OCR market could reach nearly $2 billion by the late 1970's. Others place the figure lower, but OCR growth will be a result of both the general EDP growth and the replacement of keypunch equipment.

With OCR, the machine adapts to the human environment, rather than the human adapting to the machine by changing humanly recognizable data into some sort of machine code—such as the holes in a pumch card.

A good share of OCR's growth will be in areas where a different means of data conversion such as keyboard entry or keypunching is now used. The remainder of its growth will be in cases where the volume of data is just too large to convert any other way. One great potential is the initial conversion of, or general updating of large data files.

APPLICATIONS

Direct reading of source information is OCR's ultimate function, and this is where users benefit most. This is now being accomplished in large-scale batch processing applications including processing oil company credit card tickets, postal transactions, reading information from airline tickets, and many other applications where the original information never has to be retyped or retranscribed for computer use, but is merely forwarded to a centralized data processing location in its original form.

In applications where the information is retyped before reading, such as in bank file updates, the typing merely acts as a substitute for another more traditional type of transcription. While this does have economies and advantages, such as the fact that the material is still humanly readable during every processing step and that typewriters as a means of conversion are cheaper and easier to use than keypunch or key-to-tape equipment, it is not the optimum use of OCR.

One of the uses of OCR that is almost certain to become widespread during the 1970's is the use of low-cost readers by small-to-medium-size companies or in decentralized locations where the volume of data is relatively small, but important, and must be transmitted on- or off-line to central or regional computers.

The newest of these small OCR terminals is designed to operate in ordinary working environments such as offices, factories, and warehouses and for a wide variety of applications including order writing, production and distribution, inventory control, payroll, sales analysis, and accounting. These terminals, if they are to be practical and economical, should be designed so they can be operated by the clerical or route employees, or whoever is responsible for entering the source data. This type of system offers large economies to users, because in most locations that process small amounts of information, someone is nearly always required to manually enter data that's already printed in some form. A viable OCR terminal should eliminate the expense of this extra transcription as well as the additional chance for human error.

HANDPRINTING APPLICATIONS

Since nearly half of all the data to be processed by computers originates as handprinted numbers, most OCR systems, if they are to be truly useful in real environments, should have handprinting reading capabilities. This is necessary to serve applications such as reading report information from utility meter reading and in distribution situations where routemen enter order and inventory information by hand.

Several recent test programs undertaken by OCR manufacturers have shown that the use of handprinted information is practical and that people can adapt to it with little difficulty. A large telephone company underwent a six-month test program where 80 long distance operators completed forms with handprinted information while operating the switchboard, speaking with customers, using a time stamp, keying the call, and monitoring two or three other calls at the same time. The test proved conclusively that people can successfully print numeric characters under less than ideal conditions for long periods of time and have them read successfully by an OCR system. By the program's conclusion, the document reading rate was 92 percent on the first pass with a substitution rate (reading a character incorrectly without rejecting the document, so the operator is unaware the substitution has been made) of 0.2 percent. The reading rate was on target for the test goals, and the substitution rate was 0.3 percent less than required.

The use of handprinted information in OCR applications will take hold within the next few years and will reduce the tools necessary for data input to a common lead pencil.

MACHINE PRINT

OCR's ability to read many different kinds of typewriter and line printer fonts is what makes it workable in a live customer environment and eliminates the need for retranscribing data and for industry standardization.

Government agencies, on all levels from federal to state, are finding they can process the huge quantity of forms and documents needed for data input quickly, accurately, and economically without an intermediate step. Agencies dealing in health, welfare, payroll, motor vehicle and license registration, tax, and many other areas are using OCR now, and many more will turn to OCR in the next decade. A key to OCR's success in these areas is multifont capability, the ability to read many different type styles on an intermixed basis.

SUMMARY

During the 1970's the ratio of OCR systems in use compared to total computer systems will be increased. Published predictions show that by 1975, 20 percent of the estimated 150,000 to 170,000 computers installed will use OCR. This is an estimated annual growth rate of 70 percent—a rate that industry will be hard-pressed to absorb.

Use of key-to-tape input devices will continue to grow as users look for methods to eliminate keypunching. But since key-to-tape is a direct substitution for the keypunching step, users will eventually require a method that allows direct input of source documents. By this time most users will have become sophisticated enough in data processing techniques and economics to look to OCR first.

As users become more familiar with and interested in OCR, service bureaus offering OCR will grow. Customers who are contemplating their own system will be prime service bureau customers, as well as smaller companies and organizations with seasonal peaks, such as mail order firms that have large holiday volumes.

International markets will experience similar growth in OCR utilization. Europe, in an effort to modernize their data processing, has been willing to accept new technologies and to put them to work in such areas as their postal and bank giro systems and large government agencies. As more European organizations redesign their data processing systems, they will incorporate OCR equipment as a basic part of their systems.

Who will share in this highly touted OCR market of the 1970's? Many of the newly formed OCR companies have good technical expertise, but some may not be fully aware of the problems of developing an OCR product that is workable in a live customer environment. The companies who attain the biggest share of this market will be the ones who best respond to customers' needs. They will be the companies, whether large or small, newly formed or established, who recognize the existing opportunities in the marketplace and meet them with equipment that will cost justify the users' applications.

Future technologies will include new methods for input microfilming and faster, even more versatile reading machines. However, the technological need in general is for machines that maintain the performance and reliability of OCR equipment, but with less complexity and at basically lower costs. Technology again, will be worthwhile only if it benefits the user and makes OCR more available to more users.

There will be many new application areas for OCR, such as automated typesetting in the printing industry. The industries that are now leading the way in OCR, such as banks, governments, and the credit card industry, will find OCR as commonly used as the office typewriter.

DISCUSSION QUESTIONS

1. How would one proceed in illustrating the cost relationship between OCR and other methods of input? Explain.
2. What is the gist of the article's assessment of the OCR market and applications potential?

POINT-OF-SALE SYSTEMS BRIDGE THE GAP
BETWEEN RETAILER AND CONSUMER

Richard P. Shaffer

One of the critical steps in the route toward the "cashless society" is automation at the point of purchase—the sales counter. Within the past two years, nearly a dozen major manufacturers have announced "computerized point-of-sale systems" with a multitude of configurations and capabilities. How these systems work, and what they can do to improve merchandise control, customer credit control, and customer service, will have an enormous impact on the retailing techniques of the seventies.

An automated point-of-sale system is essentially a cash register-like terminal which operates either on-line to a computer, or temporarily stores data for later computer processing. These terminals have varying capabilities. Some will automatically "read" a customer's credit card. Some will read price and merchandise data directly from sales slips. Some can be programmed to perform various sales and accounting functions. However, the two basic capabilities of point-of-sale systems which might induce the retailer to shift over from standard cash registers are: improved merchandise control, and improved customer credit control.

Source: Reprinted by permission of the publisher from *Computer Decisions,* August 1971, pp. 6-10.

HOW DO POS SYSTEMS IMPACT MERCHANDISE CONTROL?

In the area of merchandise control, automated point-of-sale (POS) systems allow the collection and processing of more merchandise data more quickly. This merchandise information has generally been coded, either optically or magnetically, onto the sales tag. This tag is then read by the terminal, either by passing a small, hand-held "wand" across the tag, or by inserting the tag into a stationary reader in the terminal.

Having this merchandise information automatically read and stored in computer-compatible form saves the retailer the time and expense of having the data converted for processing by alternative methods. The time saved may mean that the retailer can recognize a day sooner those items which are in greatest demand in each of his outlets. This may allow him to more effectively shift items from one store to another.

Speed alone does not provide sufficient cost justification for installing these systems. Such a justification can be found, however, in the impact of increased speed, accuracy, and quantity of data on the total merchandise system. This is reflected in the type of exception reports that the system will provide for the user. The difficulty here is to place a dollar value on these expanded reporting capabilities. It is up to each individual retailer to determine how much such improved information is worth to him.

Another key advantage of point-of-sale systems is in the area of financial control. These systems have the ability to tie together, through their data collection techniques, both unit and dollar information. Prior to these systems, information for unit control traveled one data path while information for dollar control traveled another—and never the twain did meet (or balance). Simultaneous capture of both unit and dollar information improves control over operations by allowing the retailer to pinpoint inventory position and make accurate adjustments. With these systems, the retailer knows that his reported "shortage" is really a shortage, and not simply an error introduced somewhere up the information stream.

SHOULD YOU HONOR THAT CREDIT CARD?

In the area of credit authorization, the techniques employed by point-of-sale systems are similar to those used in merchandise control. An optically or magnetically coded credit card is read by the terminal and the credit account is checked by the computer. All too often, POS system proposals rest heavily on credit authorization capabilities for their cost justification. There are plenty of alternate methods of credit checking available, and some of them are a good deal less costly than point-of-sale terminals. When considering an automated system, the retailer should definitely investigate alternative means of checking credit.

One of the more popular credit-checking techniques involves having the sales clerk call a central operation where another clerk will check the account in question via an on-line terminal. Since surveys show that between 90 and 95 percent of these inquiries result in simply "OK" answers, stores considering this type of system should look into on-line systems providing for voice response. Alternatively, a simple "yes" and "no" light on a separate unit, or on the point-of-sale terminal itself, could provide the same service.

This simple "yes" or "no" credit authorization technique is referred to as "negative" credit checking. That is, the files used by the system normally contain only those credit numbers which are not to be honored. If a valid account number is not on the file, the account is considered good and the "yes" light shines. More sophisticated systems can provide "selective" credit authorization giving some indication why the account is no good (e.g. a stolen credit card). Still more complex systems provide "partial positive" checking (whether both Mr. and Mrs. and daughter Sarah can use the card, for instance). The ultimate system, a "positve" credit check, tells the credit authorizer all about every account (if it is only slightly over its limit, if a high volume of charges have been made in the last few hours, etc.)

The more sophisticated the system, the larger the files which are required to service it and the more decision-making power is delegated to the system. One extremely pragmatic reason for considering some sort of automated credit-checking device is based on what your competitor is doing. If the store across the street installs a better credit-checking system than yours, the word will get around and all the wrong kind of customers will gravitate toward your door. Hence, you may be forced to improve your own system in order to survive.

In any case, the cost justification for a point-of-sale system should clearly separate those savings attributable to credit authorization from those savings attributable to merchandise control.

WHAT MAKES A POS SYSTEM WORK?

Between the cash register-terminal where the data is captured and the general purpose computer where the data is turned into useful information is a whole host of intermediate devices. The construction and configuration of these devices determines the nature of each particular manufacturer's offering.

While there are a dozen or more basic approaches to designing POS systems, these can be broken down into two basic types: those in which the terminal operates off-line, and those which operate on-line. Note well that on-line is not synonymous with real-time. Truly real-time POS systems have yet to be installed.

Under the off-line category, there are some terminals which produce transmittable output and others which produce non-transmittable output. Transmittable output takes the form of either magnetic tape cassettes/cartridges or punched paper tape. Transmission can occur by either having the main system poll the terminals periodically, or by removing the magnetic or punched paper tape from the register and placing it on a separate transmission device.

The non-transmittable output consists generally of cash register journal tape. These are then sent to the processing center to be converted (keypunched) into machine-readable form. Optically scannable journal tapes, while potentially desirable as data input media, have yet to be offered on POS terminals.

The on-line type of terminal is connected to a central device (minicomputer or collector) via a cable or a phone line. Cable units are most applicable where the required length of cable is small, 1,000 yards or less. Such configurations are thus more suited for in-store systems. The units using phone lines can be connected to the central computer via the telephone network, and are virtually unlimited by distance considerations. These would be practical in multi-store environments. It should be noted, however, that a combination of these two connection techniques is possible when a collector is used in the store to translate the register data and make it compatible with the telephone network.

If a POS terminal is to stand alone, without connection to an external computer, then all of the logic for controlling the terminal functions must be built-in. This makes for a more expensive terminal. If, on the other hand, some of the control logic is moved to a central device or minicomputer, then several terminals can share the same logic in a "cluster." This makes the individual terminals less expensive, but requires the purchase of a controlling device. Clustering terminals around a controller reduces the overall cost of the system, but makes the full operation of the terminals dependent on the continued functioning of one controller. Since the reliability of the terminals is critical in retail operations, manufacturers will frequently recommend that the critical control minicomputer be duplicated. This redundancy improves reliability while increasing costs.

WHAT ROLE DOES THE MINICOMPUTER PLAY?

The nature of the computer or collector to which POS terminals are connected varies all the way from a small, special purpose minicomputer up to the general purpose computer itself. This intermediate processor becomes a pivotal distinction amongst the different POS systems. It generally functions in one of three modes: First, it may be merely a communications link (multiplexor) between the point-of-sale terminal and the ultimate computer. In this capacity, it concentrates many small, low-speed transmission lines from the terminals into one high-speed line to the central computer. Depending on the geographical location of your terminals with respect to the central computer, such a device can be instrumental in reducing communications costs.

The second mode of operation for this communications link involves adding logic and turning it into a communications-oriented minicomputer. This additional logic may allow totals to be accumulated and may enable files to be attached to provide information on credit or merchandise on request from the terminal. The credit information can be updated periodically from the central computer. Because of the large number of customers serviced by most chain stores, this file may contain only that information pertaining to customers normally shopping in that particular store. If a customer normally shopping in one location wants to use his credit card in another location, an alternative method of credit checking would have to be employed.

While dividing the files in this manner works for customer accounts, it does not work as well for merchandise information. It would place a large burden on such a system to carry price and descriptive information for each of the multitude of items carried in that store. For this reason, some manufacturers incorporate the merchandise data in the sales tag. Thus, when the tag is read by the terminal, classification code "SKU" numbers as well as alphabetic information is caputred. Ultimately, for central control of pricing, markdowns, and descriptions, full two-way communication capability between the terminal and a large storage device will be required, as will full alphabetic capability.

The third mode of operation for the POS system is that of providing a full-scale, general-purpose computer on-line to the terminal. In such a system, larger files can be accommodated and real-time updating of these files becomes possible.

Another element in the link between terminal and central computer is the intermediate "buffer." This buffer stores and transmits data in varying-sized chunks, and has a significant effect on the system design and programming required. For example, if the buffer can transmit only 10 or 15 characters of data, then the average transaction will be placed on the storage device in sections, and will later require some sorting in order to pull a complete transaction together. In addition, some of the characters of information transmitted must be identification characters so that the bits and pieces of the transaction can be associated for subsequent sorting. These factors reduce the efficiency of transmission and operation. If the buffer capacity is several hundred characters, then the additional sort operation as well as the transmission of identification characters may be eliminated.

WHAT CAN POS DO FOR YOU?

Now that we know how the system works, it is important to consider what it can do in terms of input, processing, and output capabilities. The functions of a POS system can be combined in various configurations to provide some unique application capabilities.

For example, if the traditional cash register functions are eliminated and the device, with only an input tag reader and a ten-key number matrix, is powered by a battery, it can be used to record merchandise data on a tape cassette, and thus becomes very handy for taking unit inventory. It can be light, portable, and can be used in warehouse and store inventory-taking.

It is also possible to shrink the entire unit down and reduce the output capabilities so that it can act as a portable sales-check device enabling the clerk to carry it from one department to another during peak sales periods. In this application, since the output device has limited capacity, this mini-register must be brought periodically to the main register to transcribe its information.

There are a multitude of problems encountered by the POS system shopper. For instance, if you ask a manufacturer to quote a price for his system, he will typically give you answers anywhere between $2,000 and $5,000 per terminal. The primary reason for this wide range is the pricing concept rather than the nature of the equipment itself. A point-of-sale terminal alone may well cost $2,000. However, when you consider the cost of intermediate devices, cluster controllers, files and other communication equipment, as well as optional devices, then the cost-per-terminal of a fully operational system approaches the $5,000 mark.

One factor that can affect the total cost of the system to an individual department store is the number of terminals that can be tied into (clustered) a single control unit. There is a difference in cost between a basic module which handles eight terminals and one which handles 128. A store requiring in the neighborhood of 100 registers could be expected to look for a system which would accommodate between 100 and 150 POS terminals, to allow for some expansion. To get 100-terminal capacity might be more expensive if done by building up in clusters of eight, thus requiring about 12 such basic building blocks. It is also possible that a manufacturer may provide a variety of basic building blocks, allowing the retailer to satisfy his 100-terminal requirement by combining a building block of 64 with another block of 32. This might prove to be more economical while providing expansion capability on a modular basis rather than costing extra for excess capacity.

WHAT SHOULD THE RETAILER LOOK FOR?

There are a host of technical specifications which are not legitimately the concern of the retailer, but which manufacturers of POS equipment tend to expect from him. The retailer should not accept these highly technical decisions as being part of his problem.

For example, frequently a manufacturer will claim that his equipment is more reliable than another's because of some technical innovation he has achieved. He may claim that his use of "read-after-write" error checking is superior to his competitor's use of "redundancy" checks. It is both unnecessary and unfair to burden the retailer with this type of problem. He should not be expected to tell the manufacturer how to build his equipment.

If the technical aspects of the equipment are not to be of concern to the retailer, how then can he develop specifications for the manufacturers? The answer is, the retailer should give the manufacturer functional requirements rather than technical specifications. One functional item the retailer can specify is the reliability that he demands. For example, he may say that he wants the system to be available and in proper condition 98.7 percent of the time. He may also specify that he wants 99.99 percent data accuracy, or better. These are not unrealistic demands. Another example might be the acceptable response times. The retailer may say he is willing to wait as long as five seconds for a response to a credit check, but in all other operations the terminal operator or sales clerk should not be able to detect any delay in the entry of information. Such a specification is easily tested by simply having one of your star clerks try to outdistance the terminal.

With POS systems in general, it is probable that a manufacturer can meet all of the specifications set by the retailer, for a price. By specifying his operational requirements, the retailer can eliminate from his consideration the technical details and evaluate alternative proposals based on their price and their adherence to his specifications.

A final word about technical specifications. There is currently a considerable variety in the basic encoding methods offered by various manufacturers. Typically these employ either optical or magnetic coding. A retailer may feel that his decision to go one way or the other may seriously affect his operations in the future. However, this should not be of overwhelming concern. There is considerable evidence that technological advances in the near future will enable manufacturers to accommodate either or both of these technologies with very little extra cost to the user.

If a particular manufacturer offers a system which does not contain the ability

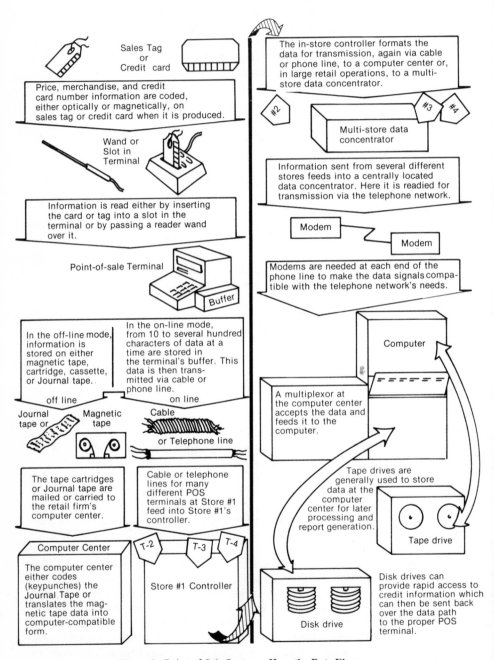

Figure 1. Point-of-Sale Systems: How the Data Flows

Sales Tag or Credit card

Price, merchandise, and credit card number information are coded, either optically or magnetically, on sales tag or credit card when it is produced.

Wand or Slot in Terminal

Information is read either by inserting the card or tag into a slot in the terminal or by passing a reader wand over it.

Point-of-sale Terminal

Buffer

In the off-line mode, information is stored on either magnetic tape, cartridge, cassette, or Journal tape.

In the on-line mode, from 10 to several hundred characters of data at a time are stored in the terminal's buffer. This data is then transmitted via cable or phone line.

off line — on line

Journal tape or Magnetic tape

Cable

or Telephone line

The tape cartridges or Journal tape are mailed or carried to the retail firm's computer center.

Cable or telephone lines for many different POS terminals at Store #1 feed into Store #1's controller.

Computer Center

T-2 T-3 T-4

The computer center either codes (keypunches) the Journal Tape or translates the magnetic tape data into computer-compatible form.

Store #1 Controller

The in-store controller formats the data for transmission, again via cable or phone line, to a computer center or, in large retail operations, to a multi-store data concentrator.

#2 #3 #4

Multi-store data concentrator

Information sent from several different stores feeds into a centrally located data concentrator. Here it is readied for transmission via the telephone network.

Modem

Modem

Modems are needed at each end of the phone line to make the data signals compatible with the telephone network's needs.

Computer

A multiplexor at the computer center accepts the data and feeds it to the computer.

Tape drives are generally used to store data at the computer center for later processing and report generation.

Tape drive

Disk drives can provide rapid access to credit information which can then be sent back over the data path to the proper POS terminal.

Disk drive

to carry out a function which you need, do not hesitate to ask if this function can be added to the system. The design of POS equipment is such that frequently these functions can be added at surprisingly little cost. One caution, however, is the ability of the manufacturer to maintain service and production on an item which is somewhat customized, as opposed to an off-the-shelf item.

Another caution is that, while there are a considerable number of manufacturers in the POS arena, a retailer cannot afford to overlook or eliminate any one manufacturer on a simple rule-of-thumb. While it is time-consuming to investigate all qualified manufacturers and determine their offerings, it must be remembered that you are dealing with a piece of equipment which has a significant impact on your total operation, not only in the present but for many years to come.

Regarding the future capabilities of POS systems, there is considerable evidence that direct-access storage devices will be larger, faster, and cheaper, and will ultimately enable point-of-sale operations in an on-line environment and record updating and processing on a real-time basis.

Such technical advances will bring closer the possibility of the totally integrated system. What does this mean to the traditional retail operation? It means a new management concept. No longer is the determination of what cash register to purchase the sole function of the control or financial department. It has now significant impact on all other areas such as merchandising, warehousing, and personnel. More and more retail decisions are going to have to be made by a committee, and it is not too soon for retailers to be thinking about how this will affect their own organizations.

GLOSSARY

"Negative" Credit Checking: A credit authorization technique which refers to a file having credit numbers that are not to be honored. Direct, on-line access to the file allows for instant verification of customers' credit status.

POS System: A technique geared to automating a collection of source data through on-line computer systems.

DISCUSSION QUESTIONS

1. What is an automated POS system? What key advantages does it offer? Explain.
2. How is credit authorization handled by a POS system?
3. Explain two types of POS systems.
4. What is the difference between a stand-alone terminal and a "cluster" terminal? What are the advantages of each?
5. Explain in 200 words or less how the data flows in a POS system. Be specific.
6. What type of problems do prospective POS system buyers encounter? How are these problems handled?

POS AND THE GROCER

Howard Merowit and Samuel Soberanes

The supermarket industry is grappling with a chain of problems that threaten to kill its profits. To industry outsiders, whose myopic view of supermarket operations is focused solely on the lines of customers, the checkout stand is the most obvious target for automation. To insiders, however, the picture is quite different. Most automated checkstands, or point-of-sale (POS) systems, only touch the surface of supermarket needs.

The manifold problems confronting supermarkets today extend far beyond the checkout counter. They span all store operations, from checkstand cash drawers through store inventories and stockpiled warehouses. They reach all the way back to corporate headquarters. Here, the midnight oil burns often and late, as it does in the offices of store managers who must nightly come to grips with their own subset of the same issues.

INFORMATION IS THE KEY

For the past few years, the store managers and their corporate colleagues have been attacking four major problems:

- Growth of sales, which are declining—rising prices and consumer demand notwithstanding;
- Price-margin management, controlling the shrinking grey area separating gross sales from gross profit margins;
- Labor productivity, getting the most effective effort from employees; and
- Inventory-space management, achieving the optimum balance among the items on store shelves. Within these categories exist particular issues which gnaw at all levels of management. For example, positive cash control, direct delivery accounting, labor scheduling and control, and integrated chain communications are industry terms whose implications are clear throughout the retail world.

The key to these incredibly complex and interwoven problems is information, the lack of which has haunted supermarket operations since the supermarket syndrome of the Post-War Era burgeoned into the pervasive social institution it is today.

Before they can even begin to deal with the problems, food industry executives

Source: Reprinted by permission of the publisher from *Computer Decisions,* April 1973, pp. 30-32.

must have timely information. In some cases it is difficult to prescribe the kind of information needed. Any information system designed to accommodate management must have enough flexibility to generate a broad range of data. This information is as vital to the individual store manager (dealing with the task of assigning store personnel to handle tomorrow's holiday crowds) as it is to the corporate buyer (determining the merchandise needs for his store while he ponders the question of raising the cash to pay for it). The typical store manager should be equipped with enough data to handle the routine operational problems he faces every day.

EASE LABOR SCHEDULING AND INVENTORY

In order to schedule the right number of checkers for any given time period, the manager needs to know what the typical customer traffic pattern is for that day. Otherwise he may wind up with too many checkers when they're not needed or too few when they are. But before he determines the number of people he needs, he also has to have some data that tells him about the productivity of each employee. The manager needs to gauge the performance of his people. He must know whether Checker No. 1 is capable of handling more customers than Checker No. 2 or if either one, or both, is not handling as much as he or she should.

The manager gets into another bind in merchandise ordering. Fortunately, computerized warehousing and electronic order entry devices have come to his aid, reducing the merchandise ordering job to the relatively simple task of punching numbers into a hand-held device and transmitting stored information to a remote receiver. As a result, he gets the goods he needs in days instead of weeks. These systems also provide a few additional benefits, such as up-to-the-minute inventory control and elimination of the costly stockpiling of merchandise in the back room.

But the manager must still attack most of his problems manually. Cash control and bookwork are the bane of his existence, and his only tools are a sharp pencil and his accounting ledger. These problems are magnified at the corporate level, where, the corporate buyer continually gropes with the dilemma of rounding up sufficient cash to buy the goods his stores need tomorrow.

The past decade has seen an enormous growth in the number of supermarkets, leading to a continuing and severe inability of individual stores to generate increased sales volume. While supermarkets grew consistently, total sales volume has spread itself across a much wider base.

The proliferation of stores has added up to increased competition rather than increased sales. Store growth rate has outstripped the market growth rate in real dollars. Many areas are plagued with supermarket saturation and, consequently, more store failures.

Some firms have tried to stimulate business by diversification: Drug and discount as well as convenience food stores are added to food chains. But firms which are dedicated solely to the food industry have yet to solve the problem of lagging sales.

Store saturation, discount food pricing, and the proliferation of products sold by the supermarkets have had significant impact on price margin management. The supermarket industry is now operating on its lowest gross margin in the past decade. In December, 1973, the national average gross margin was only 21.3 percent, with net income proportionately scaled-down to less than one percent.

This situation also points up another long-standing industry problem—the management and control of gross margins. A contributing factor to this particular problem is the incredible growth of new products which have been moving onto the shelves.

A typical supermarket stocks anywhere from 10,000 to 12,000 separate items, all of which must be individually tallied, priced and shelved according to customer demand. Unfortunately, the guesswork method of stocking leads to either under-stocking or overstocking. Most experts predict this situation will worsen: By the 1980's, supermarkets could be stocking as many as 25,000 different items.

Pricing for optimum margin management could be the answer to this dilemma but the industry has not had the techniques necessary to plan the proper pricing method to establish higher gross margins.

One key to the problem is variable pricing, relating prices and margins to the sales and turnover of specific items. But effective price control calls for the kind of information that is not now easily available to management. The lack of such information can lead to quick disaster in the discount arena, where improperly applied discounts can actually result in substantial decreases in margins and net profits.

The lack of adequate realtime information also prevents supermarket manage-ment from getting the most cost-effective performance from store employees. The problem of labor productivity, and its effect on overall profitability, is a perfect example: A productivity trap that seems to be locked into a perpetual cycle. The traditionally low wages lead to lower quality labor, which leads to low productivity. This makes it economically difficult to increase wages which, in turn, attract only marginal labor.

A REALTIME SYSTEM IS THE ANSWER

The beginning of a solution for the problems confronting supermarketing lies in a systemized approach to the realtime environment of store operations; one which will also provide the tools necessary to eliminate the next level of problems.

Consider, for example, the application of a computer-based system armed with enough software to accommodate such critical areas of store management as positive cash control, labor scheduling and control, integrated chain communica-tions and direct delivery accounting and control.

Information acquired from the system would be invaluable for building a data base that would allow management to plan inventory and space allocation.

The system should be capable of:

- Covering all store transaction areas;
- Providing interactive communications between the management and termi-nals serving transaction areas;
- Providing corporate management with instant access to in-store data files;
- Producing records on transactions, labor productivity, etc., in any timeframe required; and

• Enough flexibility for software customization.

These capabilities still address only a portion of the total problem. Still to be determined are the parameters for addressing the kind of informational needs that arise when the environment is ordered by initial controls. Meanwhile, a total system approach provides a broad and stable foundation, strong enough to attack today's problems and flexible enough to accommodate the problems of the future.

The system must be totally transparent in day-to-day operations, requiring no extra effort to implant or special attention to operate. As a result, the store manager doesn't lose control, but no longer needs to play watchdog. The system is in the office while the manager is free to concentrate on making money.

DISCUSSION QUESTIONS

1. In 100 words or less, summarize the highights of the use of POS in Supermarkets.
2. What type and capabilities of a real time system is suggested as useful in supermarket operation? Explain.

MICROFILM: PAST, PRESENT, FUTURE

Francis J. Boulanger

The growth of microfilm in the past decade has not been phenomenal, but the field has enjoyed a steady advancement. The knowledge gained in the collection, storage, and retrieval of data on microfilm has been a tremendous asset to the confidence of Government, education, business and scientific circles who require this medium. However, there still exists an aura of mystery concerning microfilm and the computer. Some planners are still unaware that computer output microfilm (COM) has combined electronic and photographic technologies by transforming output pulses to alphanumeric character images or graphic forms, for recording on microfilm.

THE MARRIAGE

The marriage of the computer and micrographics have brought significant changes in EDP. While the computer still reigns supreme in search, microfilm has become an ideal medium of storage. Together we have a rapid sequential and/or random-access

Source: Reprinted, with permission, from *Data Management,* March 1974, pp. 11-14, published by the Data Processing Management Association, Park Ridge, Illinois.

method to a vast amount of storage. As more sophisticated equipment is introduced to the market, along with more efficient uses of microfilm, there will be further innovations in computer output microfilm in all areas of data collection, storage and retrieval.

To date, microfilm is a "read only" form of storage, in contrast to magnetic data which can be changed at will. Individual pages can be accessed and read with optical devices or interfaces, but cannot be changed in a real-time or on-line environment. In contrast, magnetic media has the desired capability. Magnetic storage media is dynamic, as segments as small as a single electronic bit can be accessed, changed, or stored elsewhere at will. Microfilm is static, as once data is affixed to the film, it cannot be changed or processed into anything other than "read only."

However, for storage, microfilm has a decided advantage over its magnetic partner. Very high information densities can be attained with film. When referencing densities it becomes necessary to accurately define the density definition so as to leave no doubt of the intended meaning. A density can be the amount of light passed through the film, the amount of images stored on microfilm, or the amount of data on a given area of a magnetic media (tape, disk or drum). It is possible to store over 1,000,000 characters per square inch of surface on microfilm. The reduction ratio of microfilm can range in the area of over 200:1.

Microfilm retrieval systems can be small, medium or large-sized and can operate either on-site or remote to a film data bank. The simplest configuration may use an automated, page-seeking microfilm roll or fiche reader with look-up tables or indices to relate the film image with the material desired. A sophisticated large-scale microfilm retrieval system with multi-terminal, computer controlled film retrieval units, which can be mechanized with television camera modules, are capable of accessing data banks holding millions of documents on-line. So, the marriage of the computer to micrographics involve functions which are unique to each other. The computer processes and stores addressable data and is dynamic, while microfilm is fixed (read only) and is static.

MICROFORMS

Microfilm is an extremely versatile method of storing, retrieving, manipulation, and dissemination of data in many forms. Many variations of microforms in use today can be adapted to individual applications, but the most common are microfiche, microfilm jackets, ultrafiche, roll film (16 mm and 35mm), and aperture cards. ("Fiche" from the French, meaning "card".) It has been estimated in a recent survey of the microfilm market that ninety-five percent of the finance industry activities use microfilm in some form. In 1970, microfilming was a half billion dollar industry, 1971 and 1972 saw a bigger increase in the use of microfilm systems. It has been estimated that by 1975 the market for microfilm service products, and equipment will probably exceed one and a half billion dollars.

Microfiche is a sheer of film containing microimages arranged in a grid pattern. There are three factors which determine the number of images on a single fiche: the outside dimension of the fiche, the reduction ratio (usually 24:1), and the formatting of the images. As a result, any number of images may be imposed on a single fiche. The 4" × 6" fiche is the most commonly used; however, it is the customer's option depending upon the application and the availability of necessary equipment. It is in this area that management must be careful when ordering raw film for microfiche, because this film also comes in metric measurement of 105mm × 148.75mm, which is not quite the same as 4" × 6".

Until the 1971 National Microfilm Association (NMA) convention, there were two industry and Government standards for microfiche. One standard was the COSATI (Committee on Scientific and Technical Information) Standard with a reduction ratio of 20:1. This ratio gave 60 images on a 4" × 6" fiche. It was in the interest of standardization that COSATI voted to abandon the 20:1 reduction ratio in favor of the compaction of 24:1. The NMA is also focusing its attention on formatting options in order to reduce the proliferation of production techniques and the many models of user equipment currently on the market.

Recent advancement in color photography has made it possible to produce color microfiche which very closely resembles the original hues. There are numerous advantages of color microfiche. This fiche permits longer term viewing without eye strain, which is a definite asset in the educational field. Salesmen desire this fiche when showing brochures, as well as engineers in using color-coded engineer drawings.

To date there is also a lack of uniformity in microfiche grid standards. The rows of the grid (horizontal) are indicated by alphabetic letters, starting with the letter "A", in the left margin. The American National Standards Institute (ANSI) uses lower left as page 1. All Government agencies use upper left as page 1. Therefore, a decision is needed in this area for standardization of a page 1 microfiche starting point.

A MICROFILM JACKET is a sandwich of two pieces of clear plastic, or acetate, fused together with a series of ribs to form channels. Strips of microfilm may be inserted into these channels. The microfilm jacket is similar in size to a microfiche, but has the advantage of allowing the user to update portions of a file quickly and easily. The user merely has to remove any strip, or a portion of a strip, and re-insert the new material. A copy may be made of the entire jacket which essentially makes a microfiche. The use of microfilm jackets are ideal in maintaining and updating personnel and medical records, correspondence, legal, customer or policy-holder files.

ULTRAFICHE is a technological advance which moves microfilm away from the traditional role of dead storage and into the role of active storage and retrieval. Optical technology has made possible better and lower-cost readers and reader-printers. And, films and emulsion speeds have improved. More and better ways are being devised to pack greater amounts of information on smaller areas of film by using higher reduction ratios. However, finer optical instruments are necessary to blow the images back to normal reading size.

When using ultrafiche, literally mountains of data can be reduced to ant-hill size by comparison. Large organizations such as General Motors, Sears and Roebuck, and others, are using ultrafiche systems for their catalogs. It is much easier to reference filmed catalog pages than to wade through a huge stack of heavy catalogs or parts books. Banking systems also use ultrafiche systems to record customer transactions.

When using an ultrafiche, one must be extremely careful that the fiche is clean.

One speck of dust could blur out the images of a few pages of data. It is possible to store approximately 8,000 images on a 4″ × 6″ microfiche, giving a reduction ratio of 210:1.

THE APERTURE CARD is a standard 80-column data punch-card with a pre-cut hole over which is mounted a 35mm microfilm. This media is ideal for filming large engineering documents and drawings. In addition, data may be key-punched into the cards for faster processing of sorting, etc., or the cards may simply be hand-written upon. There may also be several 16mm frames mounted on a card. Searching and refiling in an aperture card system may be done manually by reading the data on the top of a card. Aperture cards have a major application of storage, retrieval, reproduction, and distribution of engineering data. The military services, supporting armament industries, and other large Government agencies use engineering data aperture card systems. There are certain applications which provide the nation with the rapid capability to assemble procurement packages for weapons systems with supporting elements.

ROLL FILM is the basis of many microfilm systems and these can be integrated easily into electronic data processing systems. The most widely used in this medium is the 16mm film. One 100-foot 16mm roll can hold approximately 3,000 standard letter-size documents, or can record over 40,000 bank checks. Roll film is ideal for cutting and splicing, and can remain in the roll form for viewing. The 16mm roll film may also be cut into chips (single frames), or cut into strips for inserting into microfilm jackets which makes this film size very versatile and popular with microfilm users. Another size roll film is 35mm. This medium is widely used for engineering applications as mentioned previously, by inserting into aperture cards or jackets. This size is ideally suited also for literary applications in photographing periodicals, newspapers and other publications.

In the area of film, a number of variations are in use. Silver halide film has high sensitivity, excellent density and tonal quality, low cost and good shelf life. It has the capability of being developed to produce a positive master rather than the usual negative. The disadvantage is that it requires wet processing and the requirement for venting. Diazo film produces a direct image of the original (positive from positive, and negative from negative). It is simple to process and costs less than silver film, and also has the advantage that an unlimited number of copies can be made from the original, while wet silver halide is usually limited to about 200 copies from the master. The disadvantage of diazo is that it is less sensitive than silver and requires venting in developing due to ammonia solutions. Dry silver film is developed and fixed by heat, and no venting is required. Dry silver has the advantage of being erased for corrections and it has a long shelf life under ideal conditions.

ECONOMICAL CONSIDERATIONS

Depending upon the application, computer output microfilm (COM) is a tool that should be weighed against other cost differentials. With the proper application, COM is definitely a money-saver. Cutting the corners of costs is what profitability is all about. The decision of going to COM, or not, must be weighed by management alone. Regardless of whether to microfilm or not, the following cost factors must be weighed: camera rental, the microfilm, preparation of records for filming, actual filming time, inspections, retakes, supervision, postage costs, and the costs in storing data in the original form. By weighing the above factors economically, management will be able to objectively weigh and decide whether to microfilm.

Efficiency-wise, microfilm is fast, compact, and timely in comparison to the output of impact printers. Paper, in the United States, is rapidly becoming a scarce commodity. High grade paper for impact printers is also expensive, plus it is not feasible for some printers to produce carbon copies over a four-copy depth. The cost of impact printing is three times as much as film output. A computer can write a magnetic tape in one-sixth the time it takes to write paper printout. Film can be written at magnetic tape speeds. There is less set-up time, less maintenance costs, less manpower costs and less capital expenditures than would be required for extra printers, resulting in approximately a 75% reduction in the cost of producing original information. Film duplicates may be made in whatever quantity desired and all copies are legible.

Computer re-runs are not necessary to duplicate microfilm records. The cost of duplicate copies is only 3% of printing conventional duplicates, therefore effecting a 97% reduction of duplication costs. Microfilm is approximately 45% less expensive than computer utility paper and 93% less costly than pre-printed forms. Information on microfilm is miniaturized and requires 96% less storage space than conventional paper storage. Any savings in space is a savings in the cost of floor space. Paper is extremely heavy and, in large amounts, become extremely costly. Microfilm is one-tenth the weight of paper and has the advantage of ease of handling. Paper requires decollating, bursting and binding, while microfilm does not, which results in a distribution cost savings of up to ninety percent. Information can be provided at the point of need, be more timely and usable, easier to handle and less printout problems where the computer will not become I/O-bound, with file integrity assured.

SOME DISADVANTAGES

Some disadvantages of microfilm. First, we must realize that it is not wise or profitable to consider microfilm merely as a tool for saving space. Microfilm, as with any other data processing tool, has its own place in the scheme of things. If microfilm is improperly applied, there will be waste and needless expenses. The biggest disadvantage with microfilm is the human factor. When people have not been educated to a new technique or system they have a tendency to initially shy away from it.

Traditionally, managers have become "locked-on" to hard copy print out of the impact printer and have an aversion to reading film because of unfamiliarity. If data constantly changes, or the user must interact with the data base, microfilm may not be practical. We must remember also that when we update film we must create a new film. When a large number of people are served through microfilm, there comes the added expense of a proportionate number of microfilm reading hardware throughout the organization.

There is the expense involved of training new people in the various areas of microfilm systems. These skills are different from those of the computer operator because they involve filming, film developing (even though it may be the dry process), film duplication, splicing, storing, etc. Film output must be constantly checked for proper clarity and proper alignment. People who wear bifocal lenses must view the microfilm readers through the bottom portion of their glasses and therefore must raise their heads.

Microfilm is a difficult medium to browse because if the person viewing is interrupted, it is difficult to return to the same viewing spot due to the lack of a cursor.

Another area of resistance to film is the initial costs. Management must not only account for the cost of film, but also the costs involving cameras, duplicators terminals, readers, film processors, and the whole spectrum of micrographics. Management must also weigh the advisability of engaging a service bureau to take care of his needs to purchase or lease necessary equipment. Capitalization costs must be carefully weighed in advance to avoid a needless loss in profits that are rightfully management's.

A feasibility study by management is a "MUST", no matter how small and simple a proposed microfilm system may be. The handling of information can be an expensive process. These tremendous costs restrict the systems use, and this defeats the very purpose for which it was originally intended. A system can lose its value when reports lag too far behind by not meeting timely deadlines. And, such adverse situations are not uncommon with the impact printer which may require twenty hours run-time, thus causing the system to be I/O bound.

Generally, there are five reasons why management would want to preserve records on microfilm: to conserve space; to protect vital records; to establish an information storage and retrieval tool; to have microfilm as part of an active business procedure or system; to facilitate reproduction or the transmittal of records.

THE FUTURE OF MICROFILM AND EDP

Computer Output Microfilm (COM) has become the solution to the impact printer problem. Although installations have attempted to utilize multiple printers to achieve greater efficiency in processing, it still has not achieved the efficiency of COM. Film can be written at magnetic speeds, while a printer causes any processor to become I/O bound, thus inhibiting its efficiency. Not so with image processing.

However, it must be remembered that COM is not a complete replacement for the printer. COM is only one component of a total micrographic system. EDP management is beginning to realize that to run a computer for the purpose of getting printout is a waste of the processors capability, time and money, all multiplied by the number of printouts desired. The data processing installation manager must search for ways of cutting costs and achieving greater profits in the handling of information. Microfilmed records linked to a retrieval system is the answer.

In another area of microfilm technology, film can be scanned (read) and the data translated to magnetic media in a manner or process opposite that of COM. Data from film chips (single frames) can be read and transmitted great distances over communication lines. Commercially, this type of facsimile transmission is in its early stages of development, but the potential is tremendous when one thinks in terms of engineer drawings being transmitted great distances. Here we must not overlook security of information or the integrity of the system.

Research has been progressing utilizing FOSDIC (Film Optical Sensing Device for Input to Computers) as an efficient method of handling large volumes of CIM (Computer Input From Microfilm) data. The blood, sweat and tears of the Bureau of Census, Department of Commerce, in cooperation with the National Bureau of Standards, made FOSDIC a reality, in 1954, for the 1960 decennial census. This in-house development was a major breakthrough. As each decennial census is completed, the lessons learned lead to greater efficiency for the next one.

FOSDIC-70 equipment for the 1970 census greatly improved operations. Data which took 8 hours to keypunch in 1950 before converting to magnetic tape, was converted directly to tape in 1960 in one minute and directly to tape in 12 seconds in 1970. Six FOSDIC units, the entire world's supply, made by the Bureau of Census handled the 1970 census. The 1970 census forms were microfilmed at about 50 documents per minute using forty photographic machines, and the film-scanned and recorded on magnetic tape at about 600 frames per minute.

In addition, the 1970 census processing accomplished a record. The Bureau of Census converted 255 boxcars of paper to 140,000 rolls of microfilm and from the microfilm to less than 14,000 rolls of magnetic tape as input to a computer.

The imagination and ingenuity in micrographic technology will continue to make electronic data processing more reliable and efficient. As new dynamic implications involving magnetic storage come into being with their increased speeds, many of today's problems are going to be dropped by the wayside, unsolved, in favor of the new "blue sky" concept of something new.

The application of microfilm will, in our time find an inexpensive outlet in homes and business. School text books, deliverable as microfiche, are an excellent possibility with costs no longer a deterrent. As cost factors decrease, microfilm will find its way into the small office environment. The future of microfilm will not rest on advanced technology alone, but rather on the fact that it is a superior method of managing information.

DISCUSSION QUESTIONS

1. Define the following:
   a. aperture card
   b. microfilm
   c. microfiche
2. Based on the article, answer briefly the following questions
   a. the factors that determine the number of images on a single microfiche
   b. the concept of ultrafiche
   c. the makeup of a microfilm jacket
   d. the difference between ultrafiche and microfiche
   e. the advantages and limitations of microfilm

HOW TO COST-JUSTIFY COM

Albert L. C. Chu

Although COM claims many virtues other than as a replacement for the line printer, the most common and convenient way to economically justify the use of COM is still pitching it against the line printer. Following are some guidelines and figures to demonstrate the cost disparity between COM and the line printer, and in both service center and in-house situations. It should be noted that the cost of material and rental rates are estimated averages.

To print out a 10,000-page report with four copies would take 10 hours of CPU time and line printer time, at approximately $400. The cost to deleave, burst and bind the four copies of the report is estimated at $200, considering machine time and labor cost. Cost for paper form, at $20 per 1,000, would be $200. Total: $800.

If a COM service center is used to provide four copies of the report on microfiche, the cost would begin with half an hour of computer time to create the COM image tape: $30. To produce the original copy of the report, at $15 per 1,000 frames, would be $150. The four working copies would cost about $30. In order that the microfiche copies can be used by four departments, four microfilm readers are needed. Based on a two-year amortization, the cost per month for the four readers would be approximately $40. Total: $250.

Another way to compare the cost to produce a computer output report via printer as against COM is that, using a service center in both cases, the cost to produce the COM copies would be roughly half that of the printout copies.

Some other considerations: When more than six copies of a report are needed, the line printer would have to make another run, doubling the cost, whereas COM can produce any number of additional copies at no more than $10 per copy. When a report has to be shipped to a branch location, 11 cents will airmail two microfiche; the same amount of information in a 3½ in. thick paper report, weighing over 10 lbs. would cost $5 to ship parcel post.

In an in-house situation, after the initial reprogramming is accomplished, no computer time is needed to run a report via COM. The cost of microfilm is approximately one-third that of paper form for the first copy. When more than one copy is needed, the cost disparity grows rapidly.

The decision whether to use a service center for COM service or to install in-house equipment depends chiefly on the anticipated workload. But even a company that anticipates a huge volume of computer printout reports to be converted to COM would do well to test the water a little by using a service center, before committing itself to an in-house installation. The job of selling the new

Source: Reprinted from *Infosystems*, April 1972, pp. 32-33. By Permission of the Publisher. © 1972 Hitchcock Publishing Company. All rights reserved.

medium to various user departments and to get them acquainted with the viewer will keep your staff busy for a while without having to break-in the COM operation.

What kind of workload would justify an in-house COM operation would depend on how fast a turnaround time is required, the confidentiality of the data, and the timing of the workload. As a rule of thumb, a volume of 80,000 to 100,000 frames of original copy per month would justify the cost of a minimum in-house COM operation. Looking from the other side of the fence, a COM service center reported that "when a client's monthly billing is between $7,000 and $10,000, we think he may be ready for his own COM operation."

COM service is a very competitive market. Rates charged by service centers vary greatly from area to area, and also within the same city from center to center. In Chicago, charges per 1,000 frames or original (that usually equal 1,000 pages of computer printout) vary from $10 to $25. Charges for 1,000 pages of a duplicate are between 75 cents and $2.50, depending primarily on number of copies and total volume. It pays to shop around.

Many in-house COM shops sell services to outside customers in order to help pay for the operation, if not to make a profit. Their rates are usually lower, with some as low as half what the regular service centers charge.

If you really need to have your own shop, figure your cost this way. Start-up cost includes the necessary reprogramming to restructure your tape output. Some COM recorders require more reprogramming while others require none. With few exceptions, you would also need additional plumbing for your COM room to dilute and dump the processing solutions. Depending on your location, this may cost you several hundred dollars. You also need a number of ancillary tools such as cutter, splicer and gloves.

A minimum COM operation includes three pieces of equipment: The COM recorder which converts magnetic tape data onto the film, a processor that develops the film, and a duplicator for making working copies. There is a great disparity of prices among COM manufacturers. From $800 to $1,000 per month rental for the three pieces should be a good place to start. It should be noted that most COM manufacturers have a minimum usage plan to help you get started. Under such a plan, the regular monthly rental is substantially lower for a minimum monthly usage of, say, 150,000 frames.

DISCUSSION QUESTIONS

1. What complications often limit the application of COM? What countermeasures have been taken to overcome this problem?
2. List and explain the advantages and limitations of COM.

SELECTED REFERENCES

Direct Data Input

Articles

Bellotto, Sam, Jr. "EDP Input: The Six Choices." *Administrative Management,* April 1971, pp. 40-45.

Bieser, Albert H. "Key-to-Tape and Key-to-Disk Systems." *Modern Data,* December 1971, pp. 32-36.

Chu, Albert L. C. "Data Entry." *Business Automation,* July 1971, pp. 18-23, 26-27.

Fiedelman, Lawrence A. "A Primer on Source Data Automation." *Data Processing Magazine,* September 1969, pp. 26ff.

Lachter, Lewis. "Mag Tape or Disc?" *Administrative Management,* December 1971, pp. 68-69.

Menkhaus, Edward J. "Terminals: Pipeline to Computer Power." *Business Automation,* May 1970, pp. 48-55, 68.

Murphy, John A. "Key-to-Tape Data Entry." *Modern Data,* December 1971, pp. 37-40.

Stender, Robert C. "The Future Role of Keyboards in Data Entry." *Datamation,* June 1970, pp. 60-72.

Talbot, J. E. "The Human Side of Data Input." *Data Processing Magazine,* April 1971, pp. 28-35.

"Terminal Take-Over." *Business Automation,* March 1972, pp. 23-28.

Optical Character Recognition

Articles

Canning, Richard G. "Optical Scanning: It's on the Move." *EDP Analyzer,* June 1969, pp. 1-14.

Chu, Albert L. C. "The Plodding Progress of OCR." *Business Automation,* March 1970, pp. 48-55.

"Will Optical Scanning Now Catch On?" *Administrative Management,* May 1970, pp. 18-20.

Computer-Output-Microfilm

Articles

Bellotto, Sam, Jr. "Microfilm: Easy Access, Compact Systems." *Administrative Management,* July 1971, pp. 38-46.

Canning, Richard G. "Computer Output to Microfilm." *EDP Analyzer,* June 1970, pp. 1-14.

Carding, Anthony D. K. "Microfilm: EDP's Newest Ally." *Administrative Management,* April 1970, pp. 38-48.

Chu, Albert L. C. "COM Takes On an Active Image." *Business Automation,* April 1972, pp. 30ff.

Gildenberg, Robert F. "Computer Output Microfilms Systems." *Modern Data,* November 1970, pp. 78-82.

Kaiser, Daniel C. "Fiche and Film: Forms of the Future." *Data Management,* September 1974, pp. 12-13.

McGrath, James D. "Does COM Eliminate the Output Bottleneck?" *Data Management,* May 1971, pp. 14-20.

_____. "Will COM Remain a Marketable Product?" *Data Management,* June 1971, pp. 28-33.

Menkhaus, Edward J. "Microfilm: New Power for Information Systems." *Business Automation,* May 1971, pp. 38-42.

Totaro, J. Burt. "Microfilming Cuts Computer Data Down to Size." *Computer Decisions,* March 1971, pp. 22-25.

Point-of-Sale Automation

Articles

Fiedelman, Lawrence A. "Point-of-Sale Automation,"*Modern Data,* February 1972, pp. 22-23.

Pease, David L. "POS: Another Revolution in Retailing." *Data Management,* July 1974, p. 13.

"P.O.S. Terminal Takes Over." *Business Automation,* March 1972, pp. 22-28; April 1972, pp. 26-29.

PART 4

The Make-up and Impact of Minicomputers

Since their introduction in the mid-1960s, minicomputers have been used at an accelerated rate so that today they have become a commonplace in hundreds of business organizations around the United States. Typical of organizations that use them are those that are financially unable to use larger systems, those that have limited input volume, and those that have larger computers and use minis in a supplementary capacity.

Compared to larger systems, minicomputers have less capacity and slower processing speeds. A typical minicomputer (the size of a portable television set) is generally priced betwen $5,000 and $30,000. It has word lengths from 8 to 64 bits and a core memory operating speed between one-half and one microsecond per cycle. Most minis employ integrated circuits supplied by the semiconductor industry and operate in real-time, which makes them ideally suited for process control operations and open-shop time-sharing applications. Companies in the $1 million to $10 million sales range are finding the mini ideally suited for handling such costly functions as inventory control, billing, accounts payable and receivable, sales analysis, payroll, and back-order processing.

Several characteristics of minicomputers make them attractive to organizations. The minicomputer has powerful computing capability, is highly dependable, and can operate in an environment without special wiring or air conditioning. Furthermore, the economy is a factor because an employee can be taught to operate the system in a few hours, thus eliminating the need for full-time programmers. Finally, the fact that a company has a minicomputer system offers the psychological advantage of protecting its confidential data from the inadvertent leakage that is possible in a time-shared system. This feeling of security can be a critical factor in making a formal commitment to a minicomputer system.

The readings section consists of two articles. Friedman's article is an overview of minicomputer structure and the major differences between minicomputers and larger computer systems. Hinrichs's article, "The Impact of Minicomputers on Industry," discusses key applications that are associated with a typical industrial plant, the ways of choosing the "right" computer, and the expected impact of minicomputers in the next decade.

OVERVIEW OF MINI ARCHITECTURE

Edited by Richard C. Friedman

This summary consists of excerpts from the section on mini architecture discussed in a 92-page report, published by the Rand Corporation, titled "Minicomputers: A Review of Current Technology, Systems and Applications," by Dennis Hollingworth. The Rand report concentrates on computers costing from $4,000 to $20,000 for a processor and 4K (4096 words) of memory. It deals primarily with processors employing a 16-bit word length, which is rapidly becoming a standard of the minicomputer industry.

While the various minicomputers on the market have many similarities, each has fundamental architectural differences reflecting the vendor's unique approach to solving a particular class of problems. Differences are apparent in all aspects of system architecture. Often a given minicomputer will be particularly strong in some functional areas and surprisingly weak in others. In fact, most minicomputers on the market today, even the most expensive ones, seem to have a mixture of good and bad features. It is just this fact that requires a careful match of the minicomputer system to a selected application. Unlike large systems, in which the question is generally one of selecting the optimum configuration, the question with minicomputer selection may boil down to one of picking a machine that has the necessary features to accomplish the desired objective.

FLEXIBILITY

One of the more significant architectural differences between minicomputers and large computers is reflected in the asynchronous functional modularity of minicomputer design. Most minicomputers presently being manufactured are composed of chassis and power supply, a common bus structure connecting a number of card slots in that chassis, and a number of functionally independent circuit boards comprising the processor (or processors), memory, input/output (I/O) drivers, and I/O channels. Each card is often functionally independent and transparent to the operation of other cards such that adding or deleting a card does not affect the operation of the rest of the system. Further, each module may operate asynchronously of every other module, permitting each to operate at its maximum rated speed.

Thus, one finds that additional memory or I/O drivers may be added simply by removing the back panel and plugging in additional circuit cards, and even processors may be changed or upgraded by removing one card and inserting another in its

Source: Reprinted, with permission, from *Data Management,* February 1974, pp. 12-17, published by the Data Processing Management Association, Park Ridge, Illinois.

149

place. This allows considerable versatility for configuration changes and permits easy system upgrade to faster memories and processors as processing requirements increase.

CENTRAL PROCESSOR

Features one would expect to find on a large processor may be nonexistent or optional (at additional cost) on the typical minicomputer processor. While almost every large processor has hardware multiply and divide instructions, the feature may be optional or, in some cases, unavailable on a particular minicomputer processor. Since minicomputers have a shorter word size, they almost invariably have smaller instruction sets and restricted addressing capabilities. Addressing the entire memory space, when possible, generally requires a second memory cycle to obtain the address of the operand.

Floating-point instructions are a rarity on minicomputer processors (although ingenious means may be employed to circumvent this difficulty). Decimal arithmetic is nonexistent. Yet, despite such limitations, in many applications minicomputers can out-perform some medium-sized computers presently on the market.

INSTRUCTION SET

In general, the choice of an instruction set is somewhat arbitrary, based upon the system designer's view of what basic capabilities are required or desirable for the types of applications he ultimately envisions for the processor.

When the processor is to be used in an application somewhat different from that conceived by the system designer, the instruction set may not be particularly suited to the application. Often a missing capability may be simulated through execution of a short sequence of instructions. So although a particular minicomputer lacks a desired instruction, this may not necessarily represent a serious deficiency.

In some cases, simulating a particular operation may be much more difficult, however, and require a lengthy sequence of instructions or, perhaps, iterative execution of a short program loop. For instance, lack of hardware multiply and divide might represent a particular disadvantage when such operations are frequently required—necessitating a series of repetitive additions or subtractions whenever one of those operations must be performed.

INSTRUCTION TYPES

The number and variety of useful operations that can be performed on specified operands may be quite different from the total number of instructions claimed by the manufacturer. Manufacturers tend to include every operation that may be performed on every addressable register to derive instruction counts of 400 or higher, despite the fact that some instructions may have little or no utility.

The machine type, to some degree, determines the number of instructions required to perform requisite operations. In the memory-to-memory processor, for example, the MOVE instruction performs the same function as the LOAD/STORE pair of instructions in the general-register processor. Yet a count of the number of instructions would indicate that the general-register processor had greater capability. Thus, an accurate assessment of the processor's instruction power may require a more subjective approach (such as applying weighting factors to different types of instructions and processor types) than that of merely counting the total number of instructions.

Arithmetic Instructions. Instructions for binary addition and subtraction are almost always included in the instruction repertoire. Binary multiplication and division are frequently not included as part of the standard instruction set but often are available at additional cost. Some minicomputers also have instructions for double-precision binary addition and subtraction, but rarely for double-precision multiplication and division. Thus, the latter must be simulated via software subroutines.

Floating-point capability is rarely found on today's minicomputer, despite an obvious need for it in scientific applications. When it does exist, it is generally found in the most rudimentary of forms. Occasionally, limited floating-point capability (addition and subtraction and, perhaps, even multiplication and division) can be obtained as an optional feature. Some machines presently can accommodate the attachment of an optional floating-point processor with a full complement of floating-point operational capabilities. These are processors in their own right, however, and are priced accordingly.

Data Test Instructions. The typical minicomputer is weak in this area. Often there is no COMPARE instruction whatsoever, with arithmetic comparison requiring a complicated operation sequence. In many cases there is no direct bit testing capability either.

Shift/Rotate Instructions. The characteristic deficiency found with the shift/rotate group of instructions is the lack of a multi-position shift/rotate capability, necessitating a minimum of one instruction executed for each bit position that the target-word is to be shifted.

STORAGE PROTECTION

Many minicomputers have no storage protection capability whatsoever!

The simpler memory protection schemes employed in today's minicomputers are designed to protect one contiguous block of memory from particular types of program reference. They use a single protection register (sometimes called a fence or boundary register) to determine the boundary of protected and nonprotected storage. In this scheme the lower protected block of memory is treated as READ-ONLY memory for code executing from the nonprotected block. This provides reasonable storage protection in applications where system code must be protected from user code, but is not particularly suitable for environments requiring any sort of multiprogramming.

Application of minicomputers in time-sharing and multiprogramming environments has prompted development of more sophisticated storage protection schemes designed to provide multi-user protection; i.e., protect both the system's and each user's memory space from inadvertent modification by a running program. These are typically (1) block designation schemes. (2) memory mapping schemes. Each may incorporate additional protection attributes within the confines of the basic protection scheme. For instance, selected storage blocks may be designated as readable but not writable, thus permitting user access to, but prohibiting modification of, selected areas within his own memory space.

AUTOMATIC RESTART

Auto-restart is often incorporated as part of the power failure detection feature, automatically restarting a processor that has suffered a power failure.

It should be noted here that semiconductor memories presently available for use in minicomputer systems are generally volatile with regard to power failure; i.e., power must be maintained to preserve the memory contents. Minicomputer manufacturers generally offer optional emergency battery power sources to sustain the contents of volatile semi-conductor memories during periods of power loss. These may be required for the automatic restart feature to operate.

EXCEPTION HANDLING

Exception indications in present-day minicomputer systems are generally inadequate to permit proper servicing of the exception condition. With an arithmetic exception (overflow, divide by zero, etc.), for example, the typical way the exception condition is indicated is through the setting of the overflow flag. Thus, the program must interrogate the overflow flag after each arithmetic operation if it is necessary to determine on which instruction the error occurred.

Typical of a more serious problem is the handling of nonexistent memory references. Most minicomputer processors have no mechanism for alerting the program in the event of reference to a nonexistent memory location. Typically this condition is ignored during a memory write operation; a word of zeros is returned on a memory read operation. In some systems, wraparound addressing is implemented. In this case the results are even more disastrous with all addresses generated modulo an integral memory unit size.

TIMERS

In many minicomputers the timing unit serves as either a real-time clock or an interval timer, depending on the function required. This is accomplished by either (1) implementing an interval timer that is program interrogable, in which case it may be loaded with a large interval count and treated as a real-time clock operating in a negative direction; or (2) implementing a real-time clock that is program modifiable and capable of generating an interrupt upon overflow. Such combined timers/clocks are becoming quite common in today's minicomputers.

DIRECT MEMORY ACCESS

Direct memory access is standard on the majority of minicomputers and optional on most of the remainder. DMA provides a mechanism whereby high-speed devices such as magnetic tapes, disks, and drums may transfer data directly to main storage (without processor assistance) at a maximum transfer rate approaching that permitted by the memory cycle time. This type of capability is essential for systems with high-speed peripheral devices.

PERIPHERAL SYSTEM

There are a number of peripheral devices on the market today which may be utilized on minicomputer systems. Unfortunately, many of them were designed for larger systems and are priced accordingly. As soon as the minicomputer is utilized for general data processing functions instead of specialized functions such as process control, communications and message handling, total system cost soon begins to get out of hand, with peripheral system cost far outstripping that of processor and memory. It is not particularly surprising to select a minicomputer processor with 8K of memory for around $10,000 and then find that even a minimal function peripheral system will easily triple the total system price.

Some savings may be realized in the price of device controllers, however, with those on the minicomputer system stripped down to the bare essentials, to both lower their cost and reduce their size so they can fit on a few circuit cards in the mincomputer mainframe or an expansion chassis. But because of this, many of the functions of device controllers that might be performed by the hardware must be performed by the minicomputer software.

TELETYPES

Teletypes are often the minicomputer's primary I/O device and are frequently included as part of the basic hardware offering. Their principal disadvantage is that they are relatively low-speed and do not permit any sort of off-line data preparation. As hardcopy output devices, they are rather poor performers for applications requiring anything but minimal printing.

Teletypes, optionally, come with a low-speed paper tape reader/punch combination that may offer marginal improvement in device utility and permit rudimentary off-line data preparation. Some manufacturers are offering a replacement unit for the Teletype at a slightly higher price. These are generally better engineered and offer higher printing speeds (typically 30 characters per second).

PAPER TAPE

An optical paper tape reader and high-speed paper tape punch offer significant I/O performance improvement over that of the Teletype. The disadvantages are that the system may still require some sort of printing unit; and, as an intermediate storage medium, paper tape requires operator handling because the reader and punch units are physically separate units.

MAGNETIC TAPE CASSETTES

Magnetic tape cassette units are one of the few peripheral devices well-suited for use on minicomputer systems. As a direct replacement for paper tape, they offer the handling advantages of magnetic tape at the price of paper tape systems, with an intermediate data transfer rate (750 characters per second for one unit presently being marketed, 1600 bytes per second for a competitive unit). The principal disadvantages of this new medium are lack of industry standardization and inadequate error recovery and checking.

TAPE CARTRIDGE UNITS

As an I/O medium for minicomputer systems, tape cartridge units recently became more competitive with digital cassette units through the introduction of a new cartridge. The cartridge contains 300 ft of 0.25 inch magnetic tape; data are recorded on 4 tracks at a density of 1600 bpi. Storage capacity is 20 million bits, 4 times that of a typical cassette. Transfer rate is approximately 48K bits per second. Drive units are available for $2,500.

FLOPPY DISKS

The "floppy" disk is gradually finding its way into the minicomputer industry as a standard I/O device. Floppy disks are oxide-coated mylar disks housed in either paper or plastic envelopes or cartons that are inserted in a drive unit. Storage capacities range to 2.2 million bits with maximum transfer rates approaching 1.2 million bits per second. Drive prices range from as low as $750 for slow-speed, low-capacity units, to $5,500 for high-speed, high-transfer rate units. At their lower end, floppy disk units provide a random access replacement for paper tapes and other low-speed sequential access devices. At their high end, they are encroaching on the high-speed direct access device market.

PUNCHED CARDS

Punched cards, as an I/O medium, offer certain advantages that other media cannot match: they are easy and inexpensive to create, easy to modify, can be directly read by people and, perhaps most important, represent a universal medium of data exchange between systems and installations.

With the introduction of the IBM System/3 punched card, this latter advantage is temporarily impacted, although the greater handling convenience of these small cards may eventually cause wider use and acceptance.

PRINTERS

Available devices have print rates in the neighborhood of 150 to 300 lines per minute (80 to 120 characters per line) and provide for the relatively rapid production of hardcopy listings. Unfortunately, even these slower speed line printers cost about $10,000 to $15,000, significantly contributing to the total price of the system.

MAGNETIC TAPE UNITS

At a cost of about $10,000 for a drive and controller (generally up to 8 transports may be serviced by one controller), it is the least expensive mass storage medium available. Its primary disadvantage is that it is a sequential access medium, and thus may require a great deal of tape motion and searching to position the tape at the data to be accessed.

DIRECT ACCESS STORAGE

Direct access storage eliminates the problem of the sequential nature of magnetic tape storage while still providing a high data transfer rate. The least expensive units (other than the lower precision floppy disks) are the head-per-track disk drives (fixed-head disk). While a unit and a controller (which will often service multiple drives) may run as low as $7,000, they have relatively low storage capacities (about 64K to 256K words per unit).

The direct access storage device most frequently employed in minicomputer systems is the small, removable cartridge, moving-head disk unit (of the IBM 2310 style). Although average access time is somewhat slower than that of the fixed-head disk (due to head positioning), transfer rates are about the same (around 100 thousand words per second). Costs for one unit and a controller are around $10,000. Storage capacity is approximately 1.2 million words per drive.

Large capacity moving-head drives (of the IBM 2311 and 2314 type) are also utilized on minicomputer systems. A single unit and controller will provide 20 million words of storage and cost about $30,000.

SOFTWARE

The amount and sophistication of support software provided by the minicomputer manufacturer varies considerably depending upon the manufacturer's perception of the end-user's requirements and the importance he ascribes to the role of software in marketing his product. In some cases the manufacturer seems to produce software almost begrudgingly as a necessary evil required for marketing his hardware; in others the manufacturer markets hardware and software as part of an integrated systems package assembled to address particular application areas, such as communications processing or real-time monitoring and control. Typically, however, the manufacturer offers something between these two extremes. It is likely to include an assembler, a linking loader, a Fortran or Basic compiler, a program editor, one or more operating systems, and, in many cases, some sort of real-time executive system. He may also offer time-sharing and batch processing systems, as well as serving as a distributor for special application programs developed by end-users. The assemblers, compilers, loaders, and program editors generally come in both stand-alone versions as well as on-line versions that can be invoked under the control of an operating system.

In many instances, however, one finds that different language processors and utility packages require different operating system support and, indeed, may even require different hardware configurations. For example, Basic language processing is often supported in a stand-alone interpretive processing version, but is rarely available under support of an operating system. Thus, while a vendor may offer a variety of software support packages, it may well be that all language facilities and utility packages are not available to every system.

Some vendor software is freely distributed, but increasingly one finds the minicomputer manufacturer licensing his software for use on the minicomputer system. The license fee often depends on usage of some minimum amount of the supplier's hardware as part of the configuration.

ASSEMBLERS

Invariably, every minicomputer manufacturer provides an assembler to facilitate the development of programs for their minicomputer systems. Although some of these are rather rudimentary, providing mnemonics for specifying machine operation codes and symbolic addressing to ease the job of developing program addresses and offsets, others are similar in power and flexibility to those found on larger computers, providing macro definition, assembler directives, location counter control, and other conveniences.

More frequently one finds manufacturers offering cross-system assemblers in addition to those that run on the target machine. Often developed by user personnel, these assemblers provide for the efficient development of programs for the minicomputer system by utilizing large systems such as the IBM System/360 for assembling minicomputer programs.

COMPILERS

Minicomputer manufacturers often offer one or more compilers as part of their system support software. Those most frequently found on minicomputer systems are compilers for the Fortran, Algol, and Basic languages, although one may find compilers for RPG or languages unique to the particular manufacturer as well.

Efficient compiler operation is difficult to realize in small machines with limited memory capacities, however. Most minicomputer compilers require a minimum of 8000 words of memory and often more. Thus it is not unusual to find high-level language compilers (which generate code for a minicomputer system) implemented on large, general purpose computers.

OPERATING SYSTEMS

Most minicomputer operating systems do little more than permit a single terminal user to take advantage of the conveniences offered by magnetic tapes, disks, and other peripheral devices in creating and running his program. Instead of having to load a stand-alone program editor to create his program, a stand-alone compiler to produce a binary version of the program, and a stand-alone loader to load and execute his program, the user can issue commands at a terminal to invoke these processing functions. Furthermore, such operating systems provide mechanisms to link user programs with resident I/O device drivers, permitting more convenient use of a system's peripheral devices.

A few minicomputer manufacturers offer single-stream batch operating systems, which free the user from issuing commands at a terminal and, instead, accept job control commands from a batch input device, automatically scheduling tasks at their direction.

A number of minicomputer manufacturers offer multi-user time-sharing systems. Such systems generally support 8 or more terminal users in an interactive environment. Most such systems provide only single-language support (e.g., Basic or Fortran) and run in a stand-along environment, independent of an operating system.

Many minicomputer manufacturers provide a real-time executive system as part of their software offering to facilitate the monitoring, servicing, and control of real-time devices such as those found in a production control environment. The more advanced systems of this type provide for the definition of a number of interrupt servicing tasks operating on a priority-interrupt or timed basis in the real-time foreground environment. Machine cycles left over from handling foreground tasks can be utilized for such background functions as the compilation of user programs.

DISCUSSION QUESTIONS

1. What is Friedman's definition of minicomputer?
2. In what respect do minicomputers differ from large computer systems? Explain in detail.
3. From your knowledge of basic data processing fundamentals, what is the primary difference between assemblers and compilers?

THE IMPACT OF MINICOMPUTERS ON INDUSTRY

Karl Hinrichs

The potential for improved products at lower unit cost by automation and computerization is very well known, but the implementation is still in its infancy. The recent and continuing development of minicomputers (high speed and competent machines selling for less than $20K) will provide a very rapid acceleration in industrial automation.

COST BREAKTHROUGH

The inertia that has kept us from full automation in the past is rapidly vanishing because of the dramatic economies provided by minicomputer systems. You can rent a competent minicomputer on a 40-hour week basis for approximately $1.80 an hour. This is truly a breakthrough which was difficult to predict a few years ago.

In terms of purchase price, a 16-bit competent computer with Teletype, high speed paper tape punch and reader, and four hardware interrupts was priced at well over $100K five or six years ago. This same power—except several times faster—is available today at one-tenth the price.

The rapidly expanding market for minicomputers is producing a snowball effect in industry; the more production, the lower the cost and price; the more applications, the larger the program libraries available for new uses; the wider the variety of customers, the broader the variety of peripherals available.

The large, centralized computer ("maxicomputer") will not vanish from the typical industrial plant, but will be augmented by many dedicated minicomputer installations. Some of these minicomputers will be connected to the maxicomputer, forming a hierarchical memory and computer system.

Tolerances in industry continue to decrease. Step-and-repeat operations are becoming much more common. Digital control of machinery is an accelerated trend. In all these applications, computer automation offers distinct advantages over manual techniques. Computers are wonderful for routine functions, since they do not get bored with the most tedious of tasks or strained by high precision work.

A THREE-WAY CHOICE FOR AUTOMATION

A three-way choice is available for automation. A dedicated minicomputer system may be purchased or leased to solve specific functional requirements. A computer terminal may be obtained for interaction with a maxicomputer at some remote site. A centralized maxicomputer can often be employed for automation, with inputs provided by special-purpose remote devices or batch tapes and cards.

Source: *Computers and Automation*, December 1969, pp. 28-30.

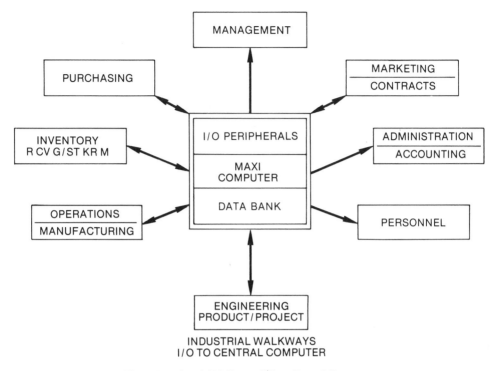

Figure 1. Industrial Walkways I/O to Central Computer

Today's typical industrial plant has a maxicomputer which serves all segments of the plant as illustrated in Figure 1. Table 1 lists associated applications. The first item, batch processing, is one where minicomputers usually cannot compete with centralized maxicomputers. Despite the high initial cost of the centralized maxicomputer, its greater flexibility, memory storage, span of peripherals, and program library offer a more economic solution to batch processing than that which can be obtained with today's minicomputers. Accounting ledgers, payroll, timekeeping, charge allocation, P/L analyses and reports, order entry, marketing records, and personnel records are all typical industrial functions economically performed by the centralized computer. A very large and valuable library of software programs has been developed for these functions, usually with specific adaptations for individual plants. Most of these essential records and reports need large amounts of memory,

Table 1. Computer-Aided Industrial Tasks

1. Batch Processing and Records
2. Inventory Accounting
3. Production Plan and Control
4. Process Control
5. Product Testing
6. Rlease and Engineering Control
7. Cost Estimating
8. Drafting and Printed Circuit Layout
9. Engineering Design

very extensive program libraries, and a wide span of peripherals. Except for new and small industries, minicomputers will not compete in the near future.

INVENTORY ACCOUNTING

Inventory-accounting is a little different from batch processing. Historically, it has been a batch record-keeping function; but we are more and more concerned with virtually real-time control of inventory and purchasing. We would like to see a system in which Purchasing, Stock Room, and Receiving Inspection are inexpensively interconnected with inputs from Engineering (Bill of Materials) and Manufacturing (kit scheduling). The minicomputer (particularly one of the larger and more powerful types) competes well in many cases with the centralized facility, since it does not require a large peripheral investment, can be easily relocated, and permits ready entry of data and program.

Production planning and control is also an area where minicomputers often provide economies compared with maxicomputers. Profuction planning and control, work-in-process reports, exception reporting, station reporting, and other nearly-real-time manufacturing information services can often be efficiently provided by dedicated minicomputer systems.

PROCESS CONTROL

Process control is the classical area for minicomputer application; and the current industry obtained its impetus from this field. Special-purpose computers have been used in processes for over 20 years. The early systems for data acquisition and control used both digital and analog computers. The economies of scale are swinging the process-control automation towards purely digital computers. Our large, complex and intertwined processes in many industrial plants would appear to recommend a maxicomputer installation to simultaneously assess and compute all parts of the control process. This grandiose concept is analogous to the universal plant Data Base. Realistically, however, there are many unknowns in the interaction between processes in total plant control; and a hierarchy of control is employed with many minicomputers and special-purpose controllers. A maxicomputer is sometimes used for centralized surveillance. For functions which are extremely well known, the minicomputer does not compete with the specialized controller. Most processes using direct digital control, however, involve functions not presently well defined or optimized. A minicomputer can be used for optimization study as well as fixed-program control. A minicomputer controller is also an excellent record keeper and performance analyzer. If the process is susceptible to improvement by the incorporation of additional loops, additional sensors, new outputs, or other modifications, a minicomputer may be the most economical answer to process automation.

PRODUCT TESTING

Product testing is also a classical area for the use of minicomputers. In the past, economics have dictated the use of special-purpose machines. Now the lower cost of minicomputers permits a vast increase in flexibility at low cost. This market is increasing tremendously in response to the testing requirements for more sophisticated products with tighter tolerances and more stringent requirements for proof of reliability and performance. One of these products, of course, is the minicomputer itself. The proof of performance of a minicomputer requires a high degree of automation for economical testing. In contrast with the applications for which the centralized computer is optimal, here the programming is minimal, few general-purpose peripherals are used, and the I/O requirements are high. Although the product testing routine does not require much flexibility, a tester must be readily modified on a day-to-day or month-to-month basis. Therefore, the general-purpose minicomputer usually out-performs the special-purpose or hard-wired test-device controller.

Engineering release and control has received a lot of attention but little actual use of computers, except in the very largest industrial installations. The availability of inexpensive minicomputers and the rapidly growing libraries of software will readily invade the engineering control area. The requirement for a very large data bank (perhaps with extensive parts specifications, vendor records, and similar files) can often justify the use of Teletype stations, CRT displays, and a centralized data bank.

COST ESTIMATING

Engineering and manufacturing jointly share cost-estimating functions in a typical industry. It is surprising to find a small extent of computer invasion in this function today. Perhaps company management is lax in forcing a marriage between the estimating staff (who do not know computer programming) and the centralized programming staff (who are often unaware of the amount of estimating under way). The situation should change radically when it is realized how efficient minicomputers with CRT and TTY can be, in assisting the cost estimating process. Time-sharing systems are also logical contenders for estimating service, although many companies will not permit their company's price files to be located outside company premises, for security reasons.

ENGINEERING DESIGN

Engineering design is the classical area for time-sharing service use. For very large plants, their centralized maxicomputer can be used with remote terminals. We are all familiar with the advantages of computer-aided circuit design (ECAP and similar programs). There are many other important engineering functions which can be improved and cost-reduced by utilizing computer assistance. The minicomputer has definite advantages for use with graphic terminals in design functions requiring intensive man-machine interaction.

CHOOSING THE "RIGHT" COMPUTER

How do you decide when to use a minicomputer, a maxicomputer, a time-sharing service, or no computer at all? The return-on-investment factors are usually straightforward. If the job is a complex one involving large banks of data, if it involves interaction with the data from many physically separated plant functions, if it can be done on a bath (non-real-time) basis, if it does not require man-machine interaction, if it can be interrupted, if it utilizes extensive programs and employs a lot of peripherals—then the centralized maxicomputer batch-processing system is the obvious solution and can be justified by a standard cost comparison.

However, if the process is relatively isolated from the data sources used by the remainder of the plant, if it is a job that is prone to change, if the solution is needed rapidly, if it involves high I/O rates, if it involves man-machine interaction, then we would want to use a dedicated minicomputer. A graphic CRT design terminal is an excellent example.

There are many industrial functions which defy computerization. Creative and intelligent human beings are also required, since you cannot buy hardware and build software to solve an undefined problem. Some urgent requirements of industry change faster than our ability to program machines. If you have a product which changes completely in six months, computerization is ill-advised. There are many classical examples of large investments in automation for processes which human ingenuity has obsoleted.

Examples of industrial functions which minicomputers should dominate by the end of the 1970's are: drafting, electrical and mechanical design, printed circuit layout, numerical control tape production, template production, data acquisition, component and system testing, and process control.

THE IMPACT OF MINICOMPUTERS

The impact of minicomputer automation will be truly remarkable in the next decade. We are apt to ignore the magnitude of change because we are watching it every day, and progress often seems slow. Drawing back for a longer-range look, however, we can readily detect some very significant impacts on industry.

The first effect, common to all improvements and efficiency, is less raw-labor content in our products. Economics cannot be denied, and we will obtain a larger production of lower-cost products with a more skilled labor force. The proliferation of minicomputers and minicomputer systems will result in a very sharp increase in trained personnel: a new class of technicians or "miniprogrammers." One of today's critical industrial shortages is that of skilled programmers. The intimate working experience of the hourly working force with small dedicated computer systems will enrich our technical labor base. Although much of the training and resultant skills will be very specific, it is a valuable background for more general programming education and in any event will free our professional programming staff from much of today's necessary routine.

The product cost reductions predicted will be particularly noticeable for complex products such as electronic instruments. Minicomputers, therefore, will continue to decrease the ratio of price to performance, both from increased volume and increased manufacturing automation. The lower prices will produce an avalanche effect not only in industrial applications, but in computer use in virtually all spheres of human activity.

It will be a big boost to small business. It will be possible for small businesses to compete with large companies in complex electronics because a minicomputer system will provide them with almost all of the functions, if not the efficiency per second, as the large companies obtain from their combination of minicomputer systems and centralized maxicomputer. Software libraries are the hold-up today, but tomorrow that will not be true. Minicomputers will be equipped with business systems and batch processors which, although perhaps not as cost-effective per dollar, will nevertheless provide small businesses with the ability to have a full set of features that the large company now possesses.

The wide application of minicomputers and computer systems will generate valuable additions to the United States' technological base in new products, new programs, technological training, and new computer system applications.

DISCUSSION QUESTIONS

1. "The large, centralized computer ('maxicomputer') will not vanish from the typical industrial plant, but will be augmented by many dedicated minicomputer installations. Some of these minicomputers will be connected to the maxicomputer, forming a hierarchical memory and computer system." Do you agree with this statement? Write a 500-word report justifying your position.

2. What three-way choice does the author mention as available in minicomputer automation?

3. Summarize the computer-aided tasks that one would expect to find in a typical industrial plant.

4. How would one decide when to use a minicomputer?

5. List and explain three industrial functions that you believe are difficult to computerize.

6. What impacts on industry does the author point out as highly probable in the next decade? Do you agree? Why?

SELECTED REFERENCES

Articles

Anderson, Walter R., and Sonn, Edward H. "How to Select a Minicomputer." *Computers and Automation,* December 1969, pp. 20-22.

Bellotto, Sam, Jr. "Minicomputers Get Smaller, Doing More." *Administrative Management,* October 1971, pp. 48-54.

Blake, Neil. "Minis: What to Look For." *Data Systems,* June 1971, pp. 22-23.

Kluchman, Allen Z. "Minicomputers on the Move." *Computers and Automation,* December 1969, pp. 24-26.

"Minicomputer: EDP's Mighty Lightweights." *Administrative Management,* June 1970, pp. 26-28.

Shah, M. A., and Stieger, W. H. "Automated Experiment Control and Data Acquisition—A Mini-Computer Application." *Computers and Automation,* December 1969, pp. 32-35.

Zack, Ray A. "Minicomputer Application—Do They Imply Something for Everybody?" *Computers and Automation,* December 1969, pp. 36-40.

PART 5

Operating Systems

INTRODUCTION

Programs written in high-level languages such as COBOL, PL/1, or FORTRAN must be compiled before they can be executed. The process of compiling involves loading into computer memory the appropriate processor program and submitting the source program to the computer via an input device so that the processor program may translate it into an assembly language and then into machine language, or translate it directly into machine language.

During processing, clerical errors made by the programmer are discovered and diagnosed by the processor, resulting in a printout of the errors. The source program and the error listing are returned to the programmer for correction and the process repeated until no further compile errors are produced. Once the programmer is satisfied of its reliability against sample data, the program is ready for a production run. From the programmer's standpoint, such program checkout or program debugging is time-consuming; often as much time is spent in debugging a program as is required to write it initially. From a computer standpoint, the time spent in loading compilers, testing, and debugging programs and then returning to a production run is wasteful.

The problem, then, is to find a way of eliminating the activities that take up time during which the computer is standing idle: changing tapes, loading different paper into printers, loading cards into card readers, making routine decisions, performing routine clerical operations, and making numerous physical adjustments to the computer system. One solution is the development of an operating system.

To put an operating system in proper perspective, consider a computer system with all the assemblers and compilers permanently stored on some on-line magnetic disk file and with a library of subroutines and frequently used programs stored on a similar device. In addition, frequently processed data files are permanently stored on an on-line basis. In this environment, a programmer need only present his source program deck to the system and request it to compile his program and to store the resulting object program somewhere on magnetic disk or tape so that he will be able to execute it whenever he wishes. This can now be done without having the operator remove any in-process production job and reloading the computer with the compiler program and then presenting the source program for processing.

WHAT IS AN OPERATING SYSTEM?

An operating system can be viewed as a framework within which all of the user's data processing jobs can be scheduled and performed. It is an organized set of techniques and procedures designed by computer manufacturers for specific systems to simplify housekeeping and speed up operations related to such areas as input/output, data conversion, and sort/merge routines.

More specifically, an operating system consists of (1) a number of processing programs (e.g., sort/merge and utility programs and user-written problem programs) and (2) a control program or monitor which supervises the execution of the processing programs in terms of job scheduling and controlling the storage, location, and retrieval of data. The monitor and other programs and hardware devices which it controls make up the operating system.

One of the key advantages of an operating system is that it serves the purpose of increasing the operating efficiency of the computer system. For example, Burroughs MCP (Master Control Program) allocates memory, loads and schedules various programs, initiates input and output, maintains a data and program library, communicates with the console operator, and distributes processing and input/output device time to multiprogramming jobs. Thus it limits operator intervention into the system, making all operations virtually automatic.

Other advantages of an operating system are (1) automatic processing of various computer programs (requiring different compilers) one after another; (2) ability to handle programs of various lengths in an overlapping fashion such that all programs are processed efficiently and on time,; and (3) input/output activities that function independently of the actual problem program.

HISTORICAL DEVELOPMENT OF OPERATING SYSTEMS

The first operating systems were developed in the mid-1950s in large scientific data processing installations such as General Motors and North American Aviation. The basic approach was to reduce idle time by job stacking. The programs for each job and the input data were loaded onto a file. A resident program called a "loader" would then take over and load each job. Upon completion, all programs transferred control to the loader; and the machine operator was instructed to execute a manual transfer to the reader program if anything went wrong. While the loading program reduced the demands to load the next job, it did not maximize equipment utilization.

The next development in operating systems involved the use of standard routines for input/output programming. Common input/output routines avoided conflicts in the use of tape units and input/output channels as the computer moved from one job to the next. The package allowed the programmer to describe his input/output requirements to the control program through the use of "macro" instructions which, in turn, provided input/output commands to the peripheral devices.

The term *macro* was used because a single command resulted in the generation of multiple machine instructions. These routines were grouped into an Input-

Output Control System (IOCS) package; the IOCS also provided effective error recovery techniques and a routine for record blocking/deblocking.

When second-generation computers were introduced in 1960, they were equipped with data channels that provided for a program interrupt when an operation was completed. The IOCS package was expanded to include a series of individual channel schedules and a group of unique processing routines to perform specific tasks such as label processing, end-of-reel and end-of-file processing, disk record addressing, and others.

From the concept of common routines for input/output grew the idea of placing common service routines, such as assembly programs and compilers, on a single file known as a system file. The system file provided a common copy of each service program for everyone's use, thus reducing modification and maintenance.

The establishment of a system file permitted operational phasing whereby each task of assembling, compiling, linking, and translation of relative program addresses to absolute memory addresses was done for a batch of programs, one phase at a time. The resulting executable programs were then stored in the system file.

The operating system provided automatic transition from one job to the next, a file search for the desired subroutine for input/output control, and output collection. The need for operator intervention was reduced by the availability of debugging aids, automatic restart facilities, and logging procedures.

With the advent of third-generation computer systems, the capabilities of the operating system were expanded to include allocation of CPU memory storage and assignment of input/output facilities among several programs. From information submitted with each job, the operating system determines the requirement of each program for memory space and input/output equipment and provided sharing of facilities as required to maintain a high throughput rate.

In more advanced multiprogramming operating systems, memory partitions are assigned according to job priority, and up to 64 different programs can occupy core storage simultaneously. Programs can be initiated and terminated independently because I/O assignments are determined by a modular schedule.

An operating system could operate on a wide variety of system configurations and is capable of accommodating several programming languages.

ORGANIZATION OF AN OPERATING SYSTEM

Executive operating systems are collections of routines for supervising the executing programs by computer. These routines reside in memory or on a direct-access device, disk, or drum.

From an organizational point of view, nearly all executive operating systems contain some or all of the following elements:

1. A hardware configuration geared to the operation of the system.
2. Monitor or supervisor.
3. Job scheduler.
4. Operations or master control scheduler.
5. Resource management program.
6. File management program.

7. Collection of service utility programs.
8. Collection of programming languages.

Hardware Requirements

The computer configuration is typically arranged to effectively use the operating systems (O/S) routines and to operate in two modes: normal mode and control mode. During the normal mode, the computer is given over to user program control and the regular production program is executed. With the control mode, it executes O/S programs and locks out all user programs.

Ability to operate in both states is tied to several hardware features. The first is the interrupt structure. A computer should be able to sense a condition which demands attention from the executive system. At the same time, it should be able to interrupt what it is doing, save the status of the currently running job, transfer control to the O/S to handle the condition, then restore the status to where it was before the interrupt and resume processing.

Another hardware feature is an interval timer that logs accounting information and also exercises control over the time each job is permitted to use the system.

In order for several operations to be processed simultaneously, a computer must have more than one channel path for transferring data in and out of the system concurrently with the processing.

It is essential for the hardware to have memory protection of individual programs that are in the system at the same time. This is usually done by hardware in the form of base and limit registers, reserved blocks protected by a program key, or by attaching special control bits for each memory word to prevent the word from being overwritten.

With several programs stored simultaneously in memory, it should be possible to load them starting at any memory address. More important, automatic segmentation should allow parts of the program to be considered as individual processing elements.

Finally, an auxiliary memory device (disk or drum) is required for allowing fast access to parts of the O/S that are not normally resident in the main memory.

The Monitor or Supervisor

The monitor is the control center which supervises the O/S functions. It coordinates the use of the various devices and operations required for program execution. The monitor also watches over interrupts which may be generated by other programs in the O/S, user programs, utility functions of the hardware such as I/O malfunctions, and operator action at the console. The monitor receives control of the O/S as a result of the interruption and can then perform functions not normally available to the programmer. Some of these functions are:

1. Allocating memory to programs requesting access to the system.
2. Occupying memory areas when notified that the areas are available for a new program.
3. Controlling the execution of shared programs which reside together in memory and providing switching of control between programs for better use of the CPU.

4. Initiating input/output operations and allowing other operations to proceed independently of the CPU.
5. Adding and deleting programs from a library.
6. Maintaining a complete accounting log of the O/S performance which can be printed out on request for analysis.
7. Loading programs into memory and passing control to the job scheduler.

Job Scheduler

The job scheduler is a part of the operating system. It receives data from job control cards and sets up a sequence of services to be performed for the program under consideration. It may allocate input/output devices, assign devices to be used as printer backup, initiate a specific sequence of job steps, alert the operator to the need for special forms, and generally perform the housekeeping functions and job control. Some schedulers are able to recognize priority jobs and shelve currently running programs off the system to accommodate the priority job.

Master Control Scheduler (MCS)

This part of the operating system facilitates direct communication with the operator and provides readable, self-explanatory messages to and from the system. Through such messages, the operator can inquire about the status of all the physical devices of the system, of currently running programs, and of all data files being processed. MCS can also instruct the operator to mount specific tape reels on disk packs in preparation for a scheduled program awaiting currently used files.

Resource Management Program

The resource management program continuously monitors the availability of all devices in the system (including channels, processors, and peripheral devices) and is capable of changing the allocation of these components to programs for utilizing new components added or to reroute the work flow around devices that have been removed from the system.

Utility Programs

In most operating systems, the monitor has control over a number of programs called utility programs, or utility systems, designed to perform basic data processing functions that are commonly required by different types of applications. These utility systems include file conversion routines, program testing and diagnosis, and sort systems.

1. File conversion routines. Frequently, a data file on a particular storage device requires storing or rewriting on another storage device. It may be desirable to rewrite a card file on magnetic tape or a magnetic tape file on magnetic disk, and so on. Equipment manufacturers have conversion programs which perform these functions in standardized ways so that installation requiring such operations can use them for that purpose.

In using conversion programs, the programmer need only indicate the format of the file to be converted and the format of the new file to be prepared. Such programs automatically provide record blocking when writing a tape or disk file; they can be instructed to generate card sequence numbering when preparing a card file; and, in other ways, they perform needed routine tasks to properly prepare a file for the storage medium.

2. Program testing and diagnosis. Even when carefully prepared, programs contain errors—either clerical or logical—that need to be corrected. Clerical errors are normally detected by the programming system employed in translating the source program into machine language. Operating systems also include testing and diagnostic routines to help the programmer discover his logical errors and to provide for their correction.

3. Sort systems. Sort systems are programs designed to sequentially order records in a given file by reference. A file of employee records, for example, may require ordering by employee number for some applications, by employee name in others. Sort systems are provided as part of programming systems to aid in arranging data by sorting with minimum programming. A programmer need only identify the field to be used in sorting the records. The rest of the sorting task is left almost entirely to the operating system. Most computer systems today include a generalized sort system in their basic software package.

Regardless of the type of operating system used, it can be generally summarized that the operating system introduces programs to the computing system, initiates their execution, and provides them with all the resources and services necessary for accomplishing designated tasks. To be effective, the operating system must be general enough to accommodate a variety of applications on a wide range of hardware configurations. It is therefore made up of a general library of programs that can be tailored to the user's requirements.

Programming Languages

All systems provide programming language translations. The more sophisticated systems can change programs from one language into another. The Honeywell OS/200, for example, allows the user to combine any of three languages to provide the most efficient solution to his problem. Each language available to the system can obtain access to files on any device.

MULTIPROGRAMMING AND MULTIPROCESSING

The efficiency with which a given program is executed depends on the efficiency and coordination of the computer hardware, as well as the nature of the program involved. Some programs require little processing but involve great amounts of output and input. Such programs are called I/O bound. That is, the total throughput time required to run the program is limited by the speed of the I/O devices used in providing the input to the CPU and output from the CPU. Other programs require considerable processing time but a minimal amount of time to record the output and are known as *process-bound* programs. Their throughput time depends on the internal speed of the CPU.

When an I/O-bound program is being executed, the CPU waits for the I/O devices to perform their function. Similarly, when a process-bound program is being executed I/O devices are idle. Multiprogramming attempts to increase the total throughput of the computer system by executing a combination of the I/O-bound and process-bound programs.

An operating system that supervises a time-sharing operation must have certain capabilities to service many users at once. Where multiprogramming or multiprocessing is involved, it schedules jobs and manages the smooth transition from job to job. The system interleaves the various tasks. It switches back and forth between the two or more programs and synchronizes the running of the tasks so that the user has the impression he is the sole user of the system.

In multiprocessing, the operating program can process two or more programs simultaneously. With multiple arithmetic and logic units, the multiprocessor can perform two tasks simultaneously. By mixing process-bound jobs with input/output-bound jobs, the use of both the computer and the I/O peripherals approaches maximum. That is, while process-bound jobs are using the computational facilities of the computer, I/O-bound jobs are using the computer's peripherals.

In real-time and time-sharing systems, users enter their jobs for immediate attention. The operating system checks the priority and operating requirements of each job as it enters the system. When an inquiry with top priority enters, the operating system has the capability of (1) suspending jobs in process by dumping them into storage, (2) entering and processing the priority job, and (3) reentering the suspended job to complete its processing.

This sequence of events is possible through the queuing feature by which the operating system can place jobs in the queue for processing. The operating system thus acts as a traffic policeman in deciding the sequence of the processing traffic and also making sure that low-priority jobs are processed within a reasonable time period. After a low-priority job has been bypassed a predetermined number of times, the operating system places it in line for processing. This prevents the low-priority job from remaining in the queue for long periods.

Computer processing can be interrupted by internal as well as external conditions. The answer to an arithmetic operation may exceed the storage location, or the electric power source may fail. The operating system must recognize the signal generated by the interruption and initiate recovery procedures. If a program attempts to write into a protected area of memory, the program should be interrupted and the operator notified through the console or some other means. User programs must be isolated from each other and protected. Since time-sharing and real-time systems are being used concurrently by many users, the isolation and protection of memory and storage are essential. The operating system must prevent improper or illegal entry and terminate erroneous programs.

The operating system keeps an inventory of all available user programs and files. As required, the system provides each user with quick and efficient access to his programs and information. When the user's request is received by the operating system, it not only searches for the pertinent program and files but at the same time checks to see that the entry is proper and legal.

All scheduling of input-output is managed by the operating system. If a printer is available, the system determines which user report will be processed. All I/O devices are assigned and reassigned by the operating system, which also checks their performance. When a malfunction occurs, it initiates recovery or emergency procedures to insure proper performance.

CONCLUSION

The incredibly high speed of modern computers and those designed for the seventies make it necessary that these machines be designed to operate with a minimum of computer operator functions. Consequently, computer manufacturers have gone to great lengths in producing elaborate but easy-to-handle operating systems. The development of operating systems has taken a leading role in the continued development of electronic data processing which caused this area to acquire an air of mystery. On the outside, a computer system controlled by an operating system is somewhat like an electronic brain under its own control; choosing the jobs to be performed, rejecting others because of errors it has found, instructing the operator to mount tapes and set switches, and in general behaving in a "dictatorial" way. This superior behavior has prompted some to envision humans soon becoming the slaves of these computers, doing their bidding. But we have to realize that the operating system is a product of man's mind, designed and written by programmers, and that the computer is limited only to what it is programmed to do.

SELECTED REFERENCES

Books

> Bohl, Marilyn. *Computer Concepts.* Chicago: Science Research Associates, 1970, pp. 311-323.
>
> Brightman, Richard W. *Information Systems for Modern Management.* New York: The Macmillan Company, 1971, pp. 277-295.
>
> Favret, Andrew G. *Digital Computer Principles and Applications.* New York: Van Nostrand Reinhold Co., 1972, pp. 142-151.
>
> Marxer, Ellen. *Elements of Data Processing.* Albany, N.Y.: Delmar Publishers, 1971, pp. 178-194.

Articles

> Boering, B. W. "Multiprogramming: Who Needs It?" *Computers and Automation,* February 1967, pp. 14-18.
>
> Flores, I. "Multiplex Programming." *Science & Technology,* September 1969, pp. 6-13.
>
> Howard, P. C. "Optimizing Performance in a Multiprogramming System." *Datamation,* January 1969, pp. 65-67.
>
> Rosin, Robert F. "Supervisory and Monitor Systems." *Computer Surveys,* March 1969, pp. 37-54.

PART 6

Real-Time Data Processing

INTRODUCTION

From the computer's early days, the speed of the central processing unit has always been greater than the speed of its peripheral devices. When tied to these devices (especially those involving card readers, punched paper tape readers, and line printers), most systems were relatively inefficient in producing vitally needed output.

The addition of direct-access devices under the direct control of the computer allowed processing to be performed on-line. Today's electronic computer enables a manager to operate his business with incomparable efficiency by having direct access to relevant information and in "real time"—that is, fast enough to respond to the problem at hand. The assumption here is that the system acts upon data as soon as it is received in a continuous flow processing scheme.

The traditional way of handling information was in batches, with inputs into a computer system collected over a period of hours, days, or even weeks before reaching the computer for processing. Little distinction was made regarding the time-dependent value of certain information included in the mass of input. Batch processing permits no interaction between man and machine, and the user receives output information at a later time. By contrast, real-time processing provides information fast enough for immediate action. Thus the response time is within seconds from the time when input data first became available to the time when a reaction is received from the computer. Actual response time may range from a fraction of a second in high-priority systems such as those used in missile launching to as long as half an hour in low-priority commercial systems.

Although real-time processing is not necessary in all data processing applications, there are situations where fast response is required, including fluctuating out-of-the-ordinary situations, high-unit inventory cost, drastic drop in sales, perishable goods, and fast product turnover.

Real-time systems can be used to reduce inventory level, contributing to a more efficient physical logistics system. A reduction in inventory is possible because the time it takes to uncover a below-minimum inventory condition is substantially reduced. Furthermore, since real-time systems permit inventory records to be updated concurrently with changes in the physical system, inventory safety stock to cover information delays can be eliminated.

Real-time systems can also be used to reduce accounts receivable by eliminating the delays between the shipment of goods and the mailing of invoices to customers. Compared to batch processing systems, real-time systems offer users competitive marketing advantages in ensuring a complete stock of goods, increased speed of product delivery, and the ability to respond more quickly to customer and salesman information requests. These advantages are more realistic, however, when the real-time system is meaningfully integrated into a management process.

A key advantage of on-line, real-time stems from the application of communications technology to real-time processing. For example, telecommunications networks enable an on-line, real-time system to be used via remote terminals over a wide geographical area. Thus, man-machine interface has the effect of minimizing redundancy and contributing to more effective control. Airline reservation and point-of-sale systems, for example, carry information continually from terminal to computer and back, providing information service to the user and accurate and current information upon request.

Real-time systems owe much to the Air Force's "Semi-Automatic Ground Environment," or SAGE, originally created to protect the United States against surprise air attack. It does the job with a network of radar-fed computers that continuously monitor the country's air space. Without SAGE there would have been no SABRE, American Airlines' $30 million real-time seat reservation system, which is probably the most complex special-purpose business computer installation to date.

Characteristics of Real-Time

A real-time system has the following seven characteristics:

1. Data are maintained on-line and stored either in memory or in random access files attached directly to the computer.
2. The computer can be interrogated from remote terminals, which means that stored information can be obtained on request from these terminals.
3. Data are updated as events occur, not accumulated (batched) and periodically updated.
4. Real-time systems are bigger, costlier, and more complex than batch systems. They have the capability of multiprogramming (more than one program in memory at a time), allowing a given program to occupy different areas of memory at different times, and allowing inputs to occur on a time-variable basis. Thus on-line real-time systems allow for many simultaneous activities, react to random sequences of inputs, and service a multitude of interrupts.
5. The systems communicate with the user in an interactive, dynamic way with fast response.
6. The systems provide storage protection (either by a hardware or a software feature) whose basic purpose is to limit the use of core by a particular program. This is important in the implementation of real-time systems for two reasons. First, it provides the executive control routines a degree of

safety from deliberate interference by programs being executed under their control. Second, many on-line, real-time systems must remain in operation continually. This means that all check-outs of new programs or changes to the current system must be performed during normal system operation. Storage protection assures that the operation of the system will not be interrupted by improper operation of unverified programs.

7. Priority interrupts are a fundamental characteristic of the systems—the ability to react to external signals. This is a hardware feature because if the job of recognizing these signals were left to software, a great deal of time could be consumed just looking for them.

Classes of OLRT Systems

On-line, real-time systems (OLRT) can be classified either by the type of applications handled or by their hardware configuration. By application, there are process control inquiry, scientific problem solving, or management information systems.

Computers used in controlling industrial processes such as petroleum refining and papermaking represent an interesting and fairly well-developed bypath in digital computer technology. The primary goal of a process control system is process optimization. It involves information routing with feedback. Input is received in the form of signals from flow transmitters, pressure transmitters, temperature transmitters, and so on, which provide the information needed to calculate optimum levels of operation. Systems of this type are used in the regulation of auto traffic, control of steel sheet thickness in a rolling mill, and fabrication of transitors and integrated circuits.

Control systems are either open loop or closed loop. In an open-loop control system, the computer provides the operator with guides to safer and more efficient operation. In a closed-loop system, the computer itself orders the necessary corrections in the process, typing out feedback information for the operator's reference only. These control systems are designed to handle tasks ranging from simple feedback control to optimizing profits through linear programming.

Inquiry systems allow human access to information currently available in the system. Among the better known inquiry systems are airline reservations and most bank savings and checking accounts.

Problem-solving scientific systems are designed to perform particular complicated tasks in mathematics, engineering, and the physical sciences, where emphasis is placed more on the computational speed and ability of the computer than on the speed and capacity of its peripheral storage. Unlike time-sharing or dedicated systems, scientific computations are nonrepetitive. A scientific program is written, tested, and run to produce a particular answer. It is a one-time application.

Real-time systems may also be classified according to their multiprogramming or multiprocessing capabilities. A single central computer without multiprogramming capabilities is usually set up for interaction with back-office terminals located away from the system. Its primary use is to process transactions after customer service has been rendered, for credit authorization on charge sales, and so on. In the case of banks, for example, checks and other financial data that are periodically collected from the mail and from the teller area are processed after banking hours.

The processed details can then be used to verify the status of various accounts for prompt action. Such a system constitutes a basic real-time system. It is the lowest in cost and in equipment reliability. Consequently, it is least dependent on business operations.

Single computers with multiprogramming capabilities are installed by many banks and savings and loan associations to interact with either back-office or stand-alone customer terminals. Systems that offer such direct customer service require more expensive and complex terminals for maintaining service, especially in situations where communication with the computer is interrupted.

The third type of real-time system provides multiprocessing with dependent users and customer terminals, utilizing two or more computers linked together for coordinated operation. More sophisticated systems have smaller computers for handling "housekeeping" duties, such as input/output assembly and processing, communication control, and file maintenance.

Planning and Design Considerations

Planning for a real-time system is generally more complex than for a conventional system. More sophisticated hardware, many simultaneous functions, receipt of transactions at random, varying peak times, and different combinations of programs required in core at one time, are just a few of the reasons for the complexity of a real-time system.

In developing a real-time system there are six major stages, as follows:

1. *Preliminary system planning.* This step is taken to ensure that the system will accomplish what it is intended to do. Representatives of various departments are brought together to participate in the planning of the proposed system, discuss its capabilities, and learn what it offers to serve the needs of their particular department.

2. *Documentation of the system design.* Documentation serves the purpose of formalizing the details of the proposed system and minimizing any disagreement or misunderstanding of what the system is designed to do.

3. *Establishment of controls, standards, and schedules.* These details serve as bench marks to test and measure the system's operations as they are accomplished. The controls keep operations within fixed paths while standards keep them within prescribed quality range. The schedules are used to develop routines for queuing and the like.

4. *Development of control and operational programs.* Such programs are established to keep the system's functions operating in a logical order. In a sense, the control program is the master, in that it determines what is to be done and relays application messages to the responsible area. Operational programs are the main computational programs of the system.

   Unlike programming of conventional systems, real-time programming involves control of the communications network and terminals, organization and addressing of random access files, and proper handling of variable processing requirements and fluctuating input rate. With these problem areas, system testing can be a difficult task, requiring a detailed and thorough debugging procedure before the system is ready for actual use. In order to achieve efficiency in real-time programming, certain points are developed:

a. Preplanned programming schedule.
b. Monitoring programming progress.
c. Budgetary control of core storage and processing time.
d. Adequate specifications and documentation.
e. Planning for the handling of all component failures and errors.

5. *Testing.* The system must be constantly tested to ensure proper performance. Initial testing is a dry run; the first step is to test all individual program segments, followed by testing of selected transactions individually. After all corrections are made, actual testing is done in an operational mode when the system is on-line and ready to function in a real-time environment.

   Prior to the completion of system testing, a conversion plan must be prepared. At this point, parallel processing is performed and the results are made available to management for its final approval.

6. *Maintenance.* Once the system becomes operational, its performance must be constantly checked so that any changes can be made as needed. User organizations with complex real-time systems often pay a premium for having an experienced staff to maintain the system on a full-time basis.

The make-up of a real-time system often involves several suppliers. A central, large-scale computer may come from one manufacturer while smaller, housekeeping computers are furnished by other suppliers. Related hardware such as memory modules, buffers, interface or switching devices, terminals, and data sets are also obtained from special-purpose manufacturers. Thus, considering the specialized nature of the task, many user organizations resort to real-time systems consultants to handle the qualifications, screening, installation, and reporting responsibility of all suppliers. The consultant can also be assigned the responsibility of developing the needed support and application programs.

In planning for memory capacity and program capabilities, the system must have (1) dynamic reconfiguration capabilities such that its software/hardware features help in providing the best possible service in any given situation; (2) dynamic recovery capabilities to handle every possible malfunction, error, or unforeseen contingency; (3) capability to recognize all activities at all times so that every input or output message is positively identified according to its origin or destination; (4) storage protection capability; and (5) priority interrupts.

Recent Application Areas

One application that is much talked about but not yet in operation is a cashless, checkless society in which all purchases will be charged directly to the customer's account by means of the computer. The store clerk will insert the customer's credit card into a telephone-like device and, within seconds, contact the computer in the customer's bank. The clerk will then tap out all purchasing information on the keyboard. At the receiving end the computer will record the transactions in its accounts receivable file. One critical factor related to this system is security. Proper safeguards to protect against unauthorized use of customer cards must be developed along with the hardware and software of the system.

Another application already being implemented is an arrangement to have a part or all of an employee's salary credited to a bank account each payday. In this case, the check-writing phase of the payroll function is eliminated. Wide use of these applications makes it necessary for banks to become broader service organizations in providing special services such as budgeting, preparation of tax forms, and issuance of periodic reports on the distribution of customers' funds.

There are a number of new computer applications in the medical field. At a 1972 medical convention, doctors heard that computerized systems were being used to read electrocardiograms, monitor intensive care facilities, and analyze subtle patterns in electroencephalograms. Hope was also expressed that an understanding of the informational processes in the brain will be applied to behavior of individuals in the hostile environment of space and in the treatment of neurological diseases.

A new real-time computer system is used in education, with the computer performing the role of tutor, responding to the student's answers and inquiries. In New York City 6,000 students in 15 local schools, using CRT units connected to a central computer, receive instruction in reading, spelling, and math through the sixth grade. Students using the system from six to twenty minutes get approximately ten times the attention they receive in the classroom.

The readings section begins with Thorne's article, "Critical Factors in the Implementation of a Real-Time System." It emphasizes five critical phases, each phase involving problems not usually found in the installation of batch processing systems. The remaining two articles are by Yourdon, in which he discusses concepts of reliability that are relevant to real-time systems and causes of systems failures.

CRITICAL FACTORS IN THE IMPLEMENTATION
OF A REAL-TIME SYSTEM

Jack F. Thorne

In recent years, the installations of real-time systems in business organizations have been increasing. From this experience, certain factors which are critical in the implementation of this type of system have been discerned. In the future, a knowledge of these critical factors should be a prerequisite to planning the implementation of any real-time system.

The process of implementation is divided into five phases: the feasibility study, the system design, the programming, the system testing, and the conversion. Because of the complex nature of real-time systems, each of these phases involves problems which usually are not found in the installation of batch processing systems. The members of the implementation team must be aware of these problems if they are to perform their duties effectively.

THE FEASIBILITY STUDY

The feasibility study is probably the most important phase in the implementation of a real-time system since the others stem from it. Serious mistakes or omissions in this study will result in inefficiencies at each subsequent stage of the installation. The results of the feasibility study include the identification of the areas within the organization where potential improvement in operations is possible and the detailed specifications on the major proposed computer applications.

The feasibility study team must understand the nature of real-time systems. This knowledge is important since available hardware must be delineated and software applicability must be evaluated. The members also must be aware of the advantages and disadvantages of real-time processing to effectively evaluate the feasibility of applications being considered.

If the environment and applications are compatible with the factors and pecularities of a real-time system, the feasibility study may recommend the installation of such a system. Following approval by top management of the recommendation, the system design phase is initiated.

THE SYSTEM DESIGN

The design calculations and estimating procedures which are necessary when implementing a real-time system are far more difficult to carry out than those needed

Source: Reprinted, with permission, from *Data Management*, January 1972, pp. 36-40, published by the Data Processing Management Association, Park Ridge, Illinois.

when implementing a batch processing system. This problem is aggravated in that the penalties for inaccuracy frequently are greater than those in batch processing. If the estimates are inaccurate in a batch processing system and the programs take more time or require more core storage than was originally expected, the computer usually can still carry out its functions (although it will need more time to do so). In a real-time system, this latitude is not available since the real-time capacity of the system cannot be expanded merely by adding on extra shift.

In designing a real-time system, a number of factors may become critical. First, the critical factors must be determined, usually through an estimating process. Then, they must be evaluated. In a typical real-time system, six types of bottlenecks are encountered: (1) computer core and/or peripheral file storage, (2) processing time in the computer, (3) channel utilization, (4) communications network utilization, (5) terminal utilization, and (6) capability of terminal operators. Each of these potential bottlenecks must be evaluated with care, and the relationship among the factors must be examined.

To have all the application programs in core storage at all times is impossible in most real-time systems since core storage is not sufficiently large. Therefore, some of these programs must be obtained from the random-access files when they are required. This requisitioning of programs is accomplished at the expense of processing time, channel time, and file-arm time.

If the processing time is limited, a remedial activity is to polish or improve the programs. Additional processing time may be obtained by other means, such as writing the programs so that they operate faster even though more core storage is required. Other alternatives include having more application programs in core, or using a fast tailor-made supervisory program, rather than a slow generalized one.

The calculation of the peripheral file storage requirements in a real-time system is complicated by the necessity of minimizing the seek times and by the addressing procedures. Seek time frequently can be minimized at the expense of tight file packing. In most methods of file organization, the longer the file-reference time, the higher the packing density of the file. However, if the reference time is long, larger queues occupying more core storage appear in the system and the channel and access-mechanism utilization is higher.

Channel utilization can be decreased by having more application programs in core storage. The same reduction can be accomplished by having a better file organization, which may require more disk space or more processing time. If the channel utilization becomes too high, queues build up, increasing core storage utilization.

Arm utilization may be lessened by reducing seek times, by distributing data more efficiently among the arms, or by considering factors which improve channel utilization. File accesses can be sifted and executed in the sequence which minimizes the timing; however, this procedure increases the queue sizes and core storage utilization.

When the communications lines are handled by a separate line-control computer, certain programs can be either in the line-control computer or in the main computer. If these programs are run in the line-control computer, more room for processing remains in the main computer but less core storage is allocated for buffering input. When the main computer handles the control of the communications lines and the buffering of input and output, processing time is increased and a considerable quantity of core storage is used.

If transactions processing is delayed because communications lines are not available, queues form at the terminals, in the main computer, or in the line-control computer. The utilization of communications lines, and hence the queues, can be reduced by increasing the number of lines or redistributing the terminals. This increase in communications lines frequently results in decreased core storage utilization.

In some real-time systems, the terminals are very heavily loaded during peak periods. This load can be reduced, however, if the response time is very fast. A fast response time requires more communications lines to avoid output delays. In some systems, the response time may be increased at the expense of core storage.

The performance of operators must be considered very carefully when terminal utilizations is high. Computer specialists tend to consider only the machinery, and thus pay too little attention to real-time terminal operators.

In a real-time system, a trade-off among these critical factors is possible. If one becomes too tight, it may be possible to relieve it at the expense of some of the others. Thus, designing a real-time system is, to a large extent, a matter of obtaining a balance among these factors.

Along with balance in the design of a real-time system, austerity must exist. Only by weighing every decision against the criterion of austerity can the designer keep the problems of implementation within manageable bounds. Since a tendency toward complexity exists in designing a real-time system, the designers must be mindful of the factors that contribute to system complexity in order that they may be minimized through the development of realistic functional requirements.

Because of the nature of real-time systems, special design considerations arise which normally do not occur in batch processing systems. These considerations are: reliability, error detection, and information protection. In real-time system design, it is preferable to begin with a basic study of the required degree of reliability. If economically feasible, this degree of reliability (with some safety factor) is included in the system being designed.

Automatic error detection and corrective action should be introduced into the system wherever possible. Unless the computer, the communications network, or a terminal has failed completely, manual error detection and correction routines are undesirable. The time constraints of real-time systems will not permit the familiar error-tracking procedures at the console.

The protection of files in real-time systems takes on a new significance and more extensive protection methods are essential. Electrical failure of storage units, accidental erasure of data through hardware failure or programming error, and physical damage by fire, flood or other disaster may cause the loss of vital records.

In designing a real-time system, three techniques usually are used which are not normally needed in designing a batch processing system—probability theory, queuing theory and simulation.

Ascertaining the time and core requirements of the computer involves probability theory and queuing theory.

To assist in preparing design estimates, simulation frequently is used. Transactions which correspond to the inputs of the proposed system are fed into a model of the system. The delays and the size of queues are measured, and the model is adjusted to make them conform with the requirements. In the simulation of a multiprogrammed system, the model can become quite complicated; however, it appears to be the best means of estimating system requirements.

THE PROGRAMMING

During the programming of real-time systems, unique problems are encountered. These problems are attributed to two main factors: the complexity of real-time systems and the management of the programming team.

A computer in batch processing normally follows a repetitive cycle which may be planned and timed in detail by the programmer. In real-time systems, however, this repetitive cycle is not present. Transactions arrive at random and vary in their length and nature. These different types of transactions requiring different programs are executed in an unplanned sequence. Because of this fact, dynamic scheduling of the work—scheduling which changes with the changing requirements—may be needed.

In a real-time system, the requirements for core storage change from transaction to transaction. A dynamic allocation of the computer memory is required since an area of storage needed for one program may be needed shortly afterwards for a different program.

Different operators are likely to enter transactions in their terminals at the same time. In fact, the system may have many transactions of different types competing for the use of the computer at one time. Some means of assigning priority among the various transactions may be necessary.

Another factor that presents problems in a real-time system is multiprogramming. In simple systems, multiprogramming may not be needed, but in complex systems, it is necessary because the time taken to handle one transaction is greater than the interval of time between the arrival of transactions. The degree of multiprogramming varies considerably from one system to another, but it always adds complications to program writing.

Because the transactions arrive at random, the system occasionally can become overloaded. Such overloads are not normal in a well-designed system and are only short-lived states of affairs. Since they can occur, however, programs must be available to handle them.

Most of the problems outlined above are connected with the difficulties of handling data that arrive at random and which vary in their nature. Other problems in real-time programming are caused by the new types of hardware that are used in such systems. The use of random-access files, a communications network, and terminals introduces new complications into the programming.

The management of the programming team is perhaps the greatest problem in the programming of real-time systems. The main difficulties arise because the work of many programmers no longer is independent as it may have been in programming batch processing systems. If a programmer makes a change in his program or in his data specifications, it is likely to affect the work of other programmers.

Thus, there are eight essential points for success in the management of programming a real-time system:

1. Plan the programming schedule in detail
2. Monitor the programming progress closely
3. Use budgetary control of core storage and processing time

4. Stress the importance of teamwork in programming
5. Write good specifications and documentation
6. Plan the handling of all component failures and errors
7. Plan for possible load or complexity increases
8. Plan program and system testing from the start

THE SYSTEM TESTING

The testing of most real-time systems, first of programs and then of the over-all system, is a complicated assignment. Because of the tremendous difference in complexity between a small single-thread system, which processes only one transaction at a time, and a large multiprogrammed system, different testing techniques are required.

In a real-time system, transactions are entered through the terminals and travel via the communications network to the computer. When testing programs, the use of predetermined input is required. Since entering all the data through the terminals is too slow, and because the terminals probably are not available in the early testing phases, much of the input used in testing must be simulated. The use of terminals in the output operations during all of the program testing is not desirable for the same reasons. Since the input rate in a real-time system fluctuates, means of varying the input must be devised in order to test the overload action.

Transactions fed to the system from tape and the results recorded on tape are common means of input and output during system testing. However, in the final stages of testing, transactions must be entered via the terminals and the communications network in order to test the complete system.

The supervisory programs probably will not be completely debugged when they are first used with application programs. Controversy may arise as to whether an error results from a supervisory program or from an application program. When two application programs are in core storage at the same time, the determination of which caused an error is difficult.

With real-time processing, transactions enter the system at random, and many partially processed transactions may be in core storage at one time. In a multiprogrammed system, many sequences of events are possible; consequently, the removal of all errors from a system is very difficult.

If an error occurs during operational running in a batch processing system, the processing is stopped and the cause of the error is determined. Because of the time constraint, this procedure is not possible in a real-time system. If program errors occur in a real-time system after conversion, they are much more difficult to find and cause more trouble than in a batch processing system.

Many of the programmers who are involved in producing a real-time system may be inexperienced. Since the work of all the programmers intermeshes tightly, many discrepancies are likely to be found when the components of the system are put together.

The testing of a real-time system starts with the first unit test of one program segment and builds up to testing the fully developed system. Although the testing of a particular system is designed for that system, the work usually involved can be broken into seven phases:

Phase #1 corresponds in batch processing to program testing except that simulated supervisory program macro-instructions are used. Non-real-time debugging takes place. During this stage, individual program segments, complete threads, and groups of threads are tested. A thread consists of all the programs needed to process a transaction. Any errors in an application program discovered in later phases may cause the program to be returned to Phase One for debugging.

Phase #2 is entered when the computer to be used in the real-time system is available with its files and with the main routines of the supervisory programs. Although the supervisory programs no longer are simulated, the communications network and terminals are simulated. Since multiprogramming is not used, transactions are entered singly. One of the difficulties of this phase is the determination as to whether errors are caused by the application programs or by the supervisory programs.

Phase #3 is a repetition of Phase Two, but with multi-thread input, and builds up to the saturation testing needed to validate the application programs working with the supervisory programs. If a system is always single-thread, this stage is not necessary since saturation testing can take place in Phase Two.

Phase #4 simulates actual operation as closely as possible without having remote terminals on line. For the first time, actual terminals are used, although the main input is still from tape or disk. Various types of switchover and fallback are tested during this stage.

Phase #5 introduces remote terminals on line for the first time. The objective of this phase is to remove all remaining errors from the system so that the cutover to actual operational running will be as smooth as possible. During this stage, the four main functions are to determine whether any errors are introduced by the use of the communications network, to train the operators, to familiarize the staff with the use of terminals, and to cause infrequent errors to exhibit themselves.

Phase #6 is the cutover or conversion phase. Files are loaded with working data and actual transactions are entered in the system. Parallel operation occurs between the new system and the previous methods of operation until sufficient confidence is obtained for complete reliance on the new system.

Phase #7 involves any testing after the system becomes operational. Regardless of how thorough the testing of the system, errors are virtually certain to occur when the system first becomes operational. Testing is necessary to find these errors. When modifications are made to the operational system, additional testing is required.

THE CONVERSION

Prior to the completion of the programming and testing stages, a plan should be prepared for conversion to the new system. This phase of implementation usually includes a period of parallel processing which terminates when management is satisfied with the results of the new system. Since conversion requires cooperation between operating personnel and the system specialists, an agreed-upon plan of action can help coordinate the effort and ensure that all interested parties are aware of the procedures being followed.

The conversion phase usually is a period of building up the system, altering the procedures, training the operators, and changing the work habits of many personnel. Since it often is a period filled with organizational, human and technical problems, careful planning can minimize these difficulties.

During this phase, support programs are needed to obtain and load the necessary data on the files and to bridge the gap between the old and the new systems. Examples of programs which might be needed are system loading programs, file loading programs, file reorganization programs, and restart programs.

Mistakes by terminal operators and lack of control over operators are major causes of difficulty during the conversion of many real-time systems. Since the system designer is preoccupied largely with the technicalities of the system, he can easily neglect the training of the operators; however, this training is vitally important in a real-time system. A sufficiently long period for training and familiarization must be allowed to prevent the conversion phase from being impeded with operator errors and inabilities. As with other aspects of testing and cutting over, it needs to be planned well in advance.

On a large real-time system, conversion normally is too difficult to cut over all the terminals at once because numerous people and various actions must be coordinated. Furthermore, programs cannot be completely debugged until some locations are on-line. Therefore, a procedure for interim operations must be devised in which some locations are off-line while others are on-line. The conversion procedure in which an off-line location goes on-line must be planned carefully.

Since many factors are involved in the conversion of a real-time system, complications would be overwhelming if the entire system were cut over at one time. Therefore, breaking the conversion into relatively simple stages is desirable. These stages may be obtained by using one of the following methods in implementation:

1. Location by location. One terminal location is put on-line, and others are added when this location is working satisfactorily.
2. Function by function. When the terminals go on-line, they initially execute only a few relatively simple functions. When these functions are free of problems, others are added.
3. Model by model. The first version of the working system is designed so that it is operational for a relatively short period of time and then replaced by a more complex version.
4. Combinations of these methods. The buildup of the system occurs with different functions and different terminals being added in a planned fashion.

Where the terminal operators update and use information from the central files, an important step in conversion is storing live data in these files. Building up the files is relatively easy when each location has its own set of files and these can be updated only from that location. Where the data in the files are used in an integrated fashion by many terminal locations, the problem is more difficult. Either the files must be loaded during a period when the data are not in use, and all the terminals which update them are cut over at once, or some other means of conversion must be devised.

In a batch processing system, the period between hardware delivery and operational running can be short, sometimes only a few days or a single week-end. With a real-time system, this period is longer since the entire system needs to be installed for the final phases of system and operator training. Only at the completion of the conversion process is the validity of the system design really tested.

The following principles should be adopted when conversion is being planned:

1. Ensure that all programs are written and tested for setting up the records, operating in the interim period, and training the terminal operators.
2. Ensure that the communications network is ready and tested on time.
3. Carry out the operator training and familiarization in advance of conversion.
4. Design the procedures to cause the minimum upheaval in the offices affected.
5. Minimize those operator procedures which are used only for an interim operation during the conversion.
6. Plan the conversion to take place step-by-step where possible.
7. Design the procedures to avoid the accidental loss of data during conversion.

While the implementation of any computer system is an intricate task, a system with real-time capabilities introduces additional complexities which are largely the result of the critical factors discussed above. A knowledge of these factors while planning the implementation of a real-time system will greatly increase the probability of a successful installation.

DISCUSSION QUESTIONS

1. What critical factors does the author discuss regarding the implementation of a real-time system? Discuss.
2. In what respect are the problems encountered in the implementation of a real-time system different from those encountered in a batch processing system?

RELIABILITY OF REAL-TIME SYSTEMS: DIFFERENT CONCEPTS OF RELIABILITY

Edward Yourdon

Several years ago an enterprising young programmer was assigned to write a real-time process control system for one of the country's largest baking companies. The computer system was to control the mixing of ingredients for chocolate cookies by opening and closing the valves through which sugar, chocolate, milk, and other ingredients flowed into the huge mixing vats. Because of the immense scale of the operation, reliability was a vital concern; a failure might ruin thousands of cookies. Faced with such an awesome task, the programmer hit upon a fiendishly simple solution. As a child, he had been told that the taste of chocolate dominated that of most other ingredients; therefore, he wrote the process control system in such a way that all errors caused a transfer of control to the chocolate subroutine. If, for example, the system noticed that it had been a trifle late in shutting off the milk valve, or that it had inadvertently mixed in a few too many tons of sugar, the remedy was simple: add more chocolate. Mothers, children, and dentists of the world, rejoice! the cookie companies of America will never let you down!

Unfortunately, most real-time computer systems do not have a chocolate routine to fall back upon. Even worse, most programmers, system designers, and technical managers do not even recognize the need for something analogous to the chocolate subroutine. If there is one universal weakness in people entering the field of real-time systems for the first time, it is their naivete. They generally tend to underestimate the number of programmers required to implement the system, the duration of the project, and the amount of money involved. These weaknesses generally reflect a lack of management experience in the field of real-time and on-line systems, and as such, are beyond the scope of this series of articles.

However, there is another area where the naivete of system management personnel leads to catastrophe, and this area *is* within the realm of a technical discussion: system failures and error recovery. It rarely occurs to the programmer or analyst that the central processor might occasionally fail, or that a critical record on the disk might become unreadable. Despite the experiences of the past few years and the gloomy forecasts of the next decade, system designers generally ignore the possibilities of failures in the communications network or the power supply. One generally has to suffer through at least one real-time system before accepting the universality of Murphy's Law: "If anything can possibly go wrong, it will. And to the degree that nothing can possibly go wrong, something inevitably will."

Source: *Modern Data,* January 1972, pp. 36-41; a revision of material originally appearing in Edward Yourdon, *Design of On-Line Computer Systems* (Englewood Cliffs, N.J.: Prentice-Hall, 1972), pp. 516-18. Reprinted with permission of Prentice-Hall.

Failures in computer systems are certainly not new. One could even argue that older computer systems were more failure-prone than current systems. However, it should be realized that most of the second generation systems, as well as a majority of the third generation, were batch-oriented. While catastrophes were not completely beyond the realm of possibility on these systems, they were at least infrequent. If the computer did fail, it was usually possible for the computer operator to re-run the program; if a file became unreadable on magnetic tape, it was usually possible to retreat to a backup copy of the file, using a grandfather-father-son technique.

In a real-time system, failures tend to be much more visible because the computer is interacting with and/or controlling the real world, e.g., steel mills, petroleum refineries, time-sharing users, bank tellers, reservation clerks, etc. Even if real-time systems fail less often than batch systems, a failure is likely to be much more noticeable.

It is also questionable whether today's real-time systems really are more reliable than their batch predecessors. Our hardware technology is certainly more reliable than that of the second or early third generation. However, today's large real-time systems involve such a vastly increased number of components (compare a 360/65 to a 1401, for example) that one doubts whether the overall hardware reliability is actually any better. On the other hand, it certainly is true that minicomputer real-time systems are very reliable; the number of hardware and software components is sufficiently small that it is possible to exercise most of the bugs from the system.

My basic purpose in this series of articles is to expand upon these introductory thoughts; in essence, to raise the level of consciousness in the area of real-time systems failures. Our discussion will be broken into six parts. In this first part, we discuss the different kinds of reliability that are applicable to real-time systems, and show how to measure them. In Parts 2 and 3, we will discuss the common causes of system failures and briefly suggest some techniques for preventing and/or recovering from them. In Part 4, we will examine some failure statistics from a typical third generation multiprogramming real-time system. Parts 5 and 6 will be devoted to a more extensive discussion of recovery techniques.[1]

DIFFERENT CONCEPTS OF RELIABILITY

Before we discuss the causes of real-time system failures in Part 2, we should first recognize that the words "failure" and "reliability" mean different things to different system designers, as a result, their error recovery procedures can take on radically different forms. We can generally identify three distinct meanings of the word "reliability":

1. Prevention of "downtime" of any kind;
2. Prevention of prolonged periods of "downtime";
3. Protection of the data base.

We shall examine each of these in detail.

[1] Parts 2 to 6 were published by *Modern Data* in its February, March, April, May, and June 1972 issues, respectively. A summary is presented at the end of this article.

Prevention of "Downtime" of Any Kind

There are a number of real-time systems which insist on *continuous* performance, often on a 24-hour-a-day schedule. Process control systems, air traffic control systems, on-line medical systems, military missile-tracking systems, and some data acquisition systems fall into this category, as do a few business-oriented systems with extremely large numbers or users (such as airline reservation systems).

The important thing here is that *any* failure of *any* duration is likely to be catastrophic. A computer that controls the machining of an expensive airplane part cannot be allowed to fail for even a fraction of a second or the part will be ruined. Similarly, a computer system controlling a steel mill, petroleum refinery, or any other large industrial process cannot be allowed to fail for even a few seconds. Even in a "people-oriented" system, the tolerance for failures may be very low. In a system with several hundred terminals, the chaos and confusion resulting from a system failure could be immense.

The standard way of describing the reliability of such a system is by its Mean Time Between Failures, or MTBF. It is interesting to note that while many control systems specify an MTBF of several thousand hours, and business-oriented systems and time-sharing systems try to survive a month (or $8 \times 22 = 176$ hours) without a failure, most time-sharing systems have a failure every day or two. Since each failure is likely to be catastrophic, most system designers shudder at the thought of specifying a *distribution* of failures. That is, the thought of a mean failure rate of one per month is so disturbing to many system designers that the idea that the same system may have a 10% probability of having two failures in one day is almost too horrible to comprehend.

As one might expect, the traditional approach to this kind of reliability involves *redundancy* of hardware. As Figure 1 illustrates, one common approach involves *duplexed* hardware, with the switchover from the primary system to the backup system being manual, partly automatic, or completely automatic. Another approach, illustrated in Figure 2, is known as a *dual* system.

Prevention of Prolonged Periods of "Downtime"

The kinds of systems described in the previous section require a different kind of reliability than the average business-oriented real-time system. Since the business-oriented system is dealing with human users, it can often survive as many as one or two failures per day *as long as the failures are not prolonged.* A failure in a management information system or an on-line sales order entry system will cause the users to grumble a bit, but it is unlikely the business will go bankrupt.

We must emphasize, however, that this type of system *cannot* tolerate prolonged periods of downtime. If the system requires five minutes to be repaired, a salesman can ask his customer to wait, a manager can chase his secretary around the desk, or a clerk can take an extra coffee break. However, if the system is still out of action after half an hour, the salesman will have lost his customer, the manager will have tired of chasing his secretary (or will have caught her), and the clerk will have forgotten which transaction she was working on at the time of the failure.

Note that the "prolonged period," or Mean Time To Repair (MTTR) to which we refer, includes *all* of the time that the system is out of action. It may take the

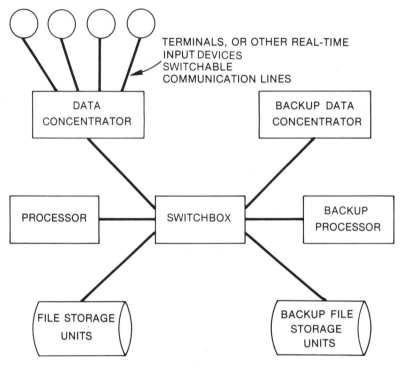

Figure 1. A Duplexed Computer System

computer operator five minutes to notice that the system is not functioning (or for the users to convince him that the system is not functioning); it may take another five minutes to correct the hardware failure that caused the system to malfunction (or to determine that it was caused by software); another ten minutes may be consumed running recovery programs to restore the data base; and finally, it may take the computer operator ten minutes to restart the system and carry on the usual "initialization dialogue" with the operating system. Meanwhile, the users will have spent thirty minutes in a growing state of hysteria, and they may or may not still be around when the system is finally repaired. For this type of reliability, it is clear that we are not only interested in the total time to repair the failure, but also the total number of such failures per day. If there is only one system failure per day, the users may be willing to tolerate a 15-minute delay while the system is being repaired. If there are two or three failures per day (and these numbers are not unrealistic), then the users will begin growing more irritable and will insist that the system be repaired in five minutes or less. If there are five or more failures per day, anything short of "instant" recovery (i.e., less than a minute) will be intolerable.

The type of recovery procedures used for this kind of reliability may involve a combination of hardware and software which, while it may be less expensive than that required for the reliability demanded by the control system, is often just as difficult to implement. In a simple case, recovery may consist of training the

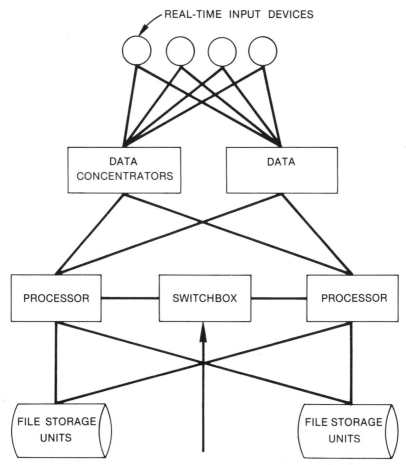

Figure 2. A Dual Computer System

computer operator to react quickly to a failure. If there is no data base recovery to be performed, the operator may be able to re-start the system in a matter of seconds. In some cases, operating systems and application programs may have to be arranged in such a way that they can be re-started with a push of a button. Finally, in situations where the failure is likely to take some time to repair, and where the MTTR requirements are particularly stringent, the duplexed hardware configuration shown in Figure 3 may be necessary.

Protection of the Data Base

Finally, we should mention those systems whose primary concern is to preserve data base integrity. There are a number of organizations, especially government

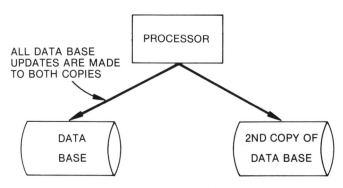

Figure 3. Data Base Integrity with a Dual Data Base

agencies, that are beginning to design on-line data bases in excess of ten billion characters. In some cases, literally hundreds of magnetic tapes would be required to keep a complete back-up copy of the data base, and several *days* would be required to load the back-up copy of the data base from tape to disk. There are other organizations which, while not so large, are building data bases that are critical to the day-to-day operation of the organization. The patient files of an on-line medical system, the financial files of any business system, and the intelligence files of our favorite government agencies fall into this category.

While it may seem an exaggeration, the people in charge of these systems will often state emphatically that they are willing to tolerate a system failure every hour, and that they are willing to let their system stay out of service all day long *as long as their data base stays intact.* In other cases, the system designer may wish to distinguish between a minor system failure, in which only one or two records are lost, and a *catastrophic* failure (e.g., a head crash or a system bug that methodically destroys data base records) in which all or a significant portion of the data base records are destroyed.

The recovery procedures for data base reliability usually take one of three forms: dual copies of the data base, disk dumps, and audit trails (sometimes referred to as log files, journal tapes, or transaction tapes). The notion of a dual data base is illustrated in Figure 3. Basically, it involves keeping two copies of the data base and wirting to *both* copies wherever the data base has to be updated. As the reader can imagine, there are a number of drawbacks to this scheme; the most obvious being the extra disk costs. It should also be apparent that the dual data base does not protect the system from power failures, memory parity errors, processor failures, etc.; nor does it prevent an errant application program from destroying both copies of the data base. Essentially, this procedure is valuable only if all of the other components of the system are duplicated. If there are plans for a backup processor, backup power supply, and so forth, *then* it may make good sense to have a backup data base.

A second approach to data base reliability is to copy the data base onto tape (or cards, or stone tablets, or some other reliable medium) at the end of each day's operation. This procedure, usually known as a "disk dump," is commonly practiced in time-sharing service bureaus and a few other types of on-line systems, but it also

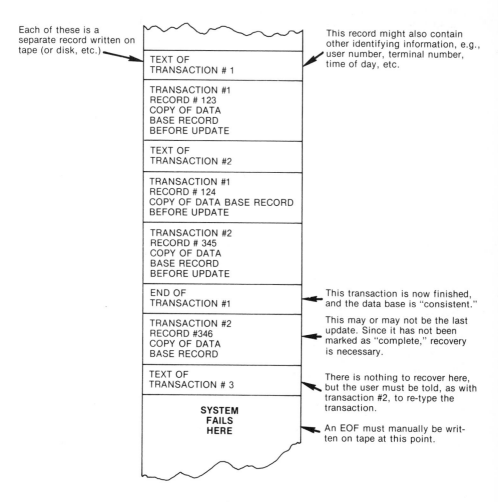

Figure 4. An Example of an Audit Trail for File Recovery

has some serious drawbacks. For one thing, it may take several hours a day to dump the data base. Also, the system designer must remember that a catastrophic failure in the middle of the day will usually cause all of the day's transactions to be lost. While time-sharing users seem willing to tolerate this limitation, an on-line business-oriented system will usually find it unacceptable. Another consideration is that repeated dumping and loading of the data base to magnetic tape may cause a slow deterioration of the data base. Sporadic undetected magnetic tape errors gradually turn it into mush.

If the system designer does decide to use a disk dump, two suggestions are in order: first, a number of backup dump tapes should be maintained to guard against situations where a damaged data base record is not noticed for several days. One of the most comprehensive procedures of this type involves keeping 7 daily dump tapes, 4 weekly dump tapes, 12 monthly tapes, and N yearly tapes (where N is the number of years the system survives). This gives the user the assurance that he will always be able to back up to a good (though possibly obsolete) version of the file or record.

The second suggestion is to build a diagnostic capability into the disk dump program. The main purpose of the diagnostic program is to ensure that the file *structure* is undamaged, that is, it should check to see that directories, indexes, bit-maps, free storage lists, and linked list structures are all intact. If time permits, the system designer might also want to check the validity and "reasonableness" of the data, though this is not commonly done. In any case, these diagnostics provide a continual day-after-day quality assurance check of the data base.

Finally, the system designer may decide to use an audit trail approach, as illustrated in Figure 4. In this case, the system keeps some combination of the following types of information:

1. The text of input messages from the terminals;
2. A copy of data base records before they are updated;
3. A copy of data base records after they are updated.

The example in Figure 4 involves keeping the first two types of information. Recovery is effected by restoring the data base records associated with transactions that had not finished being processed at the time of the failure. If only the text of input messages is maintained, then any failure will necessitate the reloading of the data base and the reprocessing of all transactions.

Measuring the reliability of one's data base is not always as straight-forward as the downtime measurements discussed earlier for operating reliability. If we distinguish between minor failures and catastrophic failures, the system design may specify a certain number of *recoverable* minor failures, a certain number of *recoverable* catastrophic failures (i.e., a failure which may take several hours or days to recover from, but which is nonetheless recoverable), a certain number of *unrecoverable* minor failures (i.e., failures in which one or two records are irrevocably lost) and a certain number of *unrecoverable* catastrophic failures.

CONCLUSIONS

In this first part, we have merely attempted to identify the different concepts of reliability that are relevant for real-time systems. Even after this brief introduction, though, it should be evident that reliability is much more difficult for real-time systems than for batch systems. If reliability really is a critical requirement for the system, the system designer and user must be willing to pay for it in terms of extra hardware, extra overhead, and extra programming.

DISCUSSION QUESTIONS

1. Identify the concepts of reliability that are relevant for a real-time system. Explain each concept briefly.
2. If reliability is truly a critical requirement for real-time system, how must the systems designer and programmer achieve such reliability?

THE CAUSES OF SYSTEMS FAILURES

Edward Yourdon

Failures in real-time systems are given special consideration in that a very intricate procedure has to be taken to re-start the job and to ensure that the data base remains intact, the proper application programs are running, and affected users are informed of the situation at hand. The procedure becomes especially complex when the real-time system's software is expected to detect predetermined errors and act upon them either by making appropriate corrections, operating the system in some "degraded configuration," or simply shutting the system.

Since the computer system occupies a major role in the recovery process, it is important to identify the various possible types of system failures to check whether the hardware or the software is capable of performing the recovery. Once identified, the system specifier may then decide on the types of system failures to ignore and to make preparations to prevent the occurrence of others.

There are eleven major sources of system failures. They are as follows:

1. *Processor errors.* These types of errors stem from the central processor's failure (particularly in new machines) to execute certain instructions properly. In such cases, the system's software is unlikely to switch to another (backup) system, communicate with the operator, or take "intelligent" steps to remedy the situation. Some operating systems, however, are designed to detect the failure and initiate proper recovery procedures.

2. *Memory parity errors.* Memory parity errors do occur, although the reliability of today's computer systems has improved to the point where processor errors are quite rare. In the simplest kind of memory error recovery, the operating system slows down the entire system, allowing the field engineer to reconfigure the memory modules. Once checked, the system can be restarted for normal processing. Another approach switches off-line the faulty memory module, making it unavailable for processing.

Theoretically, memory parity errors can be recovered without shutting the whole system. When a memory error is detected, the operating system could handle the following activities: (1) stop the execution of the application program residing in that block of memory; (2) perform the necessary recover; (3) instruct the user, if necessary, to retype his last input; and (4) reload the application program in a different memory area before restarting the run. However, this procedure cannot be implemented if memory is interleaved or if the memory parity error is either in memory module zero or in any module containing the operating system.

Source: This part is a summary of two articles by Edward Yourdon in *Modern Data,* February and March 1972, which were revisions of material originally presented in Edward Yourdon, *Design of On-Line Computer Systems* (Englewood Cliffs, N.J.: Prentice-Hall, 1972), pp. 518-32. Reprinted with permission of Prentice-Hall.

3. *Failures in the communication network.* Most of the problems that occur in the communication network are transient. Their effect on the whole system depends on the type and location of the failure. For example, failures in the terminal or in the communication line or associated modems usually only affect the operation of the terminal. On the other hand, failures in a multiplexor, in the computer itself, or in a high-speed communication line or in its associated modems may cause a total system failure. In preparing the system for operation, it is important that the system specifier check each part of the communication system to determine its reliability and impact on the system.

4. *Failures in the peripheral devices.* The electromechanical nature of most peripheral devices causes many of the transient errors in real-time systems. These errors, however, seldom cause failure of the entire system because (a) the errors are intermittent in nature and are mostly detected and corrected at their source of origin, and (b) real-time systems are somewhat independent of their peripheral devices.

5. *Operator errors.* A computer operator is often the weak link in an otherwise reliable real-time system. Most of his errors happen (a) while performing the routine for starting up the system; (b) due to improper moves in tape mounting or inadvertently feeding the wrong input data; (c) before, during, and after a system failure; and (d) resulting from incorrectly shutting down the system at the end of the day. These errors can be minimized if the operator is provided with adequate, detailed documentation about the system and when the system itself provides extensive documentation to show what the operation is doing.

6. *Program bugs.* Compared to a batch system, program bugs in a real-time system are more numerous, take longer to detect, and cause more damage. Some such bugs can throw the operator system into an endless loop while others cause an instantaneous failure of the total system.

7. *Power failures.* Power loss, though unpleasant, is easy to recognize. The more serious aspects of power failures relate to the intermittent fluctuations in voltage or frequency, especially in the summer, that are brief but enough to create problems for the computer. For systems that must run continuously, it may become necessary to provide the system with its own source of power or to use a computer with a power-on/off interrupt feature. In the latter alternative, the operating system receives an interrupt when the power falls below a specified tolerance, at which time it has twenty milliseconds to shut the system without damage to the data or the stored programs.

8. *Environmental failures.* Computer systems recently have been faced with the threat of fire, flood, drastic change in temperature and humidity, student riots, and earthquakes. Although insurance covers most of these hazards, the fact still remains that when failures occur, the total damage might be so severe as to threaten the very future of the organization using the system.

9. *Gradual erosion of the data base.* Problems in the system's data base often occur from bad records that are written without error indication or if input/output channels drop some characters or shift certain records. Communication and terminal errors may similarly result in a damaged data base. The only solution available

today is a data base diagnostic off-line program which corrects various types of errors and brings uncorrectable errors to the attention of the computer operator for follow-up.

10. *Saturation.* Failure due to saturation refers to situations where an overloaded system falls into an endless loop in attempting to handle too many transactions, too many interrupts, or too many terminals. The programmer must plan for such an eventuality if the system is to operate efficiently in a controllable state.

11. *Unexplained failures.* Several of the failures occurring in a real-time system are not properly categorized and, hence, are listed as "unexplained." Such failures are those mysterious and sudden system malfunctions with no indication or message to show whether the cause was due to hardware, software, or supportive devices. In cases where the unexplained failures are too many and continue to be unresolved, one remedy is to install a back-up processor to cope with such an eventuality. But buying such a system might prove to be a waste of money if it turns out that the unexplained failures were caused by operator error.

Each of the foregoing causes for system failures can occur in any one of the components of the system. In addition to these causes, investigation should also be made of combinations of component failures that might contribute to system failure. The larger and the more complex the real-time system, the more necessary it becomes that all possible causes of system failure be investigated to ensure a reliable and effective system functioning.

DISCUSSION QUESTIONS

1. List and briefly explain the major causes of real-time systems failures.
2. How do processor errors differ from parity errors?
3. What are some of the unexplained failures in real-time systems that the author talks about?

SELECTED REFERENCES

Books

Awad, Elias M. *Business Data Processing.* 4th ed. Englewood Cliffs, N.J.: Prentice-Hall, 1975, Chapter 12.

Brightman, Richard W. *Information Systems for Modern Management.* New York: The Macmillan Company, 1971, pp. 296-314.

Desmonde, William H. *Computers and Their Uses.* Englewood Cliffs, N.J.: Prentice-Hall, 1971, pp. 199-240.

Katzan, Harry, Jr. *Computer Organization and the System/370.* New York: Van Nostrand Reinhold Co., 1971.

Lefkovitz, David. *File Structures for On-Line Systems.* New York: Spartan Books, 1969.

Martin, James. *Teleprocessing Network Organization.* Englewood Cliffs, N.J.: Prentice-Hall, 1970.

Rothstein, Michael F. *Guide to the Design of Real-Time Systems.* New York: John Wiley & Sons, 1970.

Stimler, Saul. *Real-Time Data-Processing Systems.* New York: McGraw-Hill Book Co., 1969.

Articles

Covvey, Dominic H. "Measuring the Human Heart with a Realtime Computing System." *Data Processing,* May 1970, pp. 27-32.

"Data Networks Spread Across U.S." *Administrative Management,* February 1970, pp. 22-25.

Guertin, R. L. "Programming in a Paging Environment." *Datamation,* February 1972, p. 48ff.

Hirschfield, Richard A. "Security in On-Line Systems." *Computers and Automation,* September 1971, pp. 15ff.

"Hospital Plans Real-Time Lab System." *Computerworld,* November 10, 1971, p. 51.

"Instant Credit—Nationwide." *Data Processing,* February 1971, p. 14.

Katterjohn, John M. "Batch or Real-Time Processing?" *Automation,* August 1971, pp. 61-64.

Lecocq, Louis G. "What Is Unique in Implementing a Real Time System." *Data Management,* September 1970, pp. 47-50.

Morrissey, James V. "Three Minutes to Service an Order." *Administrative Management,* January 1971, pp. 57-59.

"On-Line System Times Powers." *Computerworld,* November 17, 1971, p. 27.

Shaw, Roy G. "Real Time Systems." *Data Management,* September 1971, pp. 18-23.

Smith, Laurence A. "Algorithm-Based, Random Access Filing System Speeds Medical Aid for 1.5 Million Patients." *Data Processing,* October 1970, pp. 29-31.

PART 7

Time Sharing and the Computer Utility

INTRODUCTION

A computer center is traditionally set up to serve one organization. Noncomputer personnel who need computer service communicate their requirements to the programmer for processing. On a batch processing system, the user is often required to wait hours, days, or sometimes weeks before he receives feedback on his program. Before processing begins, programs need to be written, recorded into appropriate input media, tested, and debugged. Even then, it may be several hours before the program is run, especially when other programs have higher priority.

Furthermore, in a single batch processing system, programs are run serially: When one program has been completed another program can begin. One job must be finished and the results printed before another job is loaded and executed, and its output is made available to the user. An inherent problem with this type of processing is turnaround time (the elapsed time between the submission of a job and the receipt of the output), or the inefficient use of the system's resources, resulting from the high-speed computer memory's wasted cycles waiting for the input data.

Thus batch processing is inadequate, especially when prompt answers are needed. This ultimately led to what is now called *time sharing,* where a modern computer, which needs so little time to execute an operating command, can switch back and forth between programs, handling a large number of jobs in a relatively short time.

Although the development of time sharing dates back to 1940, it was not until twelve years later that the first on-line inquiry system was placed into operation. Much of the groundwork was done at the Lincoln Laboratories of the Massachusetts Institute of Technology in the development of the Semi-Automatic Ground Environment (SAGE) system and its prototype, the Cape Cod System. In these early systems, time sharing was practiced in the sense that many military operations at various consoles could request and receive information from the central computing system at almost the same time. Compared to today's time-sharing systems, the systems of the 1950s were too expensive and too slow, they did not have adequate primary or recording storage capacity, and they involved extremely difficult programming.

The emergence of time-sharing systems as general-purpose, on-line facilities is primarily a development of the 1960s. Computers became cheaper and faster, programming became more efficient with high-level languages, and secondary storage began to appear, with large capacity and fast access time. A variety of service routines also have been made available for users to support activities such as sorting, merging, utility programs, information retrieval, and simulation.

In November 1961, Massachusetts Institute of Technology used an IBM 709 to give the first public demonstration of a general purpose time-sharing system, called the Compatible Time-Sharing System (CTSS), capable of handling up to eight simultaneous users. The experimental groundwork of this project paved the way for the development in 1965 of the first commercial time-sharing system by Bolt, Beranek, and Newman, an engineering consulting firm. In 1969 there were about 200 time-sharing firms with $180 million in revenue. A leading consulting firm has estimated that total revenue will exceed the $1.5 billion mark by 1975. Stiff competition has left about 22 companies in control of almost 75 percent of the market, and by 1975 it is estimated that no more than 15 companies will control about 80 percent of the market.

WHAT IS TIME SHARING?

By definition, time sharing is *an orderly organization of computers and communication equipment (hardware) and specialized programming (software) that permit concurrent utilization of the facility by several users working at remote, on-line, typewriter-like terminals.* It is user-oriented, reflecting the shared, conversational[1] nature of the system used by remote users. It reduces delays in receiving results, provides large computational and data storage capability at a substantially reduced cost, and fulfills the objective of providing many users with the services of a computer they would not otherwise be able to afford.

To process a job, the user transmits his number through the terminal. A communications controller receives and identifies the user as a legitimate paying customer and connects him to the central processor (CPU). The user now has direct access to the CPU, which processes according to a predetermined algorithm (gener-

---

[1] A survey of 1,534 questionnaire respondents was conducted by *Datamation* to find out about the heaviest users of conversational time-sharing services and the most common applications and programming languages. A summary of the findings, reported in the August 1969 issue (pp. 55-59), is as follows: (1) Industries with the highest computer usage are also the highest time-sharers. Among the heaviest users are aerospace, petroleum, electronics, and education, which have large installations and abundant programming know-how and can conveniently use time-sharing applications. (2) Except for the medical, educational, finance, and food and drink industries, the most common application within all industry groups was mathematical calculation. In the medical, food and drink, and chemical industries it was statistical problems; in finance it was investment analysis; and in education it was programming and debugging. (3) Of the time-sharing languages, 39.6 percent of the respondents use FORTRAN, 31 percent use BASIC, and the remaining respondents use COBOL, PL/1, ALGOL, and other languages including APL, CAL, JOSS, and QUIKTRAN. Regarding the average monthly expenditures for time sharing within each industry, the study reported the following: aerospace, $11,300; finance, $10,800; communications, $8,940; chemical, $8,200; petroleum, $5,500; electronics, $5,480; consulting, $5,350; education, $5,320; government, $5,200; manufacturing, $2,600; and other industries, under $2,300.

ally for one second or less). When he requests an I/O function, the user's job is swapped (transferred) from the CPU to a queue on an auxiliary storage device (disk or drum), and the user waiting at the top of the queue is moved into the CPU to begin processing. This swapping in and out of the CPU continues until all users' jobs have been processed.

The user can save an accessible copy of his program on a secondary storage device. The contents of the auxiliary device are copied each night on magnetic tape for backup purposes. Additionally, all system accounting information is written on tape, such as when the user identified himself to the system, how long he used the CPU, and when he terminated transmission.

CLASSIFICATION OF TIME-SHARING SYSTEMS

Time-sharing systems are classified according to the goal that each system attempts to accomplish or according to the design of the monitor program. Systems that are classified by goal are:

1. *Limited application systems,* in which only specialized user programs may be run. For example, the computer-assisted instruction (CAI) time-sharing system is intended mainly for administration of courses to students. Although it can do arithmetic and print output reports, it is of little utility in other applications.

2. *Limited repertoire systems,* in which generalized user programs may be run but the services they receive from the time-sharing system are limited. Time-sharing systems of this type are primarily for mathematical uses, and do not allow the search or manipulation of files stored in auxiliary storage. The user, on the other hand, gains a fast response that is economical to use and easy to learn.

3. *Unlimited (or nearly unlimited) systems,* designed to allow the programmer complete freedom in running any program he wants, or any program he could run if he were in complete control of the computer. A truly unlimited system does not exist, although IBM's TSO (time-sharing option S 360/370) approaches the concept. The system is designed to run any program that is currently running in a batch or a multiprocessing environment.

4. *Interpretative systems.* Unlike the compiled system where the user's entire program is translated into machine language before execution, the user's program in an interpretative system is left in symbolic form until a statement is ready to be executed. Interpretative systems are slower, but offer the advantage of entering and executing one command at a time. This feature is desirable when the user wants to edit results of calculations he has just entered, allowing him to change commands that otherwise would delay execution in a compiled system.

Time-sharing systems classified according to the monitor program design include the following:

1. A *commutative system* which rotates control among a set of programs, with each program taking turn according to a pre-assigned

position. This system places minimum demand on the monitor, which need only arrange for the data to be available for the user program under consideration. One further feature is that little time is lost in decision making and in evaluating priorities. Accordingly, less computer time is devoted to overhead expenses. However, this system is not well adapted to general-purpose computing, but works well in a controlled environment where the data rate and processing time are predictable.

2. *Multiprogramming systems.* They are designed to switch control only when an I/O call is issued. The core memory available to users is divided into several partitions, each large enough to contain a full program; this avoids the costs and delays of continually relocating programs. This type of multiprogramming system falls between a full time-sharing and single-program operation. Low demand is placed on the monitor and hence saves overhead expenses. When care is taken in the selection of programs to be loaded, it is possible to achieve a high degree of responsiveness, particularly if a large number of the loaded programs handle low-speed communication terminals.

3. *Multiprogramming with time-slicing.* When time-slicing or elapsed time interrupting is added to the multiprogramming features, it becomes a full time-sharing system. The time-sharing monitor takes care of addressing difficulties caused by the allocation of only a small fraction of core to any one program, and it handles all I/O operations. Queuing of requests for the use of input and output facilities is handled by the monitor. Hence the user is free to write his programs as if he were the sole client of the computer system.

4. *Virtual system.* The assumption of full memory use has led to what is called "virtual memory" in the sense that the programmer visualizes the full core memory but does not physically have the use of it. An extension of this concept leads to the complete virtual system wherein a programmer visualizes whatever system he wants and leaves it to the monitor to adjust addresses and reallocate resources to achieve the desired effect. The advantage is that the programmer can assume a very large core memory, adequate to hold all his data. He also does not have to worry about I/O operations. This is a way of having the monitor do a great deal of work that the user would otherwise have to do himself. Application of this concept can lead to highly efficient use of a computer system, even though the monitor induces some overhead costs.

ADVANTAGES AND DRAWBACKS OF TIME SHARING

Time sharing allows many users to run their programs simultaneously, improves man-machine communication, and provides better, more efficient solutions to most problems. From the user's viewpoint, a time-shared system offers the following advantages:

1. *Economy.* Time sharing operates on a subscription basis. Once a firm becomes a subscriber, it has access to the system at any time, paying only for the time used. This makes it unnecessary to commit substantial company funds to a separate computer system.

2. *Fast response.* The on-line, real-time capability of time-shared systems and their conversational mode of processing mean that users can design, change, and correct their programs with the assistance of the system and receive answers very quickly. Technical knowledge that is normally required in programming traditional computers is minimized by the use of highly simplified time-sharing languages such as BASIC. Furthermore, learning how to operate the terminal takes less than one day. An additional feature is the system's data bank, where currently stored information is readily available, providing management with relevant data at the time it is needed.

3. Other advantages includes the availability of specialists offering technical help when needed, privacy of the user's data files, and access to a multimillion-dollar system that provides most users with adequate room for most of their programs.

PRIMARY DRAWBACKS

1. *Investment cost.* From the standpoint of the firms engaged in the time-sharing industry, the initial cost is enormous. In addition to the central processor(s), equipment for secondary storage must be purchased. This is expensive, especially because a large random-access storage capacity is needed for the many users to be serviced. Terminals also must be provided for each user, and a communications network must be employed to maintain proper linkage. Add to the hardware requirements the necessary software for operating the system, and the cost of operation and maintenance could easily run into the millions. Once the system is ready for operation, enough subscribers must make commitments to enable the computer to be used to its fullest extent. Given the state of competition in the industry, it is difficult to secure enough subscribers to make a profit. This is why many of today's firms are in deep financial trouble.[2]

2. *Down time.* Several things can cause a time-shared system to stop running, among them scheduled maintenance, locating and repairing failures, adding or deleting peripheral devices, and modifications of the monitor program. When down time occurs, it leaves the users stranded until the operation is restored. Repeated frustration of this type can prompt many users to seek alternative sources—which could result in a substantial financial loss to the time-sharing firm. This problem could be minimized if two central processors (one acting as a backup system) are available. However, the total investment would be prohibitive.

3. *Speed.* The speed advantage is partly imaginary because of the size of the monitor necessary to operate such a large system. In one article it was estimated that "in a system providing 110 consoles divided among

---

[2] A special report in the July 1971 issue of *Time-Sharing Today* indicated that only 33 of the 140 time-sharing companies studied were profitable. Their success is attributed to (1) emphasis on customer service, (2) treating remote computing as a serious business, (3) experience in the field for two years or more, (4) high percentage of repetitive, production-like jobs, and (5) good reputation and respect in the time-sharing market. Companies that jumped on the time-sharing bandwagon for speculation or without advance planning have operated their systems at about 60 percent computer utilization rate, incurring substantial financial losses.

220 programmers, each using his station four hours a day, the efficiency is reduced to about 27 percent. In an eight hour period, 130 useful minutes of computing could be obtained. Divided by the number of programmers using the system, each programmer would wind up with thirty-six seconds of useful computing time during the entire eight hour shift."[3]

4. *Security.* Many users are extremely concerned about the possibility of somebody else, especially competitors, gaining access to their files. The current use of passwords to each time-sharing user does not seem to provide adequate security, particularly in view of the likely leakage of such passwords by the employees of the time-sharing service bureau. In many cases, however, the security problems are really no worse than the ones which the businessman has in his current mode of operation. It is perhaps the idea of storing one's personal files on a remotely located system that accentuates the problem. The ultimate solution is government regulation. Steps have already been taken by the Federal Communications Commission (FCC) to alleviate the situation.

5. *Processing cost.* Time sharing cannot be used efficiently for all business projects. The rise in transmission cost in proportion to speed puts severe limitations on the volume of input/output. For small users, cost of time sharing can also be substantial. It is probably safe to expect the user to spend between $75 and $100 per month for a basic teletypewriter terminal or around $200 per month for a CRT unit. To this must be added his communication costs and the cost of computer time. The advent and low cost of minicomputer systems gives the user a better choice in most cases.

TIME-SHARING SERVICES

Some 150 companies offer time-sharing service in the areas of remote-batch entry, conversational problem solving, and data base management. With the many services available, a prospective user must consider the system requirements, the classes of problems that will be run, and the costs associated with the service under consideration. Furthermore, he should evaluate (1) system reliability, especially with regard to the system's expected down time, its backup system, and the measures used in dealing with lost programs or data; (2) level of difficulty of the terminal and the programming languages used; (3) response time; (4) level of sophistication of the system's file security measures; and (5) the system's time schedule, which can range from five 8-hour days to seven 24-hour days each week.

Of the time-sharing services available, General Electric is the largest, serving 225 cities from a base in Cleveland, Ohio. Support services cover a wide variety of teletypewriters, plotters, and CRT units. Although it has a limited scale remote batch service, it offers a large number of canned programs for business and scientific applications. Each user can determine his own needs, capacity, and language with few restrictions. He can have a large or small capacity data bank, simple or complex programs, and so on. Among the other leading services are

[3] Marvin Emerson, "The 'Small' Computer Versus Time-Shared Systems," *Computers and Automation*, September 1965.

Com-Share, Inc., Control Data, Tymshare, Inc., National Service Bureau Corporation, University Computing Corporation, and Computer Science.

THE COMPUTER UTILITY

Given the general problems affecting the time-sharing industry, and particularly the tremendous amount of idle computer time, there is much talk of forming a computer utility. Although the time-sharing industry is often labeled falsely as such, a true utility would be the exclusive operator of a major, specialized, nationwide network; and, because of this monopolistic position, its rates would be regulated by the government, which would also monitor the quality of the service offered the public.

A massive central computer utility could offer computer power more efficiently and more economically than hundreds of smaller time-sharing systems. To the user it would mean lower operating costs, and he would pay only for the computer power used. The biggest obstacle to making such a network operational is the currently inadequate communications network. For a computer utility to develop, a new form of data-oriented transmission system must be created. Until this and other problems are worked out, and until the computing public begins to recognize the need and push for the development of a nationwide public computer utility, the very implementation of this concept will remain in question.

The readings section covers two articles. Donovan's article on time-sharing techniques discusses commercial services, their operation, capabilities, and costs. Gildenberg's, "The Future of Time-Sharing," summarizes the success factors in time-sharing services, with a closer look at the trends in the field.

TIME-SHARING TECHNIQUES

Stephen F. Donovan

In the early 1960's, time-sharing was found only in experimental projects such as those at MIT, RAND and SDC. The year 1964 marked the delivery of the first commercial time-sharing system sold, a PDP-6 to Brookhaven National Laboratory. The late 1960's produced an explosion of commercial time-sharing service companies; and in the last two years, we have seen many of those companies disappear. Today, we will discuss time-sharing as it appears in the current marketplace.

We will concentrate primarily on commercial services; how they work, capabilities available to the user, and some representative costs.

Source: Reprinted, with permission, from *Data Management,* September 1971, pp. 80-83, published by the Data Processing Management Association, Park Ridge, Illinois.

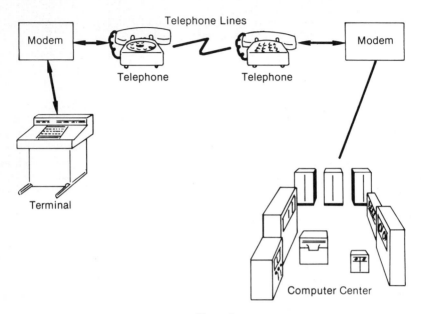

Telephone Lines

Modem — Telephone — Telephone — Modem

Telephone   Telephone

Terminal

Computer Center

Figure 1

First, let's look at the parts of a commercial time-sharing service from a new user's viewpoint. The user interfaces with a commercial time-sharing system as indicated in Figure 1. To utilize the system, he:

1. Places a phone call to the computer just as he would to a friend.
2. Identifies himself to the computer via his terminal.
3. Begins his processing.

TYPE OF EQUIPMENT

If he visits the center in person, he generally will see the types of equipment indicated in Figure 2.

Let's look at these devices as they interact with the user, who is now entering the system.

The communications controller is the first device to meet the user. It polls the telephone lines, connects the user to the CPU, and in some systems, identifies the user as a legitimate paying customer.

The user now gains control of the CPU and begins his processing according to a predetermined (in most systems) algorithm. For our purposes, let's allow the user to control the CPU for one second or until he requests an I/O function be performed. When any one of the preceding events occurs, our user is transferred (swapped) from the CPU to a queue on an auxiliary memory device (disk or drum), and the user waiting at the top of the queue is swapped into the CPU to begin processing.

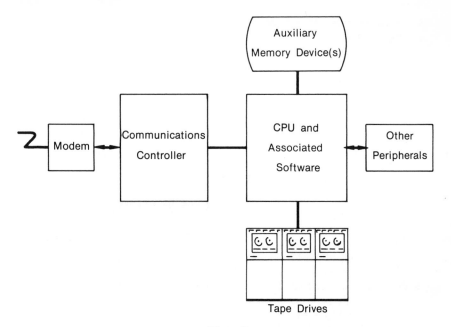

Figure 2

Assume our user is writing a new program. He will be swapped in and out of the CPU until he is satisfied with his efforts and disconnects from the system. During the same overall time period, many other users will be going through the same swapping process. The software to keep track of all this activity is called an operating system (or executive, monitor, supervisor, ad infinitum).

SPEED DIFFERENTIAL

Because of the speed differential between the high speed of the computer and the slow speed of the human/terminal combination, each of the different users will receive the impression he has sole use of the computer. Once our user has finished writing, and perhaps executing, his program, he can save an immediately accessible copy of the program on the auxiliary storage device. Each night, the contents of the auxiliary device will be copied onto magnetic tape for backup purposes. Additionally, all system accounting information will be written onto magnetic tape, such as when our user identified himself to the system, how long he used the CPU, when he hung up the telephone, etc.

Now that we have a basic idea of how the user interfaces with a time-sharing system and the different components involved at both the user's location and the computer center, let us look at what the user can do. The services available today fall into four general categories:

1. A single language service.
2. A multiple language service.

3. A virtual computer service.
4. An applications service.

A single language service allows the user to write and execute programs in one language only, normally BASIC (Beginners Allpurpose Symbolic Instruction Code). Examples of such systems are the BASIC language system implemented on the PDP-11 and the H-P2116. These systems are very easy to use, but they are limited to those who can fulfill their requirements by writing and executing BASIC programs.

In contrast, multiple language systems, such as Honeywell's 1248 system, allow the user to write BASIC, Cobol, Fortran and even assembly language programs. These systems, while offering more languages, generally are less interactive than the single language systems. One reason for this is the different method of compilation used by these two types of services. Single language systems often will compile the user's program incrementally on a line-by-line basis. The user cannot enter Line Two of his program until Line One is syntactically correct. He often will "feel" the computer is helping him write his program. In the multiple language system, the program is not compiled until the user requests compilation—normally after the program is completely written. For example:

```
SINGLE LANGUAGE SYSTEM—
      COMPILED INCREMENTALLY
NEW OR OLD
? NEW CR
BEGIN
10 LET X = 2 CR
20 LET Y3 CR
..... ARGUMENT ERROR
20 LET Y = 3 CR
30 LET X = X↑Y CR
40 PRINT "X=" X CR
50 END CR
CR
RUN
X = 8

MULTIPLE LANGUAGE SYSTEM—
      COMPILING UPON REQUEST
SYSTEM
? BASIC CR
NEW OR OLD
NEW CR
BEGIN
10 LET X = 2 CR
20 LET Y3 CR
30 LET X = X↑Y CR
40 PRINT "X=" X CR
50 END CR
CR
..... LINE 20 ARGUMENT ERROR
```

```
? PATCH CR
20 LET Y = 3 CR
CR
RUN
X = 8
```

The third type of service is the "virtual computer." The virtual computer provides the user with all the capabilities of a specific machine; for example, the TSS-8 time-sharing system provides each user with a virtual 4K PDP-8. The user can write and execute any program he could write for a dedicated 4K PDP-8 computer, including machine language programs, and he can use all system peripherals at the remote computer center such as high speed paper tape, DECTAPE, disk, etc., as well as those at his terminal. On the PDP-10 system, the user can even perform real-time servicing of laboratory instruments in a time-sharing environment.

The other service commonly available is the applications service. It may be used upon any of the other three services, and all the others offer some degree of applications service. An applications service offers the user numerous application-oriented programs for his use. The best example of such a capability is the General Electric time-sharing service. GE has catalogs of pre-written applications programs and routines. The user need do no programming. All he need do is access the program he needs, input his data in the prescribed format, execute the program, and read the results. Such a service is especially attractive to the small firm which needs some computer assistance but cannot afford either the computer or a programmer.

NEEDS OF THE USER

As one can plainly see, the advantages and disadvantages of any of these services is directly related to the requirements of the user, but whatever the user's requirements, there is a system to fill them.

The most common charges associated with these services are for terminal connect time (TCT), central processor usage (CPU) time, and on-line storage.

Terminal connect time charges consist of the time logged onto the system (from the time you identify yourself when accessing the service until the time you sign off) and normally is assessed on an hourly basis.

CPU time is a charge for that portion of your terminal connect time in which your program has control of the CPU. The CPU charge normally is assessed in terms of seconds. (Today, many systems charge Computer Resource Unit (CRU) charges instead of straight CPU charges. The CRU charge is based upon an algorithm reflecting program size, CPU time, swap time, etc. For our purposes, we will speak in terms of the CPU charge, which is easier to comprehend.)

A storage charge is the charge for keeping copies of those programs the user wishes to have saved on-line in an auxiliary memory device for future use. The total hourly cost to the user is normally a combination of the CPU and TCT charges, but commercial services do offer a variety of plans for charging the user, such as charging only for CPU time or TCT time or a flat monthly rate.

CHARGING METHODS

In selecting the proper service, the user also should try to obtain the best charging method to fit his requirements. For example, a school may prefer to be charged only for CPU time as a student normally will accumulate a large amount of TCT time but very little CPU time. A scientist or engineer using an applications service might prefer to pay only for TCT.

In the examples of hourly costing listed below, a 60-to-1 ratio (low in most cases, but a nice ratio to calculate) is used between TCT and CPU charges.

	TCT	*CPU*	*Total*
System 1	$ 4/ hour		$ 4.00
System 2	6/ hour	$.025/ second	7.50
System 3	11/ hour	.15/ second	20.00

The total monthly cost to the user is a combination of the above, plus terminal rental, telephone charges and storage charges.

For those interested in the cost of dedicated time-sharing systems, some examples are:

TSS-8 16-user system (virtual computer type): $80,000

PDP-11 RSTS 16-user system (single language type): $51,000

PDP-10 127-user system (virtual computer type): $1 million plus

It would appear from the preceding that the firm requiring time-sharing support, whether through an in-house computer or a commercial service, has a host of choices in both capability and cost. Other factors the user must consider are:

Terminals. The most common terminal is the Teletype (TTY) model 33. The TTY is noisy and slow, chunking along at 10 characters per second, but virtually every time-sharing service is designed to accept it as a terminal. Other terminals may not be as flexible in interfacing with various systems, even those claiming to be TTY compatible. If you require a more sophisticated terminal, you will want to test it in operation with the service of your choice before signing any contracts, particularly if you are buying the terminals instead of renting them. A unique terminal may bind one to a specific service.

I/O capability. What types of peripherals may appear as part of a terminal to the computer—CRT's, line printers, tape drives, punched paper tape, etc.? At what speeds may terminals operate? What code is used for transmission?

Communications. What type of modem is required? Do you want portability through acoustic coupling, perhaps reducing reliability; or do you want reliability through use of a hardwired data set? Is half- or full-duplex used for transmissions?

If your terminal is a long distance from the computer center, who pays the telephone line charges—you or the service?

Time-sharing techniques are available today to do practically anything a user wishes to do. The advantages and disadvantages of the different systems can only be discussed in terms of a particular user's requirements and the cost of such systems also must be considered.

DISCUSSION QUESTIONS

1. How does Donovan explain a time-sharing system?
2. What types of time-sharing services are available? Explain each briefly.
3. What are the alternative charging methods in time-sharing systems? Is there one best method? Explain.

THE FUTURE OF TIME-SHARING:
AN INDUSTRY EVALUATION

Robert F. Gildenberg

During the past few years, we have seen the arrival and departure of numerous time-sharing companies. With this selection process, the evaluation of the time-sharing market has gone from unfounded optimism to sober realism. In short, the time-sharing industry has done what any new industry does—matures.

SUCCESS FACTORS

Several key factors have surfaced which separate successful time-sharing companies from unsuccessful ones. First, as in any business, sufficient financial capital is required. Having this not only permits the day-to-day operations of the concern, but also ensures the second key success factor—product development.

The field of data processing is too dynamic to have a company attempting to sell yesterday's product in today's marketplace. Only those companies which have a devoted, continuous, and successful development program will be able to grow and become leaders in time-sharing over the next decade. But even the best programs and features are completely meaningless if a third factor is not present—system reliability.

Source: *Modern Data*, November 1971, pp. 38-39.

Reliability is one area in which time-sharing companies, in general, have slowly been making advances. This increased reliability is due primarily not to any technological breakthrough, but rather to a more realistic approach to the problems of the industry. In time-sharing, reliability means backup. This backup concerns not only the computer hardware, but also the software. In addition, since time-sharing relies so completely upon communications, reliability in many cases, means backup telephone lines. Microwave will help in the transmission of data over long distances, but it should not be forgotten that the telephone line will still be the final step in getting information to the user.

A fourth factor is customer support. Since many of the customers are relatively new to data processing, the responsibility of the time-sharing support staff is even greater than that of a computer mainframe manufacturer. It is the support staff's responsibility to educate its customers in evaluating what data processing can, and cannot, give them. A strong support staff is invaluable to a successful time-sharing concern.

Finally, cost is an important factor in determining the success of a company. This is not to imply, however, that cost necessarily refers to the lowest cost. It was only during last year that time-sharing companies have come to realize that the only way in which they are going to continue to grow, or just to remain in existence, is by properly evaluating not only their marketplace, but also the expense of doing business. During this time a more realistic pricing policy has been introduced by many time-sharing companies, which promises to give them a stronger financial base for continued development and operational growth.

TRENDS

Two groups of companies seem to be emerging in the time-sharing field. First, there are those companies which are concentrating on capturing basically large customers, and maintaining them with a national, or even international, sales and service force. A second group of companies are gearing their product and pricing strategy to secure greater numbers of smaller volume customers. This latter group anticipates that the total volume of these smaller customers will provide them with a sufficient financial base for operations. It will still require two or three years to fully evaluate the wisdom of either of these marketing strategies. However, it would not be unforeseeable to find that both strategies have proven successful.

Another major difference between time-sharing companies appears in the number of products which are offered. Some companies have chosen to market as many applications and packages as possible. Other companies are specializing in one or two packages. By limiting their attention to fewer products, these companies feel they will be better able to concentrate their research and development efforts more effectively. Their goal is to provide the best particular package or service that is offered in their field of specialization. As users begin to feel more confident in time-sharing, more of them will become selective, using the products of two or more vendors to take advantage of these more advanced or specialized features.

Another development taking place is the rapid expansion of the remote batch time-sharing field. Remote batch time-sharing permits user groups within a company to process selected data processing jobs by themselves, freeing the large centralized computer complex for larger and more involved work. Since many reports are nothing but listings with cumulative totals, the ability of a user group to control and modify these programs promises to bring each department increased data processing flexibility, with decreased costs.

In conjunction with the development of remote batch time-sharing, the development of very high level languages seems to be a logical growth step. Through the use of these languages, lower level management and supervisory personnel will be able to write and test computer programs on-line with a minimum amount of training and effort, and without the services of a professional programmer. The development of these languages will also afford the user the capability of making rapid modification of existing programs to generate additional reports in different formats.

One of the main reasons for the slow development of not only batch but also all other time-sharing areas is the problem of getting reliable, versatile, and inexpensive terminals. In this field, as in time-sharing itself, we have seen numerous companies come and go. As in time-sharing, a development and maturation process of this industry is taking place.

The introduction of the fourth generation of computers will also help time-sharing companies by increasing their thruput capability, while permitting them to keep their computer hardware expenses within bounds. Also, the development of more reliable OEM equipment has made it possible for time-sharing companies to take advantage of faster peripheral equipment, while retaining the mainframe of one of the major computer manufacturers.

DISCUSSION QUESTIONS

1. Explain briefly the key factors that contribute to successful time-sharing operation.

2. The author talks about two groups of companies emerging in the time-sharing field. What are they? Do you agree with his views? Explain.

SELECTED REFERENCES

Books

Awad, Elias M. *Business Data Processing.* 4th ed. Englewood Cliffs, N.J.: Prentice-Hall, 1975, Chapter 12.

Barnett, C. C., Jr., and Associates. *The Future of the Computer Utility.* New York: American Management Association, 1967, pp. 11-48.

Bauer, Walter. "The Economics of On-Line Systems," in *On-Line Computing.* New York: McGraw-Hill Book Co., 1967.

Brightman, Richard W. *Information Systems for Modern Management.* New York: The Macmillan Company, 1971, pp. 277-314.

Clark, Frank J. *Information Processing.* Pacific Palasades, Calif.: Goodyear Publishing Company, 1970.

Command System Reference Manual. Bethesda, Maryland: General Electric Information Service Department, November 1967.

IBM System 3/Model 6 Operators Guide. Rochester, Minn.: IBM Programming Publications, February 1971.

Schwartz, Jules I. "Analyzing Time-Sharing Systems," in *Electronic Handling of Information: Testing and Evaluation.* Washington, D.C.: Thompson Book Company, 1967, Chapter 23.

Watson, Richard W. *Timesharing System Design Concepts.* New York: McGraw-Hill Book Co., 1970, pp. 3-9, 78-79, 111-120.

Articles

Allen, Brandt R. "Computer Time-Sharing." *Management Accounting,* January 1969, pp. 36ff.

Bairstow, Jeffrey N. "Virtual Machines." *Computer Decisions,* January 1970, pp. 13-16.

Briggs, Peter L. "Time-Sharing Can Be a Company Tool or Toy." *Computer World,* March 25, 1970, p. 17.

Bryan, Dr. Glenn L. "Student-to-Student Interaction in Computer Time-Sharing Systems." *Computers and Automation,* March 1970, pp. 18-23.

Bueschel, R. T. "The Dual Role of Timesharing in Education." *Modern Data,* March 1970, pp. 78-80.

"Build Your Own Private Worldwide Timesharing Network." *The Time-Sharing Leader,* January 1972, GE Information Services.

Daly, Diana. "How to Choose a Time-Sharing Service." *Computer Decision,* March 1970, pp. 13-17.

Feeney, Dr. George. "A Three-Stage Theory of Evolution for the Sharing of Computer Power." *Data Processing Digest,* February 1972, pp. 26-27.

Haidinger, Timothy P. "Computer Timesharing: A Primer for the Financial Executive." *Financial Executive,* February 1970, pp. 26-35.

Hutton, Edwin W. "A CPA's Evaluation of the Business Computer Utility." *The Journal of Accountancy,* March 1971, pp. 51-56.

Levy, Joseph. "The Interactive Time Sharing Market." *Computers and Automation,* January 1971, p. 10ff.

"Market Booming, Competition Heats Up." *Computerworld,* May 19, 1971, p. 51.

O'Rourke, Thomas J. "The Many New Uses of Time Sharing." *Computers and Automation,* October 1967, pp. 48-50.

"Over 100 Minicomputers to Help Operate Tymshare's Computer-Access Network." *Data Processing Digest,* July 1971, pp. 17-18.

Schilling, Douglas. "Time-Sharing/Batch Processing." *Data Processing,* May-June 1970, pp. 230-231.

Smith, D. W. "Efficient Credit Management with Timesharing." *Financial Executive,* March 1971, pp. 26-30.

Stewart, Michael. "Will Time-Sharing Help You?" *Management Review,* June 1970, pp. 37-41.

Summers, Alan. "The Captive Computer Utility." *Computer Decisions,* January 1974, pp. 23-28.

"3 Billion of Idle Computer Time in U.S., Time Brokers' Hegan Tells Financial Heads." *Computerworld,* May 19, 1971, p. 8.

Trifari, John C. "Evaluating the National Time Sharing Services." *Computer Decisions,* November 1971, pp. 28-32.

Wilkinson, Bryan. "A Six-Step Approach to: Choosing a Time-Sharing Service." *Data Management,* December 1968, pp. 20-23.

Wolfe, Ramon E. "Multiple Mini Computers Go to Work for Large Time Sharing Applications." *Data Processing Magazine,* September 1970, pp. 33-37.

PART 8

Management Information System and the Data Base Concept

During the past decade, much work has been done to utilize the computer in helping management make more effective decisions. The management information system (MIS) is one such computer-oriented development by which the organization tells just how well it is doing.

There are various stages of MIS. One stage occurs when management inquires about the organization's performance; the answers that can be given are based on the data already created by the company's data processing system. The second stage involves projection of selected business situations from the data already on file. It takes into consideration the business organization and its immediate competitors in analyzing the external factors about the firm's ability to maintain an ongoing, healthy level of operations. The third stage is a comprehensive system which takes into consideration the entire industry and its economy. Although existing MIS have elements of one or more of these stages, the third stage is only theoretically feasible. No workable system has been devised which takes all these factors into account.

A most sophisticated, report-generator management information system in operation today is IBM's Internal Tele-Processing System (ITPS). This system is composed of 482 data terminals feeding information by leased lines through two IBM 360/50 worldwide systems located at IBM headquarters. Operating this system costs hundreds of thousands of dollars per year; its unique contribution is its ability to transmit the majority of the messages it receives to their destinations in less than ten minutes. It keeps current information on IBM's billions of dollars of sales, work backlogs, and inventory status on a daily basis, not merely weekly or monthly. This means that executives, especially the divisional operating managers, can tap management information from the source (company headquarters) directly and in a fraction of the time it takes under other systems.

An example of the second, more encompassing stage of MIS (analyzing trends and simulating the firm's performance in competitive situations) is Pillsbury's marketing information system. The system uses models to make short- and long-term projections based on such information as competitors' activities and their market share, advertising and promotional variations, and other special-purpose variables that determine the strategy of both the firm in question and its competitors. While predictions of one's competitors' activities might not be altogether accurate, any reasonably close approximation should be helpful for taking appropriate measures to compete effectively.

Although trend analysis and simulation are MIS elements, their use has only recently been implemented. The implications are clear, however: Once an organization has developed a report-generator type of management information system, the next logical stage is to extend the system so as to handle trend analysis and simulation of various types and levels of operating conditions. How well such a system is likely to develop and serve management depends to a large extent on the cooperation and understanding of management and everyone else concerned. Management must be willing to invest time, effort, and company funds in the system, especially during the development of a model and simulation.

An existing MIS can be expanded into a third stage, where the interests of the firm's executives go beyond the activities and expected behavior of the immediate competitors. At this macro level, an all-encompassing understanding of the economy and the various national indicators which affect the organization's thinking and operation is at issue. Thus a modeling system which projects such factors, especially selected industries within the economy, might be used as inputs to the existing MIS.

General Electric has developed its Management Analysis and Projection (MAP) information system, containing information from sources such as the Census Bureau, Standard & Poor's Compustat, the Federal Trade Commission, and other reliable sources. Now available for lease, the system offers a tremendous amount of statistics related to the national economy, industrial activity, and the financial status of hundreds of manufacturing firms, including stock price, working capital, income per share, cost of plant investment, and so on. Furthermore, MAP is designed to produce projections by performing moving averages, regression analysis, factor analysis, and regression factors, among others. Access to the whole system averages just under $1,000 per month.

The implication of the foregoing discussion is that there is no ready, quick method of developing a management information system that produces reliable results. Data has to be captured at its source, and models developed from the ground up are designed in such a way as to be responsive to the needs of the managers it is to serve. The key is to start at the bottom, and it is at this level that MIS encounters the most resistance.

Although each MIS is unique, they should all have the following characteristics: (1) simplicity and brevity of output, (2) emphasis on results and goals rather than methods and processes, (3) suppression of trivial and redundant data, and (4) integration with the organization's information flow at the operation level.

A humorous summary of the evolutionary stages which many organizations go through in developing an MIS is presented in *Computer Decisions,* as follows:

> Years ago, executives at my company were grateful if the payroll got out on time and all I gave them was a weekly tally. And they were delighted when I computerized the billing files. . .
>
> Then they started asking me to computerize lots of clerical tasks, including inventory and personnel records. . .

Pretty soon operating managers were demanding computerized monthly reports of shipments and weekly reports of district sales. . .

Then they started insisting on daily production schedules based on orders, current inventory and shipments. . .

Then corporate marketing people began demanding models of the company's operations so they could play "what if" games. Forty marketing guys, and they have to sit around playing games while a competitor jumps in with a new product. . .

So I hired the best model-builder I could find, stuffed data into the computer on cards, paper tapes, disks and magnetic tapes. I gave them enough "what if" games to keep 'em playing with their terminals 'till I retire. . .

Then the president calls to tell me he's been reading about this MIS jazz. So could I simulate the entire company, and give him a terminal with retrieval capability, "what if" for corporate strategy, trend projections as well as analysis of the competition?

I think I'm getting close, but yesterday the computer came up with a very interesting "what if" trend projection based on live data played off against corporate strategy. . .

The computer says that internal EDP costs will exceed the company's gross sales by 1974. Maybe the president should consider getting into the data processing business?[1]

The Behavioral Side of MIS

To enjoy the technical benefits of management information systems it is often necessary to solve the dysfunctional side-effects stemming from behavioral problems—in short, people problems. Reactions to the installation of MIS may range from failure to use the output to outright sabotage. Dysfunctional behavior such as aggression or avoidance may appear in operating personnel, operating management, and top management. Operating management, the group that should enjoy most of the system benefits, goes further than any other group in its resistance.

People tend to resist the new in favor of the old. Since unfavorable behavioral consequences often accompany any significant organizational change, it should come as no surprise when a new management information system encounters resistance. In order to minimize or prevent these negative consequences, management must not only recognize that introduction of an information system is likely to trigger trouble among its personnel, but must also have some knowledge of the particular factors that underlie this behavior. The attitude of top management should be one of full support for the system. There should also be open lines of communication between different levels of management, between management and employees, and between line and staff. The individual must retain his sense of dignity and importance as a human being along with the feeling that he is making a worthy contribution to the organization.

There is no single panacea for behavioral ills. Each situation must be analyzed

[1] "A Funny Thing Happened on My Way to MIS," *Computer Decisions,* March 1971, p. 17.

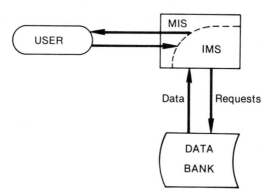

Figure 1. The MIS–IMS Interface

carefully to determine the optimal procedures for preventing or curing dysfunctional behavioral consequences surrounding the modification or installation of a system.

The dysfunctional behavior that is most likely to occur as a result of a system installation or modification varies with the type of system and the organizational level affected. The backgrounds of both the organization and the individuals interacting with the system are also important. The systems analyst must give careful consideration to these factors in solving the people problems and achieving a successful installation.

MIS Versus IMS

Before discussing an organization's data base and its relationship to MIS, a distinction should be made between a management information system (MIS) and an information management system (IMS). IMS is concerned with the manipulation of data. It neither converts the data nor generates from it meaningful information with which managers can plan and operate their areas of business responsibility. The MIS, on the other hand, is concerned with providing management with information relevant to the decision-making process. MIS uses IMS as a tool available for management use. Management requests certain information for decision making. MIS directs IMS to produce the information. IMS retrieves information from the data base and transmits it to the user. Figure 1 illustrates this interface.

THE DATA BASE CONCEPT

There are probably more buzz words in data processing than in any other field. One such buzz word that is very much in vogue is *data base*. Data base is used by itself or with other words, as in corporate data base, data base management, data base management system, common data base, data base file management, data base language.

In its Production Information and Control System (PICS) Manual, IBM defines data base as "all the operational record information needed to handle a company's business." Ward[2] asserts that data base is more an extension of old EDP techniques than a radical new method. Other definitions include:

1. A set of common data definitions and means of enforcing the use of these definitions within the organization.
2. A technique involving a common access to data files by a number of application programs.
3. Singly, a collection of files.
4. An extensive and comprehensive set of libraries of data.[3]

A more representative definition views data base as a nonredundant collection of interrelated data items processable through application programs. *Nonredundant data items* are bits of information, common to many data records, that are stored only once and limited to the records to which they belong. The phrase *interrelated data items* implies that all the records in a data base should be related in some way.

Historically, data handling evolved from the manual to the unit record, batch system, direct access technology, and data-gathering technology. Along with these changes, there have also been trends related to the rapidly increasing "people" costs and the demand for responsiveness. The data base concept appears to be a logical answer to reducing overall costs because it is expected to offer the following advantages:

1. Reduces computer process time.
2. Reduces the number of programs to be written.
3. Centralizes files for all applications.
4. Eliminates duplication of space and effort.
5. Provides a single information source for complete, accurate data processing and retrieval.

Most of the foregoing advantages are based on the notion that data are stored only once in the system and are easily accessible when needed. The result is extensive two-way communication between the various existing files.

A data base forms the crux of a management information system and is viewed as the first basic stage of an MIS structure. A complete management data base is designed to (1) accept data from internal and external sources, (2) edit the data for validity and reliability and maintain it in a data center, and (3) allow the user direct access to his own data base without affecting the integrity and functioning of other data files. Thus the design phase should ascertain that the data base is complete, accurate, unified, accessible, timely, and satisfactory for future requirements.

A viable data base must offer further separation of file and data organization. In the future it should be possible to define a file in terms of the information required by the application without regard to the organization of the data base.

[2] Dennis S. Ward, "Data Base Technology," *Computer Services Journal,* November-December 1970, pp. 15-21.

[3] Funk & Wagnalls *Dictionary of Data Processing Terms,* Harold A. Rodgers, ed. (New York: Funk & Wagnalls, 1970).

Defining a file in terms of the required information implies a frame of reference composed of objects and relationships in the real world as opposed to data objects in storage. Limited only by what information is available from the data base, it should be possible to specify a file in terms of a set of objects and the effects expected about these objects.

Data Base Structure and Maintenance

An ideal choice of a data base is one which minimizes cost while satisfying user and processing constraints. This is done by establishing trade-offs between possible file structures, maintenance requirements, and retrieval requests within a set of hardware constraints. Stored information must have some sort of structuring if it is to contribute to the efficiency of a systems operation. The particular structure is determined by the number of times the information will be accessed, by how specific the informational needs are, and by the need of other systems regarding a given subject.

The principal determination in the structure of a data base is the file organization. Random and sequential access are two major techniques in file organization. These techniques are dependent on the storage devices available or, if both random and sequential devices are available, on suitability to the established parameters of the file structure. Random access is newer, using disk or drum storage access records at any point in the file without searching the whole file. Sequential accessing is a process of accessing records in physical rather than logical order. Each of these techniques provides a set of options to make the structure as flexible as possible.

Sequential accessing is actually a subset of random accessing. Of the four ways to organize information in the data base, all are applicable to random processing, whereas only the first two are applicable to sequential access processing:

1. Sequential. The logical and physical organization are both sequential. The file is structured by predetermined sequence.
2. Indexed sequential. An index is recorded giving addresses of particular records identified by a key. The file is structured sequentially within logical groupings identified by the key.
3. Chained. Records are stored randomly but are logically connected by keeping the address of the last logical record and the next logical record stored within the currently accessed record.
4. Branch structured. Related records are stored physically in sequential subfiles, with the subfiles logically connected by chaining.

Other file organizations can be developed, but they all stem from these four.

In developing a data base structure, an attempt should be made to keep duplicate information out of the file. Duplicate information causes duplicate maintenance or, worse, updating of one record and not the other, causing disagreement between records. Software designed to minimize duplication and maximize the use of the storage space is limited. Most hardware manufacturers and many software producers are working on data base software, but nothing really new and unique has been developed.

A data base must allow for rapid updating, it must have areas for expansion, and in some cases it must clean up contaminated data and guard against its recurrence. In planning a data base as an ongoing system, the major determination is *maintaining* it to support the user's demand. In some systems (such as scheduling a fabrication shop), updating is needed almost instantly. In contrast, a personnel skills inventory may need updating only once every three months. A data base system must be designed to handle both types of requirements. Information storage allotted in the base must be flexible in order to support any record of data that may have to expand over time. By the same token, when it becomes necessary to delete certain records from the data base, provisions must be made to avoid wasted storage areas. Flexibility is the key to efficient expansion and reutilization of any record in the data base.

Contamination of the data base is a key issue in systems dealing with a large volume of data. The original information is probably the most important part of the base since any future information will be added to that and in turn will become contaminated.

New incoming data must be of high quality to ensure continuing accuracy within the system. One major step in ensuring good information is to convince the people who supply input of the importance of accuracy. Another step is to thoroughly test updating software before implementing the system. Even after both steps have been taken, a certain degree of error will creep into the system. Therefore, it is essential to identify the amount of error and make adjustments for it. One method is to purge the entire file at periodic intervals to keep the accumulated error within an acceptable level. Since this is very difficult to do in a large integrated data base, a statistical adjustment can be made or, in some cases, check procedures can be used. For example, inventory adjustments can be made by cycle-counting physical quantities and comparing them to file balances. Reconciliation can be made on the basis of some statistical parameters. In this particular example, an extended percentage of error for the entire file can be determined at the same time that adjustments are being made.

The entire idea of maintenance in a data base hinges on the concepts of updating, flexibility, and error control. The thought and planning given to these concepts are essential parts of developing a data base.

Data Base Retrieval

Determining user demand on a data base is somewhat analogous to deciding whether a city needs a two-lane street or an expressway for efficient support of the traffic flow between two points. Both a city and a data base have a "maximum traffic" and a "travel time" parameter. The parameters are interdependent.

In a data base the number of times that a file must be accessed (the amount of traffic) is totally user-controlled. If the system is designed to provide information for making routine decisions, the information must be provided quite often. For example, the system might process several hundred requests for information regarding next priority on the machines in a fabrication shop or a single request for the cost of complying with a safety law. If each type is possible, the data base must cover both.

Travel time, as a data base parameter, is concerned with the time elapsed between submitting a request to the system and receiving the information generated to satisfy the request. User needs may vary significantly depending on the use of the information. For example, a fabrication scheduler might need instantaneous information as to the next priority on a specific machine. Conversely, a user requesting the cost of complying with a safety law might not need the information for a week. Again, the system must support both requests, if applicable.

In a data base, there is a direct relationship between traffic and travel time. As the traffic increases, so does the travel time. Therefore, in planning, it is necessary to give much thought to performance in heavy traffic periods and to determine future traffic increase. The base must be sufficiently large and sophisticated to process new types of requests and handle overall traffic increases. Otherwise, a new base would have to be designed to support increased activity.

The Cost Variable

Every organization is faced with the problem of minimizing costs associated with a data base. Those costs are first calculated in units of time and then extended by some dollar rate. Some of the major variables are access time, transfer rate, number of accesses per request, and storage cost per character. Cost is not the only restriction on these variables. User constraints are also imposed. Therefore, the minimum cost is the lowest possible cost needed to satisfy these constraints.

The user requirements that control cost are maintenance and retrieval. Maintenance is typically a determination of the number of transactions that must be carried out per unit of time and the frequency of performing an update. Retrieval is concerned with the output that must be generated and the turnaround time needed. Output can be measured in terms of accesses per unit of time or, on less sophisticated equipment, as lines of output per day. Turnaround can only be determined in terms of number of accesses and processing speed. In most systems departments, cost associated with turnaround is not considered in data base costing.

Several methods of calculating times are available. By using the formulas developed from these methods, it is possible to calculate the cost of maintenance and retrieval for the particular services that the data base must supply. These costs can be calculated for each type of storage device available. The choice of acceptable combinations is dependent on the service level demanded in both the maintenance and retrieval areas.

The demands by these areas can be divided into three quantifiable terms. For maintenance, the main consideration is number of updates required per unit of time, an update being defined as the input of new data physically to the file—for example, executing a program to calculate new inventory balances based on physical receipts to and issues from the stockroom. For retrieval the two considerations are the number of accesses per unit of time and the response time required by the user. The number of accesses is the actual number of requests for information requiring an accessing of the data base. The response time is the time elapsed between the request for information and the receipt of output. Average rates can be established for these terms from studying user input or from past history.

Since we have quantified estimates for the requirements and associated times for satisfying those requirements using the available device-structure combinations, we can calculate the total systems time required using each alternative; then the alternative having the least total time for maintenance and retrieval can be chosen.

The readings section consists of two articles on MIS and two articles on data base. In "The Management Looks at MIS," Edelman emphasizes the point that an effective MIS must be relevant to and clearly understood by the managers who intend to use it. Next, he goes into some detail about the contents of a data base, the factors that determine the precise organization of an MIS, with stress on the need to develop a model if management is to have an MIS. "The Future MIS" is a most insightful approach to a conceptual framework of MIS. In this article Kriebel predicts the decline of today's orientation of MIS to data bases, the rise of personalized information systems for decisionmakers, and the emergence of distributed data processing using minicomputers.

Price's article, "The Ten Commandments of Data Base," examines ten key steps in developing a data base. This is an informative article worth reading in its entirety. Keysor's article, "The Managed Data Base" expounds on three phases of data base development.

THE MANAGER LOOKS AT MIS

Franz Edelman

What's wrong with MIS? Nothing, as long as it is not confused with clerical data handling. Real MIS is still in its infancy. It is growing in a very volatile environment. And, in spite of this, a great deal has been learned in both theory and practice.

Every management information system, to be of any value, should be designed for and by the managers who are to use it. In order to be involved in the creation of an MIS, there are certain elements of an information system, and certain relationships between these elements, that the manager should understand.

There are two "Laws of Relevance" which should govern the modern manager's style in his use of MIS technology. The first is:

"No manager with responsibility for a business—or a part thereof—will base important decisions on the outcome of a process which he, himself, does not adequately understand."

In other words, regardless of the manager's confidence in his "management scientist," he should never stick his neck out unless he fully understands the reasons for doing so.

This first law of management systems and sciences deals with the art of managing. The second law is concerned with the methodological content of the management task:

"Genuine management information consists of the quantitative (numerical) and the qualitative (relational) descriptions of the business issues at hand."

An example of the quantitiative aspect of management information would be the fact that a company has sold 10-million widgets during the first half of 1971. The number 10-million is a piece of purely numerical information which is of significance even if it is out of context with regard to the economic environment, company marketing objectives, and any other factors which imply a relationship.

Qualitative information, on the other hand, defines relationships. A good example of this sort of relational or structural information is provided by the example:

After-tax proceeds = (1—tax rate) $\times$ (revenues—expenses other than depreciation) + (tax rate) $\times$ (depreciation)

Source: Reprinted by permission of the publisher from *Computer Decisions*, August 1971, pp. 14-18.

This, too, is information even though it contains not a single numerical value. It expresses a relationship among a number of variables. It is a piece of purely relational data without regard to numerical content.

Another such example is the formula:

$$y = ax + b$$

To most people, this immediately suggests a straight line relationship between the two variables x and y regardless of what these variables happen to be.

It is important to clearly define these two different types of information—numerical and relational. To be effective, an MIS must be capable of managing two different and separate repositories—the first containing the numerical data and the second containing the relationships. The data repository is called the data base and the relationship repository is called the model.

In discussing the significance to management information systems of the data base and the model, there are three facts which should be kept in mind:

- It takes both numbers and relationships to produce results that are useful in decision-making.
- Numbers change faster than relationships.
- It is easier and more economical to change numerical inputs to a system (its data base) than it is to change programmed instructions (its model).

With these facts in mind, it is logical that the model should not only be devoid of numerical content (in order to avoid expensive program changes every time a numerical value changes) but, conversely, the data base should be devoid of structure (except that which is required by the system for retrieval). This will avoid the necessity of reorganizing a massive data base every time you decide to reorganize your business.

WHAT GOES INTO THE DATA BASE?

The contents of the data base part of an MIS system fall into two categories. The first contains historical, objective and/or factual data, and refers to measurable quantities in past and current operations.

The second category contains subjective or judgmental data. This refers to the assessments and expectations of knowledgeable managers regarding future states of the business for which they are responsible. The relative mix of historical and judgmental data is a major determinant of the capability of the MIS system.

An MIS system is *a one-to-one combination of model with data base in such relative proportion as is appropriate to the particular task at hand.* This assertion requires some elaboration. First of all, a model data base combination is a very natural thing. In fact, its parts are precisely complementary, each containing the information which the other lacks. This definition makes an important distinction between two basic types of information systems. These systems are the MIS—intended to furnish information to managers for assistance in decision-making—and the DMS (data management system) intended to help in coping with large volumes

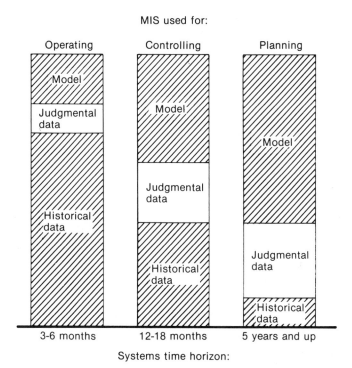

Figure 1. As the management activity (operating, controlling or planning) and its associated time horizon shift, so does the content of the MIS designed to serve that activity. At the operating level (three to six month time horizon), for instance, there is relatively little emphasis on the model, and the data base contains mostly historical data. For long-range planning (five years and up), on the other hand, the MIS emphasizes the model, and the content of the data base is mostly judgmental data.

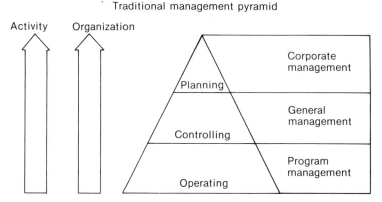

Figure 2. The traditional management pyramid model is based on the assumption that the activities of managers are subordinate to their organizational position, or vice versa. In this model, corporate managers plan, general managers control, and program managers operate.

of data and the associated-clerical tasks. A DMS is essentially a data base with attendant rules for file construction and maintenance, data storage and retrieval, but no explicit rules for processing the data into managerial information.

Within the area of MIS the relative proportion of model to data base will vary. A management system intended to influence the long-range planning process, for example, requires quite a different model/data base mix than does a system devoted to the day-to-day operational processes of a business. Practical and effective planning systems require a long time horizon—five years or more, with time advancing a year at a time—and a broad "total company" perspective. It must also do this with the *minimum degree of detail* required by the planning process.

On the other hand, a day-to-day operations system must be capable of dealing with things as they actually happen in the real world. For example, an operations system for manufacturing must produce daily schedules for specific products to be

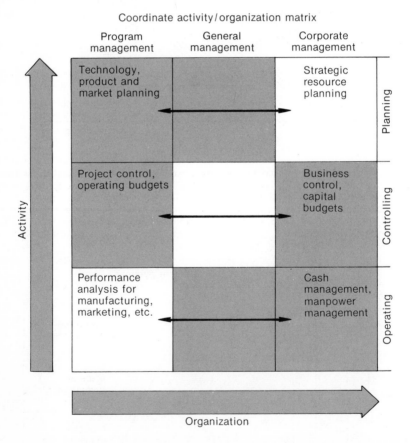

Figure 3. The coordinate activity/organization matrix adjusts for such activities as are ignored by the traditional management pyramid. This matrix represents activities on the vertical axis and organizational position on the horizontal axis. Although most of the action takes place on the ascending diagonal (light area) corresponding to the traditional pyramid model, exceptions are also included.

made on specific production lines. An operations system, therefore, does not require scope, in the interfunctional sense, but rather the ultimate in detail from the particular function under consideration. Consequently, the horizon of an operating system cannot and should not be long—certainly no longer than three to six months—and the report period should advance weekly or daily. In addition, the data base used by a long-range planning system has a far higher ratio of judgmental to historical data than that used by an operations system.

THE "WHO" AND THE "WHY" OF MIS

The precise organization of a management information system depends on two things—who is to use the MIS, and to what purpose. For purposes of illustration, we can define the *who* in terms of the traditional corporate organization chart, separating it into top (corporation), general (division), and program (major operating department) managerial levels.

The *how* of the MIS depends on what the managers do when they manage. Unfortunately, there is no organization chart for the activities of managers. However, again for purposes of illustration, we can oversimplify the activities of managers into three basic categories—planning, controlling, and operating.

These three management activities are differentiated by the time horizon which they address. As the time horizon of a management system gets shorter, it also tends to get more involved in day-to-day detail. A useful analogy to the horizon/detail tradeoff is the common road map. When driving from Boston to St. Louis, for instance, two different types of route information are necessary. First, one must have a general overview of the main route to be taken (long or planning horizon), and second, a detailed map of the cities which will have to be navigated along the way (short or operations horizon).

The planning process is concerned with information that covers a wide time horizon (generally five or more years), and is structured only two or three levels of detail below the top of the enterprise or operation being modeled. For example, representation of product and market structure, in the planning context, is generally accomplished by aggregating everything into product families within major product lines or customer groups within industry segments. You would not want to take the planning process down to the ultimate level of detail where you deal directly with the individual product (by catalogue number, so to speak) or with the individual customer (by name and address).

The second level of managerial activity is the controlling level. The control process is concerned with interpreting the near-term portion of the long-range plan by translating this into a more detailed near-term business plan (this might be called the annual budget). This is done by means of more detailed (tactical) resource allocations, and established and/or expected seasonal patterns. The control process is also expected to signal the planning process if long- and near-term prospects are mutually inconsistent. Thus, the control process covers the middle range of detail over a 12- to 18-month horizon.

Finally, the third level of managerial activity is the operating process. This operations level performs the day-to-day tasks of the enterprise and is concerned with measuring actual outcomes, applying specific exception rules to ascertain performance and signalling to the control process for corrective action if a discrepancy develops between reality and expectations. The horizon over which this is generally feasible is a period of three to six months.

It should not be assumed, however, that detail on operations is the sole responsibility of program managers, or that generalized planning is the sole domain of corporate managers. Such an assumption is the result of thinking in traditional terms of the management pyramid model. This model is based on the belief that the activities of managers are subordinate to their organizational position, or vice versa.

Such a pyramid model may be relevant to a small, monolithic firm, but it doesn't work very well when applied to a large, diversified and complex enterprise. For instance, a function such as cash management involves short-term operations with a close attention to detail. According to the traditional pyramid model, cash management should, therefore, be handled by program-level managers. But it obviously is not. Because of the large amounts involved, it is carried out within corporate headquarters by top management.

To adjust for such activities which are ignored by the management pyramid model, a coordinate relationship model can be suggested. This model, with activities represented on the vertical axis and organizational position represented on the horizontal axis (Figure 3), will include such activities. At the same time, it should be noted that most of the action takes place along the ascending diagonal of this coordinate chart corresponding to the traditional pyramid model. The main advantage of the coordinate model is that it recognizes and identifies the unique management systems requirements of each cell. This breaks the systems task into manageable chunks. And, furthermore, it facilitates the synthesis of those chunks into a consistent whole.

Managers sometimes ask why it is not possible to design a single, "integrated" MIS which combines the horizon of planning with the detail of operations—all under one roof. This is the equivalent of asking for a Boston-to-St. Louis map having full street details for every city and town along the way.

It is simply not practical to attempt to create a single, integrated MIS. To produce useful results, it is absolutely necessary to partition the total job into manageable segments. These segments are then tailored for each particular level of management and for each particular managerial activity. This is not to say, however, that each of these segments is incompatible with all of the other segments. Just the opposite should be true. By providing the system with a conceptually and technically sound blueprint as a basis for action, and by employing imaginative, intelligent, experienced design techniques, a consistent whole can be synthesized from each of the segments.

WHAT ARE YOUR MIS PEOPLE DOING?

In a diverse company seriously concerned with the use of MIS, the manager can see what his MIS people are working on by trying a simple two-part test.

First, select two or three of current, high priority MIS design projects slated for your particular use. Be sure, in advance, that they are MIS and not DMS projects, since the latter do not depend on a model and, therefore, do not meet this test. Ask the designers to explain to you the model of each MIS—the collection of analytically expressed relationships relevant to the task at hand. This should be a group of equations, anywhere from ten to several hundred in number, containing symbols representing the variables involved (no numbers, please). Most often these will be simple arithmetic statements and not esoteric mathematics.

In any event, *you*, as the manager for whom this MIS is intended, must understand the model and how it relates to your specific requirements and responsibilities. If you don't, if you and/or your MIS designers have ignored our First Law, then the chances are that you will never get any returns from your investment.

Do not settle for flowcharts (block diagrams). They mean something else, usually system logic rather than business relationships. If the designers cannot produce such a thing, you have probably discovered that this MIS is really a DMS. It is not that I underestimate the value of DMS's, for they have a most useful purpose, but managers are very rarely interested in retrieving raw data for control or planning purposes. They need to have raw data processed—filtered, condensed, distilled, interpreted, interrelated, etc. The rules for filtration, condensation, etc. are precisely what we mean by model. It comprises the manager's mental image of his responsibilities.

Thus, a system without a model cannot possibly be an MIS.

If the designers come up with proper models for their MIS designs, you should next turn your attention to the data base used by this MIS. Select at random from the data base dictionary a dozen or so input definitions to the system. If all of the inputs turn out to be historical variables, repeat the test. If you continue to be unable to discover a satisfactory collection of genuine judgmental variables, then you have learned something else. It is most likely that the model you are looking at is of a statistical variety (correlation, regression, or what have you), probably being applied to some forecasting task or other. Now, there is nothing wrong with statistical models per se. However, well conceived ones, intended for use in forecasting, must always contain at least some judgmental data. It is patently impossible, nonsensical in fact, to say anything relevant about the future of a dynamic business which is based entirely on statements about the past.

If you have found a system that has both a model and an acceptable judgmental component in its data base, then you have found an MIS. That is not to say that the mere existence of a model proves its reasonableness. Would that this were so! An adequate data base is also a necessity.

An example might well serve here to guide your search for an MIS. Consider the granddaddy of all data processing applications—the payroll. In the strict sense of the word, this application has only two missions: the issuing of paychecks and the reporting of total payroll, taxes, deductions, etc. to accounting for housekeeping purposes. The payroll system per se is practically all data base with, at most, a rudimentary model containing some of the relationships needed in the calculations. In addition, the traditional payroll data base contains only historical and current data. The payroll system would, therefore, rightly be classified as a DMS. Clearly, the basic payroll system has nothing to do with any decision-making process. But, once you have a payroll system, it seems sensible to extend it to give you labor distribution. Now things begin to change. Immediately, you must ascribe a structure to your labor force and, hence, your production processes and perhaps even your basic product or service organization. What is that? A model, of course! Once you have done such structuring, it would be a pity not to take the next step and extend the system to do analysis of such things as performance and turnover. This requires two things. First, a considerable extension of the model is needed since we are now defining and structuring performance. Second, for the very same reason, the data base has acquired a sizable chunk of judgmental data (how else can you model performance?). The next steps are obvious: compensation studies, productivity and resource analyses, among others. We are by now knee-deep in genuine MIS.

As implied by the previous example, the creation of an effective MIS system requires that the managers be directly involved every step along the way. The manager contributes his entrepreneurial skills and instincts to the design of an MIS in two ways. He participates in the building of the model which becomes an organized, systematic description of his own mental image of his basic responsibilities. Clearly, unless he does this the model is not likely to assist him in discharging these responsibilities. Second, he must express the quantitative judgments regarding goals, alternatives, expectations, priorities, uncertainties, etc., implied in the model he has helped structure. These are to be inserted into the judgmental section of the data base.

The model now performs the analytical operations indicated, using the content of the data base, and presents the manager with the results. He will examine the results and most likely decide to change one or more of his assumptions. He might modify his goals, try other alternatives, reorder his priorities in order to ascertain the likely impact of changed conditions. In this manner, the manager and his MIS become involved in a *management process* that consists in alternating hypothesis with experiment and using one to improve the other. This is the essence of scientific method, and is the very "raison d'être" of management systems.

DISCUSSION QUESTIONS

1. "To be effective, an MIS must be capable of managing two different and separate repositories." What are these repositories? Explain their relationship and importance in an MIS.

2. In what respect do the elements of a model/data base combination compliment each other? Explain briefly.

3. What is the relative model/data base emphasis in the operating, controlling, and planning activities of management? Illustrate.

4. "A system without a model cannot possibly be an MIS." Do you agree with this statement? Why?

THE FUTURE MIS

Charles H. Kriebel

The continuing exponential growth in raw computing power prompted Art Buchwald recently to editorialize on "The Great Data Famine" of the 1970's. According to Buchwald's expert source, by January 12, 1976 " . . . every last bit of data in the world will have been fed into a machine and an information famine will follow." To cope with this impending disaster, a crash program is urged in which (1) "no computer can be plugged in more than three hours a day"; (2) the government will spend $50 billion to set up data manufacturing plants and their output will be mixed with soy bean production; and finally, (3) a birth control program will be advocated for all computers—provided "the Vatican's computer gives us its blessing."

Instead of a "data famine" the technological issue today is that computers haven't been able to do all that was expected of them. In stronger language, Isaac Auerbach has said that the performance obtained by users of computers for business data processing shows: 20% are successful, 40% are marginal, and 40% are failures. Reviews by others of computers in management information systems also sharply criticize the notable lack of results in spite of great expectations. If true, this is a dismal return for a $40 billion investment in equipment. What went wrong? Who is at fault?

We can gain perspective on the problem by briefly probing the issues involved. A conceptual framework is particularly important in this case because the broad connotation of MIS and misunderstanding are the source of most of today's difficulties.

The phrase "management information systems," or "MIS," has gained popularity as a descriptor for information processing activities in support of management. If one explores the environment of management it is soon apparent that decision-making is the primary function that distinguishes managerial activity from other behaviors. In fact, management decision occupies a singular role in management literature, since other behavior—such as planning and control—is often defined in terms of decision activity. Thus, an understanding of the central issues in MIS might logically begin with the concept of management decision.

A parsimonious description of the decision process would include four identifiable stages of activity: observation, inference, evaluation and choice. The process begins with *observing* states of the environment; measurements are taken, and data are collected, encoded and stored. The second stage in the process involves analysis of the recorded data as a base for *inference* and prediction. Stage three is initiated by the need for a decision. Inferences and projections are analyzed to identify action alternatives and these in turn are *evaluated* with respect to goals, constraints

Source: Reprinted from *Infosystems*, June 1972, pp. 18-19ff. By Permission of the Publisher. © 1972 Hitchcock Publishing Company. All rights reserved.

and efficiency. Finally, an alternative is selected which is preferred (or "best") under the criterion of choice, the action is communicated, resources are committed, and the *decision* is implemented. The process actually perpetuates itself through cycling and feedback, since upon implementation the decision becomes a source for new observations, and so on.

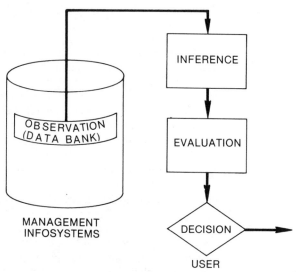

FIRST LEVEL

Consider the development of information structures in support of this process. The simplistic decision model can serve to characterize four levels of the relative maturity (or sophistication) achieved by an information system. In its most elemental form an information system is simply a repository or data bank, encompassing only the "observation" activities of the model. The raw data has been organized in some convenient manner and is stored, say, in a computer file; upon interrogation, the computer gives a report to the manager, who performs all subsequent analyses from inference to decision. Most accounting systems are of this elementary form. Simplicity, *per se,* is not a criticism of such systems; their shortcoming in application is that typically they do not discriminate between vital information and trivia. Thus, managers interacting with an elementary data bank system often become frustrated by the lack of relevancy in large volumes of data.

At the second level of maturity in development the data bank system has been expanded to include most of the activities of inference as part of the formal system. In addition to exception reporting, the system now includes the capacity to forecast and to artificially test the consequences of implicit decisions. Here the manager can interrogate the system with "What if ... " questions, and receive an array of consequences in response for his evaluation. The hidden danger in this dialogue is that the manager is usually insulated from factual data in the system by a host of assumptions imbedded in the model which provides the inferences. It is surprising how readily individuals are lulled into believing that "realistic-looking" output is fact.

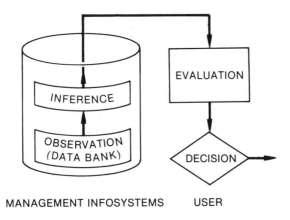

MANAGEMENT INFOSYSTEMS   USER

SECOND LEVEL

At level three, evaluation activities have been programmed into the selective-inference structures so that the information system now encompasses action recommendation. Here the need for a decision is triggered within the formal system on the basis of monitored observations and predetermined rules of a time-scheduled event. Procedures are programmed to evaluate alternatives against assigned goals as the situation requires, the "best" course of action is chosen and the recommendation is communicated to the manager. At that point the manager either implements a decision based on the recommendation or he rejects the alternative and further analysis may be initiated. The most common form of this action-recommending information system in organizations today is the advisory staff group or committee. In this case line management delegates authority for a certain area of responsibility to a staff department, but retains final control for decision through review and certification. Another variant of this system has appeared in the form of large-scale optimization models, particularly linear programming applications in industrial

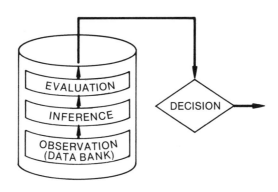

MANAGEMENT INFOSYSTEMS   USER

THIRD LEVEL

scheduling. In many of these cases, systems originally designed for "action recommendation" have reverted back to "selective inference" systems as limitations of the model became apparent.

In the final stage of maturity the entire decision process has been automated within the information system. All activities from observation to choice and the ability to initiate action, commit resources and monitor results have been programmed. In effect the manager is now outside the structure, having fully delegated his authority, although he retains the power to revoke the delegation at some future time. The simplest form of the automated decision system is the "standard operating procedure" in organizations; a more sophisticated example would be a computerized process control system in a petroleum refinery. Modern factory inventory control systems are another common example. Obviously, automated decision systems require extensive knowledge of the decision process for the given application and consequently their development has been limited to well-defined environments.

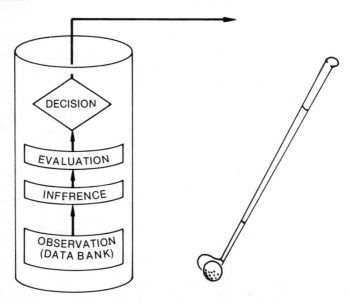

MANAGEMENT INFOSYSTEMS   USER

FOURTH LEVEL

The MIS in a modern organization today is not one of these information structures; it is a composite of all four types. Said differently, the two basic components of design in any information system are (1) a model of the user, and (2) a data store. The former defines the output interface of system application, and the latter constitutes the environmental image or system input. For MIS, the user model reference is management decision processes. In the evolution from "data bank" to "automated decision" the user model becomes technologically more sophisticated as more activities of the process are formalized and programmed into the system.

But decision processes exist at all management levels in an organization hierarchy. Thus, one finds information structures of different maturity at different management levels. The most mature computer automated information structures in MIS today are still confined to lower management levels. The lackluster results vis-à-vis expectations realized in MIS to date can be attributed in part to the fact that the implicit model of the user has remained naive.

As total costs increased in spite of gains in computer hardware efficiencies, the third generation systems of the mid-to-late 1960's saw a shift in emphasis toward consolidation—though not necessarily of the "total systems" variety. The output-oriented, management function user models in large measure were abandoned for an input-oriented data base model with the goal of data processing efficiency. The development orientation in MIS focused on a corporate data bank which stressed input data format, flows, and files with little attention to the specific output requirements of end users. Working applications programs in the system were de-coupled from data files through the imposition of file management software. Most formal information systems today are still in this stage of evolution.

This raises several questions concerning future developments in the user model dimension of MIS technology. For example, the profit center organization is a move toward the information utility concept; but is "information processing" a homogeneous commodity? Divorcing the system design from specific user needs is an attempt to make the technology independent; but is MIS technology inert? The contemporary orientation on data input and EDP technology implies that resource efficiency is a major bottleneck; but has EDP utilization been the key barrier in MIS implementation? The data base model development of an MIS seeks to establish a corporate data bank, often building from the bottom up; but do information structures for managers draw upon common data?

In anticipating the next ten years, my first prediction is the demise of the present-day data base orientation as the dominant user model image in MIS development. Instead, the development focus will shift back to an output orientation that is user dependent. The emphasis will be on basic decision processes and problems of the specific organization and manager without regard to the functional environment. Information structures will be developed to solve a particular manager's problems; some of the structures will be generally applicable to other situations in broad outline.

The user model image that focuses on *critical decision* processes for MIS development, however, is only one aspect of the new technology. Allied with the change in orientation will be a rise in the application of operations research and behavioral science in developing and implementing these information structures. It is common knowledge that many of the basic methods and known results in operations research are not being used by managers today, even though many of the techniques have considerable potential as decision aids. This issue has been labeled a "communications gap."

The empirical evidence on MIS implementation suggests: (1) except for the most routine activities, managers actively resist attempts (real or perceived) to erode their authority base; (2) the executive's orientation is toward the "people" in the organization, his self-concept is as an individual who directs the activities of others; (3) there is relatively little understanding of upper management decision processes.

Emerging information structures in the next decade will increasingly incorporate behavioral parameters in their design which reflect organizational associations, leadership style, and management attitudes as a means toward improving acceptance and effectiveness at the user/system interface. Before the end of the decade I anticipate appearance of more "personalized" information structures which better match the users' needs. Within the data processing industry the emerging trend toward companies which provide "information services" will continue; they will be the developers of the new technology which solves the user's problems.

EDP technology encompasses a broad domain beyond "the computer," from firmware to peripheral devices and communcations, from POLS (Procedure Oriented Languages) to data management software and supervisors, from system configuration to systems analysis and people. The most distinguishing characteristic of third-generation EDP system operations was the emergence of teleprocessing, facilitated by multi-programming and data communications technology. This development is significant for at least two reasons. First, it provided the basic framework for distributed data processing; second, it turned the centralized vs. decentralized operations debate into an academic issue to be decided on a relative basis by organizational philosophy.

The distributed data processing (DDP) approach employs a hierarchy of EDP centers, ordered on the dimension of capacity and interconnected through direct communication lines. (Increasingly in the future these lines will be used for data transmission rather than modifications of voice networks.) At the lowest level in the DDP grid the point-of-origin device for data capture and interaction will be an "intelligent terminal," ranging from a Picturephone-like device to a minicomputer with local data processing capacity. Where on-line access and speed are not important, data cassettes will provide communication linkages. In more sophisticated applications computer networking will be employed for direct communication between computers and multiprocessor centers. Although thus far the DDP concept has been employed primarily in experimental systems, I believe it will be commonplace in the future.

The distributed data processing approach in one sense is a natural outgrowth of the time-sharing principle to extend system utilization while capturing some of the economies-of-scale in hardware technology. However, experience has shown that the massive "universal" system approach rapidly leads to substantial diseconomies in software overhead and administration. By analogy, the computer is not a universal machine; "a truck, a motorcycle or a racing car—each has a different engine which is designed for high performance and in the specific use intended." The computer system and MIS that seek to be all things to all people in one package is doomed to failure at the outset. The cost balance in configuration is between operating control over a fragmentation of diverse specialiazed systems which may be locally optimal but globally expensive, and the universal system "dinosaur."

The basic difference under DDP is not to integrate but, instead, to provide a well-defined interface for relatively independent subsystems. Data managers have been a first step, and in the future these systems will be dedicated to subset applications as required. What emerges then is a portfolio of technology (packages) optimized with respect to the portfolio of user information structures. Some of the elements in the overall portfolio will interact, some will not; however, all elements will be highly modular. That is, one application may periodically require augmented computer capacity from the sector or regional centers in "competition" with other applications, others may share certain master files for data and still others may be locally self-sufficient.

The economic rationale by management in making the commitment to EDP and MIS was essentially to replace labor with capital and improve productivity. What has happened, however, is that total costs have increased. Even if one examines only the apparent costs of systems operations and development, the capital/labor ratio advantage has not materialized; equipment hardware cost continues to decline as a percentage of the total which includes systems personnel and administration—today ranging between 35% and 45%. Furthermore, as most of the trade literature reports, apparent costs are only the visible portion of the economic "iceberg" in MIS when we include such hidden cost factors as the drain on management time, inadequate priority analysis of competing applications (and the foregone opportunities), abandoned projects due to vacillating support, security in the EDP department, inefficient software, etc. The constant advance in the sophistication of the new technology will continue to raise the economic stakes for payoff in MIS as this total cost base expands. Sunk cost notwithstanding, the decision many companies are beginning to face is whether or not they literally can afford to be in the MIS business.

This economic crossroad in MIS is not to suggest that management is contemplating a nostalgic return to the Dark Ages. More realistically, they are weighing the practicality of making it themselves or buying it on the outside. Today information services companies sell pieces of an MIS; you can buy information problem solutions as a complete package and for a price contracted in advance. Often this opportunity does not exist in-house and cost estimates are notoriously biased. The large corporations with the requisite capital base and absolute system constraints will retain in-house technology for their MIS. Increasing numbers of companies in the $50 million annual sales or less category, however, are going to buy their MIS technology over the next ten years. Few companies today generate their own electrical power requirements; many companies buy their legal services as needed; most small companies buy their accounting services. The distributed data processing approach will facilitate a comparable opportunity for EDP technology. Management will decide how much of it to "buy" and how much to "make" in establishing an economically viable MIS. For the data processing industry, establishing the centers, developing the technology, and regulating operations will be determined in the marketplace by the user, or the government, or both.

DISCUSSION QUESTION

Write an essay in 500 words or less, explaining the four levels of relative maturity achieved by an information system.

THE TEN COMMANDMENTS OF DATA BASE

Gerald F. Price

A data base stores all organization information in a single, multi-phase system. The importance of the data base to organization operations places greater emphasis on design planning and control. These "commandments" reduce the risk of failure, provide security recovery, reduce development time, provide project controls, assure investment justification and achieve system objectives.

If you were among those who converted from second to third generation hardware, you can recall the pain of changing data files, programming languages, and the subsequent testing of those revised programs. It was a bitter experience at the time; however, the data processing industry focused its view on some basic inadequacies in documentation, standards, and technique uniformity within an installation.

As we look back, we can be thankful for the lesson gained through the conversion experience. Thankful, especially, because this lesson was learned prior to the era of integrated systems and data base technology. Today, we have applied these experiences to avoid the need for future conversion efforts. We now enjoy freedom from hardware, software, and data bases. Our programs are independent, dealing strictly at an applications problem level. Our analysts now concentrate on application problems and technology is left to software specialists. We have taken advantage of the painful conversion experience. Or have we?

If you look back to the number of programs operating in your installation at the time of the conversion effort, you will find that today you operate two or three times as many programs. Would another conversion today be twice as difficult? Three times? We, of the data processing industry, must insure our firm's system investment by avoiding the need for re-programming efforts. Problem level languages and hardware, software, and data independence is one way to avoid future costly conversions. It can be done.

DEFINING A DATA BASE

Before looking at how one develops a data base, a definition is required of what a data base is. A data base is an orderly collection of business facts stored to serve information requirements. Data bases are frequently stored on direct access devices to provide rapid information retrieval. A dynamic business environment dictates

Source: Reprinted, with permission, from *Data Management*, May 1972, pp. 14-23, published by the Data Processing Management Association, Park Ridge, Illinois.

that data bases be adaptable to change. The information storage technique must accommodate data entry, maintenance, and retrieval.

The ideal data base would contain all information required in the process of conducting your business. This ideal data base would contain current, historical and forecast information which would be stored in a logical manner and available for retrieval as need demanded. Ideally the data base would provide only the information necessary to satisfy each request, however cost considerations frequently rule out maintaining a data base at this ideal level. Information stored is limited to the more practical level of *active* data. If the cost of insurance (*storage*) exceeds the cost of the accident (*usage*), it may not be practical. A data base can be scaled to a practical level to contain the significant information while omitting information which can be stored more economically in a different manner.

In the days of second generation hardware, each application operated with its own independent set of data files. There were two choices in moving to third generation equipment. The first, *conversion* on an immediate basis, the most costly, was rarely selected. The second choice, *evolution,* provided the user an opportunity to convert one application at a time while he continued to operate his new third generation machine as if it were second generation. Evolution worked the last time, but under an integrated data base, it may never work again. How would you convert one application at a time when your entire company data is stored in an integrated data base? With a large number of programs depending on the data base, development efforts must avoid unnecessary conversions. Advancements in data processing technology and hardware occur regularly. To take advantage requires an ability to adapt rapidly with minimum effort. There are basic steps which can help us avoid future conversion problems. The "Ten Commandments of Data Base" identify some significant considerations in data base development.

IDENTIFY DATA ELEMENTS

Close examination reveals that most business decisions are based upon a relatively small collection of data elements. These elements must first be recognized. A data dictionary to define standard elements can be developed with uniform data names and field characteristics (Figure 1). These elements are combined to form information in input documents, stored file records, and information retrievals. All data elements identified in the dictionary can be cross-referenced through a data directory to provide a data usage record (Figure 2).

The process of identifying the data elements requires an examination of existing transactions, files and reports. Document these elements in a dictionary in this basic identification step. A matrix can then be established to relate the identified elements to transactions, files, and reports. These study documents provide a basis for the data directory (Figures 3, 4, and 5).

After examining the use of significant data elements in existing systems, data inconsistency and redundancy identification is common. Variation in field lengths, edit rules and data interpretation contribute to the inconsistency between the independent files on nondata base systems. Information stored in multiple files requires redundant maintenance. Early recognition of data element conflicts provides added intelligence for data base planning.

```
┌─────────────────────────────────────────────────────────────────────┐
│                                                                       │
│  DATA DICTIONARY                                                      │
│                                                                       │
│  ELEMENT              DATA NAME          CHARACTERISTICS              │
│                                                                       │
│  Accumulated Average  Accum-Av           3 Numeric XX.X%             │
│  Accumulated Credits  Accum-Cr           3 Numeric                   │
│  Assignment Grade     Assign-Grade       3 Numeric XX.X%             │
│  Birth Date           Birth              6 Numeric XX-XX-XX          │
│  Class Days           Class-Days         5 Alpha MTWTF               │
│  Class Link           Class-Link         3 Numeric Storage Address   │
│  Class Year           Class-Yr           4 Numeric 19XX              │
│  Course Code          Course-No          3 Numeric                   │
│  Course Name          Course-Name        10 Alpha                    │
│  Days Absent          Days-Abs           2 Numeric                   │
│  Final Grade          Faculty-Name       15 Alpha                    │
│  First Grade          Final-Grade        3 Numeric XX.X%            │
│  First Name           First-Name         8 Alpha                     │
│  Next Class           Next-Class         3 Numeric Storage Address   │
│  Next Student         Next-Student       3 Numeric Storage Address   │
│  Number Credits       No-Credits         1 Numeric                   │
│  Registration Number  Reg-No             3 Numeric                   │
│  Room Number          Room               3 Numeric                   │
│  Sex                  Sex                1 Alpha                      │
│  Student Link         Student-Link       3 Numeric Storage Address   │
│  Surname              Surname            18 Alpha                     │
│  Test Grade           Test-Grade         3 Numeric XX.X%             │
│  Time of Class        Class-Time         4 Numeric HR-MN             │
│                                                                       │
└─────────────────────────────────────────────────────────────────────┘
```

Figure 1

A review of the evaluation results with pertinent-using-organizations provides additional intelligence for defining control responsibility over each data element (e.g., grade assignment = faculty responsibility). Additional data elements and future control needs are identified in these reviews.

```
┌───────────────────────────────────────────────────────────────┐
│                                                                 │
│  DATA DIRECTORY                                                 │
│                                                                 │
│  ELEMENT          USAGE                     T    F    R        │
│                                                                 │
│  Class-Yr         Student Application       X                   │
│                   Student Master                 X              │
│                   Grade Report                        X         │
│                   Transcript                          X         │
│                                                                 │
│  Course-No        Schedule & History             X             │
│                   Course Master                  X              │
│                   Grade Report                        X         │
│                   Transcript                          X         │
│                   Course Definition         X                   │
│                                                                 │
│  Course-Name      Course Master                  X              │
│                   Transcript                          X         │
│                   Course Definition         X                   │
│                   Grade Report                        X         │
│                                                                 │
└───────────────────────────────────────────────────────────────┘
```

Figure 2

DATA EVALUATION ARRAY-TRANSACTION TO DATA ELEMENT

TRANSACTION \ DATA ELEMENTS	ACCUM-AV	ACCUM-CR	ASSIGN-GRADE	BIRTH	CLASS-DAYS	CLASS-LINK	CLASS-YR	COURSE-NO	COURSE-NAME	DAYS-ABS	FACULTY-NAME	FINAL-GRADE	FIRST-NAME	NEXT-CLASS	ETC.
FACULTY ASSIGNMENT					X			X	X		X				X
STUDENT APPLICATION	X	X		X			X						X		
CLASS ASSIGNMENT					X			X	X				X		X
TRANSFER REQUEST	X	X		X			X						X		X

Figure 3

DATA EVALUATION ARRAY-FILE TO DATA ELEMENT

FILE \ DATA ELEMENT	ACCUM-AV	ACCUM-CR	ASSIGN-GRADE	BIRTH	CLASS-DAYS	CLASS-LINK	CLASS-YR	COURSE-NO	COURSE-NAME	DAYS-ABS	FACULTY-NAME	FINAL-GRADE	FIRST-NAME	NEXT-CLASS	ETC.
STUDENT MASTER	X	X		X	X	X							X		X
SCHEDULE & HISTORY			X					X		X		X			X
COURSE MASTER							X	X	X	X					
FACULTY MASTER				X						X	X		X		X

Figure 4

DATA EVALUATION ARRAY-RETRIEVAL DOCUMENT TO DATA ELEMENT

RETRIEVAL \ DATA ELEMENT	ACCUM-AV	ACCUM-CR	ASSIGN-GRADE	BIRTH	CLASS-DAYS	CLASS-LINK	CLASS-YR	COURSE-NO	COURSE-NAME	DAYS-ABS	FACULTY-NAME	FINAL-GRADE	FIRST-NAME	NEXT-CLASS	ETC.
GRADE REPORT			X		X		X	X	X	X	X	X	X		X
TRANSCRIPT	X	X		X			X	X	X		X	X	X		X
COURSE-SCHEDULE					X			X	X		X		X		X
CLASS ROSTER	X	X		X	X			X	X	X			X		X

Figure 5

DEFINE FILE REQUIREMENTS

The three most significant elements which influence files are record size, quantity of records and retrieval requirements. Retrieval influences the data management technique and will be examined later. This phase considers file content and size as criteria for planning and economic evaluation.

A master file is organized through use of a key data element which identifies the record and provides storage control. Master file information relates to this key data element in a static sense. Maintenance activity in a master file consists mainly of record adds and deletes.

A subordinate file provides opportunity to extend a master file by a variable number of detail records. These detail records increase the available intelligence known about the key element at minimum storage cost. (Figure 6.)

The student master record contains information which applies to each student. This information does not change throughout the school year. Limited updating is performed on an annual basis. The subordinate record provides opportunity to record a student's current schedule and prior course completions. The number of records per student depends on his class year and current schedule. The example shows a subordinate file supporting two masters.

Each data element is a candidate for either master or subordinate file storage. Basic identification of each data element by file type provides a basis for an initial file layout. This layout is preliminary and will be changed as specifications are solidified.

Once the file content is available, review with the system-using-organizations is required. This review initiates a communication with the system user which must continue through the entire development cycle. The user is best qualified to estimate the number of master and subordinate records by type. A requirement to

MASTER NO. 1 - STUDENT FILE

REG NO	SURNAME	FIRST NAME	SEX	BIRTH	CLASS YR.	ACCUM AV	ACCUM CR	CLASS LINK

SUBORDINATE - SCHEDULE & HISTORY

COURSE NO	REG NO	ASSIGN GRADE	TEST GRADE	DAYS ABS	FINAL GRADE	NEXT STUDENT	NEXT CLASS

MASTER NO. 2 - COURSE FILE

COURSE NO	COURSE NAME	FACULTY NAME	CLASS TIME	DAYS	NO CREDITS	NO ENROLL	ROOM	STUDENT LINK

Figure 6

document this estimate frequently improves the estimate validity. Modifications in record content are identified through these user communication meetings.

Completion of this phase has provided a knowledge of what we are dealing with (data elements), how the elements are structured (file definitions), and storage requirements (volume estimates).

DESIGN GENERAL SYSTEM

Boundaries of an information system extend far beyond computer processing. They encompass the entire information flow from the condition which triggers initial action through the final result. It includes actions and responsibilities of all organization areas affected by the system. The basic design defines primary procedural flows, responsibilities, processing requirements and controls. Economics of the system have not been examined. Documentation of the general design provides a basis for economic review and development effort of approved projects. System complexity controls logical limits of resource expenditure in this phase.

System objectives are fundamental to design. What end will the system accomplish? Objectives are defined as a shared user and development group responsibility. Systems developed without user participation are viewed as "ivory tower" logic by users and frequently fail. The user must be equally committed to the result. Documentation of objectives can be narrative. They must identify data usage, frequency, and volume (Figure 7).

Flowcharting provides a simple means of information flow display. The flowchart communicates the means of producing results to satisfy the objectives. The flowchart provides understanding of procedural requirements and organization responsibilities. Changes in responsibilities can be considered in terms of manpower requirements and logic. (Figure 8.)

Processing logic and controls are documented through use of decision tables. Decision tables contain identification of variable conditions and corresponding actions. The decision tables of the general design are not adequately detailed for

---

OBJECTIVES - STUDENT RECORD SYSTEM

1. Provide a grade record for each student containing current and historical course information. Maintain accumulated credits and grade average.

2. Maintain course grade records for assignment grades, test grades, and final grade. Include absentee record by course.

3. Maintain record of course to faculty member assignments.

4. Provide course record of students enrolled, class days, time, and room number.

Figure 7

STUDENT RECORD SYSTEM FLOWCHART

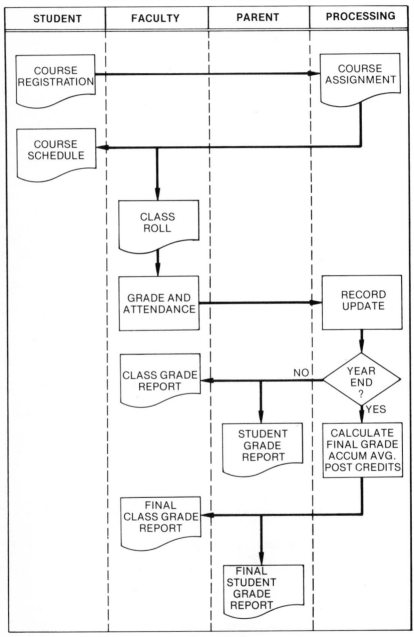

Figure 8

development programming. They are intended only to document the primary logic considerations. (Figure 9.)

Working with the user, the general design must further identify development responsibility. There are three data associations in an information system; data gathering, purification and use. Gathering refers to the initial file creation action and subsequent file expansion. Purification provides maintenance capability to improve data accuracy. Usage is application of data in achievement of the objectives. Data base system logic incorporates control disciplines. Information failing to satisfy the logic disciplines is rejected. The using organization has responsibility for rejection response during and following the file creation and implementation effort. A data audit performed by the user during the development elapsed time may reduce file load rejections.

EVALUATE JUSTIFICATION CRITERIA

Are the objectives of the new system currently being accomplished? If not, the development and operating costs of the new system will be added operating expense. If a current method of achieving the objectives exists, it must be either operating at greater cost or producing unsatisfactory results. Unless the proposed system reduces cost or increases benefits, why expend the development effort? The justification for development and future operating costs must be supported by improved results and/or cost reductions.

System operating costs are the direct result of resource expenditure. The resource is either labor or equipment. Clerical effort to get the job done today and equipment including non-data processing machines which have maintenance, rental, and service contracts are primary cost considerations. The cost evaluation should consider all major elements associated with the system.

A similar cost evaluation should be developed in support of the system proposed. Clerical efforts and equipment requirements should be estimated and included. Development costs of the new system fall mainly in the category of manpower and equipment expenditures. The manpower portion must consider

CONDITION	1	2	3	4	5
Applied This Course	N	Y	Y	Y	Y
Prerequisites Satisfied		N	Y	Y	Y
Credit Already Earned			Y	N	N
Vacancy Available				N	Y
ACTION					
Reject Application	X	X	X	X	
Enroll					X
Notify Faculty Rep.					X

Figure 9. Enrollment Decision Logic

		JUN	JUL	AUG	SEPT	OCT	NOV	DEC	JAN	FEB	MAR	APR	MAY	JUN	JUL
I. Development Cost															
A. Programming/Analysis	160 Hrs./$10	$1600	(800)	(800)												
B. User Participation																
1. Supervision	60 Hrs./$10	$ 600	(200)	(400)												
2. Clerical	90 Hrs./$4	$ 360		(180)	(180)											
C. Computer Costs																
1. Compilation & Test	6 Hrs./$50	$ 300	(100)	(200)												
2. File Conversion	8 Hrs./$50	$ 400		(100)	(300)											
D. Total Development Cost		$3260	(1100)	(1680)	(480)											
II. Operating Cost																
A. Computer Cost	12 Hrs./$50	$ 600				(100)	(50)	(50)	(50)	(100)	(50)	(50)	(50)	(100)	(50)	(50)
B. Keypunch/Verification	30 Hrs./$4	$ 120				(20)	(10)	(10)	(10)	(20)	(10)	(10)	(10)	(20)	(10)	(10)
C. Program Maintenance	2 Hrs./$10	$ 20							(10)				(10)			
D. Total Operating Cost		$ 740				(120)	(60)	(60)	(70)	(120)	(60)	(60)	(70)	(120)	(60)	(60)
III. Savings																
A. Part-Time Typist	$250/Mo.	$3000	250	250	250	250	250	250	250	250	250	250	250	250	250	250
B. Rental Typewriter	$30/Mo.	$ 360	30	30	30	30	30	30	30	30	30	30	30	30	30	30
C. Transcript Copies	$.20/Copy	$ 200			20	20	20	20	20	20	20	20	20	20	20	20
D. Total Savings		$3560	280	280	300	300	300	300	300	300	300	300	300	300	300	300
IV. Cash Flow			(820)	(1400)	(180)	180	240	240	230	180	240	240	230	180	240	240
V. Cumulative Flow			(820)	(2220)	(2400)	(2200)	(1980)	(1740)	(1510)	(1330)	(1090)	(850)	(620)	(440)	(200)	40

Figure 10. Cash Evaluation & Flow

analytical programming and clerical tasks required to satisfy systems objectives. Include the effort required by user personnel during development. One-time charges for forms design, freight, and building modifications should be identified. Equipment costs for programming and data conversion are additional cost considerations.

Elimination of one hour per day of a person's time does not reduce operating costs. True savings must result in a reduction of operating costs. Cancellation of a rental or maintenance contract is a true saving. Elimination of an existing position or the need to increase headcount are true savings. Such reduction of operating costs are tangible benefits. Associated with new systems are many intangible benefits which can be documented. The system user may not be able to identify the precise dollar value of intangible benefits for information control, accuracy, or timeliness. If the development effort is a business expense, a user estimate of intangible benefits is required to adequately identify the system value.

Development and operating costs, including one-time charges, can be calendarized over the life span of the proposed system. Experience tells us that this should not exceed five (5) years duration in most justifications. Identified savings can be spread over the system cycle in a similar manner. (See Figure 10.)

Knowledge of the cost versus savings criteria identifies the cash flows to calculate economic justification. Systems justified without a detailed approach frequently provide inadequate or unrecognized benefits. The expenditure for data processing equipment and manpower will contribute most to an organization which requires that each project developed contribute through reduced operating costs.

PROJECT PLANNING AND CONTROL

Many projects developed have critical implementation dates established by fiscal or annual considerations. Elimination of project planning is commonly considred as a development time reduction. If the result supports the development endeavor, planning is the insurance of result achievement and quality. The elements of planning are essential to success. Satisfaction of the design objectives requires achievement of all system aspects. Planning identifies the elements and provides a record of project status. Early recognition of project delay provides for corrective actions. Failure to plan results in overlooked considerations which may result in system failure.

A development network diagram identifies project tasks and task relationships. (Figure 11.) The network provides documentation of the project efforts and

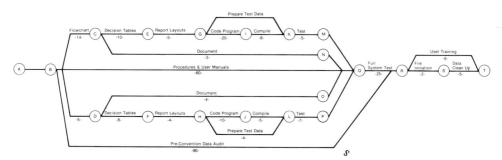

Figure 11. Student Record System Development Plan

highlights critical activities. It includes all tasks required from project approval to completion.

Project work programs provide specification details relative to specific assignments in the project (Figure 12). They show the timing schedule, available information and required activities. The work program identifies responsibilities of both the development and user personnel. Documentation of a system is not an afterthought. The work program identifies specific documentation requirements provided from each work step.

The combination of the network diagram and work program provide progress

---

DEVELOPMENT PROJECT WORK PROGRAM

Project Description: Course Assignment-Student Record System

Start Date: June 1   Completion Date: July 31

Estimated Project Time: Development   56 Hrs.   User   17 Hrs.

A. information Provided:
  1. Basic logic flowchart
  2. Basic logic decision tables
  3. Internal control rules
  4. File data layouts
  5. Data Dictionary/Directory
  6. Data Management Standards

B. Development Activities:

	Develop Hours	Used Hours	Document Created
1. Develop logic routine flowcharts	14	0	X
2. Prepare logic decision tables	6	4	X
3. Prepare report layouts	3	2	X
4. Code program	20	0	
5. Prepare test data	0	8	
6. Compile and omit diagnostics	8	0	X
7. Test and desk check (3 tests)	3	2	
8. Finalize documentation	2	1	X
	—	—	—
Total	56	17	5

Figure 12

measurement tools. Completed activities can be noted on the network diagram for achievement recording. Project managers can inspect and approve satisfaction of each activity, including documentation required. These documents provide the ability to measure actual time expended versus plan. Since planning is an estimating process, knowledge of the deviation provides a basis for refining the estimating technique. Most significant, however, is the control it provides over resource utilization. The project was justified on the basis of economic feasibility. Lack of control can delay development, fail to recognize realignment of assignments and thus hide true project costs.

The general design was the basis of estimating. Modifications to the design specifications must be evaluated and documented. Significant changes may require review of the economic factors and plan revisions.

DATA MANAGEMENT CONTROL

Data management is the process of disk data-base control. The Data Management Routine (DMR) initializes files and provides record add, delete, retrieval and update functions. The principle of data management promotes independence between application programs and file management technology. (Figure 13.) The DMR can be measured in terms of performance on retrieval efficiency, storage utilization, file restructuring conversion time and contributions to simplification of application programming. Application of data management concepts promotes standard conventions and control over applications programming which reduce programming costs.

The DMR may be identified in simple terms as a data base input/output control program. Information is stored on direct access files by a sequential or random access method included in the DMR. The problem program communicates with the DMR through modular programming linkage techniques. The application-programmer regards the management routine as a tool to achieve a system objective. Data management packages are available from equipment suppliers, software companies or can be independently developed.

The DMR responds to system requirements for action and control relating to file organization, access and maintenance. A data base by definition is a collection of information. This information includes multiple master and subordinate files. The routine must support all master and subordinate files and maintain file relationship linkage.

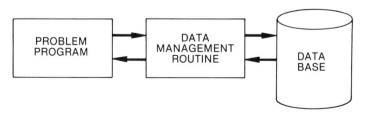

Figure 13

Master files are sequentially or randomly organized. A specific record is located through a key data element. Subordinate master files are loaded by a controlled load through the DMR. Record availability and usage control must be recognized by the DMR.

A random access record has four segments: file address, key, data and linkage. Data includes all stored information including the key. The key also serves as record identity and access control. File address is the physical device storage location for the record. Linkage provides a path from a master to a subordinate record. Subordinate files are stored by the DMR and require no external key. Instead, accuracy verification controls are required. (Figure 14.)

In the example, the STUDENT FILE is sequentially organized by SURNAME. The COURSE FILE is sequentially organized by COURSE-NAME. Follow the student CLASS-LINK path to trace academic history or course schedule. Now, follow the COURSE MASTER STUDENT LINK to obtain class enrollment. Other master files (i.e., FACULTY-MASTER) can be linked through additional subordinate files.

MASTER NO. 1—STUDENT FILE

ADDR	REG NO	SURNAME	FIRST-NAME	SEX	BIRTH	CLASS YR	ACCUM AV	ACCUM CR	CLASS LINK
1,3	4,5,2	A,N,D,R,E,W,S	T,H,O,M,A,S	M	0,5,2,7,5,7	1,9,7,5	0,0,0,0	0,0,0,0	0,8,0
1,9	4,5,3	A,T,K,I,N,S	S,H,I,R,L,E,Y	F	0,6,2,0,5,6	1,9,7,4	8,8,6,0	0,0,4	0,8,4
2,0	4,5,4	B,A,K,E,R	S,A,L,L,Y	F	0,3,1,7,5,7	1,9,7,5	0,0,0,0	0,0,0,0	0,9,2
2,1	4,5,5	B,R,O,W,N	R,O,B,E,R,T	M	1,1,2,0,5,7	1,9,7,5	0,0,0,0	0,0,0,0	0,9,6
ADDR	KEY	KEY	KEY		DATA				LINK

SUBORDINATE—SCHEDULE & HISTORY

ADDR	COURSE NO	REG NO	ASSIGN GRADE	TEST GRADE	DAYS ABS	FINAL GRADE	NEXT STUDENT	NEXT CLASS
8,0	M,2,6	4,5,2	0,0,0,0	0,0,0,0	0,0,0	0,0,0	0,8,4	0,8,1
8,1	S,0,1	4,5,2	0,0,0	0,0,0	0,0	0,0,0	0,9,1	0,8,2
8,2	E,0,1	4,5,2	0,0,0	0,0,0	0,0	0,0,0	0,9,5	0,8,3
8,3	F,R,1	4,5,2	0,0,0	0,0,0	0,0	0,0,0	0,9,7	E,N,D
8,4	M,2,6	4,5,3	9,5,0	9,3,4	0,2	9,3,2	0,8,7	0,8,5
ADDR	CONTROL		DATA			LINK		

MASTER NO. 2—COURSE FILE

ADDR	COURSE NO	COURSE NAME	FACULTY NAME	CLASS TIME	DAYS	NO CREDITS	NO ENROLL	ROOM	STUDENT LINK
3,1	M,2,6	A,L,G,E,B,R,A	M,R,.,N,O,L,A,N	0,8,3,0	M,T,W,T	1	2,7	1,2,6	0,8,0
3,2	S,0,1	B,I,O,L,O,G,Y	M,R,S,.,P,I,E,R,C,E	0,9,3,0	M,W,T,F	1	2,4	2,1,8	0,8,1
3,3	S,0,4	C,H,E,M,I,S,T,R,Y	M,R,.,A,D,A,M,S	1,0,3,0	M,W,F	1	2,8	2,2,2	0,9,0
ADDR	DATA	KEY		DATA					LINK

Figure 14. Loaded Data Base

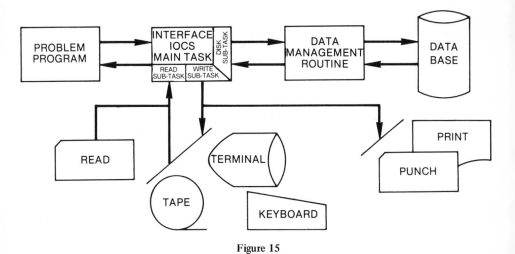

Figure 15

An application program requests a collection of data by field name from the DMR. The DMR responds with the data only and need not provide address or linkage information. It communicates at a data element level rather than record level. Modifications to the file organization or record sizes do not affect the existing application programs. This provides data independence. Additional independence is possible through development of a standard interface to handle ALL input/output functions. This routine resides between the application program and the DMR. (Figure 15.)

Fundamental COBOL without input/output is similar between all equipment manufacturers. The standard interface routine provides hardware and software independence. It provides conversion capability to accept new advancements in our industry with minimum application program change.

Data management is a tool. Use of this tool requires a skilled "craftsman" and brings a new specialist to our data processing scene. This man, the data base administrator, must achieve efficient response and maximum throughput through his technical skills. He must understand all tools of his trade including DMR's, access methods, and storage devices. His function relieves application programmers from storage technology and frees them to concentrate on the application problems.

DEVELOP, TEST AND DOCUMENT

Throughout the preceding phases of our project, development personnel were involved with other assignments. Other projects were being evaluated simultaneously. We have defined the objectives, prepared a plan, identified justification and employed a data base administrator to satisfy our technical needs. We are now ready to deal face-to-face with our system. Personnel assignment is step one on our project network. Where does this project relate in priority to other application projects? Who in the organization has authority to make this decision?

It is a decision which requires judgment and communication. An Information Services Steering Committee comprised of executive representatives can direct the development priorities based upon need and operating cost/return-on-investment factors. Economics may justify staff expansion or use of external services to achieve project objectives. Activities of prior phases have provided defined specifications for external quotations.

The user-development relationship is already a reality and now our project priority warrants personnel assignment. From here to implementation the two units become a single team. Too often, we see systems representatives resort to "walking the halls" in pairs following implementation of a system. Coordination and team-work at this time is the best assurance a system has for success.

Case No. 1—After Implementation Without Coordination
User: "Your system fails to recognize this condition; fix it!"
Case No. 2—After Implementation With Coordination
User: "I failed to recognize this condition. How do we change our system to include it?"

It may not be quite that easy, but it definitely helps. All members of the development team have responsibility for the result. The user has participated in logic, testing and preparation. At implementation time he is aware of what the system does, how it does it and the expected results. He lacks this knowledge if he sits back with an attitude of "call me when you're done."

What is job achievement? How do we recognize when we are ready for implementation? The Computer Standards Manual must define the required criteria to be satisfied to classify a project as complete. It must include documentation, test satisfaction and mutual user/development agreement of achieved objectives.

The phase of development, test and document is a roll-up-the-sleeves working "party." It is the springboard to achievement. This phase frequently extends over a prolonged elapsed period if inadequate preparation preceded start-up. The efforts are more efficient if performed in an organized manner. Each step we have performed is essential to success and is required either before or during development.

PLAN SECURITY PROTECTION

The Pentagon fire, university and industrial vandalism and unauthorized time-share data access were given front-page coverage in business and data processing tabloids. Unfortunately, need for data processing security can be recognized too late. Data security is an insurance which protects the system investment, assures continued processing of data and permits data processing managers a few extra hours of restful sleep.

Protection needs include equipment, data, programs and documentation. Unintentional accidents occur from program and operator errors, floods, power failures and equipment malfunctions. Economic justifications reveal the cost of system development and operation. They fail to identify the effect a prolonged operational failure has on operating costs. Imagine your organization reaction to a prolonged operational failure. Redevelopment of a data base or procurement of

CONDITION	1	2	3	4	5
Data Restricted	N	Y	Y	Y	Y
Terminal Authorized		Y	N	N	N
Proper Key			Y	N	N
Proper Password				Y	N
ACTION					
Serve Request	X	X	X	X	
Reject Request					X
Log Unauthorized Request					X

Figure 16. Confidential Security Decision Logic

replacement hardware could exceed several weeks. Security is a primary responsibility of information services management.

Major security considerations include confidentiality, data recovery, equipment protection and program/system back-up. Back-up equipment agreements, restricted computer-room access and elimination of glass computer rooms protect hardware. This development phase addresses the other aspects of data base security.

Confidential security restricts dissemination of the information captured by a system to persons authorized access to the information. Data bases may store available and restricted information in a single file or bank of files. Remote terminal access requires computer control over information dissemination in addition to prior administrative controls. Basic control by terminal identification can be incorporated in the interface subtask to restrict confidential responses to authorized terminals. Key or password access can also be incorporated to restrict access to an authorized individual. (Figure 16.)

Data security implies the ability to recover from data destruction without loss of the information validity. Cause of data destruction is not important when the data base is destroyed. Concentration rests on recovery and the ability to react. Previous tape systems provided the natural generation back-up procedure. Protection of data bases requires periodic capture of the file images on tape or disk packs. Back-up frequency is determined by considering the recovery duration and the effect on organization operations.

The file image changes in a data base system as a result of transaction processing. Reconstruction of a data base following destruction is a process of restoring the most current back-up and reprocessing the interm transactions. It is necessary, therefore, to retain the processed transactions between back-ups for accurate recovery. A multi-level security procedure for a data base can be initiated. In this procedure, each back-up level may require higher organization authorization to initiate restore action. (Figure 17.)

Programs and software require similar protection. A system requires both data and programs to satisfy its objectives. Security protection requires librarian controls over program decks, listings and documentation. Recording procedures to identify program modification details aid in debugging and protection.

DATA BASE BACK-UP PROCEDURE

File Number_____1262_____Name___Back-Up_____

Frequency_____Daily_____Retention___4 Generations____

Transaction File Ident___No. 286 Daily Batch_____

Generation	File Loc.	Trans. Loc.	Rotation Inst.	Authority to Use
1	Tape Library	Computer Room	Move to Gen No 2	Shift Supervisor
2	File Vault	Tape Library	Move to Gen No 3	Data Base Administrator
3	Payroll Vault	File Vault	Move to Gen No 4	Data Processing Manager
4	Bank Vault	Payroll Vault	Scratch	Director Information Services

Figure 17

System documentations is a volume of hand-written, computer generated, and correspondence papers accumulated from the initial specification through actual implementation. Much is using unnecessary drawer space. Some is valuable reference material which requires protection. Microfilm is a compact means of duplication and storing documentation at relatively low cost.

Computer management realizes the importance of security. They are responsible for its success and must enforce compliance with security standards. Unrecoverable loss of a data base would be difficult to explain to operating management.

EDUCATE AND IMPLEMENT

Implementation is an elapsed period rather than a point in time. Implementation tools are information flow procedures and system user manuals. Preparation of these documents has been accomplished during the development cycle.

Procedures are written, published, distributed and maintained by the development group. The procedures identify organization responsibilities and manual controls as information flows between organization units. "Playscript" method is a brief simple method of procedure writing which identifies actions by responsible area.

The user manual documents detailed actions within a single organization unit. The user manual contains system flow diagrams and decision tables. Written action steps can also be written in playscript style. The user manual is an extension of the procedure and shows step-by-step actions to satisfy procedural information flows.

The user area representatives can be assigned responsibility for publishing their segments of user manuals. Writing assistance may be required from the procedures analyst; however, he should not write the manuals independent of the user.

Prior to implementation, procedures and user manuals must be presented to and discussed with persons who will work with the new system. These sessions are intended to clarify the responsibilities, actions and objectives of the system. Both development and user representatives should participate in these presentations. If multiple sessions are necessary, all should be presented by the same individuals. Be prepared to repeat training following system start-up as required.

Programs, procedures and education are completed. The system start-up can begin. The development representatives must be available to assist the user through retraining and answering questions. He must physically locate within the user area to be available to all user personnel. As system flows operate smoothly, and questions reduce, he can withdraw and return to his home area. A random sample of transactions should be traced to assure accurate data base results. Rejections must be examined and controlled. Rejection logs must verify that response and corrective actions have occurred. The development department is responsible to inform the user of any program modifications which affect the data rules. The stored data must never be altered without user control and participation.

The user is responsible for the information accuracy. Data base information is the result of gathering data from multiple sources. The establishment of a data base can reveal past data inaccuracy which requires corrective action. Post-implementation clean-up must be a user responsibility.

Proper planning and adherence to the steps outlined pave the road for implementation. The approach outlined avoids undesirable surprises since adequate planning, coordination, testing and education have preceded implementation. The combined participation of system and functional skills, sharing accountability for the result, leads a system to achievement of its objectives.

AUDIT AND EVALUATE RESULTS

The system audit is a post-implementation review of operating costs, savings and investment security. The audit will be conducted by a person or group other than the development project leader or user. Large organizations may identify a system audit function. Others may assign this responsibility to a financial or data processing manager. The auditor has the economic study documents, development costs and operating records as the basis of his review.

A comparison of the economic evaluation to actual costs requires a comprehensive review. Transaction volumes, file sizes, computer operating costs in addition to user responsibilities must be examined. Projected savings, both tangible and intangible, must be reviewed for achievement. Additional costs or savings should be included in this audit study.

The audit report should be a brief narrative which describes the findings. It should be supported by an evaluation and cash flow similar to the economic study document (Figure 10) plus a comparison of plan to actual. Project audit and evaluation reports should be submitted to the Information Services Steering Committee.

Each organization has its own attitudes and opinions toward systems responsibilities. These "Ten Commandments of Data Base" provide a procedure for systems development. They identify ten fundamental steps to follow in the development of data base systems. These steps may be applied to any information system design. A data base stores all organization information in a single, multi-phase system. The importance of the data base to organization operations places greater emphasis on design planning and control. These guidelines reduce the risk of failure, provide security recovery, reduce development time, provide project controls, assure invest-ment justification and achieve system objectives.

Through this ten phase method we can enjoy freedom from hardware, software and data bases. Our analyst will deal at a problem level and new technology may enhance but shall never restrict our development endeavors.

GLOSSARY

Data Base: An orderly collection of business facts stored to serve informa-tion requirements in a single, multiphase system.

Data Dictionary: Defines standard data elements. The elements are com-bined to form information in input documents, stored file records, and information retrieval.

Data Management Routine (DMR): Initializes files and provides record add, delete, retrieval, and update functions.

DISCUSSION QUESTIONS

1. How does the author view a data base? An ideal data base?
2. In the article ten basic considerations in data base development are listed and explained. Summarize the ideas underlying these considera-tions.

THE MANAGED DATA BASE

Frederic Keysor

A new dimension in data processing, as we know it, is receiving increased attention in the emerging era of information processing. This dimension is the recognition of data as the third resource, together with hardware and personnel resources, required to develop information.

The problems resulting from non-recognition of data as a resource can be solved with effective data management. With this new approach to the data resource, three phases of data base development can be identified. Phases I and II are application oriented. Phase III is application independent.

Data base control is a documentation problem. Now, the capability of solving this problem is available through the recently developed PRIDE, a proprietary system methodology. This methodology provides data base control through effec-

Source: Reprinted, with permission, from *Data Management*, May 1974, pp. 15-21, published by the Data Processing Management Association, Park Ridge, Illinois.

tive documentation and is a technique which can be applied to systems design problems in the traditional file oriented environment and to analysis and control of data as a resource.

As data processing has developed over the past 20 years, emphasis has been placed on management of personnel and hardware. Personnel development and utilization, and hardware selection and performance have been the major management problems.

In the 1970's, an important change in approach has been evident. The hallmark of the change is "INFORMATION." Systems have become "management *information* systems (MIS)" and data processing has become "*information* processing." The emphasis on information reflects the recognition that the computer oriented system is to be replaced by the information oriented system.

The problems experienced in development of management information systems result from a static computer/application oriented data base used as a source for the dynamic information required by MIS.

Separation of the data base from the application systems producing information is essential. New information needs are met in a managed data base environment by writing new procedures.

DEFINITIONS

The revised concept of information processing has required specific definitions of data, information and subsequently, of data base. Data is defined as the representation of a fact or event. Information is the result of the collection, analysis and summarization of data. A data base is the entire accumulation of data necessary to meet the information requirements of an organization.

Several observations are relevant to these definitions. The definitions are not new. What is significant is the interrelationships which become apparent as data, information and data base are considered together. Data has no intrinsic meaning. Information is derived from data. A data base is not an entity to be created in the future—it exists at the present time and is composed of computer *and* manual files.

The data resources contained in an existing data base present an immediate problem. Current management of personnel and hardware resources must be expanded to include data resources. Only recently has the recognition of this trichotomy led to identification of a new management area, termed data management or data administration.

The problem of data management did not develop overnight. It has been present during the development of data processing and existed prior to the advent of the computer. As noted by the definition of data base (the entire accumulation of data necessary to meet the information requirements of an organization), the problem is fundamental to organization, per se.

THREE PHASES OF DATA BASE DEVELOPMENT

Three phases in data base development can be identified. Phase I is the Manual Data Base (Figure 1). Phase II is the File/System Data Base (Figure 2). Phase III is the Managed Data Base (Figure 3).

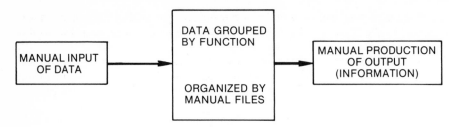

Figure 1. Phase I The Manual Data Base

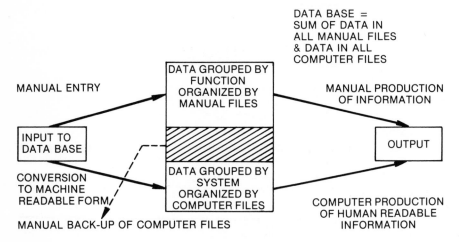

Figure 2. Phase II The File System Data Base

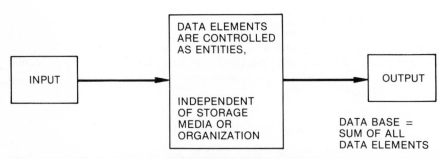

Figure 3. Phase III The Managed Data Base

Phase I represents the data base of an organization prior to the introduction of data processing. Even in a completely manual environment data bases have been conceptualized in terms of files and records.

Phase II represents the data base of an organization using data processing. The file/system concept remains dominant. If the existence of a data base is recognized, it is compartmentalized into files within systems and the interrelationship of manual and computer files is ignored or neglected.

Before examining Phase III, a recapitulation of the problems resulting from the file/system orientation of Phases I and II follows:

1. The data base is not considered as an entity. The dominant entities are files and records.

2. Additional fragmentation results in Phase II when the dichotomy of computer and manual files is introduced.

3. Control of the data base is lost, resulting in redundant data and storage of information. It should be noted here, that only data should be stored in the data base. Information, which is produced from data, should not be stored. Information should be produced from data as output is required.

4. Physical file security is the dominant consideration—data security is neglected.

5. Input and output are related to specific files.

6. Information on the data base as the sume of data resources is not available.

Phase III represents the managed data base. Data elements, not files and records, are the basic entities. The data base is the sum of all data elements regardless of storage media or file/record organization. Using this approach, solutions to the problems resulting from the file/system orientation are available.

BASIC CONCEPTS

The basic concept of the Phase III managed data base is data oriented, not processing oriented.

Traditional Data Processing Concept

INPUT   → PROCESSING   → OUTPUT

Data and the action taken on the data are represented as equivalents. The central body of data, the data base, it omitted.

Phase III The Managed Data Base Concept

INPUT   → DATA   → OUTPUT

This representation relates to data which must be available for processing to take place. Processing is represented by the arrows. Processing is required to produce information from the data base and enter required data into the data base.

Expanding the revised concept of the Phase III managed data base, it is now possible to relate the data management documentation as designed in PRIDE, to the existing data base present in all organizations. It is important to remember that the data base storage can be either completely manual or manual and automated.

"PRIDE" DATA MANAGEMENT DOCUMENTATION

Input	Data	Output
Descriptions	Descriptions	Descriptions

INPUT ⟶ DATA ⟶ OUTPUT

Organization
shown by:
File Descriptions
Record Descriptions

The data base is documented by data descriptions. The information to be produced from the data base is documented by the output descriptions. The data required to develop, expand and maintain the data base is documented by the input descriptions.

The data base is not a formless mass of raw data. It must be organized. Organization is accomplished through files and records within files. This organization is documented by file and record description.

ORGANIZING THE DESCRIPTIONS

It is apparent that the methodology's data management descriptions outlined above must be organized to perform two functions. First, they must be available to assist the data manager in solving the problems resulting from the file/system oriented data base. Second, they must be available to the analyst/designer to respond to information requirements from the data base.

As the Data Management Forms Usage Diagram (Figure 4) shows, the organization of the descriptions by the data manager corresponds to the concept of the Phase III managed data base. Manual files of descriptions are established by description, i.e., input, output, data, file and record. The descriptions are logged with serially assigned description numbers and filed sequentially by the description numbers. This organization contributes solutions to problems resulting from the file/system orientation as follows:

1. The data base is now considered an entity which can be managed and controlled.

2. The dichotomy of computer and manual files is eliminated because all data elements are documented as components of one data base.

3. Because the data base is now subject to analysis and control, the problems

ORGANIZED BY THE DATA MANAGER:

INPUT A	DATA a	FILE A	OUTPUT A
INPUT B	DATA b	FILE B	OUTPUT B
INPUT C	DATA c	FILE C	OUTPUT C
	DATA d	RECORD 1	
	DATA e	RECORD 2	
	DATA f	RECORD 3	

ORGANIZED FOR THE ANALYST:

INPUT A	FILE A		OUTPUT A
DATA a	RECORD 1	RECORD 2	DATA d
DATA b	DATA a	DATA d	DATA e
DATA c	DATA b	DATA e	DATA f
	DATA c	DATA f	

Figure 4. The Data Management Forms Usage

of redundant data and storage of information can be identified and solutions developed.

4. Data security can be achieved in addition to physical file security because information on the data base components is available.

5. Input is now related to the data base, not specific files. Output can be produced from the entire data base, not specific files.

6. Information on the data base as the sum of all data resources is available to meet information requirements of the organization promptly and accurately.

Again referencing the Data Management Forms Usage Diagram (Figure 4), the organization of descriptions for the analyst/designer reflects the real world environment in which systems must be designed. The data base can only be accessed through files and records within files. Therefore, file descriptions and record descriptions are presented to the analyst/designer with associated data descriptions.

Output and input are defined as human readable. Examples of output include listings, COM and CRT displays. Examples of input include forms, applications and other source documents. Output and input descriptions are prepared with associated data descriptions.

Finally, the descriptions organized for the analyst/designer provide detailed system documentation which is continually updated. This is one of the outstanding features of PRIDE data management.

DATA MANAGEMENT INTERFACE

The analyst designer and the data manager must work in close cooperation during system development. The system's methodology defines nine phases of system development during which this interface takes place.

The interface between analyst/designer and data manager involves three basic steps. Systems development is initiated by the analyst/designer in response to a user request for additional output. The procedure followed by the analyst/designer is related to the Output Formula.

OUTPUT FORMULA

$$\text{OUTPUT} \quad - \quad \frac{\text{EXISTING DATA}}{\text{ELEMENTS}} \quad = \quad \text{INPUT}$$

Definition of the output provides a list of required data elements. After determining the existing data elements in the data base, any non-existent data elements must be entered in the data base through input.

THREE-STEP INTERFACE

STEP I Output Definition. The analyst/designer defines the output required and lists the component data elements. The data manager catalogs the output description.

STEP II Data Definition. The data manager compares the data element list to the data descriptions. After identifying existing descriptions, the remaining data elements fall into two classifications. First, data elements may exist in the data base but have not been described. The analyst/designer must describe these. Second, data elements not in the data base comprise the input components. The data manager now organizes the descriptions for the analyst/designer as shown in the Data Management Forms Usage Diagram, (Figure 4). At this point new data descriptions, file and records descriptions providing organization for the new data in the data base and input descriptions are missing.

STEP III Input Definition. The analyst/designer describes the new data elements and related input descriptions. With the assistance of the data manager, new or revised file and record descriptions to organize the new data, are prepared. The data manager now organizes complete sets of descriptions for the analyst/designer as shown in the Data Management Forms Usage Diagrams, (Figure 4).

DATA MANAGEMENT FORMS

When discussing the **PRIDE** data management forms, the primary responsibility for documentation control entries is assigned to the data manager. The designer/analyst is responsible for the descriptive information.

Each data element comprising the data base, including manually and computer stored data is to be defined using the methodology's data description. Documentation control entries include a serially assigned data description numbers and names for cross reference. Descriptive information includes data names, type of data, narrative including code lists if applicable, physical characteristics, data source and validation requirements.

The organization of the data base is defined by file descriptions and one or more record descriptions associated with each file: "File descriptions" are linked to associated "Record descriptions" which in turn are linked to associated "Data descriptions" for each data element or field in the record.

A file may contain several records, e.g., header, detail, and trailer. A record may be present in more than one file, e.g., a transaction record appearing on both a transaction file and an error file. Data elements appear on inputs, in the data base in several records, and as output components.

Each record is to be defined using the system's record description. Documentation control entries include a serially assigned record description number (RD No.). File description numbers and names relate the record to each associated file providing cross reference to data base organization. Data description numbers and names relate the associated data elements providing cross reference to record composition. Descriptive information includes record names, record grouping (sort keys and/or access keys), record length and security. Record layout forms should be filed with the record descriptions. These are not provided with PRIDE, which is hardware independent.

Each file designed to organize the data base is to be defined using the PRIDE file description. Documentation control entries include a serially assigned file description number (FD No.), associated record description numbers and names, and program or subsystem identifications referencing the file. Descriptive information includes file names, file type, file organization, size, blocking factor, media, retention, and security.

Input and output are human readable. Following conversion of input to machine readable form, organization of the data is in the file/record hierarchy. Prior to creation of output the data also is organized in the file/record hierarchy.

An input source document is converted to record(s) within files at the time of data entry, e.g., key-to-disk. In the case of manually maintained data, physical filing of the source document converts it into a record(s).

A listing, COM, CRT display or manual report is not classified as output until it is human readable. Print tapes, data communication messages or manual records used to prepare reports are still classified as records within files.

Each input document is to be defined using the PRIDE input description. Documentation control entries include a serially assigned input description number (ID No.), and associated data description numbers and names. Descriptive information includes input name, function, preparation requirements and data conversion and transmission information.

Each output listing, COM, display or manual report is to be defined using the system's output description. Documentation control entries include a serially assigned output number (OD No.) and associated data element numbers and names for both copied data elements and generated data elements. Descriptive information includes output requirements, purpose, grouping and sequence, frequency, and form.

IMPLEMENTING THE SYSTEM

The implementation of PRIDE data management includes establishment of description logs, preparation for indexing the descriptions, developing routine procedures for processing descriptions, planning analysis of the data base and preparing for conversion to the new documentation.

The descriptions of data, files, records, inputs and outputs should be logged for control purposes by the data manager. Individual logs are maintained for each type of description.

Indexing the descriptions is a vital responsibility of the data manager. The problem is complicated because the existing data base has not been developed systematically. One flaw in the Phase II file/system data base is data redundancy.

Related to this is the haphazard assignment of data file, record, input, and output names. Effective indexing depends on assignment of standard names.

During conversion to PRIDE data management, it is necessary to create a lexicon for name standardization. Using this lexicon, standard names are developed for use on the descriptions, in systems documentation and programming. Nonstandard names are linked by description number to the appropriate description.

The lexicon should be developed to meet individual requirements of the installation. For example, five hundred terms could be selected from which all standard names would be developed using one or a combination of terms. The selection of terms should be a joint effort involving analysts and data management personnel. Currently used terms and abbreviations should be included when possible.

The primary indexing problem is related to the data descriptions. Also indices and/or alpha listings may be required for file, record, input and output descriptions. Note, that linking of diverse names to a description with a standard name requires human judgment.

Indexing will be facilitated by developing a data management system. An indexing subsystem could be implemented using a card master file. Updates to the master file would be manual with indices produced by card-to-tape or card-to-disk sorts resulting in two listings. First, an alpha list of current names with associated description numbers would allow reference by current names. Second, an alpha list of description names with associated current names would provide cross references to be attached to the descriptions.

Consideration should be given to including additional data on the master file records to provide for analysis of the data base as descriptions are accumulated.

Conversion to PRIDE data management requires routine procedures for processing descriptions. As discussed above in the section on "organizing the descriptions," a manual filing system for data management control of the descriptions must be established.

Preparation of a data management handbook for use by analyst/designers is recommended. The contents of this handbook will facilitate education, communication and description processing.

DATA MANAGEMENT HANDBOOK

- Educational material includes explanation of data management contents and procedures for using the handbook.
- Copies of frequently used descriptions will be maintained for convenient reference.
- Standard names will include the lexicon and listings of standard names entered on the system library.
- Indices required by the analyst/designers for reference will be maintained.

Analysis of the data base will be a continuing function of data management. Planning should provide for analysis of redundant data, stored information, optimization of file structure, record organization, input redundancy and output requirements. As the data base is documented, analysis requirements will develop which are not apparent at the outset.

Preparation for conversion to the PRIDE data management documentation will be required. Commitment by management to the concept of data management is essential. It is also essential for management and the data manager to plan the evolutionary implementation of data management. Direction from management will be required to insure the acceptance of data management by system personnel.

1. Education—the use of PRIDE data management will provide excellent education in systems concepts.
2. Documentation—the PRIDE methodology provides many features designed to upgrade system documentation. One of the most important is the data management documentation which will be created and/or updated as systems are designed or modified.
3. Data base control—this includes reduction of redundant data and stored information, data security capabilities, and a data base inventory.
4. Data management system—this system will provide indexing of the descriptions, COBOL translation to standard names and the basis for an on-line documentation system.

CONCLUSION

The era of information processing has brought recognition of the data base as an existing resource requiring management control. Data bases exist in three phases of development: manual, file/system oriented and managed.

The current status of most data base development is file/system oriented and compartmentalized into manual and automated segments. Using a revised concept of information processing centered on the data base, PRIDE has developed documentation of data elements with files and records providing data base organization. Input and output, defined as human readable elements, are documented and associated with component data elements.

The system's descriptions are organized for the analyst/designer in the traditional file/record hierarchy. The data manager organizes the descriptions by type to control the data base, define data organization and document input into and output from the data base. The organization of the descriptions relates to the interface between the analyst/designer and the data manager. This interface involves output definition, data definition and input definition.

PRIDE provides data management description forms for data elements, files, records, input and output.

The implementation of PRIDE data management requires development of an indexing scheme, preparation of routine procedures for processing descriptions, commitment of management support, planning for analysis of the data base and preparing for the conversion to PRIDE data management.

This data management system provides the concepts and approach necessary to separate the existing data base from application systems and define the data base to meet dynamic information requirements effectively.

DISCUSSION QUESTIONS

1. What is the primary "message" of this article?
2. Briefly describe the following terms:
   a. data base
   b. phases of data base development
   c. data base interface
3. Distinguish the difference(s) between the traditional and the managed data base concept. Explain.

SELECTED REFERENCES

Management Information System

Articles

Field, Roger. "MIS Curves Percolating Up the Organization." *Computer Decisions,* March 1971, pp. 14-19.

_____. "Bringing the Universal MIS Down to Earth." *Computer Decisions,* June 1971, pp. 12-16.

Fry, James P. "Managing Data is the Key to MIS." *Computer Decisions,* January 1971, pp. 6-10.

Gerdel, J. K. "The Fundamentals of a Management Information System." *The Office,* May 1972, pp. 62-66, 149.

Head, Robert. "The Elusive MIS." *Datamation,* September 1, 1970, pp. 22-27.

Data Base

Articles

Canning, Richard. "Creating the Corporate Data Base." *EDP Analyzer,* May 1970, pp. 1-14.

_____. "Data Security in the Corporate Data Base." *EDP Analyzer,* May 1970, pp. 1-14.

_____. "Organizing the Corporate Data Base." *EDP Analyzer,* March 1970, pp. 1-14.

_____. "Processing the Corporate Data Base." *EDP Analyzer,* April 1970, pp. 1-14.

Foster, Caxton C. "Data Banks—A Position Paper." *Computers and Automation,* March 1971, pp. 28-32.

Harrell, Clayton. "Maintaining a Healthy Data Base." *Business Automation,* February 1972, pp. 16-18.

PART 9

Computer Security
and the
Issue of Privacy

Man has always been concerned about the privacy of information affecting his personal and business activities. Since the computer became commercially available, the massive volume of information stored in data banks has made it increasingly important that security measures be implemented to safeguard private information from unauthorized use. Thus, computer security and security measures are vital areas of interest both to the data processor and to the consumer.

This part consists of an editorial and three articles. The editorial by *Business Automation* (presently, *Infosystems*) criticizes the relatively ineffective steps taken to date by government committees on the invasion of privacy issue and urges user groups, societies, and associations to begin taking a stronger role in data security.

Welke's article makes clear that the role of the data center manager is to keep his employees from "diddling" with customers' data. The customer, on the other hand, should check the security precautions of a data center before committing his data there. He might also want to commit the center to agree to an independent "surprise" audit of the work being processed.

Scaletta's article points out that, while computers have been the solution to the information explosion, they are a threat to our individual privacy. Under nearly all circumstances involving computerized information, the individual is deprived of control over both accuracy of and access to information about him. Although the government maintains that allowing access to stored information about individuals affects national security, Scaletta suggests that a balance be established between what seems to be the national interest and personal privacy through legislation reinforced by statutory civil remedies and criminal punishment.

Finally, Scoma's article lists examples and results of cases where individuals have sabotaged or gained unauthorized access to computerized data using magnets and other ingenious methods. He lists 10 commandments of EDP security that management should follow for achieving optimal protection of computer facilities. The alleged success of a magnet in destroying data on tape, however, is highly controversial. How such a technique is used is not explained in the article. Perhaps the key point of the presentation is that computer and data security must be strengthened if today's organizations, highly dependent on computerized data, are to survive and continue to function in a dynamic environment.

THE PRIVACY THING

For a couple of weeks in February, the people most affected by data banks and other potential infringements on their rights to privacy were made aware, once more, of the tissue thin nature of those rights. Spurred by disclosures of surveillance of civilians by the military, Sen. Sam Ervin's (D-N.C.) subcommittee on constitutional rights mounted an investigation and the subsequent hearings produced newspaper, TV and radio reports that, presumably, reached the "masses."

So what happens now? Will an aroused citizenry get itself organized and campaign for laws that will protect them from peepers? We doubt it. Will politicians campaigning for election to Congress and state legislatures wield a platform plant that says, in effect, "A vote for me is a vote for your privacy?" We doubt it, though most assuredly a few champions will arise if their research tells them the "privacy thing" will garner a few votes that otherwise might be lost. Will those in the best position to put in perspective the whole matter of the use of computers, data banks and the right to privacy, speak out? The Ervin subcommittee hearings are not encouraging on that score.

At the hearings, computer manufacturers were represented by Honeywell, IBM and BEMA; the latter submitted a statement, but chose not to make a vocal presentation. One users' group was represented, but somewhat obliquely. Robert P. Bigelow, chairman of ACM's special interest group on computers and society, testified "as an individual." The other users, members of the military, were called on the carpet because of publicity they received for surveillance activities. One can only conclude that the commercial users had no voice before the subcommittee, and that's a tragic situation. Because, as the spokesmen for the manufacturers implied, the impetus for protection of privacy should come from the users. The manufacturers can supply the hardware and software that can be used to protect data files, but it's up to the user to decide how and where the techniques are applied.

The problem seems to be that privacy invasion is something that always happens to "the other guy." Someone else lost his credit rating because of decisions based on bad data. Someone else is being inundated by junk mail because he got his name on a computerized list. Someone else is in those data banks in Washington.

Source: Editorial, reprinted from *Infosystems,* June 1971, p. 80. By Permission of the Publisher. © 1971 Hitchcock Publishing Company. All rights reserved.

Further, data banks would not appear to represent a "clear and present danger" to many people. Used properly, they could be a clear and present blessing. The question is: Will they be so used? Or will a law be passed that pretends to solve, but really ignores, the problem by tossing out the data banks? Those who use computers are going to be affected, no matter what type of law is passed—or even if no law is passed. It's time for at least some of the user groups (almost every major manufacturer has at least one), societies and associations of users, to begin speaking out, where it counts.

WHAT ABOUT SECURITY?

L. A. Welke

A good data center manager or salesman can wax poetic on the subject of his data center. If you want a different tune, ask him about security, especially as it applies to your data in his center. His answer will probably be that your data is better off in his shop than in your own because his employees are disinterested. Disinterest apparently comes in several shapes and sizes. In this case, an employee is interested enough to be accurate and disinterested enough not to care!

If this *non sequitur* fails to satisfy, he will then cite the volume of work as being so large that no one has time to diddle with your data. Or he will point out that volume is so small that no one could afford to risk fiddling with your facts. Both arguments are interesting expressions of sentiment and say a good deal for the emotional disposition of data center management. Neither, however, quite answers the question of what is being done to protect your data. The implication is that somewhere between the two, a great middle ground for manipulation and abuse exists.

It's possible that your data does not have an element of confidentiality or that you do not care who knows your data. Facts and figures, after all, need interpretation and can be meaningless without further information. But few businessmen have a charitable view regarding information about their company. They are inclined to be close of mouth and tight of lip. The competitive commercial animal seems to prefer non-disclosure to the open kimono act. This being the case, data centers might do well to come to better grips with the problem.

Employees who handle customer data must know this data. It becomes management's task to control data center employees. It's a matter of personnel

Source: *Modern Data*, September 1971, p. 34.

selection, training, supervision, policy, and belief. As they say at the local bank: "Knowing a man's account balance is usually more important than knowing what he does with his evenings. We don't talk about either."

Keeping the situation under control because the employees lack the comprehension to understand the data is no excuse. Customers can come in contact with data not their own, inadvertently or by design. This can be minimized with locked containers and also by curtailing tours through the computer installation if not eliminating them altogether.

Security violation by data center management itself is most difficult to eliminate, although there is seldom a direct attempt by management to misuse information by selling someone's customer list or revealing income figures to a competitor, etc. The violations lie elsewhere. Reference selling will usually disclose some particulars on volumes and numbers. Any discussion of operating problems, troubleshooting calls, or new application development can include commentary on someone else's data and this constitutes a violation of privacy. In short, it takes a concerted and conscious effort to avoid disclosure of information.

The whole point being: what should or could a customer do to prevent or minimize these violations or, at the very least, is there any recourse through litigation? Litigation, while currently popular with the press and always popular with attorneys, is a last resort as a business maneuver. The courts will probably be on the side of the customer, but this is small recompense for the time lost and money spent in proving you were right.

Using an "ounce of prevention" approach, a customer is well advised to check security precautions of a data center prior to committing data to that center. Has the management shown what policies are in effect? Talk directly to employees and note the pick-up and delivery procedures. Check housekeeping rules in the computer room.

If procedures are not formalized, the odds are that the center's practice is not either. If the data center management is concerned enough about the subject, they will have issued some edicts to reflect their concern. And if you're allowed into the computer room to check its condition, you probably should not allow your data into it.

A customer might want to get a data center agreement to have an independent surprise audit of work being processed. The contract should clearly state who owns what in the line of data, programs, back-up files, etc., who has access to the information and under what circumstances.

If this entire discussion has left you feeling slightly paranoid about your data being in a data center, it was worth reading. If you feel quite comfortable, you probably were in good hands to begin with. Or does the problem still elude you?

THE COMPUTER AS A THREAT
TO INDIVIDUAL PRIVACY

Phillip J. Scaletta, Jr.

Computers and automatic data processing machines of various types and descriptions have already become an integral part of American business and government, and the 1970's will see an even broader expansion of services and application of the EDP industry. We have become dependent upon the computer for our very existence and survival without realizing it.

Without the computer we would have long ago drowned in our own sea of paper. Without the computer we could not have achieved space exploration, nor the standard of living which we enjoy and take for granted. Without the computer we could not successfully defend our country. It has become as much a part of us as our shadow.

While admittedly computers and EDP have been the solution to the information explosion problem, and have been a great boon to mankind, they have also created a host of new legal problems.

The most serious problem, however, is not strictly legal per se, but is a problem that immediately affects every man, woman and child in the United States. This problem is the threat the computer poses to our individual privacy.

For the past decade banks, finance companies, insurance companies, credit bureaus, motor vehicle bureaus and clubs, mail order houses, medical groups, retail businesses both small and large, federal agencies, police record centers, state agencies, the armed forces and a host of others have been amassing great volumes of data of personal information about their customers and potential customers, competitors, enemies and friends.

Many of the possessors of this personal information data, sell this data on individuals in the form of credit reports, lists for solicitation purposes, and various other reasons, to anyone who wishes to have the information and is willing to pay the price. For example, the California Department of Motor Vehicles for a nominal price sells information which it has on California autos and people who own them. Information such as name, age, address, sex, physical description, marital status, driving record, and whether the individual needs glasses to drive can be secured.

What is happening to our individual privacy? What guarantee have we that all the data about us in the computer is accurate, properly explained, etc.? When can we face our accuser—the computer?

While the U.S. Constitution does not in specific terms guarantee rights of privacy, our courts have always assumed the role of guardian of the privacy of the individual. The Supreme Court back as far as 1880 even prevented Congress from

Source: Reprinted, with permission, from *Data Management*, January 1971, pp. 19-23, published by the Data Processing Management Association, Park Ridge, Illinois.

looking into the private affairs of the citizen, and there have been numerous court decisions in the last decade reaffirming the individual's right of privacy. Does the fact that business, industry and government now depend on these large data reservoirs of personal information (about some 200 million Americans) to expand their operations and serve their customers more efficiently justify the death of individual privacy?

FEDERAL DATA CENTER PROPOSED

Approximately five years ago, the Bureau of the Budget proposed that the federal government merge all of its computer operations and create one mammoth federal data center which would be available to industry and researchers as well as for government use. There are more than a score of federal agencies and countless private agencies that now have extensive data about individuals in the United States. In terms of cost and efficiency, the establishment of a federal data center seemed to be eminently reasonable. Many states also proposed similar data centers on state levels as well as other data centers for medical records of patients, for academic records of students, etc.

Such a center would have brought together all of the information reported to the various federal agencies, and all of that material would be potentially available to anyone who could gain access to any part of it. The scope of information is frightening when one considers the records in even a few of the agencies involved, the Internal Revenue Service, the Bureau of Census, the Immigration-Naturalization Service, the Social Security Administration, the files of the FBI, the Civil Service records of federal employees, and possibly even medical records of people treated in government hospitals.

The Subcommittee on Administrative Practice and Procedure of the Senate Judiciary Committee and a subcommittee of the House Committee on Government Operations both held hearings on this issue. Opposition to the establishment of a federal data center stressed the threat to the individual's right to privacy. Information which is outdated, incomplete, or inaccurate can cause grave injustice to a citizen. He can be damaged by data in the bank which he is not even aware of being recorded there. In that situation, his right to face his accuser is infringed.

Many have also expressed great concern that if a federal data center is ever established, the computer could become the heart of a surveillance system that would turn society into a transparent world in which one's home, financial affairs and associations would be monitored, causing radical changes in the manner in which one acts and interacts with others. Visualize the potential capability of this system to create a "womb-to-tomb" dossier on each of us, with the observation that success or failure in life may ultimately depend upon what other people decide to put in our files, and upon the programmer's ability or inability to evaluate, process and interrelate the information. Scary, isn't it!

The controversy concerning the National Data Bank was helpful since it did play a useful role in focusing attention on the problem of computers and the threat to individual privacy. The proposal for the National Data Bank has now been effectively laid to rest.

This growth in concern over personal privacy in the computer age has directly paralleled the growth of the "time-sharing" method of computer utilization. In sharp contrast to the old "batch process" method of computer utilization under which programming jobs are run sequentially, often leaving the heart of the computer idle while data is being read in and results are being written out, time-sharing now allows nearly full utilization of the computers capacity by enabling more than one user to use the computer at once. Each user has his own input-output terminal connected to the computer, and by means of a complex master program the computer is able to switch its attention among the commands of the various users virtually instantaneously, giving the impression to each of the users that he alone is using the machine.

Thus some users may be inputing data and others outputing results while still others are having their programs executed by the computer's heart—the central processor. Under such a time-sharing arrangement the computer is used more efficiently and economically than it is under the old batch processing arrangement, the net result being that each user is given the functional equivalent of his own computer at a fraction of the price that a computer of his own would cost him. However, under a time-sharing arrangement there occurs the simultaneous exposure of several distinct bodies of data in the machine, creating the risk that one user might gain access to the files of data of another user, thus compromising the privacy of the other user and of the third parties whose personal data was being stored or processed in the time-sharing system.

The problem of protecting personal data has been heightened by the input-output terminals away from the central processor to strategic locations in regional offices of national corporations, or federal agencies or an important customer's place of business. Such "remote" terminals are connected to the computer's central processor and memory units by means of communication channels which usually utilize telephone lines for data transmission. Although other communications media—private microwave systems, the telegraph, and communication satellites—are not far behind the telephone companies in their ability to provide mass transmission of digital data, utilization of telephone circuits is by far the most prevalent means of data transmission used by time-sharing users today.

In fact, the use of telephone circuits promises to become even more widespread with the conversions by the telephone companies from electro-mechanical switching equipment to electronic equipment, resulting in the faster transmission of digital data over telephone lines, and even to the eventual transmission of voice communications in digital form. Unfortunately, however, telephone circuits are relatively low-security communications channels, and little is being done to make certain that computerized digital data will be any safer from snoopers or line tappers than private telephone conversations have been in the past.

TIME-SHARING ENVIRONMENT

The increase in the application of computer technology resulting from the time-sharing, remote-access terminal approach to computer utilization, and other cost-reducing procedures that have been implemented has caused profound changes in the manner in which the industrial and academic, and even the federal sectors of our society regard information and the uses to which it is put. Institutions in all of these sectors are employing computer technology for assistance in decision making, record keeping and various forms of analysis.

As a result of the increased value that is being placed on information by contemporary institutions, a substantial portion of information that previously has been treated as private is now considered as "appropriate grist for the computer mill and fair game for the data collector." There can be no doubt that we are in the midst of a change in attitude toward what is and what is not to be recorded as private information. Not only are we in the midst of an information explosion; but also an information revolution.

VAGUE CONCEPT OF PRIVACY

It has often been said that few concepts in our law are more vague and less easy to define than the concept of privacy. More and more frequently, however, the position is being taken that a basic aspect of an individual's right to privacy is his ability to control the flow of information concerning or describing him—a capability that is often essential to the establishment of social relationships and to the maintenance of personal freedom. When the individual loses his ability to control his flow, he becomes to some extent subservient to those individuals or institutions that gain access to such control. Thus, it has been suggested that the individual whose data profile is bartered or sold has become little more than a commodity.

In the past, informational privacy has been relatively easy to protect for a number of reasons: (1) large quantities of information about individuals have not been collected and therefore have not been available, (2) available information has been relatively superficial in character and often has been allowed to atrophy to the point of uselessness, (3) the available information generally has been maintained on a decentralized basis, (4) access to available information has been difficult to secure, (5) people in a highly mobile society are difficult to keep track of, and (6) most people are unable to interpret and infer the revealing information from the available data. Obviously, in a highly technological computerized environment these conditions no longer hold true.

Deprivation of an individual's control over who accesses the computerized information about him can come about in various ways. Improper access may be obtained to the information files containing the individual's record by means of unauthorized duplication or outright theft of the file.

Machine-readable records in memory banks, or on tape, drum, or disk, can be duplicated more rapidly and with less effort than their paper counterparts (a tape with 50,000,000 characters of data can be duplicated in a few minutes, leaving no traces that such a duplication has taken place). Theft of such a file may take place by such duplication of the tape, or the snooper might attempt to "eavesdrop" on the computer while a system is operating by monitoring the electromagnetic energy radiating from the computer. This energy could be then reconstituted elsewhere in the form of the data in the system at the time the radiations were captured.

Within a time-sharing system, there is the previously mentioned possibility that the computer's rapid switching from one user to another might leave a residuum of one user's file in the core of the machine, ready to be accessed by the next user. There is also the possibility that the file protection mechanisms in the time-sharing system might be inadequate, allowing one user to reference the stored files of another user.

Even if the time-sharing system employed access codes as protection to gain material from the memory bank, it is still possible to break the access code and gain the unauthorized information. At Massachusetts Institute of Technology, the home of time sharing, students were able to break elaborate codes that were supposed to protect the privacy of the users of its Project MAC computers. In one instance, the students even tapped into lines carrying transmissions from the Strategic Air Command in Omaha. Once such an access code is broken, the intruder has the ability to display and manipulate data stored in the system.

PERSONNEL SECURITY

The personnel employed to program the system are another potential source of weakness in security, for they could program "doors" into the control program which would allow unauthorized individuals to enter the system unnoticed, bypassing all the protective devices and leaving no trace after they had copied the material. More simply, the computer's operator could simply reveal the access code to snoopers. Or perhaps a corrupt repairman could rewire the machine so that certain instructions appeared to behave normally whereas in fact the protective mechanisms could be bypassed, also, the simple technique of wiretapping could be used where the telephone lines are used as a method of transmission.

Although some of the techniques mentioned may seem quite esoteric, none of them is technologically impossible, and in fact most are already feasible and most have been used. Experts have flatly stated that most programming languages are easily deciphered, that "digital transmission of data does not provide any more privacy than . . . Morse code," and that "modest resources suffice to launch a low-level infiltration effort."

Deprivation of an individual's control over the accuracy of computerized information about him can also come about in other ways. For example, a minor mechanical failure in the system might randomly distort data, a speck of dust or a fingerprint on a magnetic tape may obliterate some information, the machines, after all, are vulnerable to such accidents.

But even more serious are the possibilities for human error. Out of carelessness, maliciousness, or sheer stupidity, much damage can be done by administrators who introduce errors into the records. Unthinking people are just as capable of injuring others by unintentionally rendering a record inaccurate, losing it, or disseminating its contents to unauthorized users, as are people acting out of malice or for personal gain. It is simply unrealistic to expect personnel in clerical positions to understand the basic principles of individual privacy and to implement the subtle standards of care that the upholding of these principles requires. We have all read about individuals who have suddenly lost their credit ratings, only to find out after tedious backtracking and checking, that clerical errors had been made in record entries at the credit bureau level.

Serious problems of contextual accuracy are also created by the centralization of data. Information can be wholly accurate in one context and wholly inaccurate in another. It has been suggested that the widespread implementation of time-sharing systems across the nation, combined with the linking of regional data banks and the resulting interchange of data, will virtually guarantee the misinterpretation of that data by means of faulty inferences and false implications. Illustrative of this type of distortion is this example. A terse entry is made that the subject was arrested, convicted of a felony, and sentenced to a penitentiary for a number of years. The impact of such information would surely affect the individual's ability to gain employment or to get a credit rating, yet the "felon" may have been a conscientious objector who could not meet the requirements for exemption from military service that existed at the time he was to be inducted. If the events occurred in the past or if social attitudes had significantly changed, such information could be doubly damaging.

Of course other difficulties may also arise to increase the risk of inaccurate interpretation. Items of data that appear to be "hard" and "factual" often take on different shades of meaning, and the individual who is asked to provide explanatory details in one instance may not have the opportunity to do so at a later date when his file is reviewed for some other purpose.

The presence of such information in an individual's computerized file can be especially detrimental if it is stored without the necessary explanatory material detailing the limitations of the data. The probability of the inclusion of such supporting material is small, particularly since the trend seems to be toward oversimplifying that data which is recorded.

Under nearly all circumstances involving computerized information files, the individual is deprived of both accuracy control and access control, in one or more of the manners previously outlined. Thus a very real threat is posed to an individual's privacy by the computerization of information about him. But even more serious are the implications for personal privacy that the computer would have if used as the heart of a surveillance or intelligence system for the federal government. Yes, a very real threat of the potential capability of the government's computer system to create a comprehensive "womb-to-tomb" dossier on each of us.

"BIG BROTHER" CONCEPT UNDERWAY

Furthermore, consider the following possibilities. We may be quite near to a cashless, checkless society in which all of our financial transactions would be taken care of by a credit card which would be inserted in a remote computer terminal to register each transaction. The telephone companies could use their systems, which in essence are computers, to keep track of all calls we make. The postal department could use optical scanners to compile data on persons with whom we correspond. Some of the airline reservation systems are already maintaining passenger lists for two to three months after each flight, so that these lists may be accessed by investigators who are checking on the travels of certain individuals.

Suddenly it becomes apparent that "Big Brother" could be watching if he so desired, and that virtually every move that an individual makes could be documented. Hence, it is easy to understand why you should become concerned with the matter of individual privacy in the computer age, particularly in light of our government's interest in establishing a National Data Center.

How, then, can a balance be established between what seems to be the national interest, and personal privacy? The answer, it would seem, must come in the form of enabling legislation passed by Congress. Such legislation must provide sufficient or even excessive safeguards for the privacy interest. The legislation must also be reinforced by statutory civil remedies and criminal punishment.

Following are a few suggestions for such legislation. Incoming data for any

Federal or State Data Center should be suitable for "statistical" usage only, the specific kinds of data associated with "dossier" systems, such as those of the FBI, the IRS, Government hospital records—physical or psychiatric, and military records should be specifically omitted; mechanisms must be installed on all time-sharing systems to identify the caller and verify his right to access the material; transmission of digital data over telephone lines must be limited to statistical data only, prohibit transmission of potentially embarrassing data over such low security lines; require all computer equipment to be shielded to prevent theft of electromagnetic radiations; set up standards for competency for computer programmers, perhaps tests and licensing procedures. There are many other safeguards which will be necessary before such a system should be allowed.

DISCUSSION QUESTIONS

1. What is the main theme of the article? Elaborate.
2. In what respects is the computer a threat to individual privacy? Explain.

PROTECTING YOUR EDP

Louis Scoma, Jr.

Commercial empires will tumble unless business and industry take steps to prevent "computercide"—destruction of their computer centers which today are the nerve center of many corporations. The "guerrilla war" against the business establishment is feeding on recent successes and will widen its thrust in the months to come. Supercomputers encourage centralization of corporate EDP, and consequently increase the vulnerability of a company to natural and planned disasters. Millions are spent for fourth-generation hardware but many companies are still using first-generation security procedures. The dependence of the data generated and stored within computer centers and its validity suggest that stringent security measures be implemented immediately.

A magnet, the size of a quarter, can destroy a magnetic tape library of up to 50,000 tape reels in a matter of minutes. The crime is silent, neat and clean. The scrambling effect on the data may go undetected until a particular tape or series of tapes is called from the library. The accompanying list contains examples of actual cases.

Source: Reprinted with permission from *The Office* Magazine, September 1971, pp. 53-54.

THE INCIDENT

1. Large chemical company, makers of war materials, invaded by group armed with magnets.
2. Disgruntled employees stole customer master file containing two million names from encyclopedia distributor.
3. Computer service engineer inadvertently scrambled 80,000 customer credit records on a disc pack.
4. Five men rigged computers at two New York banks.
5. Rioting students at a Canadian university held computer as security, destroyed hundreds of thousands of records.
6. Bank's programmer altered savings account program to transfer round-off cents in interest calculations to a fictitious account.
7. While cleaning interior of a magnetic drum cabinet, employee adhered magnetic flashlight to sidewall, destroying part of data on drum.
8. Dissatisfied employee destroyed virtually every file and program in his company.
9. Member of ladies garden club touring insurance company's EDP facilities took an EAM card from the center of a box as a souvenir.
10. Students at a western college hurled Molotov cocktail through window of data center.
11. Dissidents from a western university tore through a bank's offices, destroying magnetic tapes and other records.
12. Army officer, dissatisfied with assignment and awaiting retirement, erased Army purchasing data from magnetic tapes.

THE RESULT

1. Damages estimated at $100,000 for 1000 magnetic tapes destroyed.
2. File data was sold to competitors. Estimated loss of over $3 million in sales.
3. It cost the company $10,000 to recreate files from hard copy which, fortunately, they still had.
4. Loss of $1 million.
5. Unestimated cost to re-create lost records.
6. Large sums were withdrawn from fictitious account.
7. Company lost six days' computer time reconstructing the data.
8. Auditors doubted that company could continue in business.
9. Confusion as to what was causing a program problem.
10. $500,000 computer destroyed in fire.
11. Thousands of dollars spent to recreate records.
12. Projects delayed and many dollars spent to remake files from duplicate data.

Conventional security at most firms today can be broken. Office management can check this out themselves by having people masquerade as repairmen, cleaners and guards, enter a facility and see if they are challenged by any of the personnel working there. A disgruntled employee can do untold harm by destroying such records as payroll, accounts receivable or payable, personnel records, production or inventory control, budgets, even stockholders' records. It is possible for an employee to have metal objects in his pocket or tool box that have been magnetized sufficiently to damage magnetically stored data. Degaussers can be taken into most data processing installations unnoticed in pockets, attache cases or purses. Unintentional damage has the same effect as does intentional sabotage.

EDP security is a highly specialized field. Among the many devices which we have developed to thwart computer theft and sabotage is an electronically controlled double door entry system from corridor to computer center. Once a person enters the first door, he is subjected to an electronic search by concealed probes for magnets and other "illegals." If the person carries anything creating a magnetic field into the buffer zone between the doors, a scanner detects it, freezes the lock on the second door and automatically alerts security personnel. The buffer zone prevents a mob from entering a computer center. The security guard at a closed circuit television can see and talk to a person trapped between both doors. Also, our system will signal if someone attempts to remove a reel of magnetic tape. A special label (patent pending) is affixed permanently to each reel and it cannot be taken from the facility without triggering the alarm. This label helps companies in inventory control. Recently one EDP manager confided that his company was missing 1000 tapes, each containing vital corporate data. Programers have walked off their jobs with program tapes and, within 30 days, a new company was born with a full assortment of programs.

STOP SHOWING OFF YOUR COMPUTER

Many companies invite trouble because they regard their computer centers as corporate showcases. They are proud to show visitors the winking and blinking lights, the clean looking, tastefully done facility. They do not realize the computer center is vital to the organization's daily operations. Each employee having access to a company's data center should be given a security check, including the night cleaning crew. Computer centers and data banks should be separate from other areas within a company. Utilities (power, air conditioning, heating and water supplies) should be hidden from view and provided with electronic protection.

Corporate management clearly has been increasing the need for better security by centralization, while the risks continued to escalate. It is now imperative that management establish a professional plan to prevent, as well as to catch, would-be thieves or saboteurs if it is to avoid potentially heavy expenditures and corporate loss. Management can achieve optimum protection of computer facilities and magnetic tape files by adhering to Ten Commandments of Security:

TEN COMMANDMENTS OF EDP SECURITY

1. *Thou shalt not take security for granted.* Protection of vital records and processes is a growing problem and demands serious investigation.

2. *Thou shalt provide for adequate personnel clearances.* All prospective employees, regardless of the level within the company, who have dealings with computer operations and the facility should be thoroughly screened as to past employment and personal background before they are hired.

3. *Thou shalt establish restricted areas.* Only authorized persons should be allowed to enter the computer center.

4. *Thou shalt provide fire control and prevention measures.* Foremost should be installation of fire suppression systems. No-smoking regulations should be enforced and flammable materials not be stored near the computer. Smoke can cause serious damage to the computer core and hamper its effectiveness.

5. *Thou shalt provide for theft detection.* All data storage media should be equipped with detection devices to prevent unauthorized removal.

6. *Thou shalt provide for sabotage detection.* All devices which could be harmful to magnetically stored data should be barred from the computer area.

7. *Thou shalt establish riot and mob controls for entry and egress.* All entranceways should be designed to limit the number of persons who can enter or leave the computer center at one time.

8. *Thou shalt not overlook backup equipment requirements.* There should be adequate and independent on-site electrical power and air-conditioning facilities in the event of a public utility failure.

9. *Thou shalt generate backup data bases.* A secure off-site storage facility should be utilized to protect essential and necessary vital records from loss or destruction. Management should have written agreements with other facilities to provide computer processing time during periods of emergency.

10. *Thou shalt be security minded in the physical planning of computer facilities.* Management should take extreme care in locating the data processing facility within a building. The computer room and tape library should not be alongside an elevator shaft. There should be easy access to water and air supply as well as sufficient electrical power, from public and back-up equipment.

DISCUSSION QUESTIONS

1. One way of safeguarding data against unauthorized access is to hide the computer from public view. Do you agree with this statement? Why?

2. Evaluate the security plan recommended by the author.

PART 10

Data-Processing Management

The bulk of published work in data processing during the past 20 years has focused on developments in computer hardware, programming languages, and general computer systems. In contrast, relatively little attention has been given to the management of computer facilities. True, some progress has been made, but only the surface has been scratched. Data processing management is the most critical determinant of the computer facility's success or failure. It is important, therefore, to include in a publication of this type a representative section on various areas of management relevant to a data processing facility.

The 10 selected articles making up this part discuss three major topics: Computer productivity, computer and personnel selection, and personnel management. The first two articles discuss computer productivity. Schroeder's article, "The Part-Time Computers," points out that poor productivity of most computer systems stems from the ineffectiveness with which EDP managers manage the EDP function. Examples include the following: (1) Over 50% of computer time is used inefficiently; (2) 25% of manned hours are wasted; (3) lost time is greatest in large data processing centers, and (4) over one third of the computer system's available time is idle. Most of the blame is attributed to inadequate instructions for computer operators, absence of internal controls, and improper computer scheduling.

McCollum begins his article, "Some Major Computer Diseases and How to Effect a Cure," by noting that much dislike or even distrust of computers is due to "diseases" that plague many computer installations. Management is aware of certain deficiencies in its computer functions and continues to have this attitude until the problem is solved. The rest of the article is a diagnostic procedure which begins with determining the nature of "the symptoms," and is followed by suggestions for a "cure." Some of the symptoms include underworked computers, dissatisfied users, poor scheduling, late reports, inability to handle certain jobs, and slowness in implementing new applications. The practical cures vary with the circumstances involving each installation.

The next four articles represent topics related to computer and personnel selection. Gotterer's article, "Selection Techniques for Data Processing Personnel" discusses the pros and cons of hiring and training inexperienced personnel versus hiring trained and experienced personnel for data processing. The author also explains the uses and techniques of interviewing, testing, and evaluating prospective data processing applicants.

Davis' article, "Internal Recruitment and Training of Data Processing Personnel," has the theme that hiring people from within the organization for data processing jobs can be a better approach than hiring from the outside. He proceeds by listing the advantages of internal recruitment and predicts that widespread training and transfer of personnel from other departments into data processing will probably become more frequent in the next few years.

Interviewing is a key step in screening and selecting job applicants. Cornwell and Hallam present guidelines for selecting the right programmers. The controversy of "buying" rather than "producing" programmers and other data processing personnel is discussed by McMurray and Parish in their article, "How Can We 'Produce' More People for the Computer Industry?" They blame the academic community's failure to produce data processing talent on the computer industry's failure to clearly state its needs. This means that the solution to the data processing manpower problem must be assumed by management within industry. The recommendations presented in the article are aimed at establishing greater stability within the data processing operation and the overall industry.

The last four articles address themselves more directly to the area of personnel management. The main thrust of Guin's article, "Killed by Computer," is that a computer facility requires a qualified manager for effective control. Without such control, the computer can afflict the entire company operations either from failure to provide adequate service or from budgetary requirements greater than its productive value. The manager who lacks computer knowledge either closes his eyes to this area of responsibility or abdicates it to specialists whose dictates could dominate the entire facility. Thus, in the long run, without the effectiveness of a qualified computer facility manager, the company can be "killed" by its own computer.

The main theme of Coleman's article is that while programmers are generally preoccupied with solitude and knowledge related to programming rather than human relations, there are programmers who could learn the skills necessary to become effective managers and at the same time best serve their own interest. Computer industry managers should take steps to identify them and develop the skills they will need as managers.

Newlin's article, "The Changing World of the Data Processing Administrator," emphasizes current changes in attitude affecting the data processing administrator. These attitudes are concerned with management's viewpoints of the computer's role in business, the administrator's perception of his role in the company, and the increased protection and utilization of company investments in data processing. According to Newlin, these changes have occurred as a result both of the technological advances in computers which made the field highly specialized and of management's increased knowledge about computers and their profitability. These and other factors are forcing the data processing function into a new maturity with increased need for effective management skills.

The last article by Irvine speculates on the role of the EDP manager in the future. The author feels that today's manager has a unique opportunity to be the change-agent of the organization. Managers who have succeeded in meeting the new challenges of the EDP field should be well equipped to accept greater responsibility in the future.

THE PART-TIME COMPUTERS[1]

Walter J. Schroeder

Predictions concerning the future of the computer are not difficult to find. Everyone, it seems, has at one time or another felt compelled to make a prognostication about where electronics would lead us in managing business enterprises. It is an intriguing fact that about the only major forecast to be achieved was the number of computers installed. There, we have exceeded expectations.

But in other, more fundamental aspects, the predictions have largely failed to materialize. Consider some of the following which were widely held beliefs during the 1960's:

That there would be a reduction in the number of middle management personnel required by corporations as the computer began to take over the routine decision-making functions. There is certainly no evidence to support any conclusion this has been achieved. If anything, there are more middle management positions today than there were five years ago.

That profitability and return on investment will improve when EDP functions fulfill their primary purpose of providing faster and better information. High speed information should result in better management decisions and improved performance. Although there are some instances where improved information has led to improved performance, there are many more where it did not come to pass.

What many top management people and most EDP personnel have overlooked is the fact that decisions are made by people. If people are going to become more effective, they not only need good information but: they need to be motivated to change and they need to be taught how to change.

Few EDP functions adequately address this problem let alone even recognize it as the really fundamental objective of their activity. In case after case, from hundreds of interviews and consulting assignments in this field, I have found the EDP manager turning into more and more technician and less and less business manager.

It is small wonder, therefore, that the third, desperately held view, has not come to pass. *Many people have believed that the EDP manager, by virtue of his*

Source: Reprinted from *Infosystems,* January 1971, pp. 18-22. By Permission of the Publisher. © 1971 Hitchcock Publishing Company. All rights reserved.

[1] Refer to Bain's article (selected references) for a rebuttal.

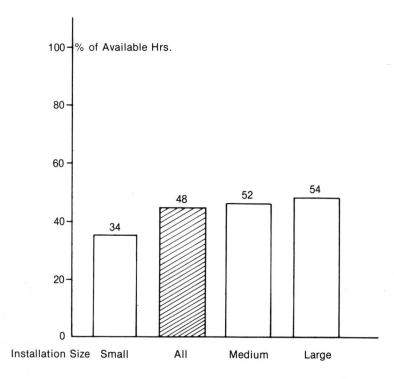

The average productive time of the 155 computers in the survey is 48 percent.

Figure 1. Productive Use of Computers

analytical training and understanding of the business through the information systems, will become the general manager of the enterprise. A few EDP managers have crossed the barrier into the ranks of functional or operational management positions. Most of these are in staff jobs and only a very few are in line positions. Those who achieved top management status did it mostly by starting their own businesses in the EDP service industry. A large number of these have proven to be less than capable as testified by the large number of business failures in this industry.

In general, there is little about the systems and data processing field which trains a man to be the future president of the company. He learns little about the true nature of competition, choosing product or pricing strategies and use of risk capital. Many in the EDP field have become so engulfed with the hardware and software they do not even relate well with their fellow man—an important ingredient in leadership needed at top corporate levels.

Some EDP managers, particularly those under 35 years of age, have had work experience only in the EDP function where they started their careers as computer programers. Unfortunately they often know very little about the business.

Those are major expectations of the past that have largely not come to pass. What then is the current status of the EDP manager?

Recent surveys indicate a trend toward moving the EDP organization out of the corporate accounting or financial area and placing it higher in the overall corporate structure. Many EDP departments located in the financial areas of the business have concentrated on financial information systems and have done very little to help in other problem areas. About 50 percent of the EDP managers now report to non-financial executives. The larger the corporation, the more likely the EDP manager will report to the president or other high-ranking officer.

WHAT'S YOUR ROLE?

The effectiveness of the problem solving application system development service provided by EDP functions is heavily dependent upon the way in which the EDP manager views his own role in the business.

Some consider the proper role one which is closely related to the technical computer environment. They concentrate on the development of highly capable computer complexes and rely upon the users to ensure the realization of economic benefits. The EDP manager with this view is likely to describe his functions as one of supplying better information faster.

The other perspective is to view the job as one of solving user problems, such as too much inventory, excessively high cost of operation, inadequate customer service. I endorse this as the proper role of the EDP manager. However, if that role is to be fulfilled effectively, the EDP function must be fully absorbed into the operations of the business. EDP cannot stand alone or be isolated from the line and other staff activities. We have found that the degree of EDP absorption into the business is revealed by the extent of its planning for the future and how well those plans are integrated with the operating functions' plans. Only a minority of EDP departments have really effective long-range plans.

Another topic concerning the current status of the EDP manager is the effectiveness with which EDP managers manage the EDP function. A research study recently undertaken by A. T. Kearney & Co. reveals some significant facts about the effectiveness with which EDP managers use the tools they have.

A stratified random sample of companies in several major industries was chosen from the mailing list of a well-known financial service. Each company was asked to provide explicit information about its computer operations. First, a small sample of companies was contacted and results summarized. Later, a larger sample was analyzed and the results compared with the earlier sample to test the validity of the study. The two groups were highly correlated, indicating the results are statistically valid. Eighty-nine companies and 155 computers were included in the statistics.

Interestingly, though the study sample was broken down by industry, the data revealed no significant differences among industry groups. Briefly, the six most revealing findings are:

1. Only 48 percent of available time is used productively.
2. Computers are operated only 64 percent of available time.
3. Twenty-five percent of manned hours are wasted.
4. Large centers have the poorest performance in all categories of lost time.
5. Forty-two percent of the companies reporting do not maintain accurate records on computer performance.
6. Firms using multiprogramming achieve higher production.

Of the total available machine hours (three shifts, 30 days per month = 720 hours) the average computer in the study performs productive work only 48 percent of the time. Productive work is defined as the time equipment is used to process production runs and testing, without regard for how effectively the computing power of the machine is being used at any one time or the value of the information produced. Based on our experience, there is a high probability that the computers are not working to capacity when doing productive work. Therefore, productivity is even less than indicated by the study results.

Computing centers are manned and operated only 64 percent of available time, a major factor contributing to low computer utilization. Significant differences exist in hours manned as between large and small installations. The larger installations tend to operate much longer hours. Several companies reported that their computer centers hardly ever close.

The percentage of manned hours to total hours converts into shifts per week as follows:

Size of Installation	Machine Rental Per Month	Number of Shifts Per Week
Small	Up to $10,000	10
Medium	$10,000–$40,000	14
Large	Over $40,000	16
Average		13
Available		21

Despite the availability of computing capacity we frequently receive inquiries from companies regarding the need to secure new, faster, more costly equipment. The alternative of expanding the number of manned shifts, or improving throughput by using available technology are often not considered.

A comparison of productive time with total hours that a computing center is manned and operated is most revealing. This comparison indicates that 25 percent of costs are wasted due to idleness, reruns, machine maintenance and down time.

Significantly, larger installations suffer about 40 percent greater losses for these same reasons than smaller ones. This suggests that huge computing centers are less efficient, experience greater scheduling problems, are more difficult to manage and are more likely to have highly structured, inflexible organizations resulting in lack of coordination and a negative impact on efficiency.

The substantially higher rerun percentage (4 percent for small installations vs. 6 percent for large installations) suggests that large installations need better controls and need to provide improved training for personnel.

We have seen from other studies of individual computing centers that the technology of massive hardware and complex configurations of devices create an environment which may not be fully understood and controlled by the staff. Trial and error play major roles in managing these installations.

It is readily apparent management should evaluate the productivity ratios of the computer installation before authorizing multiple shifts and new equipment. During the time the computers are manned but idle, the company is paying for both rental and payroll. Sixteen percent idle time translates into a cost to U.S. businesses of about $960 million annually. The 4 percent average reruns cost American industry about $240 million per year.

On the average, the companies in the study are incurring these annual losses due to idle time and reruns:

Size of Computer Installation	Annual Costs Due To:	
	Idle Time	Reruns
Small	$ 30,000	$ 2,000
Medium	$ 84,000	$18,000
Large	$280,000	$94,000

These costs represent inadequate management in the truest sense and result from such factors as: inadequate instructions for computer operators, absence of internal controls and improper or non-existent computer scheduling.

The 155 computers in the survey represent a total capital investment of approximately $110 million purchase price. The lost utilization indicates that management is not giving its attention to the performance of this expensive equipment. This is substantiated by the fact that 42 percent of the respondents report the data submitted is *estimated* because accurate records of computer utilization are not maintained.

Approximately 28 percent of the computers in the study are operated in a multiprogramming or multiprocessing mode (processing more than one application program at any one time). Those with multiprogramming achieve a ratio of productive time (production and testing) to total available hours of 62 percent compared with only 42 percent for non-multiprogramming operations. This indicates that, as some companies require processing in multiple shifts, they also seek more ways to increase throughput per hour of processing.

To validate this conclusion, we compared meter hours with total operating time. Meter hours are widely held to be the only convenient measure of how near capacity a computer is operating.

Multiprogramming computers have a 94 percent relationship between meter hours and operating hours. Non-multiprogramming computers have only a 75 percent ratio.

It is easier but more costly to increase throughput by going to multiple shifts than it is to install multiprogramming.

Although many installations have the technical competence and hardware/ software capability to increase throughput of their computers with multiprogramming, they do not avail themselves of this added capacity due to: desire by the technicians for more powerful and costly equipment; a large residue of computer

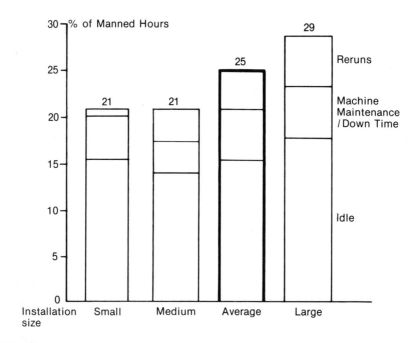

The idle time of the average computer, 16 percent of manned hours, translates into a cost to U.S. businesses of about $960 million annually. The 4 percent loss due to reruns costs businesses about $240 million annually.

Figure 2. Wasted Man Hours

programs written in second generation or non-compatible programming languages; management's failure to understand the true capacity of equipment on hand.

Only 22 companies, out of the 89 in the study, reported productive time compared with available hours exceeded 60 percent. The results of these 22 companies were segregated from the total sample to establish performance criteria that might suggest goals or objectives for less efficient operations. As a group, they operate their computers longer hours and achieve 68 percent productive time compared with only 40 percent for the other respondents.

As a percentage of manned hours, these high performance companies turned in these results:

Performance Indicator	Percent of Manned Hours	
	Multiprogramming	*Non-Multiprogramming*
Productive time	81 percent	70 percent
Idle time	10 percent	20 percent
Reruns, machine maintenance and down time	9 percent	10 percent

All industry groups and all size classifications were represented among these high performers. In rerun performance alone, this high performance group had a poorer result than the rest of the respondents—6 percent vs. 5 percent. It appears that even the best computing installation can find opportunities to cut waste.

It has become more and more apparent to both EDP specialists and general management that selection and management of computer system projects has suffered from lack of management attention and direction during the decade of the 60's. It has often seemed that frustrations generated by delays and escalating costs of system projects causes executives to breathe deep sighs of relief once the systems are installed. They quickly and gladly turn attention elsewhere, and the result is waste and inefficiency in the computer room.

This study demonstrates clearly the opportunity available to the company which has the interest, determination and know-how to measure and improve the performance of computer operations. Tools can be utilized to monitor the computing center. Once such tools are in action, goals can be established and performance gradually improved.

The EDP community has tended to think of computer scheduling in terms of the dynamic interactions which take place internally where multiple problem programs are contending for the limited core, channels and peripheral devices. They need to recognize the vast improvements which simple block scheduling techniques can provide.

Similarly computer performance measurement today is discussed in terms of dynamic measurement of internal operations involving hardware probes and constant monitoring. Don't overlook the tremendous performance improvements which simple approaches can generate.

Regardless of the industry, managing a computer center has virtually all the characteristics of managing a manufacturing plant. Many of the same disciplines and techniques apply.

It is time to apply some of the concepts of Management Information Systems to the management of computers. Although millions upon millions of words have been written about information systems that schedule and control manufacturing processes, and millions upon millions of dollars have been invested in such systems, there is seeming reluctance to apply similar techniques to the data center.

A machine tool costing $50,000 may be scheduled, loaded and measured in terms of minutes and mills. A complex of accounting, routing, standards and methods are used in this process; while even a modest size computer, costing 10 times that amount, is operated with inadequate or non-existent management tools.

Management has the option of applying generally known planning and control techniques to the computer center or employing one of the more recently developed services—facilities management (where an outside vendor takes over operation of the customer's computer center, sometimes including systems and programing activities, and physically removes operations to the vendor's data center). Such an approach is not without trial and tribulation.

When the computer is used effectively and becomes an integral part of the business, it usually is due to an intensive involvement by top management. The systems and information with which the business is operated are as vital to its success as the products or services it sells. Thus management does not have the choice of managing these systems and computer activities or turning them over to someone else. They must be well managed irrespective of where they are performed and those responsible for the success of the enterprise are responsbile for the successful conduct of all its vital functions.

The findings of this study suggest that the EDP manager of the 1970's must become a much more effective manager of his resources. At the same time he must continue to struggle with difficult user relationships and hopefully fulfill some of the prophecies of the 1960's.

DO AS YOU SAY

A great deal of credibility is lost by the EDP manager who does not look to the effectiveness of his own managing techniques while trying to advise users on how to solve their problems.

Those who have seen the opportunity to improve the EDP performance have been rewarded by substantial performance and economic gain. They usually accomplish that by following a five-step process:

Find out where you are. How good or bad is the current situation. Which aspects are satisfactory? Which are not?

Define objectives. Determine and define the role and mission of the EDP effort within the organization.

Establish measures of performance. On the basis of objectives, systems and data processing activities should be analyzed to establish those specific performance factors that will be measures of effectiveness. Care must be taken to identify items that can be measured with some precision and accuracy, such as costs, quality, schedule adherence, utilization of personnel, utilization of machinery.

Develop goals and plans. For each measured activity standards of acceptable performance should be agreed upon between senior management and EDP management.

Measure and motivate. Senior management should demonstrate its sincere desire in seeing that standards are achieved. This requires the personal time of the interested executive.

The wave of criticism, of both computers and those who work with them, seems to be in some ways justified. The status of the EDP manager is best characterized by one word—opportunity.

DISCUSSION QUESTIONS

1. Elaborate on the major findings of the study regarding inefficient use of the computer.
2. How does the author explain improvement in the performance of the EDP manager? Explain.

SOME MAJOR COMPUTER DISEASES
AND HOW TO EFFECT A CURE

Ralph C. McCollum

Tales of computer goofs are legion. A computer programming error recently caused the simultaneous destruction of 117 high-altitude weather balloons. A lapse in IRS computer tape controls caused duplicate refund checks to be sent out to large groups of taxpayers.

But, to the voices who seem to say, Never Trust a Computer, there is a remarkable record of reliability.

Banks and utilities use computers to handle billions of checks or bills each year, airlines to keep flight reservations up-to-the-second, and manufacturers to automate production, forecast sales, etc.

The U.S. has gone from 10 or 15 computers in 1955 to an estimated 88,000 in 1972 (and a projected 100,000 by 1975). First-generation computers which could do 17,000 additions per second have been supplanted by third- and fourth-generation computers doing up to 1,500,000 additions per second. Computers obviously can absorb and emit vast quantities of information accurately, and they can perform gargantuan tasks in arithmetic and logic at tremendous speeds.

Why then the distrust, unease, or even dislike for this technological Aladdin's lamp? Perhaps this attitude on the part of many managements is due to "diseases" that plague many computer installations. Top management in many firms recognizes deficiencies in its computer activities and, until these problems are overcome, the whole technology will be subject to distrust.

THE FEVER CHART

The onset of most diseases is signalled by a fever in the patient. Similarly, in a computer installation, the onset of problems is signalled by the "rising temperature" of abnormal costs. Project costs are "overrun" and departmental budgets are exceeded on the monthly cost statements.

The ramifications of computer costs go well beyond the monthly rental or investment in computers. There are salaries for programming and operating personnel, plus clerical staff, and cost of supplies. In addition, there are the indirect expenses that too few firms attempt to evaluate—stock outages because of inefficient operation, inability to meet peak demand, customer dissatisfaction, etc.

The monthly cost statement can offer useful signals on the health of the installation, but to rely on it to define a computer ailment is like letting the

Source: Reprinted, with permission, from *Data Management,* July 1973, pp. 26-29, published by the Data Processing Management Association, Park Ridge, Illinois.

thermometer diagnose a hernia. The so-called "cost excess" is a direct function of a cost expectation—which might be in error. We frequently have no foreknowledge permitting us to say that an expenditure is a cost overrun. Accounting procedures vary among firms and no two operations are exactly alike.

Special analyses are needed, first, to determine the nature of the malady, and next, the cure—whether to go to the medicine cabinet for a pill, whether to take medicine prescribed by a doctor, or whether to enter the hospital for surgery.

The symptoms of some major computer diseases and what can be done to prevent or correct their occurrence can be identified.

SYMPTOM: UNDERLOADED COMPUTER ANEMIA

The large investment in computer hardware suggests that the computer should normally have a workload requiring at least two shifts a day. If usage is consistently below this level, steps may need to be taken to assure more economic operation. If the installation is new, short-term time sharing can be offered to outside firms. (Where a long-term plan is developed before the original installation is made, the initial slack-use period can normally be minimized by the debugging of new applications.)

When the workload on a computer is less than optimum, it may be possible to substitute lower-speed equipment or auxiliary hardware of another manufacturer to reduce the rental cost of the installation, while keeping the operating time of the system within acceptable limits.

After all worthwhile applications have been mechanized and excessive unused time still remains, a computer service bureau or some form of joint computer use approach can be considered to share productive capacity and the cost of a large-scale system. This joint-use venture approach was employed in the city of Owensboro, Kentucky, where the municipal utility, the city administration, and school board are successfully served by a common installation.

The supporting staff of systems men and programmers must also be in balance with the capabilities of the hardware. If there is a shortage of skilled personnel, the implementation of new applications will be slow, and idle computer time may result. Frequently, the manpower requirements for updating and maintaining existing computer applications is overlooked. As a consequence, manpower is diverted from new application conversions, causing the staff shortages.

On the other hand, inadequate computer facilities can result in a multitude of complaints, including a frustrated staff. Skilled programmers must wait to debug their programs, and systems personnel cannot plan further new applications in the face of an already congested computer.

SYMPTOM: COMPUTER FLU OR STAGNATION

The growth in computer technology and in the rate of obsolescence points to a future of infinite applications. Keeping pace becomes not only a technological but often a competitive necessity.

This is an overlying reason for constantly upgrading operations and finding new applications, apart from system needs. But many operations are stagnating, without responding to this challenge.

It is important to expand basic applications into the areas of "exception reporting" to concentrate the user's attention on unusual situations requiring human review. The computer can conserve human time, can assure attention to critical items, can spot missing tickets, reports, overrun conditions, etc., and can coordinate the flow of data to all levels of management in accordance with the importance of the exception. Unless the computer system is upgraded periodically, maximum utility will not be achieved.

After the basic historical accounting system has been mechanized, it is normally possible to expand the system to provide day-to-day information to field managers for the control of operations. Comparative reports showing information such as "costs compared with quantity produced" permit unit cost comparisons and "actual versus standard" cost analyses. In this manner, operating managers can be supplied with comprehensive, up-to-date information, without adding significantly to the cost of the basic accounting system.

In many cases, computer operations remain marginally productive until the system can smoothly take hold of an entire industrial or service organization. One must recognize there is a normal metamorphosis in this taking hold, a progression of applications, typical of most industries. If the pacing goes awry at an early stage, computer "hangover" often results.

1. Usually, the first computer installations are devoted to bread-and-butter applications, such as payroll, material control, customer accounting, etc. The primary benefit is the replacement of clerical effort, justified by reducing manpower or enabling fewer clerks to absorb substantially increased workloads over a period of years.

2. The next stage of development is normally devoted to "management" applications. These computer uses involve the planning, dispatching, accounting and control of all company activities which help management control the business. These controls cover engineering, construction, manufacturing, transportation, marketing, etc. and are run on the computer periodically (versus on line).

3. The third stage of development is the use of the computer for "dynamic applications." By making the computer an active part of the process on a real-time basis, in which the computer participates directly on line, significant improvements can be incorporated into the entire process. The computer logic can be used to audit and edit human activities and can assist these activities with information from a vast data bank under the computer's control. These uses are sometimes referred to as interactive terminal applications. Airline reservations operations, utility order entry operations, and automatic bank teller applications are illustrations of this approach. Very shortly, retail chain stores will be installing similar devices on a large scale.

It is important to install these applications in the proper sequence. Critical errors have been made in attempting to implement dynamic applications before achieving a sound underlying system, including integrated procedures, a comprehensive data base, and management control capabilities. Costly installations have been abandoned and some firms have nearly gone bankrupt due to the improper selection of the workload for the computer.

SYMPTOM: DISSATISFIED USER SYNDROME

How many executives have heard their departmental heads complain: "We converted to a computer last month, and now I don't know what's going on in my own department!" Or another favorite comment, "The computer department keeps taking over one function after another, and soon it will be running the entire company!" Such attitudes may be a harbinger of diseases.

When the using departments fail to have a part in the process, the resulting computerized system frequently overlooks significant conditions, develops impractical systems, and leads to intracompany conflicts when the system is installed.

Such problems disclose a lack of proper computer-organization planning. Management has delegated responsibility and authority to specific groups such as the sales, manufacturing, distribution, and accounting areas. The installation of a computerized system is no excuse for the functional managers to abdicate their responsibilities of understanding and controlling all processes dealing with their areas.

Departmental responsibilities and new computer techniques can be reconciled by establishing the proper relationship between the user and the data processing center. Each user should loan staff to the computer effort and should be in on the project at the system design, programming, and system acceptance stages. The user department should also furnish test cases and examples for the new system to prove that it meets all departmental requirements.

All formulas in the computer programs should be clearly set forth in "decision tables" and other documentations to insure that the user departments understand and approve them.

Then the "wails" of the users will be replaced by a *proper sense of pride for a job well done, or a sense of joint responsibility in patching up the inevitable omissions.* Failing to respond to this "wait" symptom can lead to disruptive clashes.

PREVENTIVE MEDICINE

As more and more vital company functions are mechanized—including payroll, accounts receivable, and management control applications, the company is increasingly exposed to computer system failures. The protection and backup for the computer system may become vital to the survival of the firm and therefore should be periodically reviewed at the executive and other levels rather than being delegated to the data processing manager alone.

The system design of each application should include internal controls over the accuracy of all files and reports in the system. In addition, provision should be made for external audit totals over the internal control files to detect programming or data problems that may creep into the system.

Another method of obtaining efficient hardware usage is a subcontracting arrangement for Facilities Management. Under this plan, the computer installed on the firm's premises is owned or operated by a contractor, relieving management of responsibility for supervising the installation. Since the contractor is free to rent the unused computer, more efficient utilization can be made of the hardware.

SYMPTOM: THE SCHEDULING VIRUS

Poor scheduling, like a viral infection, leads to major disorders such as conflicts between departments and serious losses of efficiency.

When users complain that results from the computers are late, or when work cannot be run because of a peak load, scheduling needs to be examined.

The daily planning of computer operations is important to total effectiveness. Balanced scheduling of "background" and "foreground" programs in a "disk operating system" computer increases total throughput of the system and can therefore solve many scheduling problems. Enforcement of input document receiving schedules also improves the ability to schedule computer runs.

By selection of the proper time of day for each run or application, the usefulness of computer results can be improved. As an illustration, engineers and research men work with iterative problems. Therefore a one-half hour period on the computer twice a day will normally provide better service to such users than a five-hour period once a week.

Of course, when warranted, the ultimate goal in computer accessibility is the installation of an on-line system. By installing terminals in various user departments, one computer can interleave the demands and provide better service to all personnel needing rapid information.

SYMPTOM: THE HYPERTENSION OF IMBALANCE IN THE COMPUTER SYSTEM

In many installations, repeated excuses are given for late reports, inability to handle special jobs, or slowness in implementing new applications. The data processing manager can frequently be heard to exclaim "The printer is all tied up," "I'm short of programmers," or "We need more systems men."

All of these comments suggest a possible imbalance in the total computer system. The input and output capabilities of a computer should be in the same range of magnitude as the internal processing speeds of the equipment. Otherwise, there is either a bottleneck in the throughput of the computer or unused capacity in one of its components.

Each application should also provide for the periodic backup of master files, operating system and programs on magnetic tape to be stored away from the computer site. If disaster strikes, these tapes can then be taken to another computer to re-establish the system.

It may be desirable to make mutual aid agreements with other organizations having compatible hardware. When an agreement is reached, it is desirable for the parties to exchange plans on hardware changes to maintain this compatibility. Sometimes a period of peak work may warrant the rental of time on a nearby computer system. These periods can be used to test out backup procedures before an emergency exists.

Backup of manpower is also essential. By means of cross-training, every complex program and system should be understood by more than one person. In addition, the data processing manager should have a designated assistant to take over the reins in case of an emergency and the unavailability of the manager.

It makes good sense to call in an outside "physician" for a periodic checkup on the computer system's state of health." Top management can obtain worthwhile independent appraisals which might catch and correct a "cold," improve the "working life" of important systems, or even detect early signs of a "fatal" weakness.

Examination of computer systems can cover either the full range of plans and operations or specific elements on a rotating annual basis.

THE CHALLENGE

There is ultimately another dimension to the computer, going beyond most current usage—freeing the efficient manager for the task of making decisions, say in the heuristic, marketing area where no compiling or rearranging of data can create an infallible decision.

Awareness of the computer's versatility is essential to such flexibility. For example, a major logging and wood products company uses the computer as a forest simulator. Information about the size, spacing and age of the trees is fed into the computer. One of the printouts is an overlay that can be placed on a map to show the condition of the timber—even the degree of insect infestation. Another system converts the harvesting plan to logs available—by species, grade and diameter. Through such means a log allocation is made to the mills. These methods give top management a model for planning—and decision.

Learning to live with the computer as a helpmate is the challenge of the future when the computer may be as commonplace as the telephone is today. That milestone can only be achieved through integrating computer operations into the management fabric of the total organization. When data processing is properly planned and "diseases" are controlled, fear of the computer will disappear. The computer will then achieve its rightful place as a productive, manageable genie of the future.

DISCUSSION QUESTIONS

1. What problems or diseases does the author emphasize that plague many computer installations? Do you agree with his approach? Explain in detail.
2. What stages of application development does a computer installation go through?

SELECTION TECHNIQUES
FOR DATA PROCESSING PERSONNEL

Malcolm H. Gotterer

In the brief history of data processing there have been major shifts in attitude toward the problem of selecting data processing employees. These have ranged from attracting bright people from other disciplines and then training them, selecting employees within the organization and then conducting extensive in-house training programs, recruiting trained and experienced personnel, and recruiting trained but inexperienced personnel.

Each of these personnel philosophies have been both satisfactory and unsatisfactory depending on the environment, people doing the selecting, available labor, and performance expectations by management. In this paper the subject will be discussed from two points of view: first, hiring inexperienced personnel, and, second, hiring trained and experienced personnel.

THE SELECTION PROCESS

There are at least seven steps in the normal selection process:

1. Attracting potential job applicants
2. Receipt of application for employment
3. Tests and their evaluation
4. Interview by personnel department
5. Interview by data processing department
6. Verification of application data and reference check
7. Review of qualifications

THE PERSONNEL DEPARTMENT

For many years a number of data processing managers bypassed the personnel department in the employment process. Among the arguments for this action were that personnel did not understand the needs of data processing, good computer personnel would not put up with the inflexible personnel procedures, the personnel department took too much time and candidates would be lost, and finally job candidates would lose interest in the job if they were interviewed by personnel experts rather than data processing experts.

Source: Reprinted, with permission, from *Data Management,* September 1972, pp. 66-68, published by the Data Processing Management Association, Park Ridge, Illinois.

In times past some of these attitudes were valid. But with a growing labor market from which to draw job applicants and a trend toward standardizing data processing jobs a change is required. The traditional role of the personnel department is now valid in data processing as well as the other departments of the organization.

The major contribution of the personnel department in the employment process is to recruit and screen applicants, verify claimed experience and education, check references, advise other departments on individual candidates, maintain personnel files, and assist the supervisor in placing a newly hired person in a suitable position.

JOB DESCRIPTION

Central to the selection process is an understanding of the requirements of the job to be filled. Ordinarily this is accomplished by a formal written document called a job description. Among the information in a job description is the educational and experience requirements of the job, the job duties, the place of the job in the data processing organization, and the knowledge required to perform the job satisfactorily.

It has often been pointed out that there is no set of generally accepted job descriptions in data processing. The job called "Senior Analyst" in one company may be "Programmer" in another. There is little likelihood of any universal job descriptions acceptable to a major segment of various data processing managements. The reason being that various organizations have different requirements, traditions, policies and procedures. Rather than wait for the general descriptions each data processing manager should prepare, or have prepared, detailed job descriptions for the positions in his organization. These can then be the basis of the recruiting process.

ATTRACTING APPLICANTS

Assuming that job descriptions have been prepared, the next step is that of attracting job applicants. The company will, if it has a good reputation, receive a certain number of unsolicited job applications. Many of these will be from well-qualified people who want to work for the company. They should receive application blanks to complete.

Advertisements in both local and national papers and data processing publications are valuable sources of job applicants. In using this approach a large number of marginally qualified responses should be expected. Advertising in national newspapers or data processing publications is most effective when seeking very specialized personnel. For more general skills local advertising is frequently preferred.

The number of educational institutions offering training in data processing and computing has been increasing at a rapid pace. The graduates of programs are a primary source of well qualified but inexperienced personnel.

Finally for untrained and inexperienced personnel the non data processing employees of the company itself is the first, and frequently the best source. After this source is exhausted then, and only then, should an effort be made to recruit people in this class from the general labor market.

In summary the task of attracting job applicants is not very difficult when the skill and experience levels of the desired new employees has been defined. The hardest part of this step is therefore preparing meaningful job descriptions and forecasting staff needs.

THE APPLICATION FORM

Usually when the job applicant approaches the company he will submit a letter or résumé or both. These should be reviewed by a member of the personnel department and a company application form sent to those who appear to be qualified for the staff openings. Many of the questions and a great deal of the data requested on the application form will duplicate that originally submitted by the applicant. Nonetheless the company form should be required before further consideration is given to the person.

The company form will have been organized and standardized over a period of years. Company personnel when evaluating an application are aware of exactly where on the form various items can be found. Further they are assured that the data they normally consider in the employment process is present. Neither of these two objectives are met if the applicant's résumé is used.

Company application forms will not be discussed because it is assumed that one is available. If it is well designed and standardized, it will most likely also serve for recruiting data processing personnel. If for any reason this is not so, either the form can be revised to include the necessary data or an addendum added for use by data processing applicants. In this addendum the questions pertaining to data processing experience and training missing from the standard application can be added.

TESTS AND EVALUATIONS

Tests have had extensive use in selecting programmers. Their use has been at a much lower level for selecting operators or systems analysts. Almost all computer manufacturers have offered their customers the use of one or more tests to determine the ability of prospective data processing personnel. In fact at one point in time in the history of data processing the test, as supplied by the computer manufacturer, was the primary step in the employment process. A greater recognition of the limitations of available tests and the results of judicial review of testing have caused data processing managers and personnel administrators to re-evaluate these procedures.

Research over the past decade has demonstrated the difficulty of identifying the qualities measured by particular data processing oriented tests. Often is forgotten the fact that most of the programming tests were originally developed to measure the applicant's ability to *learn* programming, not to test his competency. Therefore it would be a gross error to use that test in evaluating a job applicant who has programming experience. Therefore the use of tests has to be divided in terms of whether or not the applicant has experience.

For the inexperienced job applicant a battery of tests may be desirable, provided they are not in violation of the law as discussed later. Among the types of tests to be included in this test battery would be interest, aptitude and intelligence tests. A cut-off score is then used to indicate whether or not the applicant has met the minimum acceptable achievement level. It should be noted that his test battery is but one of a series of steps and one piece of data in the final decision. It should not be the sole basis for the final decision.

For experienced job applicants there is no point in giving aptitude tests for their past job history will disclose aptitude as well as job interest. There may be some argument for the use of intelligence tests for this class of applicant because if the test has been validated in your data processing department it may then be a valuable guide in determining the relationship between the applicant and the other people in the department. Where possible an achievement test for the job should be used. Some achievement tests for programmers are now becoming available. But, as discussed earlier, it is still necessary to validate the test in the local environment.

A combination of laws, both federal and state, and recent Supreme Court decisions have forced organizations to evaluate their personnel selection procedures to insure that there is no built in bias or discrimination against applicants or groups of applicants. Typically tests of the paper and pencil variety have cultural and language bias. In an opinion by the U.S. Supreme Court it was stated that employers must demonstrate the business necessity of personnel procedures which may have an adverse effect on minority groups. This can be extended from minority groups to any group. Therefore it is necessary for the personnel department together with the legal department to develop a company policy on testing. This is not a decision within the authority or competence of the data processing executive.

Testing therefore should be used with caution. Under proper conditions such procedures may be both useful and legal, but their use should be limited to those cases where it can be shown that this is actually true.

PERSONNEL DEPARTMENT INTERVIEW

After testing, if any, has been performed and it has been determined that the applicant meets the minimum cut-off score the next step is an interview by a member of the personnel department. Interviews are one of the more controversial steps in the selection process. Critics of interviews fail, however, to come up with a suitable alternative.

The purpose of this first interview is to determine if a job opening exists for which the applicant is both qualified and interested. The interviewer armed with the application form and test results must therefore probe to determine both of these qualities in the applicant. Then the applicant can be compared to the job descriptions for the positions that are open. During this interview the applicant can be made aware of the company's personnel practices and policies and their implications. If a job vacancy exists for which the applicant may be qualified then the next step is an interview with representatives of the data processing department.

DP DEPARTMENT INTERVIEW

Two primary questions are to be answered when the applicant is interviewed by the data processing manager and his subordinates. These are, first, does the applicant have the qualities necessary to successfully carry out the requirements of the job, and, second, will the applicant fit into the concept of the data processing department. Hence, this interview should revolve around technical questions concerning the applicant's ability and attitude toward the technical concepts.

During this interview an effort is made to gather more and specific data concerning the applicant's past experience. Exactly what was done, by whom, using other's, if any, advice, etc. In this type of probing environment an estimate of the applicant's actual experience is obtained. An error frequently made by data processing interviewers is that of not probing deeply enough into both experience and training. That is the purpose of this interview and if error is to be made it should be on the side of thoroughness rather than superficiality. In a large data processing department the applicant may be interviewed by several people.

DATA VERIFICATION

In filling out the application form the prospective employee has provided certain data that should be verified prior to further consideration. This checking should be done by both the personnel and data processing departments.

The personnel department may well want to confirm the applicant's job history, dates, salaries, company history, and reason for leaving. In similar fashion the claimed education can be verified. References can then be obtained as indicated by the applicant on his application.

The data processing manager wishes certain other information than that being obtained by the personnel department. He, through a subordinate in a large department, wants more technical data concerning the type of work actually performed and the level of responsibility of the potential employee in that work.

Through the joint effort of the two departments, personnel and data processing, a thorough picture of the candidate's prior experience and education can be obtained. This step should not be taken, however, without prior approval and knowledge of the candidate.

REVIEW OF QUALIFICATIONS

At this point the reports of both departments are available to the data processing manager or the subordinate who is to make the decision. A great deal of data is now available which when compared to the job description will not directly produce an answer as to whether or not to hire the applicant. Judgment is necessary. For example, an applicant may have worked on similar problems but different hardware, or the same hardware but different applications. In either case training will be necessary and the manager must judge whether or not the trade-offs are favorable to him. The data processing manager will make many such decisions and being a manager it is not unreasonable to ask for these types of judgments.

The selection process is a long and detailed sequence of steps. No longer is it necessary to bypass good management procedures to hire data processing personnel. The long history of data processing projects being completed late and costing substantially more than estimated in itself suggests that greater care should be exercised in personnel decisions.

The procedures suggested are essentially the same if the person under consideration is currently an employee of another department of the company. Much of the data collection and verification will have been done at an earlier data and be available. The individual steps should still each be taken, for errors can be made in personnel transfers as well as hiring.

DISCUSSION QUESTIONS

1. What steps are taken in selecting EDP personnel? Explain each step in detail.
2. How are tests important in the selection process?
3. From the company's viewpoint, do you believe a job interview should be a key factor in a decision to hire an applicant? Why?

INTERNAL RECRUITMENT AND TRAINING OF DATA PROCESSING PERSONNEL

Sidney Davis

It is surprising in today's personnel-hungry market that so many companies seem to ignore an available and potentially fruitful manpower pool from which to fill their data processing department vacancies—their present administrative and clerical personnel.

These people know the company's operations, have proven employment histories, have evidenced a degree of loyalty, but lack one thing—data processing and computer programming knowledge and training, a factor that can be remedied.

If these people have the aptitude, and this can be determined by testing, they may, with proper education and training, be upgraded to data processing personnel. This is not theory. This has been done successfully at a number of far-sighted companies.

Widespread training and upgrading and transferring of personnel from other departments into DP will probably become more frequent in the next few years.

AVAILABLE MANPOWER

All available information indicates that the gap between trained computer data processing personnel and job openings will continue to widen for at least the next few years.

Source: *Computers and Automation*, September 1969, pp. 38-39.

The widening gap between personnel needs and available manpower is basic to the rapid pace of computer installations. Computer production and installation is simply outstripping DP personnel training.

Where are these people going to come from? Present training falls far short of the constantly expanding need. Just consider promoting 30,000 experienced programmers to fill the demand for analysts and managers.

Obviously, companies with large DP departments must consider imaginative solutions to their data processing personnel needs.

ADVANTAGES OF INTERNAL RECRUITMENT

One answer is an internal recruitment and training program. There are several factors in its favor:

1. Retraining in computer programming usually means upgrading and promotion from within—a policy that builds employee morale and helps attract new employees.

2. Recruiting and training from among present company personnel also can be an effective method of reversing the high rate of turnover that is common in many DP departments.

   As pointed out earlier, by promoting people with several years' experience in the company, DP employees are selected who have demonstrated a tendency to stay with the company—they evidence loyalty and have seniority.

3. If the company has a pension or retirement plan, or a profit-sharing program, the employee with several years' experience would hesitate to leave for a small or moderate increase in salary and risk loss of other benefits.

4. Training these people can be done in the evening, during non-working hours through a recognized responsible programming training school. Thus, the employees would remain productive in their present positions, and could be transferred into entry-level DP positions at the appropriate time in their training.

TURNOVER

As any DP department manager knows, keeping trained personnel is as difficult as finding them. Turnover continues at a frightening rate. The pressure of supply and demand tends to cause salaries to rise rapidly after only a year's experience—and usually at a faster pace than in other areas in the company. The allure of higher salaries elsewhere—combined with the possibility of working with highly advanced and more sophisticated machines and applications—are principal reasons for high turnover of DP personnel. The influence of these factors can be lessened by training and promotion from within.

There has been, traditionally, one other brake applied to the attraction of computer programmers, the demand for a college degree. Happily, this arbitrary requirement is no longer as widespread, and we find more and more non-college graduates being hired for business applications programming.

The non-college graduate can do the job. For over a dozen years, high school graduates have been trained in computer programming, and successfully placed in thousands of companies across the nation.

QUALIFICATIONS

What are the general qualifications that a programmer must have? It is generally accepted that the ingredients necessary for programming are aptitude and motivation.

Computer programming does not require a heavy background in advanced mathematics. Rather, it calls for an orderly, logical mind that can analyze business information and instruct the computer to process it. It requires a grasp of basic numbers, of arithmetic, and an aptitude for working with these figures.

Aptitude tests to be used for screening company personnel are available from several sources. Electronic Computer Programming Institute (ECPI), for example, has administered such tests to company personnel, and has assisted in screening potential programmers for computer training.

It is interesting to note that many DP departments recruited their programming staffs from within the organization when computers were first being introduced. A principal yardstick used to measure an employee's potential was his past history and record with the company.

"Had he performed well? Yes! Does he have the aptitude? Let's test him and find out! Let's send him to programming school and see how he performs." And the system worked.

Yet, these same companies, when replacements or expansion required them to hire additional programmers, sought men with past experience and often with college degrees. They forgot or ignored, their earlier successful recruitment techniques.

GETTING THE JOB DONE

The existence of functioning, qualified computer training schools means that companies interested in recruiting and training data processing personnel from their present employee group, need not set up self-administered screening, training and computer education programs .. with the operational and manpower investment it would entail.

The entire training program could be accomplished with the cooperation of any one of a number of outside organizations.

DISCUSSION QUESTION

Discuss the advantages and limitations of hiring from within the company. What factors are at issue? Explain.

INTERVIEWING PROGRAMMERS?
GUIDES FOR SELECTING THE RIGHT PEOPLE

R. C. Cornwell and Stephen Hallam

The demand for programmers has skyrocketed ahead of the supply, creating a shortage of skilled people. Since most programmers are hired on the basis of an interview—or a series of interviews—here are guidelines to help assure selection of a good candidate.

The selection process can be divided into two major parts: general questions contained on an application form, and specific questions during an interview

The application form can be quite valuable if it clearly identifies the applicant as to name, address, sex, and type of job desired. It should also determine the applicant's educational level and work experience, and obtain some indication of his character. Such application blanks are fairly standard and serve to eliminate the obviously unqualified.

Although the application form serves a useful purpose, an interview is necessary to obtain more specific information. The interview should obtain specific information in the general areas of education, work experience, and personality. The interview should also provide the potential employee with information about the nature of the job and the company.

EDUCATION

Some guidelines in regard to obtaining information concerning the applicant's education are:

1. Determine if the applicant has taken specific courses in computer programming.
2. Exactly which programming languages were taught in these courses?
3. If the applicant has taken a course in systems, what did the course contain?
4. Did the applicant take any of the following data processing courses: unit record equipment, micro programming, macro programming, operations analysis, comparative programming languages and data processing management?
5. Did the applicant take any of the following courses which might be related to the data processing field or demonstrate his analytical interests and

Source: *Administrative Management*, September 1969, pp. 37, 42.

ability: mathematics, statistics, accounting, symbolic logic, communications and business machines use?

Information you should gather concerning the applicant's work experience would include determining the extent of his data processing laboratory experience while in DP courses, and determining if the applicant worked in a data processing laboratory while in school and the nature of this work. Identify the specific systems with which he has worked. Also it would be advisable to know if the applicant has worked with such peripheral equipment as tapes, disks, data cells, high speed printers, cathode ray tubes, badge readers, and various types of terminals.

Practical experience with converting existing systems to computer usage should be noted as well as the type and quality of programs written by the applicant.

PERSONALITY

Information concerning the applicant's personality can be obtained in several ways. First determine if the applicant prefers to work in groups rather than alone. Ask him to evaluate himself as to his ability to get along with others in a cooperative work effort, and how he would rate himself as to patience and perseverance. Find out if he enjoys doing creative work, and if so ask him to provide evidence of his creative ability.

The interviewer also has to provide information to the potential employee. Remember that programmers are in short supply, so some selling of your company might be in order. Let the applicant know where he would fit into the organization, and what his chances for training and advancement are. Keep in mind that an inadequate applicant for a programming job might be very adequate for other openings in data processing. Consequently, a courteous treatment of all applicants is in order. You should also spell out how the job is challenging without scaring the applicant away.

Explain how the data processing function fits in with the rest of your company's business. Is data processing located within the finance area or is it an independent department? Don't forget to define the duties, responsibilities and rewards of the position. Salaries must be competitive, but other factors can be of almost equal importance. Allow the potential employee to meet other people with whom he may be working. Don't create discord with present employees by hiring a new man who doesn't fit into the work force.

Of equal importance to the success of this process is the background of the interviewer. Although preliminary questioning could be handled by an interviewer with no programming experience, the specific questions concerning education and experience regarding programming could best be asked and the answers evaluated by an experienced programmer. Some people can talk about programming far better than they can actually program and thus fool an interviewer who has not had experience in this area.

These guidelines suggest a selection process which has the disadvantages of complexity and of consuming valuable time, but the advantages of selecting a good programmer will justify the effort.

DISCUSSION QUESTIONS

1. What are the advantages and drawbacks of using the guidelines suggested by the authors? Explain.

2. Summarize the recommendations offered by the authors for producing more people for the computer industry. How practical are these recommendations? Discuss.

HOW CAN WE "PRODUCE" MORE PEOPLE FOR THE COMPUTER INDUSTRY?

J. A. McMurray and J. R. Parish

The greatest challenge faced by the computer industry today originates from within its own structure. It has failed to propagate its own kind. Our industry is underpopulated. The magnitude of the current manpower shortage demands that we recognize our collective errors and take action.

Perhaps our most serious failure has been our inability to communicate effectively with the academic community. For the first time perhaps in modern history, a profession has been forced to develop with little participation from the universities.

In the past, when industry has needed engineers, accountants, or geologists, the need was made known and the colleges responded. Within a reasonable period of time, adequate numbers of trained personnel became available.

But we, the computer industry, have never adequately voiced our growing personnel requirements to the academic community. We have never clearly indicated what it is we need. As a result of our inaction, few universities have initiated meaningful degree programs leading to career positions in data processing. Unfortunately those schools frequently give the curriculum too much of a scientific orientation. In so doing, they misrepresent to the student body at large the type of skills which are in tremendous demand throughout industry.

We therefore conclude that only token assistance will come from the universities in the next decade or so. We review this limited response by the academic world to demonstrate that it provides no panacea, and that the solution must be generated by concerned management within industry.

Source: *Computers and Automation,* September 1969, pp. 28-30.

In our search for this solution, we must become aware of existing practices which work to the detriment of our overall personnel objectives.

HIRING EXPERIENCED PERSONNEL ONLY

One of the most obvious problems is the common policy in the industry of hiring experienced personnel only. Rather than "produce" the programmer or specialist needed to meet a predictable requirement, the EDP manager too often turns to the open market. He "buys," at the going price, an individual whose résumé indicates the desired qualifications. As a group, EDP managers have become "buyers" to such a degree that fifty thousand technical positions remain unfilled today in the industry.

Why this swing to "buying" rather than "producing" the programmers and other computer-knowledgeable people who are needed?

The typical reasons set forth are:

- We inherited rather than created the current manpower dilemma. We are so fiercely engaged in solving today's problems (and sometimes yesterday's) that we have no time to find and train new people.
- We are reluctant to invest in more than preliminary training of our people. Experience has taught us that when they reach a respectable level of EDP knowledge, they will be "purchased" by a "buyer" in the marketplace.
- It is difficult to schedule a comprehensive training curriculum from the list of available courses offered by computer manufacturers.
- The dollar cost involved in thoroughly training our computer people often causes a luxury tag to be placed on our efforts.

Each of these philosophies of management requires close examination, lest they be allowed to excuse our "buyer" club membership. Taking them in order, let us challenge the validity of each.

CREATING A "GOOD" EMPLOYEE

1. The philosophy which allows us to "live it one day at a time" has no more justification in computer work than in any other professional business activity. A manager must always look to the future, for the good of his company, his staff, and more personally, in the interest of his own career.

Of the many resources which he must manage, his people become his primary concern. If he has a personnel shortage or an inadequately trained staff, he must recognize this deficiency and take steps to correct it.

Many managers overlook the most practical answer in favor of a short-range solution of their programmer shortage. New, inexperienced personnel *can* be made productive in a realistic time frame. An efficient training program *can* be designed to meet the requirements of any data processing environment. The training may be a program 6 to 12 weeks in length. The cost will vary depending on the approach taken in designing the programs: the site chosen, internal education strength, degree to which standard manufacturer courses apply, contractual services required, amount of computer time utilized, etc.

The important fact is that good professional people can be created in a short period with the proper initiative and investment through training. Honeywell regularly conducts such programs for its own entry level personnel, and over the years has found them as productive as individuals "bought" in the marketplace with up to two years of experience.

KEEPING EMPLOYEES

2. The philosophy which asks "Why propel a man, via good training, into an ex-employee status?" speaks of weak management. It darkly hints of résumé updating and weekly screening of newspaper employment sections. Yet, industrial psychologists assert that the appeal of money runs far behind achievement, responsibility, recognition, and growth as dominating factors in employee motivation.

The EDP manager faced with "buying" an employee to stay in the organization after the employee has attained advanced EDP training is indeed in an unfortunate position.

The manager without this problem is the one who wisely helps his people grow professionally through training and other means. Satisfied employees seldom can be "bought" away by another company solely by the standard 10 to 15 percent increase in salary.

EDUCATION FROM MANUFACTURERS

3. The philosophy which cries "The manufacturer is to blame for my education problems because his schedules won't allow comprehensive training in a reasonable length of time" is invalid today. While not all manufacturers can plead total innocence of this charge, we have seldom seen a bona fide case of a well-motivated manager being foiled in his attempt to send an employee to school because a manufacturer's schedule wouldn't allow it. When a reasonable effort is put forth by management in terms of flexibility in schedule and in travel policies, it is certain that his education request will be met.

COSTS

4. The philosophy of "My gosh, do you realize what it costs me to send one man to a two-week course in . . . . . ." is a short-sighted one. The real expense here, unfortunately, is the cost involved in "not" sending the man to the given course, assuming that he needs the training.

The computer, we assert, is a tool like no other tool. Its potential has yet to be measured. Its ability to simulate the marketplace, control inventory, load the factory, forecast sales, and generally help move the company ahead is widely acclaimed. We buy it or lease it for sums which total hundreds of thousands or millions of dollars. Isn't it paradoxical that we won't invest the final few thousands necessary to truly educate our computer people to the required level for reaping dividends from computer dollars? The dilemma of modern management is that sufficient numbers of computer-knowledgeable people are unavailable "anywhere" to help harness the total potential of management's greatest tool.

CONSTRUCTIVE ACTION

Various philosophies effectively impede proper use of and proper return from computer systems today. We will have matured as an industry when we are able to face the problem collectively, in full awareness of the causes, and in full resolve to effect a successful solution. These manpower philosophies must be eliminated. But this will not be enough. They have already done tremendous damage. Constructive action is called for. It must be positive; it must be massive; and it must be effective.

We must start now. Our industry needs a massive influx of new people if it is to grow at predicted rates. We need to put forth a unified campaign to attract qualified people to our industry. We must start now by selling our industry to qualified people seeking a career. In so doing, we must tear away the mysticism which shrouds computers and the EDP industry in the eyes of the public in general.

In this regard, we must eliminate the ignorance which caused a college senior last fall to give us this evaluation of our industry: "I wish I understood where there is any room for personal creativity in the field of data processing." Another senior started his evaluation in these words: "This era has been called the Age of Computers, and I'm afraid it is so . . . ."

The public does not recognize, as we would like to think, that computers are ingenious "tools" which require high imagination and intelligence on the part of the people who program and otherwise direct them. The young people who might enter the field are discouraged by the seemingly cold, structured, and passive role played by the people in our EDP industry.

Too many of the highly motivated and idealistic people our industry needs are rejecting EDP as a career. We never get the chance to reveal the opportunities in computer-related work.

We must change this situation. Computer involvement represents unexcelled career satisfaction. It is a further paradox of our industry that, having so much to offer, we attract so few people.

TRAINING COLLEGE GRADUATES

Honeywell EDP has addressed itself to this overall problem. It has instituted a tuition-based "Postgraduate Education Program." College graduates attend the program for twelve weeks. They participate in an intense curriculum which is designed to equip them as systems programmers with an understanding of the primary management role of computers. The program stresses a high ratio of computer interaction with lecture, workshop, and case study modes of learning. Upon graduation, students may assume technical positions throughout the industry.

Over 200,000 college students have had the career potential of computer-related work revealed to them through Honeywell's efforts to recruit students for this course. Results have been significant. The campaign has rooted out misconceptions and apprehensions concerning computers and related career positions. Students who might otherwise have eliminated EDP because of their liberal arts or business administration backgrounds are learning that computers have diverse areas of application. The misconception of mathematical wizardry being required for computer-related work is debunked.

The Honeywell "Postgraduate Education Program" is one example of what a computer manufacturer can do toward helping to solve the people problem in the EDP industry. More effort from computer manufacturers is needed.

RESPONSIBILITIES OF COMPUTER USERS

But computer users also have a duty to perform in this industry campaign. They must act now and with determination. "Buying" must give way to "producing." The employee merry-go-round must be stopped. EDP managers must discard the manpower philosophies discussed above and start applying good management techniques to their personnel problems.

Every opportunity must be taken to train existing employees. This will produce several values. It will guarantee a productive employee, whose knowledge will exceed the actual requirements of the job. It will provide a challenge, which may be the missing ingredient in an otherwise satisfactory position. It will insure the continual flow of ideas which is the lifeblood of an effective computer operation.

PROFESSIONAL GROWTH

Hand in hand with formal training should be a program designed to provide professional growth. Allow each staff member to represent your company to a professional society. Encourage him to use and contribute to your manufacturer's user group resources. Provide a library and applicable textbooks or at the very least, pay the cost for a periodical of his choice.

Develop career paths and goals for individual employees and assist each along the path toward meeting his particular objective. A useful step toward management responsibilities might be the assignment of a junior man for counseling and professional guidance. In any environment, an individual's self-esteem can be enhanced by having him teach his fellow employees in a subject in which he has an outstanding capability.

Look ahead to future personnel needs. Your present employees will do so, and if they sense inaction on your part, their résumé will soon appear in the marketplace.

Be determined to have one or more trainees in your department at all times. Look inside your company for these people. Take the individual who may be going stale in his present occupation, yet exhibits aptitude for EDP. After a three-month coordinated training effort, you will often have an employee who is "turned on" by the challenge of EDP. Incidentally, he will display a degree of loyalty to you and your company unparalleled by the experienced fellow you may be tempted to "buy" from external sources.

GREATER STABILITY

These recommendations sound expensive, but they are aimed at establishing greater stability within your operation and within the overall industry. A reduction of a modest 25 percent in your employee procurement costs would provide sufficient funding to cover these recommendations.

Our industry is being challenged from within. Only through concerted effort by the manufacturer and user segments of the industry can the challenge be answered. Together, they must address themselves to the single imperative: "produce."

DISCUSSION QUESTIONS

1. Explain the primary reason(s) for buying rather than producing computer personnel.
2. Under what circumstances do you believe a company should definitely consider "training people from within" for meeting its computer personnel needs? Discuss.

KILLED BY COMPUTER

John A. Guin

One of the great dangers any firm can court today is placing the responsibility of its computer facility into the hands of an unqualified manager—one who has no technical knowledge about computers; one who permits the responsibility of the facility to be usurped by his subordinates; one who fails to exercise control and authority over the facility and its staff. With such a person at the helm, it is but a matter of time before disaster sneaks up on the department in the form of an overmanned staff and underused facilities. Nor will the situation automatically reverse itself. A computer facility out of control is an insidious malignancy that makes its fatal presence known all too late. With no control the computer can afflict the entire company before it is awakened to the threat, crippling or strangling the company either from failure to provide adequate services or from budgetary requirements greater than its productive value.

The key to control of the computer facility is the facility manager. Without a well-qualified one the company, indeed, can be killed by its own computer.

Source: Reprinted, with permission, from *Data Management,* March 1972, pp. 10-16, published by the Data Processing Management Association, Park Ridge, Illinois.

COMPUTER SPECIALISM

Computer programmers and systems analysts are the *computer specialists* we are concerned with. There are others, to be sure, but none that are significant to the matter at hand. The terms *computer specialists* or *computer specialism* refer to computer programmers and systems analysts. Computer operators, although decidedly specialists in the true sense of the word, will not be included in the term unless specifically noted.

Understanding the nature of the jobs of computer specialists is critical for the facility manager, assuming, of course, he understands the nature of his own job. It is the job of the specialists to cause the computer to carry out or perform certain tasks in the operation of the firm which will enhance the collective performance of the organization. It is *not* the job of the specialists to determine which tasks will be committed to the computer. As a rule, if the decision is left to the specialists, all tasks, needed or not, will glut the computer's schedule. Management, as both the *principal* and the *principle* of organizational function, defines the area and scope of application; the analyst designs the architecture of the application; and the programmer designs the performance of the computer in effecting the application. (The 1960's unfortunately have cast the systems analyst in the role of *computer* systems analyst, grossly limiting the scope of his work to but one dimension of several in existence.) It is one of the segments of managerial responsibility to *control* all facets of the computer facility—i.e., equipment, staff, performance, etc.—constantly making sure that whatever use the computer is put to stems from functional need and not from unilateral preferences of the specialists.

THE SPECIALISTS IN CONTROL

The manager who out of lack of computer knowledge either closes his eyes to this segment of responsibility or abdicates that responsibility to the specialists must shoulder the blame alone when the facility fails in its assignment or is misused. Practically no computer specialist when given responsibility for overseeing use of the facility will allow a computer to remain idle. Since he is almost entirely computer oriented, he believes that all work regardless of nature—must be channeled through the computer. He knows that when the computer is idle the status of jobs and equipment comes under question. Consequently, just to keep the machine busy, he may propose or permit any use that comes to his or anyone else's mind.

Thus irrelevant or trivial use of the facility takes a strong foothold to the extent that machine time for subsequent *necessary* uses is pre-empted, leading to the inevitable demand for bigger, faster, and more powerful equipment, more staff, and, of course, more money. The bubble is thus inflated, and the facility manager, who by his abdication of control in the first place finds himself "subordinate" to his specialists, has no alternative but to support the proposal. He isn't about to reveal his lack of control resulting from his own ineptitude. In fact, since most other computer facilities are experiencing similar "growth and expansion," he finds no fault and actually considerable confidence in going along with proposals for more of everything, trusting implicitly the decisions of the specialists to stay in the running of the vicious and never-ending computer race.

Once control is out of the hands of the manager, the dictates of the specialists dominate practically every aspect of the facility. The specialists are free to propose whatever they fancy to keep the bubble inflated—anything from the reasonable to the absurd, from the legitimate to those special interests that somehow manage to grow into little empires. In some instances the facility manager innocently goes to bat for proposals to senior management outlining three or four times the computing power and processing capability the firm presently needs or ever will need. Indeed, many firms are totally remiss in even having a computer despite what the computer specialists claim. It is a standard excuse to blame computer vendors for overselling their products. Specialists who take up this line of defense during a managerial inquisition usually have themselves to blame, if, indeed, overselling has been committed. The intelligent specialist cannot be oversold, while the loyal specialist would not allow it to happen to his manager.

What then can management do to establish the kind of control over the computer facility that will insure the integrity of the system and secure maximum efficiency, honesty, and loyalty from the specialists? The answer lies, of course, in the appointment of a qualified computer facility manager who not only fulfills first the traditional expectations of a manager, but also fulfills expectations of the leadership of an important and highly specialized branch of the organization.

TECHNICAL PREPARATION

The computer facility manager must first prepare himself with technical knowledge about computers—systems design, programming, the function of the computer in his firm, his own firm, policies of senior management concerning the role of the computer, and so on. In other words, the facility manager is not merely a person in charge of a section or department like some worn out teacher put out to pasture in charge of a study hall; he is to be an integral part of that department, exercising control and leadership to their fullest extent. Active participation requires knowledge and understanding that must be included in the manager's make-up *before* he takes over his command. If the manager is uninformed in any of the foregoing areas, his effectiveness as a manager will already have begun to erode. Without technical knowledge about the computer, for example, he has but one course of action—let the computer specialists take over that segment of his responsibility. What can happen from there on already has been cited.

STOP PLAYING THE COMPUTER GAME

Secondly, the facility manager must stop playing the computer game and begin to make the computer play the game for the firm. He must assume that much of the work undertaken heretofore by the computer is unnecessary, irrelevant, or trivial. He must take steps to purge such uses from the computer work load. Indeed, before entertaining any proposals for equipment changes, he should require of the specialists a massive overhaul of the computer work load accompanied by a thorough investigation of other methods *more appropriate than the computer* to achieve less important work. The watchword should not be, "Can the computer do the job?" but rather, "Should the computer do the job?" Above all, he must adopt a rule-of-thumb attitude that the computer is an expensive tool to be used only when other available processing means cannot meet the demands of the job. He must constantly weigh the value of the computer output against the cost of achieving that output and be prepared either to make corrective procedural changes or to purge the job from the repertoire if the cost cannot be justified. It is vital the manager understands that growth and expansion do not automatically require a new set of equipment to keep up with the Jones Company. Few computer facilities are performing anywhere near capacity, a fact which suggests that management had better begin to question the performance capacities of those persons responsible for putting the computers to work.

CONTROL THE SPECIALISTS

The facility manager must be prepared to subject the specialists to a down-to-business policy of operation and control. If the facility is to work for the firm—and it is here assumed that such is the purpose of all computer facilities—then *someone responsbile to the firm* for the output performance of the computer must "call the shots" as to its use. Under no conditions is that person to be one of the computer specialists, for, although the specialist is trained to exploit the computer, the emphasis of such training is something quite apart from exploitation from the managerial point of view. The two approaches are almost diametrically opposed in terms of the firm's interests. Whereas the specialist is concerned with justifying the existence of the computer with a simple preponderance of work load, the facility manager is concerned with justifying the cost of the means with the value of the production output. Control of the specialists is the name of the game; control them and management controls the computer.

One final word to the facility manager in regard to his relationship with the specialists. Dishonesty in computer specialism is the exception, although recent disclosures of cases have been on the increase. There is, however, no telling how many other cases have yet to be uncovered, and it is impossible to ignore the possibility that today's disclosures may give rise tomorrow to many that are as yet but some obscure notion. Incompetence or just plain laziness are more apt to be the root of much tourble in the specialist department. Empire building is probably the most prevalent as well as the most devastating evil that threatens the computer facility. It is through empire building that firms find themselves face-to-face with a million dollar facility and a quarter-million dollar output. Empires that survive undetected have a treacherous way of becoming the breeding grounds for dishonesty. Ironically, empire building occasionally thrives unintentionally; even so, it is one of the most difficult trouble spots to eradicate before it takes its excruciating toll.

COMPUTER BUBBLE

It is no surprise that the computer bubble should have burst. It was inevitable either with or without the aid of the current international unemployment crisis. It was inevitable that computer users throughout commerce, industry, social services, government, schools, etc. should eventually come to the conclusion that their facilities were frantically computing the mad race of computers and ignoring the competitive needs of their employers! It was inevitable throughout the 1960's that someone in the managerial strata should realize that the mushrooming costs of computer facilities were far outstripping the output value from these facilities. The switch had to be pulled before the insatiable appetites of computer proposals and budgets had sucked the lifeblood out of the operating resources.

CAUSE OF THE COMPUTER BUBBLE

The basic cause of the computer bubble in the first place was not so much the hordes of programmers and analysts pouring out of educational institutions all over the country and bloating the staffs of computer facilities, but, rather, the hordes of programmers and analysts hired to work on misdirected, trivial, outdated, and unnecessary projects "to keep the computer busy." Just how many times the wheel has been re-invented in the last decade of computer specialism is a matter of conjecture. Suffice it to say, if the truth were known, the ratio of actual productive hours to the total invested specialist hours would doubtless be a shocking pittance. If, in fact, every proposal for computer service or equipment expansion included a 40 percent waste factor, those budgets would be more realistic. But endless projects of senseless computer use have distorted and bloated the "need" for a computer, and, of course, have increased demands for staff and other equipment to keep the bubble inflated and the lights blinking.

EFFECT OF THE BUBBLE BURST UPON EMPLOYMENT

One of the results of the current international unemployment crisis is that for the first time since the initial impact of commercial computing, the computing industry is suffering an employment drought during which thousands of computer specialists have been terminated without a sign of hope for rehire. The real tragedy in this gloomy picture is that these highly skilled experts—some with master's and Ph.D. degrees in their field—are "too well qualified" for employment in other fields, and in some dire cases are forced to resort to menial labor to survive. Meanwhile, management has discovered that computer facilities can continue established operations without a huge staff of programmers and analysts milling around looking busy just to keep the bubble inflated. In fact, if the jobs of all specialists were suspended at this very moment, computer facilities could continue operation of established assignments indefinitely.

This, of course, is not intended to encourage such drastic measures. To be sure, the reader is soundly cautioned against the dire consequences that could result by unadvisedly following such a course of action. This does show, however, the tenuous nature of the jobs of computer specialists—that is, totally dependent upon a never-ending process of expansion or change within the firm. It shows that some firms may find certain advantages in having no permanent staff of specialists and merely calling in a firm of consultants (specialists) to handle such matters if needed. It suggests that a major upheaval in staffing computer facilities may be in the offing, that more effective means of control must be developed as a result of those changes, and that attitudes on the part of programmers and analysts will necessarily change to accommodate to a more controlled working environment. Ironically, while harnessing the rest of the working staffs to devised systems, the systems and programming experts have been the least systematically controlled throughout the development years of the 1960's, and the results of that lack are no more plainly evident than in the disappointing fulfillment of brilliantly predicted achievements by computers during the decade. But computers do not inhibit themselves. It takes people to do that.

NEED FOR PERSONNEL CONTROLS

Few computer facilities have yet attempted any substantial means of checks and balances on personnel, especially not in the programming and analysts staffs. Undoubtedly the reason for this failure heretofore has been the lack of managerial guidelines based on long-term experience dealing with problems of specialist personnel. It may be simply that management has yet to become aware of the serious threat that an incompetent programmer or systems technician can pose to the welfare of the company. The bitter fact remains, nonetheless, that lack of control of the specialists during the 1960's has produced a slovenly monster that must be dealt with both quickly and radically if computers are ever to fulfill the role cut out for them. If management fails at this time to take positive action, the same inflated bubbles will soon enough reappear, and the same mad race to keep up with the Jones Company will be revived.

DECADE OF NONCOMPETITIVE SPECIALISM

During the 1960's computer programmers and systems analysts lacked three factors in their work: control, competition, and teamwork. Although exceptions are bound to exist, in the main, programmers and analysts have pretty well been the masters of their own destinies throughout the decade. They have been well paid; they have named their hours of work; they have hopped from job to job with impunity leaving behind deskfuls of chaos; they have been wined and dined, coddled and humored, promoted and pampered. If ever a group of employees rose from normalcy to Cinderelladom overnight, the computer specialists were that group. And why? With no qualified authority to challenge their work, they pretty well controlled their own activities. They were immune to control; they were immune to discipline; they were immune to challenge; they were immune to competition. What they divined, management swallowed as the holy word, and the holy word was that the computer could do no wrong. Although one can accept the near-perfect truth in that concept, it is the credentials and motives of the declarers that unfortunately have remained unchallenged even in the face of obviously incompetent use of the facility.

Competition breeds efficiency, and challenge is the root of competition. But for years programmers and analysts have plodded along in their modern ivory towers, each in his own way inventing and re-inventing the wheel week after week, all at the expense of their employers without so much as a blink at the costs or a "thank you" for the paid experience.

The process has been slow, tedious, boring, and expensive—especially expensive when a specialist departed for employment elsewhere leaving behind half-finished projects without documentation. The fact that half-finished work almost certainly guaranteed one's continued employment did very little to speed productivity. Indeed, the more work remaining in a state of "near-completion," the more secure one's job became.

Throughout the 1960's thousands of specialists held on to their jobs because not only did management lack control over them, but also management had been misled into believing that it required gargantuan staffs to keep the computer lights blinking to the tune of 50 percent efficiency. But it doesn't require genius to observe that computers work at 50 percent efficiency because those responsible for making them work do so at only 50 percent efficiency.

Looking back over the decade of specialism, it is reasonably clear that by having matters much their own way, the specialists have failed to rise above their own level of incompetence largely (or, perhaps, fully) because there was no challenge, no competition, and no qualified demand. Further, because no one knew what the other person was about, islands of indispensability flourished. Great and important projects dragged on interminably because some "loner" specialist was unable to put the finishing touches on his segment of responsibility so that the whole project could come together. To the specialist it was essential that no one else knew his job so that no one could challenge his work and threaten his job security. At the same time, there were those specialists who just couldn't be bothered, and who knew that if they were terminated, some other company very soon would put them to work playing the same bubble game.

TODAY'S REACTION BY MANAGEMENT

Thus, the facility manager interested in promoting control, efficiency, and economy in his sector of responsibility is today confronted with two frustratingly contradictory demands: (1) maintaining at least the status quo in productive output, and (2) trimming the budget drastically.

Most managers have responded to the dilemma simply by recognizing that production can carry on effectively without huge staffs of specialists working on future projects. Thus, the reason for the tragic employment crisis in computer specialism.

An alternative to specialist decimation, however, is the introduction of *competitive specialism,* or, if it happens already to be in operation in the firm, the tightening of controls and demands upon the competitive system. The general guidelines follow, but it is to be recognized that numerous variations can be rendered to fit varying needs.

FRAMEWORK OF COMPETITIVE SPECIALISM

1. All programming and systems work would be performed in teams.
2. Two competitive teams would be assigned duplicate work in which the two teams would attempt to outdo each other in the competition. Appropriate rewards and penalties (?) would go to the respective "winners" and "losers" of the competition.

3. Choice of "winner" would be made by the facility manager. A bonus would be awarded the winning team.
4. Team and individual member achievement records would be maintained.
5. Losers would have the responsibility to review the winning work. Appropriate compensation would be made for accepted suggestions by deducting the compensation amount from the winner's bonus.

TEAMWORK EXPLAINED

The team approach is categorically recommended because (1) it provides an effective deterrent against private empire building; (2) it spreads the responsibility of the project over several persons; (3) it stimulates mental activity through common-interest contact with other members of the team. The immediate effect will be that of any single individual ceasing to be indispensable to the organization. He can be terminated at any time without endangering the successful conclusion of the project. Every member of the team has an assigned segment of responsibility, but that segment, by virtue of its relationship in the team effort to other segments, must be openly available to all other members at any time, such that in an emergency practically any member of the team can assume that segment of responsibility either to its conclusion or until an appropriate replacement can be made.

COMPETITIVE TEAMS

Two competitive teams in each of programming and systems would bring out the best in practically all of the staff. The nature of specialist personnel is not unique—they, too, crave attention and praise despite their seeming indifference to the plaudits of others. In fact, much of the cause of the notorious reputation of disloyalty to the firm (as evidenced by the frequent job-hopping) may be brought on not so much from desire for job or reward improvement, but more from a persistent lack of praise from a respected superior. Competitive specialism provides a true outlet for recognition in this field as well as job status, and a further stimulant to professional improvement. With teamwork and competition as driving forces, the cost of parallel staffs might well be less than the losses brought on by exclusive, individual effort. Those endless days of waiting for a specialist to produce workable results could, under competitive teamwork, become hours. At present, there is really no substantial force to put the programmers and analysts through their paces to get the job done and done well.

PENALTIES AND REWARDS

Endless methods of penalties and rewards exist, but generally they will be most effective if they have a monetary base. One possible method is to guarantee the staff a minimum salary to be augmented by bonuses or commissions for "winning" work. The "loser," however, is not without recourse; during his review of the winning work, he stands to gain much in rewards by making suggestions for improvement. Whatever system of rewards is adopted, competition, challenge, and teamwork will provide the motivation for continued professional growth and improvement. One very practical modification of the competitive team system is to provide for regular rotation of team members to lessen the possibility of collusion taking root and to cater to the need for continual critical scrutiny of the specialists' work by those who work directly with and understand current techniques. The company stands to be the real winner, while competition will push the standards of computer specialism to a level never before attained within the department.

Records of achievement will play an important part in the competitive system. They will enable management to observe the quality of performance not only by individuals but also by particular combinations. A member who shows up continually on the winning team is one to watch for promotion, while those who persistently lose perhaps should be considered for termination or for placement elsewhere within the company. Those combinations that prevail as winners may be selected for special bonus projects, the individual members even then being set apart in competition with each other. The attention to individual achievement can reward the effective workers and fail to reward (not penalize) the ineffective workers.

THE FACILITY MANAGER PARTICIPATES

The one person to choose the winning work should be the facility manager or a team of judges he may appoint. But if the manager is to maintain control, his stamp of approval must be felt in the choice. The worthy manager will be able to evaluate clearly and fairly. If he delegates the authority, he must be able to justify either his confirmation or his rejection of the judgment. It is essential that the manager control the facility, and, to do so, it is imperative that he make the ultimate decision as to the plans, designs, and programs to be used in the facility. Certainly, such demands call for exceptional qualities in the manager. But his position in the company is critical and deserves exceptional attention. Decisions he makes can have far-reaching ramifications, in some cases involving commitments or profits and losses of several million dollars.

CONSTRUCTIVE CRITICISM AND CHALLENGE

When the winning team project has been selected, that project must be exposed to the critical eye of the "honorable opposition" so to speak. When one knows his invited criticisms may be recognized and rewarded, he takes much greater pains to seek out concealed trouble spots. At the same time, the winning team will be concerned with preventing the honorable opposition from finding such trouble spots by eliminating them before the opposition can study the plan. The ultimate incentive to produce faultless work would be to deduct from the winner's bonus any amounts awarded for critical improvements by the opposition. Where money is concerned, team efforts will become more cooperative and tightly knit. The prima donna computer specialist will be forced either to join forces with the rest of the group or to go his own insulated way. Deadwood personnel will be forced to change their habits and attitudes in order to survive. A continued attitude of non-cooperation will promptly eliminate much of the deadwood simply by demand from the cooperating members. Consistent winners and losers can be dealt with according to standing policy. The prevailing fact that all work must come under the watchful eye of competitive specialists will elicit the best from most, if not all, personnel.

For those who consider the competitive system economically unfeasible, it should be pointed out that the cost of duplicate teams will be offset by faster and more accurate individual work. Additionally, the quality of systems and programming cannot help but improve notably, while policing and control within the system are automatic. As long as the work of every member is subject to the scrutiny of any other member, there is little chance that incompetence, collusion, fraud, deception, or empire building will escape detection for long. In the long run, the company should discover that economically it has never done better in its computer facility while concurrently improving decidedly the efficiency and control of the department.

One possible way of reducing the costs of the competitive system would be to periodically use a consulting firm of computer specialists as the honorable opposition instead of maintaining a permanent "duplicate" team. At no time, then, when the regular team was assigned a particular project would the members know whether or not the consulting firm would be actually working in competition. By using the consulting firm only for occasional spot checks, the costs may be reduced somewhat.

At a time when most computer facilities are divesting themselves of highly qualified (and expensive) technicians, it appears contradictory to recommend a course of action in the opposite direction. But if ever there was an appropriate time to clean house throughout the computer field, now is that time.

The need for computer assistance in today's society is well established and perpetual, very much as any company depends upon the telephone for competitive action and information.

Although others may stumble along with crippled staffs throughout the present crisis, the astute facility manager will recognize an opportunity not only to hold on to talent and genius, but also to put it to work constructively reorganizing the computer facility from the ground up.

Whatever the opposition to the competitive system because of the cost of maintaining duplication, one reply emerges quite clearly: It is far better to spend the "extra" money to openly control and expedite operations than it is to spend the same amount or more to support unknown and entrenched elements of incompetence, deception, precious empires, and even fraud.

The time has come for the public to begin to realize dollar-for-dollar value from the computer, for, ultimately, it is the public who is footing the bill. Every needless use of the computer is a needless addition to that bill, and every effort to vie with the Jones Company for superiority of equipment is a sorrowful multiple of that bill. The present national computer expenditure is, indeed, a national tragedy because of the shocking wastelands to which the public has been led by incompetence, mismanagement, and ignorance. If our computer experts continue their practice of using an expensive and powerful tool to resolve trivial problems, the wastelands will never disappear, and John Public will go on and on paying twice what he should.

DISCUSSION QUESTIONS

1. "The key to control of the computer facility is the facility manager." Do you agree? Why?
2. Who is the facility manager? What are his functions and responsibilities?
3. Evaluate the author's views toward the team approach in programming and systems work.

THE PROGRAMMER AS A MANAGER

William E. Coleman

In the current tight economy, organizations critically need effective managers. With the software industry experiencing its first recession, the quality of its managers may well determine whether a company will survive. Although the last 15 years have enabled the software industry to spawn some good managers, this writer believes that the number is insufficient to meet the urgent needs of the industry. It is the author's view that technical managers are developed through direct experience. Formal courses and education may provide some of the tools, but the concepts must be seasoned through direct exposure to enable the individual to readily identify the problems that must be handled, the priorities to be assigned, ultimate solutions, and ways of judging results before the financial statements are in.

THE IDEAL MANAGER

Although it may be possible for senior officers of a corporation to manage activities without having technical competence in these areas, this does not work at lower levels of management. The manager of a systems analysis or programing group must have a strong understanding of the work for which he is responsible. He must be able to judge how difficult different tasks may be, how long they should take, whether the approach being taken is technically sound, etc. Thus, we cannot borrow managers from other disciplines and expect them to solve our problems. In addition to technical knowledge, studies of effective managers have shown that they also possess good communication and human relations skills, high energy levels, and are assertive and decisive. Thus, the ideal candidate for programming manager would possess all these attributes.

Source: Reprinted with permission from *The Office* Magazine, May 1971, pp. 14-15.

Over 20 years ago, the U.S. Department of Labor started a project to identify the attributes of people who perform successfully in each of the broad range of jobs in our country. Results of this vast effort are contained in Part 2 of the 1965 edition of the Dictionary of Occupational Titles (DOT) which described a programmer as being primarily concerned with data, rather than with people. He tends to work by himself, independently, rather than spending most of his time working with others. Thus, this lack of contact with other people is a hallmark of the programmer.

THE PROGRAMMER'S DILEMMA

Further substantiating the DOT description of programmers, many psychologists have tried to identify characteristics which might be used to select successful programmers. These efforts have indicated a dilemma for the computer industry and for programmers themselves. The studies show that programmers place great emphasis on what they know, and that successful ones like to work by themselves—completely engrossed in their formulas, logic diagrams and design specifications. Most are not concerned with skills related to communication, relations with other people, persuasiveness or assertiveness. Their apparent preoccupation with solitude and knowledge sets them apart from members of professions involving public contact, such as salesmen, physicians, attorneys and teachers. Thus, the computer industry suffers from a severe shortage of potential managers, and the programmer suffers from a severe shortage of the skills required either to become a manager or to develop his full potential to benefit himself and his industry.

The dilemma for the industry is that it needs good programmers, but it also needs effective managers of programmers. The attributes of a good programmer normally do not include the human relations skills required of managers. The programmer's dilemma is that he takes pride in his work and the way he does it, but he generally lacks the skills he must have to achieve a management position. Further, lack of these skills puts him at a distinct disadvantage if he is unemployed and trying to sell himself to a prospective employer.

What can the industry do about this? How can people who take delight in working alone be made articulate, persuasive, self-confident, energetic, perceptive and results-oriented—all within a framework of sensitivity to the needs of other people? If one is to succeed as a manager, or to sell himself to a prospective employer, these characteristics are necessary. Can they be developed? They can if the person is able to understand why people behave the way they do, wants to be sensitive to the needs of others, and perceives himself as being capable of continued growth in the many roles he must play as a total human being.

It seems clear that the industry would be ill-advised even to attempt developing these human relations characteristics in some programmers who are content to work on their logic diagrams in their own cubicles, and who are resistant to any change. However, all are not alike. Some may actively aspire—based on sound reasons and adequate qualifications—to management and to development of the human relations skills required of a manager. Few in number but easy to identify, they are most likely to succeed in carefully developed, progressive, manager development programs.

INTROVERT AND EXTROVERT

Between the "cubicle" group and the management-aspiring group are a good many who, for one reason or another, have not given much thought to human relations or to becoming managers. Many of them could learn the skills necessary to become effective managers and, at the same time, best serve their own interests. Computer industry management must take the responsibility to identify them and to do everything possible to help develop the skills they will need as managers. One way management might identify programmers with management potential is through close observation of their performance on certain assignments. Some questions that might be considered in making the evaluation are:

1. How well did he handle himself when he was called on to interact with a user?
2. How well did he present a briefing or report to management?
3. In leading a project team, did they work well together?
4. What was the quality of the work?
5. Was it done in a timely way?
6. How easy is it to communicate with him?
7. Does he give any indication of having set some definite goals for himself and is he striving to reach them?

Another approach used quite widely is to have an industrial psychologist assess the individual's personal qualifications. Through psychological tests and a depth interview, the psychologist seeks to determine whether the person possesses the attributes needed to be a successful manager. There will be both successes and failures in attempts to identify programmers who are likely to succeed in management positions. However, the main point is that management should make such attempts. Failure to do so amounts to a disservice to all.

SOFTWARE INDUSTRY'S PROBLEM

To remain viable, and to grow, the computer software industry must look to its own ranks for its own managers—at all levels. Since the industry consists primarily of trained programmers, they must get special emphasis as a source of potential managers. Identifying and motivating them toward management roles is not an easy task. However, it is a vital task, worth the expenditure of substantial effort. To succeed in developing effective managers is in itself gratifying. It is also productive and economical, in terms of increased efficiency and in developing the potential of people to succeed in their profession and in their personal lives.

DISCUSSION QUESTIONS

1. What is the author's view of the "ideal" manager?
2. According to the article, how could one expect a programmer to become a successful manager? Explain.

THE CHANGING WORLD OF THE DATA PROCESSING ADMINISTRATOR

Clarke Newlin, Jr.

Looking back over the past 20 years of the computer industry, we could label the five year segments thus: the first five years as a period when the new tool for business was spearheaded by the younger set, the second five years as the period when computer uses were expanded despite high costs, the third period when technology mushroomed equipment and applications, and the fourth period when management decided to harness the computer for profits.

While no one concerned with computers is a novice to change, data processing administrators have been guilty of not always recognizing and properly analyzing change; as a result, we have not prepared ourselves nor our company data processing operations adequately to maximize benefits for our employers not for ourselves.

Changes now occurring in data processing which affect the data processing administrator are not technical but are rather changes in attitude and viewpoints which can very well determine the future of our careers, salaries and positions.

Three major areas of change in attitude are concerned with: (1) Management's view of computers and the computers' role in the company; (2) The view data processing administrators have of themselves and of their role in the company structure; (3) The increased concern for the protection and utilization of company investments in data processing. Several factors have effected these changes. First, the great proliferation of computers into almost every line of business and in most application areas. Today there is far more exchange of ideas and of experiences with computers so that data processing operations come in for more scrutiny.

Secondly, the advances of computer technology, both in hardware and software, has made the field of computers highly specialized, and specialization always exacts greater emphasis in the management of the total activity.

Third, management has become far more knowledgeable about computers and what makes them profitable and is demanding better performance from the data processing administrator.

Recent trends in the economy which have management taking a closer look at expenses also carry expectations for better returns on the computer investment.

Since jobs in data processing have tightened up, many are finding that they have to try harder and be more professional in their work than ever before.

All these factors are forcing the data processing function into a maturity that is somewhat new and somewhat uncomfortable.

Source: Reprinted, with permission, from *Data Management,* February 1972, pp. 35-38, published by the Data Processing Management Association, Park Ridge, Illinois.

CHANGING MANAGEMENT'S VIEWPOINT

We haven't done too well in convincing corporate management that a data processing administrator is capable of joining their ranks with qualifications equal to those who came up through sales, marketing, controllership or engineering. It all gets back to administrative capability, and not in proving how important you are because you understand what's required to handle a large terminal control program!

Corporate management seems to view the data processing administrator as not having adequate executive abilities because the data processing administrator has done such a great job of proving to management how technical and how different are the demands of his work from those of other company functions. Yes, of course, there are differences, but they should not be emphasized so that management thinks "once a technician always a technician!"

In our efforts to advance to a top level management position, we would do well to keep in mind that few if any members of the corporate management team came up through data processing. As an industry data processing wasn't even around when many of them started out in the business world. Because of this, management may view us as different and may find it difficult to consider us in the same light as another prospective management member who is working in the very job the president once held. We must overcome the possibility of such shortsightedness, by speaking management's language, and concentrating on using data processing to enhance profits and dominance in those areas in which management is keenly interested.

IMPROVING COMMUNICATION

Computer jargon is a source of much trouble. We speak too much "bytese" or "COBOLese" when we should be using the language management uses—good ole' English. It's not the company president's responsibility to communicate with you, it is your responsibility to communicate with him. He can easily replace you if he desires better communication; it's a little tougher for you to try the reverse action to solve the problem.

To improve communication with management:

1. Determine what corporate management wants and needs to know about your data processing operation. It's not core size nor channel limitations. Management is interested in profit and dominance. What are your schedules of manpower, budget, progress and other items by which they can measure your contribution to profits and dominance?

2. Involve management in long-range planning of data processing as a dovetail to the long-range planning of the company.

3. Concern yourself with management's concerns, otherwise you'll have them saying, "there goes data processing on another harebrained tangent."

4. Subject your operation to the same scrutiny of reporting on performance which every other department in your company has.

5. Speak management's language. We've been telling them for years to learn ours; it's time we used theirs.

THE COMPUTER AND THE BUDGET

Management now views the computer operation for what it is—a big part of the total company operations. Thus the position of the data processing function has taken on a new importance and so have the positions of personnel in data processing. This increased importance of the function has increased requirements needed to attain the top data processing jobs. Many firms have sought to find the answer through facilities management services or by going outside the company to get top data processing administrators. The need to go to external sources for personnel almost always results when the internal data processing people do not recognize and do not respond properly to the changing demands for their services.

Data processing people are said to be unrealistic in projecting and estimating costs because they are not "cost conscious." This notion probably stems from a mistaken belief held by many data processing personnel that the value of their position is directly proportional to their data processing equipment and personnel expenditures! This is complete folly. It is generally true that a bigger installation requires more qualified people, it does not follow, however, that merely increasing your expenditures will enhance your position. This might have worked in the early days of computers, but it will probably have a reverse effect today, and any data processing manager who practices this philosophy is in for some rough times ahead.

CHANGING THE VIEWPOINT OF THE DP ADMINISTRATOR

At the Houston DPMA Conference (June 1971), it was interesting to note the strong emphasis in seminar topics on management rather than on the technical aspects of data processing. This is a clear indication of one of the changes our industry has recognized—the need for each of us to be better administrators, not only technical experts. This was highlighted in the editorial which appeared in the August 1971 issue of *Data Management,* which reads in part thus:

> "Data Processing offers an unparalleled opportunity to reach a position in corporate management. Its benefits can be utilized in virtually all of the company's activities, and effective implementation crosses virtually every organizational boundary. The daily operations of the company, and its future planning, center increasingly about the efficient application of Data Processing. The individual at the head of these operations is a logical and valuable addition to the management team.
>
> "Why, then, do some have difficulty in making 'the big step'? In many instances, it may be because they can't see the forest for the trees.
>
> "Management regardless of whether it's managing a fleet of trucks or a multi-divisional international corporation, involves one's ability to handle the resources of the business. These resources include machines, people and money. The resources allocated to a Data Processing Manager include computers, peripheral equipment, data communications, programmers, analysts, operators . . . and, of course, money.
>
> "Too many Data Processing Managers associate themselves with their function . . . their equipment . . . their personnel. With technology . . . and procedure . . . rather than their objectives. They are too close to the trees to see the forest.

"Too many become involved with the 'tools' of their trade rather than with the task of *managing* those resources to assure their optimum utilization. They are outstanding employees, but too often they think at the level of their employees, rather than at the level of their management."

Another change, which is a healthy sign, is our own critical review of what we are doing, of where we are heading, and the alternatives for us in data processing. There used to be a feeling that the only way to get anything done in DP was to do it yourself. The result was re-invention of every wheel in data processing at least several hundred times over. The smart DP manager now considers how to get the greatest return for the money and achieve management's objectives most efficiently—even if it means purchasing outside services, acquiring someone else's system, or accepting less than the ultimate system when that's the most profitable thing to do.

We've sometimes been guilty of making a god out of a concept. We've taken terms like "Management Information System" and built it up as if the term itself was our corporate objective. I remember one seminar in which the audience was asked to define a "Management Information System." After listening to some of that discussion I was inspired to jot down this definition:

MIS—a system concept put forth as the major thrust of a joint conspiracy of DP professionals and consultants, formulated and used to increase their own salaries, to confuse what otherwise would be a record of minimal accomplishment, and to retain their position in the organization by using the MIS effort as a means of retaining their staffs until the next generation of computer is released.

Perhaps facetious, but it does point up the futility of pursuing any data processing concept without giving due emphasis to what we're hired to do, that is, use DP to help our companies gain profits and dominance.

Data processing administrators now are using better administrative tools in performing their work, many of which have always been available but were not utilized. These include standardization, rigid documentation, realistic scheduling and estimating, and measuring the return on software and hardware investments. The current business slump has forced the data processing administrators to recognize that constant reprogramming to upgrade equipment is contrary to profit and dominance objectives of the company.

Perhaps the one change in viewpoint which will effect the greatest benefit for the data processing adminsitrator is his acceptance of the fact that the computer must make a profit for the company. He will, therefore, use a different approach to computer costs and the computer operation when viewing them as a profit center for the company. In several instances, forward thinking data processing people have helped their companies get into new profit-making businesses through the use of the computer.

PROTECTION AND UTILIZATION OF THE COMPANY'S DP INVESTMENTS

Today, security is a big issue, not just for the large companies but for installations of all sizes. Some sad losses have occurred, accidentally and intentionally:

"Thus a discontented employee stole the company's master file of more than 2 million customer names and sold them to an eager competitor. Estimated loss to the firm was $3 million ... A bitter employee of a West Coast electronics firm managed to destroy virtually every one of the company's computer files and programs.

"It seems almost incredible how easily a computer tape can be destroyed. At one company, an employee inadvertently attached his magnetic flashlight to the side of a tape cabinet while he was cleaning the interior. Result: The company lost six full days of computer time while it reconstructed the data the magnet had erased from the tapes. Another computer service man forgot he had a magnet in his toolbox while working near tapes. His oversight destroyed some 80,000 of a credit company's customer records, which had to be recreated from hardcopy files at a cost of $10,000."

The first reaction is probably to explain how our installation is different and this could never happen to us. The real issue is that we are responsible as DP professionals to face these issues and avoid any such losses before they occur.

As a part of their audits of companies, several auditing firms now are beginning a thorough check of the protection of the DP assets covering site security, extent of documentation, protection of programs, protection against fraud, and recovery procedures.

The details demanded in two questionnaires used by one CPA firm, each 14 pages long, would prove quite embarrassing for many installations. The partner in the firm using these said he was reviewing with one DP manager the items needed in covering program documentation. The DP manager blurted out, "If I let you see all of the items you've requested, I'd lose my job!"

How would your installation score on some of these questions?

1. What is the physical location of the computer facility? Is it removed from centers of magnetic or radar activity? Is it remotely located and not open for public display?
2. Are all doors to the computer facility kept locked? Is entry restricted?
3. Is one person ever alone in the computer room?
4. Is the computer facility subject to possible damage through flooding or water seepage?
5. What fire-prevention steps have been taken?
6. Do computer center personnel know emergency procedures? Are drills ever held?
7. Have fail-safe devices been installed to halt operations if power drops below satisfactory operating levels? ... if power reaches marginal levels? Are computer operators familiar with procedures should this occur?
8. Are computer center employees, who are fired or resign, immediately relieved of all duties if they were employed in sensitive areas?
9. Is there adequate insurance coverage to replace equipment, programs, and files?

As to program security:

10. Are master copies of all programs, listings, documentation, and operating manuals kept off the premises in a fireproof vault? Are they current? What procedures assure their being current?

11. Do programmers retain copies of operating programs?
12. Who assigns, reviews and approves changes to active programs?
13. Do programmers have access to "live" data? If so, why?
14. Do operators have program listings?

No DP manager should delude himself into saying, "We'll do those things when we find enough time," or "My management has me working on so many projects that I don't have time to do all of those things the way I'd like to." It's our responsibility to point out to management the costs of not doing these things. When we do, they'll see to it that we take the time to do them, and they'll also think more of our administrative abilities!

These are only a few of the many changes now affecting data processing administrators but it is imperative that we recognize those changes, prepare ourselves to meet the challenge of those changes and follow through with making the necessary adjustments.

We must learn from top level management and must involve ourselves in various computer industry related activities, such as DPMA, to be more knowledgeable, to increase our abilities, and to learn from one another through personal contact. Most corporate executives involve themselves in many such activities to keep informed of changes. We must learn to view the business scene the way corporate management does, and we must think the way they do. We must strive for professionalism. We must take time to plan, otherwise we cannot be data processing executives.

DISCUSSION QUESTIONS

1. What areas of change are affecting data processing administrators? Explain in detail.

2. "Unrestrained growth and expansion have come to a halt. Management has decided to harness the computer for profit." Explain this statement. Do you agree? Why?

WANTED: A FUTURE

Eleanor H. Irvine

Speculation about the role of the EDP Manager in tomorrow's world is becoming a popular topic. Some theorists claim it will be a minor role, supportive and technical in orientation. Others view it as a consultative position to top manage-

Source: Reprinted, with permission, from *Data Management*, June 1973, pp. 22-25, published by the Data Processing Management Association, Park Ridge, Illinois.

ment. More optimistic predictors foresee the role as one of policy and decision making. The most inspiring viewpoint states it will be a leadership role, helping to shape the destiny of the organization and even that of society's.

All these forecasts have merit because the role that any EDP Manager plays in the future will be primarily a personal, individual decision. The position today affords ample opportunity to plan and prepare for a pivotal position in tomorrow's organization. But the effort must be made to be ready for whatever form and shape the new organization takes in the years ahead. Otherwise, one's position will depend largely on which philosophy one ascribes to and adopts for a course of action.

The harbingers of doom are always with us and have been plentiful of late. They fill one with disillusionment, pessimism and negativism. Rachel Carson's *Silent Spring* and other disturbing forecasters have provided new evidence to support their perpetual recommendation to concentrate on today because there will probably be no tomorrow. Ross A. Webber expresses another group's approach when he writes: "Managers tend to avoid real thought about the future because it is ambiguous."[1] Members of this class play the "wait and see" game. Eric Hoffer, longshoreman turned writer, is a good spokesman for the camp followers of optimism who anticipate the future as challenging and exciting. His experiences on skid row for eighteen years and on the docks most of his adult life have given him an appreciation of the capacity of this country to find the solutions and to excel.

To predict precisely what EDP's management role will be in the future appears to be an exercise as perilous and futile as Peter Drucker tells us is the prediction of the impact of new technology.[2] People are the enigma and for centuries have defied predictors of their behavior. *It is more realistic to assess the assets and liabilities that exist in the present role when considering the potential for leadership in the world of tomorrow.* EDP has developed an unique place for itself in most organizations and provides its management many distinctive opportunities to acquire assets for a leadership role. Several of these assets are worth specific mention.

CHANGE-AGENT

Today's EDP Manager has an unusual opportunity to be the change-agent of the organization. EDP has affected almost every segment of an organization in a very few years. Its unprecedented acceptance has made it one of the fastest growing industries and subject to constant changes in hardware, software, applications and systems. Its management has been required to be innovative, a constant student and able to grow rapidly and well. Many of its members have been infants in the management field, pushed too rapidly into senior status without preparation or guidance. They have matured rapidly and are becoming equal to the challenges presented by their more experienced and conditioned peers. Few managers today have been exposed to a more rigorous or dynamic environment. There is strong evidence that the dynamic nature of the field will continue and require equally dynamic management. Managers who have succeeded to date and continue to meet

[1] Ross A. Webber, *Time and Management,* Van Nostrand Reinhold Co., 1972.
[2] Peter Drucker, *Management: Tasks; Responsibilities; Practices,* Harper & Row, 1973.

the field's new challenges will be well equipped to accept greater responsibilities in the future.

BROADER SKILLS REQUIRED

Management of EDP has required a broader skills capacity than other positions in the organization. A technical knowledge of the field is imperative and administration without it has proven ineffectual. Ability to serve the user well is equally important and calls for substantial knowledge of systems and applications. Awareness of the latest trends in the behavioral science field is important to keep updated on the shifting needs and behavior patterns of people. Only then can realistic systems be built around the human element and the highly diversified and professional group of EDP employees be managed properly.

The manager's task as change-agent requires a sales capacity, diplomacy and ability to cope with entrenched ideas and resistance. General knowledge of special disciplines, operations research, information retrieval, communications and scientific applications are needed when under the guidance of the EDP area. EDP Management must be versatile and flexible to be prepared to serve every function of the organization. Few positions offer a better opportunity to develop a broader overview of an organization and to gain a head start on major accomplishment in the years ahead.

Another special feature of EDP Management is the character of its communication. The normal channeling of communication in today's functional organization is vertical. EDP communication is in all directions both inside and outside the organization. It must be equally adept vertically and horizontally to deal with the many segments of the organization. It crosses lines to communicate with peers, top management and all levels of the hierarchy. Seldom are managers exposed to this diversity although organizational developers recommend it as a way to improve present communication shortcomings. The future organization that is reshaped to fit the demands of a rapidly changing business environment may well benefit from the communication experience that will be brought by its EDP Management.

NEW, UNTRIED EDP EFFORTS

The recent addition of EDP to most organizations frees its management from the usual precedents that exist in most areas of the business. Freedom from these traditions make it easier and more necessary to be creative and original. So much of EDP's efforts are new and untried that imagination and perception are equally important in the design of sound systems. Few opportunities exist for so many measurable savings from one's personal efforts and approach to problem solving. How well this is done is reflected immediately on the balance sheet. Achieving the capacity to create within such restraints should be good practice for whatever lies ahead.

EDP Management has one of the best on-job training experiences that is possible for top management grooming. It rivals the programs offered by graduate schools of business because of its work setting. Learning takes place by observing and doing; and teaching is given by those responsible for the subject matter. The most comprehensive training is received by EDP Managers who are responsible for installing a Management Information System. Tremendous insight is gained by fitting the individual pieces together into a total concept. But even the improvement of existing systems and initiating new ones provide exceptional opportunities to listen and learn. The most appealing aspect of this training is its continuance *for it never comes to an end.* All systems change constantly and require modifications and redesigning. The EDP community is kept busy just being aware of new hardware and software offerings and their numbers show little signs of changing. The EDP area as a laboratory of learning offers its management one of the best insurance policies available against obsolescence.

JOB SATISFACTION, TREMENDOUS POSSIBILITY

The nature of EDP work provides its management with extraordinary capability to meet the needs of its members. Job satisfaction through meaningful work and personal growth is more possible in EDP than in most departments of an organization. Fluid work structures, task forces and project teams, eliminate the usual divisions of work and frustrations from a lack of accomplishment. Temporary assignments throughout the organization help develop its personnel and through comparisons better appreciate their permanent work location. The continual introduction of new specialities creates new positions for promotion of personnel. These may be specialist and consultative positions which carry equal status as those of management.

The diversity of EDP membership in backgrounds and skills makes its environment stimulating and unusual. It represents the type of environment and climate that all organizations will wish to adopt to attract tomorrow's workers and to keep them happy. This observation may well prompt one to ask: "If this is true, why hasn't EDP made a bigger impact on its organizations?"

There are two major reasons that have made this impossible. One is EDP's location in the organization chart and the other is the qualifications requirement set for its management. These can be serious liabilities to EDP Management when evaluating its future chances and require further consideration.

EDP SUFFERS A BAD IMAGE

EDP was initiated into most organizations as a replacement for manual or punched card systems. It was considered an expensive and necessary evil to handle the increasing volume of paper detail. This conception of its use placed it in the controllership or equivalent area as a service and staff function. Top Management's lack of EDP know-how and the emphasis on its technical capabilities resulted in its general acceptance by all members of the organization as a helpful tool to handle routine, repetitive, menial and cumbersome details of their tasks.

Rapid changes in hardware did little to change this image. The emphasis on technical advances merely pointed up the need for better technicians. Even changes in the reporting structure seldom advanced its status in the organization. Forceful functions like manufacturing and marketing yielded none of their influence and at times caused showdowns to establish which was superior in the hierarchy. Rarely did top management rock the boat by deciding otherwise. EDP proved a poor match in these power plays and faced constant frustration in proving and providing the full capacity it could offer.

Only now does it seem possible to prove EDP's full value to an organization. But it is still limited and identified by its location in the organization. There is little hope that this will change until organizations abandon their functional approaches for something which places EDP in a more influential position in the new design.

Top Management's attitude of a low status level of EDP, and the role EDP played in the organization, colored its thinking on the credentials of the new EDP Manager. Primarily he should be a top flight technician since he was the only one who knew the capabilities of the computer and how to install it successfully. The position was filled by promoting the former punched card Manager, if the organization had one, or by hiring someone who had installed a computer previously. The computer manufacturers did not discourage this impression because there was added assurance to them that everything would go smoothly when trying to prove EDP's worth to the organization.

In the early days of computers this may not have been a bad idea, up to a point. However, too much latitude was given this technical management with weak guidance from the inner sanctum. EDP moved rapidly from one generation of equipment into another, a maverick in the organization causing unprecedented expenditures and alienation of needed supporters. Costly errors in judgment and application brought constant changes in its management and did little for the computer's general reputation.

Today finds the computer reporting frequently to a capable young executive who has learned enough of the mysteries of the computer to be its master. EDP Management is still the second-class citizen who keeps the hardware running smoothly, the users happy and the EDP budget in line. Requests for replacements of the position still specify the magic numbers and names of hardware, software, applications and related qualifications. Seldom do requirements include such considerations as ability to work with and understand people, capabilities for senior management, planning and decision making experiences and a sound knowledge of business principles and practices. It is obvious that today's business leadership rarely considers EDP Management for promotion into its arena.

The history of EDP to date and the resultant liabilities need not prove fatal to the EDP Manager who wishes an enlarged role in the coming years; they are hurdles that must be recognized and overcome. Although EDP is a staff function the assets of its present workshop are strong ones and provide sufficient exposure to make a substantial contribution to the organization. What is needed is a new conception of EDP Management and better public relations with the entire organization. This requires a personal program of growth which each Manager must undertake on his own. Such a program is never easy because it requires a realistic appraisal of one's own shortcomings and determination of how best to overcome them. Consideration of some of the common failings in the field may be of assistance.

COMMON SHORTCOMINGS

EDP Managers have a tendency to overreact to their organization's environment. Most organizations are conservative and weigh changes very carefully. Considerable groundwork is necessary to convince policy makers and management of proposed areas of change to alter direction and disrupt satisfactory operations for unknown and untried substitutes. Enormous patience, sound evaluation, indisputable facts and persuasive speaking ability are necessary requirements. Possession of all these qualities is lacking in most EDP Management. Rebuffs prompt leaving the organization, cries of "politics," an emphasis on professionalism rather than consideration for the corporate good, and reacting rather than listening and gaining insight.

The heavy involvement of EDP Management with technology frequently results in little involvement with people. EDP offers an unending fascination and it is easy to become more absorbed with its complexities and problems than with those of its personnel. EDP Management has gained a reputation with many of its employees as unsympathetic to their needs because it has held itself aloof and delegated personnel responsibilities to its middle management team. The EDP Manager alone must be a leader, a teacher, a counselor and a guide. These duties are priorities in today's organizations where people are the most important asset, and, at the same time, are the most challenging to manage of any time in the history of modern business. Their influence has never been greater and any management insensitive to their new and growing capacity may look forward to difficult times. EDP management has an added dimension in its need to like and understand people, their shifting requirements and behavior patterns. The constant interplay with a wide variety of users, and the design of systems which must always consider the human factor, call for more than average ability in personnel management.

FEW MODELS OF LEADERSHIP

EDP has developed few models of leadership. This requires disciplines which are foreign to the life styles of most of its managers. Lack of constant exposure to a leadership environment is partially responsible. Equally at fault is the acute unawareness of the personal demands required for such membership. EDP Managers need to develop more natural ease in any social situation, whether it be a platform, a conference room or a boardroom.

They function at a disadvantage when taken out of their daily habitat and become ill-at-ease when faced with strange situations and people. Moderation in personal indulgences in all circumstances claims few practitioners. This is evidenced with superiors and subordinates alike and indicates not only poor judgment but obliviousness to the importance of a good example. A high standard of personal values is frequently missing.

Greater commitment to programs which improve the quality of life is needed, within the organization and in the community at large. This requires replacing selfishness with selflessness, developing a social consciousness and spiritual values. It is in this direction that leadership must go to obtain the respect, admiration and personal commitment of its followers. *Dedication to people has strong appeal when choosing one's leader.*

The demands of this style of leadership may appear too onerous to be worth the effort and too difficult to achieve success. It depends principally on how badly one wishes to achieve such a goal and how much effort one is willing to put forth to reach it. The decision to plan such a program and pursue it with full commitment can bring the individual one of the most exciting and rewarding periods of life.

Achievement of the goal could make the difference between a mere existence and a rich, full, active, and meaningful life.

One discovers what real living is all about by developing these disciplines of leadership within oneself.

DISCUSSION QUESTIONS

1. Summarize and discuss the special features and skills required of data processing managers.
2. In what respect can one view a data processing manager as a change-agent? Explain.
3. Do you feel that an EDP manager's on-the-job training is adequate preparation for top management grooming? Why?
4. According to the author, in what way(s) does EDP suffer a bad image? Do you agree? Explain.

SELECTED REFERENCES

Articles

Bain, Dennis A. "Another Look at the Part Time Computers." *Business Automation,* April 1971, pp. 39-41.

Black, Dexter. "Job Hunting in 1970." *Computers and Automation,* December 1970, pp. 28ff.

Bouldin, Robert W. ' Guidelines in the Selection of Data Processing Personnel." *Data Management,* September 1971, pp. 89-91.

Braun, R. J. "Computers in Management: An Outlook into the Future." *Data Management,* August 1971, pp. 28-31.

Carlson, Walter M. "Make Your Computer Profitable." *The Office,* January 1972, p. 49ff.

Chapin, Ned. "Successful Planning Techniques for Data Processing Managers." *Data Management,* September 1972, pp. 35-38.

Dinter, Heinz. "Criteria for the Organizational Effectiveness of Data Processing." *Data Management,* July 1971, pp. 31-35; August 1971, pp. 32-35.

Donati, Frank R. "The Evaluation and Appraisal of Programmer's Performance." *Data Management,* October 1971, pp. 18-19.

Judd, Dudley F. "The Need for Systems Analysis." *The Office,* January 1972, pp. 120-121.

Karush, Arnold. "Performance Measurement.' *Data Management,* July 1971, pp. 36-40.

Lineback, Edward O. "Better Management of EDR." *The Office,* January 1972, p. 70.

LoRusso, Paul M. "The Operations Manager's Job." *Data Management,* September 1972, pp. 38-40.

Schroeder, Walter J. "The EDP Manager—and the Computer Profit Drain." *Computers and Automation,* January 1971, pp. 14-18.

Sobczak, Thomas V. "A Systems Approach to Job Hunting." *Computers and Automation,* August 1971, pp. 31-35.

PART 11

Computing in the 1970's

THE SUPERSONIC SEVENTIES

As the nation slips, slides and stumbles into the supersonic 70's, there is no little concern and uncertainty about the direction and distance that lies ahead. On one hand, there is the pall of social, environmental, philosophical and inflationary problems that at times seems bent on smothering all hopes for a brighter tomorrow. On the other, is the eloquent testimony of past technological and economic progress made possible by the free enterprise system, promising a future of accomplishments that taxes all but the most vivid of imaginations.

We'll bet on the second hand, confident that the supersonic 70's will produce a boom that will minimize, if not solve, a majority of the nation's ills, and break down the barriers that separate and segment the various people of our society.

The success of the 70's will depend greatly on the ability of management, in business, industry and government, to harness the technological power already available and that to come, in order to bring new dimensions to management's decision making processes.

Actually, most of the problems of the new decade are carryovers from the last. There is the people problem; the need to train vast numbers, minorities in particular, to become productive members of the information processing industry. Likewise, the problem of preparing students in the use of information processing techniques, and perhaps more important, the problem of who will teach the teachers so that they may instruct the students.

Then there are the social implications of vast nationwide information networks, private and governmental national data banks, and the threats they pose, if any, to the individual's privacy. There are the problems and potential of "unbundling" to the user and the industry. Also, the possible effect of further government antitrust actions.

And with data traffic exceeding voice traffic in the 70's, data communications faces the problem of overloaded and unreliable transmission lines, which could seriously hamper the growth of information processing.

But whatever the other issues of the 70's, the overriding challenge will be for

Source: Reprinted from *Infosystems*, January 1970, pp. 44ff. By Permission of the Publisher. © 1970 Hitchcock Publishing Company. All rights reserved.

343

management to finally master the technology and get on with the business of developing effective management information systems.

Rewrite the Rulebook

This, of course, is easier said than done. For the technological developments continue to run far ahead of management's ability to understand and apply. As one speaker at '69 Fall Joint Computer Conference commented, "We can't stand 40 more years of machine improvement without improving the people that operate them, and the rules under which the machines are operated."

The 70's may well mark the decade of "catch up" for management. There will be improvements in cost-performance of computers, due to advances in circuitry design and manufacture. But there are no present indications that the user will be faced with another painful transition from one family of computers to another, such as characterized the move to IBM 370's.

MANAGEMENT

What will be the prime EDP problems facing management in the 70's? Most likely the same problems that were faced in the 60's and even the 50's—how to take advantage of EDP power. Take, for example, the following quote: "We at Univac are concerned that . . . there are users who continue to struggle under the unnecessary burden of unprofitable and unsuccessful installations." That statement is most applicable to the average user today, but it was actually uttered some nine years ago, by Gordon Smith, who was then director of marketing for Sperry Rand Corp.'s Univac Div.

The facts are that management has long had available more systems power than most have known what to do with. We have only to look at man's conquest of the moon to realize what the successful marriage of technology and management can accomplish. It took a total management information system to provide roundtrips to the moon. True, the talent and dollars involved were far beyond the scope of any business enterprise. But then, so were the objectives. The point is, that put in the proper perspective, the systems planning that assured success for the Apollo projects can produce similar accomplishments for business management.

At the risk of oversimplification, the reason MIS worked for the space agency was that they followed the rules for developing a management information system. They started with an objective, they established a desired timetable, then set out to measure the means already available and those that must yet be discovered in order to successfully complete the project. And at every critical step of the way, management—all management—was heavily involved in the system.

But in the business world, management for the most part is yet to really get involved in the systems function. Surrounded by technological revolution they remain reactionaries, clinging to past methodologies, seeking to isolate themselves from the changes they seem unwilling to understand.

In other words, if the Apollo projects were at the mercy of the average management approach to computer utilization, there would be no capsule, no engine, no crew, no timetable, and probably little agreement as to the target. But, undoubtedly the computers would be busy grinding out the payroll and other historic data.

Is this too damning a charge to toss at management? One has only to examine the many studies conducted by research and consulting firms to find ample justification for the charge. They show, with few exceptions, that management has failed miserably to profitably apply the tools made available by technological advances.

The problem, as one observer has put it, is that the time has long passed when management can afford to leave the direction of the corporate computer effort largely in the hands of technical staff people. Yet the identification and selection of new computer applications are still predominantly in the hands of computer specialists who, despite their professional expertise, are poorly qualified to set the course of the corporate computer effort.

Marshall McLuhan has stated, "The computer is the LSD of the business world, transforming its outlook and objectives." Putting aside the objectionable overtones of drugs, the analogy isn't bad. But few management people have taken the trip. For most, the computer is still an accounting machine and operating at a rather poor cost-performance ratio.

And so it will be, until management understands more about management sciences and their relation and relevance to modern business management; more about the characteristics of management science computer applications and how they differ from the traditional business uses of the computer, i.e., recording the past versus understanding the present and predicting and molding the future.

Management must understand the contributions of time sharing and real time systems to scientific decision making processes, and how the return on computer investment can be improved with management science applications. They msut understand models, data bases and scheduling techniques such as PERT and the Critical Path Method.

Management must come to grips with simulation and how it helps in dealing with uncertainty; how to apply simulation and risk analysis to the problems of inventory and production management, capital investments and profit planning.

Why "must" management have a working understanding of the management sciences? Basically because such an understanding is essential if the computer is to become a competitive weapon and a contributor to the increased profits of the enterprise. And if the computer does neither, it is little more than a million dollar quill pen.

Why then has management shied away from the principles of scientific management? One reason is the natural fear of the unknown. A large number of today's managers received little if any formal indoctrination to the concepts of scientific management during their academic years. Accordingly, there is a tendency to look upon scientific management as "way out" and something that requires a Ph.D. for understanding.

The latter tendency is not without justification. A majority of the "experts" on SM spend a good deal of time communicating with each other and have done little to explain scientific management in terms that the average management man can understand. Fortunately, the SM authorities are coming down from the ivory towers in increasing numbers, and the 70's should find more and more firms gaining a deep understanding of just what the principles of scientific management are all about. When this happens, computer payoffs will finally become more than a salesman's promise and management's impossible dream.

Another area that needs management exploration and understanding in the years ahead is the subject of facility management. Reduced to its simplest terms, facility management is a sort of "leave the driving to us" approach to information processing, wherein a firm of specialists take over the total responsibility of the customer's computer installation, including equipment, personnel and results. In some cases the latter is guaranteed in writing, which should provide considerable temptation, considering that most installations have difficulty producing the desired or anticipated results.

Facility management companies have two basic methods of operation. They either take over the installation on site, or, and most seem to prefer this approach, they absorb the customer's computer operations in their own service bureau complex. At the moment there are few case histories available, but the fact that facility management entrepreneurs are mushrooming around the country indicates there will be considerable action on the subject in the future.

The mounting costs of information processing and the problems of personnel turnover and escalating salary demands could well move management to serious consideration of some sort of facility management program.

PEOPLE PROBLEM

In the 1970's, the people problem will ameliorate to some degree. Part of the easing will be due to two major factors: (1) the larger birth rates of the post-World War II era will be felt, particularly in the managerial class; and (2) the end of the Vietnam War should free a large number of eligible young men for the EDP employment market.

However, by 1980, a shortage will still persist, mainly because the EDP industry is so volatile and, as such, gobbles up talent with an insatiable appetite. What will really be needed to keep the people problem within manageable limits will be a concerted industry effort to recruit, train and retrain employes for the demands of data processing in the 70's.

Following Russia's launching of Sputnik I in 1957, the U.S. Government helped rally nationwide support for recruiting and training engineers and scientists. Prior to Sputnik I, there was a horrendous shortage of these people; by the early 60's there was almost a glut on the market.

To achieve some of its employment goals in the 70's, the EDP industry may also have to rely on governmental help in galvanizing the lay community.

Most assuredly, some government aid will have to come in the form of grants to local school districts to staff and equip meaningful computer curricula. On the average, individual school districts simply do not have the money necessary to do it.

Before looking into some of the reservoirs of talent to be tapped in the 70's and the major training sources for computer employes, let's look at the scope of the problem.

There have been many guesstimates as to the need in the 70's. According to Dr. G. Truman Hunter of International Business Machines Corp., there were about a half million people working in the computer industry in 1967. It is estimated that 125,000 were operators while 375,000 were managers, programmers and systems analysts. By 1975, according to one projection he cites, 450,000 operators and 1.5 million managers, programers and systems analysts will be needed.

"It is interesting to compare this with the number of people needed in some other professional fields which includes 300,000 lawyers, 650,000 scientists and 1.4 million engineers by 1975," said Dr. Hunter. "Therefore, it is estimated that the data processing industry will offer more new career opportunities than almost any other major field between now and 1975!"

Robert Half Personnel Agencies Inc., which specializes in placement of financial personnel and which includes 21 branches in principal U.S. cities from coast to coast, conducts an annual salary survey, and the organization has projected salary ranges for 1975 and 1980 in various categories (see Table 1). In 1975, for example, experienced programers will be earning between $12,000 and $15,000 in large installations and $10,000 to $12,000 in small ones. Systems analysts will get between $17,000 and $19,000 in large installations and $12,000 to $14,000 in small ones.

By 1980, the figures for experienced programers will soar to $22,000 to $27,000 in large installations and from $28,000 to $35,000 for systems analysts.

Robert Half, president, added the following predictions for the 70's:

1. More and more college degrees are becoming a requirement. As we get further into the 1970's a college degree in computer science will become a requisite.

Table 1. Projected Salaries for EDP Personnel

Position	1975			1980		
	Large	*Medium*	*Small*	*Large*	*Medium*	*Small*
Programer, Jr., Exp'd	12,000– 15,000	11,000– 14,000	10,000– 12,000	22,000– 27,000		
Programer Analyst	16,000– 18,000	14,000– 16,000		22,000– 27,000		16,000– 18,000
Prog. Lead/Sr.	18,000– 22,000			24,000– 30,000		
Systems Analyst	17,000– 19,000	14,500– 16,500	12,000– 14,000	28,000– 35,000		
Systems Anal. Mgr.	22,000– 25,000	17,000– 20,000		17,500– 22,000		
Operations Mgr.	15,000– 20,000	13,000– 18,000		30,000– 50,000		
Mgr. Data Proc.	26,000– 45,000	20,000– 26,000	15,000– 18,000			23,000– 27,000

Salary projections by Robert Half Personnel Agencies reflect the company's expectations that there will be no medium scale computers by 1980 and also, by then, the manager of data processing job will change—he'll be divorced completely from the financial area.

2. Manual systems will be reemphasized. For the last few years the manual systems areas have been ignored. Companies are realizing that computers must tie into a complete system.

3. Job jumping, common with EDP specialists, will be frowned upon by employers instead of encouraged by them.

4. By 1975, the programmer as we know him today will reach the final stage of obsolescence. Instead, programmer analysts will develop complete systems and specifications while coders will prepare instructions for machines.

5. By 1980, the data processing manager will be divorced completely from the financial area. The EDP manager will not report to the controller or treasurer but to an administrative vice president or an individual who will be in charge of the total EDP function.

6. There will be fewer recruiters of EDP talent by 1980. Why? Freelance recruiters who once worked for one of the computer manufacturers and went into business placing their friends and former associates will vanish.

7. IBM's unbundling will create a greater demand for systems managers and software specialists.

8. There will be an increased number of EDP specialists in law, medicine, accounting, engineering, dentistry and other professions..

One of the industry's greatest challenges will be to interest young people in becoming involved in EDP. Some steps have already been taken in this direction— but a great deal more needs to be done.

The Data Processing Management Assn., for example, has helped in developing a merit badge in computers for the Boy Scouts of America; and the Business Equipment Manufacturers Assn. is conducting annual Careers Day programs.

Another reservoir of talent lies among the disadvantaged, the undereducated and underemployed and the minority groups. The National Alliance of Businessmen is shooting for better than 600,000 placements in all types of industry by June 1971. A large number of these individuals will moved into the EDP community, and although training costs are high and results still questionable, it is an avenue the computer industry cannot afford to overlook. Aside from providing needed people, it also helps to alleviate a nationwide problem affecting a large segment of a have-not population. Failing to ease this larger problem could blunt growth efforts of the U.S. in all areas. And the problem that persists is also a moral one—while most whites are sharing the prosperity of the age, the majority of blacks are not and seem to have little hope of ever participating in the society as full-fledged members of it.

In the 1970's, major training sources for people needed in the EDP community will be high schools, colleges, private EDP schools and industry itself.

There is doubt, however, that they will be able to meet the projected needs of the 70's, without recourse (as pointed out above) to a concerted industrywide effort funded in part and given publicity impetus and perhaps leadership by the Federal Government.

Historically, high schools and colleges have been slow to adjust to changing academic needs. Pedantic approaches are often rigid and costs are another stumbling block. Getting qualified instructors in the EDP area is another barrier. In the 70's, the EDP community must make an effort to get curricula changes incorporating "how-to-teach" computer courses in the normal schools (teacher colleges).

Private EDP schools have their own shortcomings. As Half says: "Most of the computer school graduates do not have either the quality or quantity of experience that industry requires. Most companies will not accept graduates of many computer schools."

Another problem facing the private EDP school is one of reputation. More than 700 EDP schools have sprung up in the past 12 years. The number changes daily as new ones enter the field and operators of others, whose only goal is to make a fast buck, move on to other exploitable areas. In their wake are graduates no closer to jobs in data processing than they were before spending their time and money for worthless diplomas.

EDUCATION

Educational institutions implementing computer systems, or upgrading existing ones, during the next decade would do well to contemplate a point made by the President's Science Advisory Committee in 1967. The point is " . . . to keep in mind that computing should not be thought of as primarily a new subject to be taught in addition to all the other important material now in the curriculum."

There are two basic educational needs in the years ahead, so far as the business automation industry is concerned. Computer scientists will be needed to build and program the machines. People in nearly all occupations will need to know how to use computers effectively in their jobs. It is expected that virtually all of the existing 2,200 institutions of higher education would be making computer instruction of some degree available to students by 1980. But, there are two problems: making sure that the instruction is available to a majority of students, rather than to only computer science majors and researchers; and, accelerating the growth in "computers available" to compensate for the expected increase in the total number of institutions of higher learning.

The experiences at Dartmouth College, and at other pioneering schools where students and faculty have free access to computing power, show that given an opportunity, students and faculty will discover a multitude of new areas and new ways in which the computer can be applied effectively. More colleges will follow Dartmouth's lead and no doubt computer access will become a "recruiting carrot" held out to prospective scholars. This will occur in part because an increasing number of high school graduates will have been exposed to the computer and will know how to use it by the time they're ready to scout college campuses. It will also occur because business will need computer-assisted talent in large numbers, and that need will be recognized.

The transition, however, will be slow. The main problem: money. The secondary problem: inertia. The President's Science Advisory Committee placed the estimated annual cost of providing adequate computing facilities for undergraduate students at $60 per student per year. But, as the committee noted, that figure is sufficiently high that "there is no place for it in the already tight budgets of America's colleges and universities."

The committee made several recommendations, most involving increased government assistance, but so far they have not been put into effect.

The availability of time sharing computers will help put students on-line at a price most schools can afford, but, in most cases, for rather limited applications. Also, minicomputers—a booming segment of the industry—are available at a relatively low price. Again, these are limited systems, but they offer the opportunity for meaningful experience.

Right Pictures, Right Minds

Taking into account all the "positive" factors—growth in number of computers on campus, expansion of time sharing, availability of inexpensive minicomputers—it seems rather certain that by 1980 nearly all college and university graduates will have been exposed to computer use. Moreover, most high school graduates will have a basic knowledge of EDP. For the vast majority of students, becoming a programer or computer scientist will not be a goal. However, curricula to produce scientists at all the degree levels—bachelor's, master's and Ph.D.—will be available in most major universities and a large number of small colleges. This training will be for the upper level jobs that the computing industry requires.

Entry-level talent will continue to come from the vocational and private EDP schools, and from the two-year, or community, colleges. The latter's role will become increasingly important as they become centers for continuing education in numerous fields, including EDP.

Before leaving the subject of computers in education, some attention to computer-assisted instruction is in order. The technique has barely had a chance to prove or disprove itself, partly because when the door became ajar a few years ago, there were overly aggressive attempts made to exploit it. Countering those efforts was overreaction that gave birth to a sort of scare slogan—"teacherless classrooms." The technique still isn't proven, but it shows enough promise to merit further exploration. There is little doubt that many aspects of learning can be enhanced by having the student interact with a computer. The specific aspects, and the programs to facilitate interaction, must be further identified, developed and tested.

As mentioned previously, cost is a big barrier, and inertia another. The problems were expressed this way by Prof. J. C. R. Licklider of MIT: "If most of the opinion leaders of our society had in their minds clear pictures of what computers could do for education—of education as a self-motivating, self-exciting interaction through computers with responsive knowledge—it would take only a very short time to get the computer industry, the education profession and the government all working together along a constructive course in the overall interest of society. The trouble is that, by and large, the right pictures are not in the right minds."

COMMUNICATIONS

If the 1970's are to be the gateway into an era where the tremendous power of computers is fully harnessed and made readily available, greatly expanded data communications capabilities must be forthcoming.

The present trend towards the use of large scale, time shared computers and development of advanced terminals have led to the estimations that, within the next decade, more than half of all computers used will be communications-oriented, used in remote time sharing mode; that this country's communications need will more than double its present level; and that data communications will exceed voice communications in volume, i.e., the volume of communications among computers will exceed that among humans.

This three-dimensional evolution will see: (1) the present wireline, cable and microwave systems become the backbone of an integrated complex of communications networks which also include a number of new vehicles such as private microwave systems, a broadband network, Community Antenna Television (CATV), a communication satellite system, and possibly a laser beam transmission system. Playing supplementary but increasingly important roles: (2) a redeployment or expansion of the control base for the communications setup; and (3) substantial increase in data communications efficiency.

The whole situation now hinges on the answers to three questions: (1) Should present regulated common carriers remain in firm control of the communications system? (2) Should common carriers be allowed to enter the data processing business? (3) Should data processing services be placed under the regulatory jurisdiction of the FCC or some other form of government supervision?

The FCC has conducted an inquiry into the interdependence between computer and communication services and facilities. An analysis of the issues involved as well as the testimonial materials collected has been made by the Stanford Research Institute. A report has also been made by the President's Task Force on Communications Policy, originally appointed by President Johnson in 1967.

So Far, So Little

So far, little action has been taken by the FCC, except for the Carterfone decision, whereby the FCC rules that telephone users are entitled to the use of attachments other than those supplied by the common carriers in order to extend the telephone's capabilities. This means telephone users now can take advantage of the numerous coupling devices available to more efficiently transmit digital data via regular phone lines. Another important decision being considered by the FCC involves whether common carriers should be required to open their systems to non-common carriers, such as the private microwave systems, for inter-system connections.

Based on all information available, we expect that in the future, a number of competitive communications vehicles will spring up to meet the growing need for data transmission, and will be connected to the basic system of the common carriers in order to reach the end users. These will include, in the immediate future, one or more microwave systems, CATV and a domestic satellite system; and in the more distant future, a broadband network and laser beam transmission.

The FCC has recently granted, after six years of proceedings, permission to Microwave Communications Inc. to build a microwave system linking Chicago and St. Louis. At least four other applications to build additional microwave legs under the same concept are now on file. Eventually these will form a nationwide network to supply microwave communications channels to multi-location companies for interoffice or interplant communications at low cost. Typical use for such a system would be instant access to computer centers, transmission of data, pictures, radio communications to mobile units and to remote control stations. It will offer an alternative to the similar service now offered by the common carriers, which would be most beneficial to those smaller users who cannot afford the present service.

At least one other company has filed applications to build a microwave system. University Computing Co., through its subsidiary Data Transmission Co. (Datran), plans to build a $375 million, 255-station digital microwave network and estimates the rates would be 50 percent of the Bell System's rates.

An Interactive Society

A domestic communications satellite system consisting of from one to four synchronous satellites and a number of ground stations to transmit television signals, facsimile computer data, and news dispatches, is most likely to come into existence within the next decade. Such a system has been proposed by Comsat and the President's Task Force on Communications Policy, and has been warmly endorsed by the television networks. Such a system would provide economic feasibility for communication distances of 800 miles up, and would bring the cost of long distance communications down to as much as one-fifth of land line cost. This domestic satellite system would be supplementary and not competitive to the existing international communications satellite system.

CATV is also likely to become a supplementary means to locally relay data signals to end users for not only entertainment but also business purposes.

A huge switched wideband communications network with capability to handle tens of thousands of data channels, using coaxial cable as a basic medium to link together video terminals across the country, has been proposed by the Electronic Industries Assn.'s Industrial Electronics Div. Such a network, according to EIA, will serve both business and consumer data communications needs, and will be instrumental in the formation of an "interactive society" in the 1980's. Interconnected with the domestic satellite system, it will provide two-way transmission of digital as well as visual information to all connected terminals in the country or even overseas.

Laser beams have been successfully used to project images and to transmit signals. It is expected that in the future they will become the basic means for transmitting massive volumes of data at high speed.

Facing powerful challenges to their regulated monopoly, the common carriers are under tremendous pressure to upgrade their services in order to retain their commanding position in the communications industry. The Bell System has greatly improved the data transmission efficiency of its voice grade lines, and will gradually phase in the electronic switching system (ESS) which will further increase the speed of data transmission via phone lines and will provide new services such as an automatic transfer of phone calls.

Another significant development now being carried out by Bell is Pulse-Code Modulation (PCM) to replace the present amplitude modulation. PCM measures signals from the ordinary voice channel and breaks them down into 8-bit codes that can be electronically modulated and transmitted at much higher speeds than presently possible (from the present 2,400 bits per second with voice grade lines to as much as 1.5 million BPS). As a result, the phone line can also be used to transmit visual information, facsimile and other types of signals, making every Touch-Tone phone a virtual data terminal.

The Bell System will also introduce its Picturephone in the early 70's to make face-to-face communications available at a reasonable price. Bell is now offering, on a trial basis, a wideband communications service called Data-Phone 50, which provides a switched 50 kilobit-per-second transmission speed, and is charged based on distance and time.

It is inevitable, inasmuch as it will be necessary, that the above mentioned new communication vehicles will be put to widespread use and be interconnected with the existing system. The question is, who will run the integrated system, and who will provide the data processing services which will be interdependent with the communications services? The trend appears to be more competition in both data processing services and communications. Some common carriers offer data processing services. Some data processing service companies are eyeing the communications field. Meanwhile, the FCC is trying to decide whether this trend should continue.

Eliminating Distance

In determining whether common carriers should retain their commanding positions in the communications field, the FCC has to determine whether they have sufficient facilities and capabilities to meet the present and foreseeable communications requirements of the computer industry, and whether such a regulated monopoly is to the best interest of the user public. The common carriers, obviously, are constantly building up their capabilities in order to retain their commanding positions, but pressures are high in the data processing industry to open up the market to private system operators.

What does this evolution of the communications industry mean to data processing users? First, the coming of the satellite communications network means distance will be eliminated as a determining factor in the pricing of communications channels. The availability of alternative communications vehicles as well as better designed, more efficient terminal equipment means that the cost of communicatons will decrease, and that services will be more responsive to the specific needs of the user regardless of its size.

This evolution also means that data processing users will need more competent personnel to design systems that would take full advantage of the alternatives available and of the technological advances. They will also have to be able to project their communications needs well in advance in order to take advantage of the new communications setup.

This increasingly close relationship between data processing services and communications has inevitably led to the question of whether the teleprocessing services industry should be placed under the regulatory supervision of the FCC just as the common carriers are.

Primary proponents of government regulation for the teleprocessing services industry are the regulated common carriers, for obvious reasons. However, various industry organizations, including the Assn. of Data Processing Services Organizations (ADAPSO), the National Assn. of Manufacturers (NAM), and the Business Equipment Manufacturers Assn. (BEMA), are up in arms in opposition to such a proposal. Significantly, the President's Task Force on Communications Policy has also recommended that government regulation of the teleprocessing services industry is unnecessary.

Their primary argument is that the teleprocessing services industry is still in its stage of dynamic growth. None of the common reasons that call for government control in order to safeguard public interests, such as concentration of market, unrestrained price increases, has occurred and none is expected to happen in the foreseeable future. On the contrary, due to the low cost of entry into the market and the variety of services being offered with more to be developed, it is unthinkable that any concentration of market will be able to materialize in the near future.

Further, the unit cost of data processing in remote access mode has dropped drastically in the past few years, and is expected to continue to decrease as better hardware and software are developed. Free competition can only help drive down this cost and work for the public's interests.

Unconstrained Forces

Opponents of government regulation of the teleprocessing services industry also point out that the industry includes a great variety of remote access data processing services, and can by no means be considered as a monolithic entity offering services that can be uniformly priced.

These opponents also suggest that the FCC should encourage the communications and data processing services industries to work together to set up standards and practices that would serve a self-policing function, and that relevant governmental agencies make periodical surveys of the teleprocessing services industry to determine whether the unconstrained forces of competition continue to stimulate improvements and cost reductions in its service to the public.

As for the safeguard of personal and proprietary information being abused, they submit that at this stage of the game, government regulation will not solve the problem. They suggest that government and all industries involved should combine their efforts to find ways to achieve such safeguards.

PRIVACY

"The contemporary era of electronics and computers has provided the final coup de grâce to the technological premises on which the classic American law of privacy has been based. Microminiaturization, advanced circuitry, radar, the laser, television optics and related developments have shifted the balance of power from those who seek to protect their conversations and actions against surveillance to those who have access to the new devices. What was once Orwell's science fiction is now current engineering."

Privacy can be said to include everything from garbage snooping to electronic eavesdropping to curbing the activities of credit bureaus to the proposal by the U.S. Bureau of the Budget nearly four years ago that a national data bank, housed in a National Data Center, be established. The function of such a center would be to improve the availability of interrelated statistical data for economic and social analysis. It would serve as a central repository for data now scattered among various government agencies. The idea of a National Data Center has caused many individuals in the business automation community and outside it to choose up sides.

As Prof. Westin of Columbia Univ. has stated: "One position . . . is to oppose creation of data centers and intelligence systems completely. The need for better statistics for policy analysis or of richer information systems for criminal justice purposes is seen as inadequate when weighed against the increase in government power and fears of invasion of privacy that such systems might bring.

Self-appointed Defenders

"A second view . . . assumes that traditional administrative and legal safeguards, plus the expected self-restraint of those who would manage such systems, is enough to protect the citizen's privacy.

"The third position . . . assumes that neither the 'total ban' nor the 'traditional restraints' positions represent desirable alternatives. What is called for is a new legal approach to the processing of personal information by authorities in a free society and a new set of legal, administrative and system protections to accomplish this objective. The fact is that American society wants both better information analysis *and* privacy."

The entire National Data Center issue came to national attention thanks to hearings held in the summer of 1966 by a House of Representatives Special Subcommittee on the Invasion of Privacy of the Committee on Government Operations. Chairman of the unit, Rep. Cornelius E. Gallagher (D-N.J.), was a little-known congressional figure outside his district prior to the hearings. At the end, he was a nationwide figure, being lauded in the press by such self-appointed defenders of public privacy as Vance Packard.

The role of the heavy in the hearings fell to Raymond T. Bowman, assistant director for statistical standards of the Bureau of the Budget. His job was to present the Bureau's case for the National Data Center.

There was a strong indication, although it cannot be proved obviously, that Gallagher was riding a publicity wave—and a safe one at that. As safe as supporting motherhood and not kicking dogs. He gets plenty of mention in the press and was called on by many organizations because he began to represent to the public the defender of its privacy.

But Gallagher's crusade has had a salutary effect on the business automation industry: it has awakened it to what the computer has wrought! Gallagher was quite correct in saying that "America . . . cannot be the same America after a centralized computer system, a system which neither forgives nor forgets." And, further: "If we have learned nothing else from previous technological revolutions, we must have learned that these revolutions have changed man's outlook on society and man's concept of himself."

Gallagher helped make the business automation community sharply aware of its inadvertent complicity in and responsibility for some of the invasion of privacy allegations centered about credit bureau "dossiers" on individuals.

Myron Benton, in his book *Privacy Invaders,* perhaps put the problem for the public into perspective when he wrote: "You began the process of losing your privacy the day you first opened a charge account, took out a loan, bought something on the installment plan or applied for a credit card."

The 60's focused attention on the privacy issue. It will be left to the 70's to deal with it effectively.

The business automation community will be most concerned with two aspects of the issue: the establishment of a National Data Center and regulation of credit bureau information banks.

It is obvious that some central repository of data for the Federal Government is needed. But safeguards must be ensured first, including access to the system by authorized individuals only.

An Ominous Offshoot

Prof. Westin has put it this way: " . . . A network of legal controls is absolutely essential. For example, a Federal statute could specify that the data put into a statistical center is to be used solely for statistical purposes. It could forbid all other uses of the data to influence, regulate or prosecute anyone, making such use a crime, and excluding all such data from use as evidence in judicial or governmental proceedings. It could forbid all persons other than data center employes to have access to the files, and the data could be specifically exempted from subpoena. An Inspector General or Ombudsman-type official could be set up to hear complaints about alleged misuse, and judicial review for such complaints could be provided for."

Overall, after much haggling and concerted effort by the business automation community to develop safeguards, the National Data Center will become a reality in the 70's. The overriding factor will be that it is needed, and this need will be "the mother of invention" for spurring the industry to provide the necessary safeguards.

The other "hot" aspect of the privacy issue, delineated in the 60's, is the dossiers compiled by credit bureaus.

Associated Credit Bureaus Inc., a trade association which represents more than 4,300 local credit bureaus and collection agencies in the U.S. and abroad, has recommended operating procedures for the protection of consumer privacy.

Despite this move, Sen. Sam J. Ervin (D-N.C.) proposed late in 1969 that a Federal agency be created to regulate the use of personal data stored in data banks across the nation.

In the 70's, abuses of information in credit bureau data banks will be noted with increasing frequency, partly as a result of the proliferation of credit cards and a move toward the so-called cashless and checkless society.

Federal regulation in this area will be demanded and undoubtedly will come. An ominous offshoot, however, will be a move by Congress to regulate the entire EDP field.

There will be several reasons for this development: (1) the business automation industry has, in the past, been slow to regulate and police itself, and historically this reticence in other industries has resulted in the government moving in to regulate and control; (2) the abuses in the credit data area will cause a violent public reaction and the Congress will be swift to act in response (some will believe, rightly so, that the reaction will be precipitous); and (3) the psychology of the approach and nearness of George Orwell's 1984 will provide fodder for overeager consumer press and media people to dramatize what will happen if effective controls are not imposed on the business automation industry; Big Brotherism will make good headlines.

DATA PROCESSING: 1973 ± 10 YEARS

James A. Campise

If we were able to examine the track of data processing upon the continuum of time and were asked to select a single twenty-year period which spanned the most events of lasting significance which occurred in the last half of the twentieth century, it is likely that we would select the period between 1963 and 1983.

1963 was a key year in the evolution of the computer era. It marked the national dedication to the space program following the tragic assassination of President John F. Kennedy. The result was an acceleration of technological development unmatched in history (with the possible exception of World War II). There is certainly no period during which so many major concepts in data processing were simultaneously undergoing intensive study, experimentation, and development. The technology of operating systems, multiprogramming, multiprocessing, high-level and user-oriented languages, timesharing, data communications, hardware miniaturization, and operating speed were all subject to well funded, intensive research in both the private and public sectors of the economy.

Furthermore, our educational institutions were awakening to the need for more people with better academic training in data processing. During the period between 1963 and 1973 educational institutions at all levels inaugurated programs in computer science and data processing. (Hopefully, one of the significant changes in the 1973-83 period will be the attainment of a maturity level that recognizes that processing data *is* the purpose of all computing, no matter what the source of the data, so that the imaginary boundary between "computer scientists" and "data processors" will disappear.)

If we can accept the premise that the sheer volume of published material is indicative of the amount of work being done in a field, then we must focus on 1968 as a banner year in data processing. Periodicals published in the field flourished and a very prolific group of book writers were active. By 1971 over 800 books had been published by more than 150 publishers, not to mention the dozens of periodicals which range from daily publications to quarterly and annual journals.

1963—1973

So the 1963-1973 period found more people working simultaneously on more problems of lasting significance, at a time when major concepts were in their developmental stages, than ever before in data processing. As the concepts became

Source: Reprinted, with permission, from *Data Management,* May 1973, pp. 13-16, published by the Data Processing Management Association, Park Ridge, Illinois.

experiments and the experiments became practice, the patterns of the future were set. Technology would undoubtedly continue to advance, but the *directions* of that progress were set in the period between 1963 and 1973, and the environment for the changes in emphasis was established.

But the first ten years of our selected period are already recorded for all to see. Without the vantage point of a higher plane of reference, we must examine the second ten year period through the distorted window of speculation.

As a further basis for our speculation let us recall some influencing facts: Most of the major contributors to the field during the next ten years will be those who entered it during the last ten years or will enter it in the next year or two. Consider also the fact that none of these young people have been influenced or had their thinking or responses conditioned by either the depression of the 1930's or World War II. Couple this difference in mental attitude (from their predecessors) with the additional fact that they have never known a time when there were no stored program computers.

These factors mean that we now have among us a group of dynamic young people who are less concerned with potential economic disaster, they are not preoccupied with acquiring possessions; leaving them free for considering the social impact of their technology. They are not prone to be constrained by the economic considerations of doing things as cheaply as possible, don't seem to have the feeling that the Government must be supported at the expense of the individual, and see the computer as a familiar and necessary tool to be used to improve the welfare of man. This, then, will be the springboard to discovery during the next ten years.

ATTITUDE CHANGE

This difference in background and attitude of the currently maturing practitioners and academicians will cause the previously referred to boundary between "computer scientists" and "data processors" to disappear. This same difference will be the reason that the application of the computer to the social and environmental problems of man will receive major emphasis.

Another significant occurrence during the latter half of our first ten year period was the first real recession that the computer industry has known. The resulting consolidation and adjustment may have taken place without the general economic recession, but it was certainly the precipitating factor. Since the entire economy suffered, top management in most organizations were forced to probe into what they were getting for their computing dollars. This probing led to a conscious awareness of what most of them already knew; that the computer had become an essential part of the organization, but one which could be managed as well as any other major and essential asset. The consolidation resulting from the recession had a maturing effect upon the industry and set the stage for the period during which many of the people who were involved in the birth of the computer industry were moving into positions of executive management—providing a heretofore missing link in the chain of communication between "computer people" and executive management.

Now that we have established the attitudinal environment and the directions of the changes to come, let us examine the nature of some of the change we will see.

Let us consider hardware, and examine the impact of the trend toward miniaturization upon the future of computers, and, in turn, upon the various segments of our society.

COMPLETE CIRCUIT CHIP

The era of the complete circuit "chip" is just beginning. It is reasonable to assume that within the next ten years we will see a complete computer (CPU) on a single chip. A "microcomputer" with about 8-16000 words of storage, an instruction set of 64 to 96 commands, about 16 general purpose registers, and an I/O bus on a single chip which will probable be a reality within two or three years. In ten years such a computer chip will probably sell for under $10, possibly as little as one dollar! The impact of this kind of microcomputer will be felt in every walk of life.

An area of major change will be that of education. The use of machines as an aid to thinking will begin to permeate the educational process all the way down to the primary grades.

Consider the impact of a small computer, similar to the current miniature electronic calculator, selling for about five dollars or less at retail. A pocket computer will be as common and as essential as today's pencil and workbook. There will be no need to teach the mechanics of arithmetic—no drills on the "time tables." Classroom time will be spent teaching the thought processes required to solve problems with the computer as an aid to do the mechanics of arithmetic and recording, except that the "classroom" will not be a classroom at all but a learning laboratory centered around computer-aided learning techniques under development today but made practical through better man-machine communication and the microcomputer.

The next ten years will bring the beginning of the end of the classroom building as we now know it. All classroom activity will take place in the home or in a community learning center. The campus buildings of educational institutions will become laboratories for research and experimentation.

IMPACT ON SOCIETY

Let us examine the impact of the "computer on a chip" on other areas of our society. Consider the impact of the microcomputer built into consumer products such as an alarm clock with a built-in hundred-year personal calendar. It would be pre-programmed to awaken its owner at an appointed hour on each day of the year, skipping weekends and holidays, of course. The same device could be built into a wrist watch to serve as an appointment reminder for the business man. A credit card with an individual's entire credit history stored in an imbedded microcomputer could eliminate the need for credit reporting if point of sale terminals could be made to record each transaction in the credit "card." The same card could serve to activate the lock on its owner's home, office, or automobile, in addition to activating the bank's money dispenser, a pay telephone, etc. (A microcomputer in the lock would remember who was authorized to open it.) Think of a computer chip in your electric typewriter, your telephone, television set, refrigerator, range, etc. The possible list is almost endless. Toymakers could make *truly* educational toys!

Now, if your imagination has started to work on the potential of our microcomputer in the area of consumer products, let's examine the possibilities in the field of data processing.

MICROCOMPUTER IN DATA PROCESSING

It is the opinion of this writer that the microcomputer chip will be the basis for the next *true* generation of computing equipment.

Programming as we know it will not exist for the new equipment. Instead, user languages will be developed which will be microprogrammed into language interpreter chips. These may be built into the user's terminal, but they will also be available in the central system. The user's terminal will call a central system whose communications chips will establish communication with the terminal's communication chip, synchronizing such things as transmission speed, character codes, and invoke the appropriate user language or compiler chip in the central system. This, of course, will be preceded by appropriate security checks performed by "watchdog" chips appropriately microprogrammed to prevent unauthorized access to either the data lines or central computers. (Scramblers will be used for sensitive or confidential data.) Following security clearances and validation, the watchdogs will invoke the internal accounting microcomputer so the system utilization can be properly accounted for (bookkeeper chip).

When the preliminaries are completed, the operating system or "traffic cop" chip will be notified of the presence of the user and will handle the traffic required by the user program. When files are required, a file manager chip will consult the file directory chip, go to the backup storage controller chip and get a copy of the user's program or data or both. The file manager will also consult another series of "watchdogs" in the file security section to make sure that no unauthorized file accesses are performed and to prevent conflicts in the event of multi user access to the same files.

All programs will be executed by appropriate language interpreter chips. Input and output will also be handled by "traffic-cop" chips and since each peripheral unit will have its own microcomputer, these units will require very little attention.

A "doctor" chip will aid the service engineer in diagnosis and repair of the entire system by calling a central maintenance system which has the maintenance history files of all similar systems. When the "doctor" chip and the central maintenance system arrive at the most probable cause of the malfunction, the "doctor" chip will either notify the maintenance engineer or switch in a substitute part from the built-in bank of spares, recording the use of the spare in its parts inventory file and notifying the bookkeeper chip so it can re-order the component if necessary.

SHOEBOX SIZE

Incidentally, except for certain large peripherals, the entire central system will be no larger than a shoebox! Site preparation will consist of wiring to the telephone and data transmission circuits, and providing for the peripherals.

In general, we see that each function within an entire system, starting with a remote user and ending with the replacement of repair parts, has a microcomputer assigned to look after its proper operation and each resource in the system is managed by a microcomputer. In other words, the next generation of hardware will not be a single coherent giant but a community of hundreds of "ants" (micro-computers), each busily doing its own thing.

From these speculations, we can see the character of the jobs in data processing changing dramatically within the next ten years. The emphasis will be on systems analysis, with the definition of "system" expanded to include the psychological and sociological aspects of using computers. In other words, the direction that we set during the 1963-1973 period was to create a user oriented emphasis during the 1973-1983 period. Pre-occupation with jargon, programming problems, and hardware technology must give way to pre-occupation with service. Popular acceptance of the computer will depend upon our ability to adapt to an environment which emphasizes the importance of the user for the services which the computer professional offers.